ON POETRY AND PHILOSOPHY

ON POETRY AND PHILOSOPHY

Thinking Metaphorically with Wordsworth and Kant

Brayton Polka

☙PICKWICK *Publications* · Eugene, Oregon

ON POETRY AND PHILOSOPHY
Thinking Metaphorically with Wordsworth and Kant

Copyright © 2021 Brayton Polka. All rights reserved. Except for brief quotations in critical publications or reviews, no part of this book may be reproduced in any manner without prior written permission from the publisher. Write: Permissions, Wipf and Stock Publishers, 199 W. 8th Ave., Suite 3, Eugene, OR 97401.

Pickwick Publications
An Imprint of Wipf and Stock Publishers
199 W. 8th Ave., Suite 3
Eugene, OR 97401

www.wipfandstock.com

PAPERBACK ISBN: 978-1-6667-0126-5
HARDCOVER ISBN: 978-1-6667-0127-2
EBOOK ISBN: 978-1-6667-0128-9

Cataloguing-in-Publication data:

Names: Polka, Brayton, author.

Title: On poetry and philosophy : thinking metaphorically with Wordsworth and Kant / Brayton Polka.

Description: Eugene, OR : Pickwick Publications, 2021 | **Includes bibliographical references and index.**

Identifiers: ISBN 978-1-6667-0126-5 (paperback) | ISBN 978-1-6667-0127-2 (hardcover) | ISBN 978-1-6667-0128-9 (ebook)

Subjects: LCSH: Kant, Immanuel, 1724–1804—Philosophy. | Wordsworth, William, 1770–1850—Philosophy. | Poetry, Modern—18th century—History and criticism. | Philosophy in literature.

Classification: PR5892.P5 P65 2021 (print) | PR5892.P5 P65 (ebook)

[Scripture quotations are from] Revised Standard Version of the Bible, copyright © 1946, 1952, and 1971 National Council of the Churches of Christ in the United States of America. Used by permission. All rights reserved worldwide.

[Scripture quotations are from] New Revised Standard Version Bible, copyright © 1989 National Council of the Churches of Christ in the United States of America. Used by permission. All rights reserved worldwide.

Table of Contents

Acknowledgments vii

1. Introduction: In the Beginning Is the Critical Practice of Metaphor 1
2. Thinking Poetically with Wordsworth 17
   Introductory 17
   Coleridge on Wordsworth 47
   Shelley's *A Defense of Poetry* 69
   Conclusion 80
3. Reading Wordsworth's *The Prelude* 83
4. Thinking Philosophically with Kant 117
   Introductory 117
   Kant and Religion 128
   Conclusion 172
5. Reading Kant's Practical Philosophy 174
   Preliminaries 174
   The Critique of Pure Reason 180
   The Critique of Practical Reason 210
   Conclusion 240
6. Conclusion: The Metaphoric Critique
         of Poetic and Philosophic Practice 246

Notes 257
Bibliography 273
About the Author 283
Index 285

Acknowlegments

I am pleased to thank my friend and former student, Geri Das Gupta, for her generous yet always critical support. I also want to express my gratitude for the financial support that I received from the Faculty of Liberal Arts and Professional Studies at York University for the publication of my book.

CHAPTER 1

Introduction

In the Beginning Is the Critical Practice of Metaphor

KIERKEGAARD INITIATES PART II of *Works of Love*, in his "Christian deliberation" entitled "Love Builds Up," with the statement that "all human speech about the spiritual, even the divine speech of Holy Scripture . . . is essentially metaphorical speech" (209).[1] The issue that I undertake to examine in my book is whether or in what sense both poetic speech and philosophic speech, the language of both poetry and philosophy, are "about the spiritual" and so "essentially metaphorical speech." The term *meta-phor* in Greek is identical with the term *trans-fer* (*transferre*) in Latin and so also in English: to transfer, to carry over, to bear across.

Kierkegaard proceeds to tell us that it is "in the order of things and of existence" that all human speech about the spirit is metaphorical "since a human being, even if from the moment of birth he is spirit, still does not become conscious of himself as spiritual until later." Indeed, Kierkegaard points out that human beings begin their lives in acting "sensately-psychically," that is, as body and soul but not (yet) as spirit. He immediately adds, however, that, when their spirit awakens, their sensate-psychical part is no more to be cast aside than the awakening of the spirit "announces itself in a sensate-psychical way. On the contrary, the first portion is taken over by the spirit and, used in this way, is thus made the basis—*it becomes the metaphorical.*" While in one sense, Kierkegaard continues, spiritual persons and sensate-psychical persons say the same thing, still "there is an infinite difference . . . between the two: the one has made the transition or let himself be *carried over* to the other side, while the other remains on this side; yet . . . both are using the same words." The persons in whom spirit has awakened remain in the finite, visible world of nature and use the same language, except their language is now "the metaphorical language" (209).[2]

The argument that I make fundamental to my book is that the language of both poetry and philosophy, when each is truly comprehended, is what Kierkegaard calls transferred or metaphorical language. It involves the "transfer" of human beings from the finite, visible world of sensate-psychical nature, what Kant calls the natural world of sensibility and understanding, to the infinite, "invisible" world of spirit (what Kant, together with Wordsworth, associates with reason). The issues, consequently, that I undertake to examine, to work through, and to explicate in my study are exciting, arresting, and, I believe, profoundly revelatory of our human condition. They involve, as we shall discover, implications, at once historical and ontological, that so very seldom have been properly and truly comprehended by the scholarly or the larger intellectual community.

One of the arresting elements in Kierkegaard's observation that all speech about the spirit is metaphorical is that it includes "even the divine speech of Holy Scripture." If biblical speech is metaphorical, are we, then, to conclude that, insofar as poetical and philosophical language is metaphor, it is biblical and that, consequently, the Bible is at once poetry and philosophy? What, in other words, is the relationship between the Bible and both poetry and philosophy? Other truly engaging questions follow. If the divine speech of the Bible is, as spiritual, metaphorical, how would we undertake to distinguish between the spirit of the Bible and the spirit of the discourse of modern thinkers, at once poetical and philosophical? In other words, is all properly spiritual poetry philosophical and religious? Equally, is all properly religious language poetical and philosophical? If poetry and philosophy are each religious, is there, indeed, no critically ontological or historical difference between poetry and philosophy or between poetry and philosophy, on the one hand, and religion, on the other?

Other critically significant questions, historical and ontological, also begin to emerge. If poetry and philosophy, insofar as they involve and express the metaphorical or transferred language of spirit, are biblical, how, then, are we to understand the concept of modernity as secular and the concept of the secular as modern? What, in other words, is the relationship among our concepts of modernity, secularity, and religion as they are articulated by both our poets and our philosophers? Or we may ask: Is the Bible, in embodying the spirit of metaphor, the metaphor of spirit, and so in being at once poetical and philosophical, no less secular than it is religious? We may recall that St. Jerome, in his translation of the Bible into the Latin Vulgate of his Roman times (in the late fourth century CE), rendered "eternity" as the *saecula saeculorum*: the ages of ages. What, indeed, is the eternal spirit of God and so, no less, of humankind? Is the spirit, in being both human and divine, at once secular and religious?

We thus find ourselves before the awesome question of temporality, of historical time, of time as historical, of beginnings and ends, of alpha and omega. The eternal God of the Bible is the God of history. This is the Lord of creation and the covenant who launched, not the fleet of a thousand ships but the metaphorical story of the historically infinite spirit of human practice. Indeed, we may recall that when, as we read in the story of Genesis, God expels our forebears Adam and Eve from the paradisiacal garden of Eden to the covenantal life of labor, conception (both physical and spiritual), and death, he reflects on the fact that human beings are like their Lord in knowing good and evil. The issues embedded here are, yet again, immense. But the basic question on which I presently focus is historical. "What are human beings," the Psalmist asks, "that you [Lord] are mindful of them, mortals [the sons of man] that you are mindful of them, mortals that you care for them? Yet you have made them [but] a little lower than God, and crowned them with glory and honor" (Ps 8:4–5). Human beings, we read earlier in Genesis, are created in the image of God (Gen 1:26–27). If, then, human beings are God's metaphor, if God is the metaphor of human beings, if, as Kierkegaard writes, human beings are born spirit yet must—historically, eternally—effect the transfer, the transition, from the sensate-psychical to the spiritual, from, in other words, natural temporality to the spiritual temporality of history, how are we understand those non-biblical peoples, i.e., pagans, who are suspended for ever—at once temporally and eternally—within the contradictory opposition between time as without end (chance or *tyche*) and eternity as without beginning (fate or *moira*)?

In simple terms, what we shall see, in multiple ways and contexts, as we proceed in our study is that the ancient Greeks, from Homer (in the eight century BCE) through Socrates and Plato to Aristotle (in the later fourth century BCE), were ignorant of metaphor, spirit, and history. In the biblical sense of transferred language, the ancient Greeks had neither poetry nor philosophy, although our modern terms originate in the ancient Greek of *poesis* (making) and *philosophia* (the love of wisdom). We shall find throughout our book that we must learn to distinguish, systematically and comprehensively, that is, at once historically and ontologically and so hermeneutically, between spirit and soul, metaphor and simile, concept and term, and communication and language. Again, in simple, introductory terms, not all images are metaphors, and not all terms (like poetry and philosophy) are what Hegel calls the concept (*der Begriff*) when understood as embodying the spirit of infinite self-consciousness. The ancient Greeks, like all non-biblical peoples, possessed, within their soul, similes and terms but not metaphors and concepts. They had language but not communication. They could not imagine that each and every human being, in being like God in knowing (in being responsible for) good and evil, belonged to the community of ends all of whose members shared the absolute duty of doing unto others what they wanted others to do unto them. Indeed, we may say that what it was that the Bible brought to the people of the book and continues to bring to its readers today is the revelation that they have the duty of enacting the critical transfer, of confronting the crisis, the trial, of ever making the transition, historical and ontological, from soul to spirit, from simile to metaphor, from term to concept, and from language to communication.

As I say, we have before us immensely profound and freighted issues, at once historical and ontological. We shall want to make our way, deliberately and methodically, in discussing them—by way of Wordsworth and Kant. But why this particular poet and this particular philosopher? Other poets and philosophers of their stature come to mind: Shakespeare, Milton, Whitman, and Stevens, in the English tradition of poetry, and Spinoza, Vico, Hegel, and Kierkegaard, in the continental tradition of philosophy, while not taking into consideration any of the great figures in the history of the European pictorial, sculptural, architectural, and musical arts. I want to indicate here my basic reasons for choosing Wordsworth and Kant as my exemplars, respectively, of poetry and of philosophy, with the understanding that the true justification of my choices constitutes my very book itself.

Before, however, taking up the question of why I choose Wordsworth as the exemplary poet and Kant as the exemplary philosopher for my study, there is yet a more fundamental question to consider. Why take up the two questions—Who is the poet (what is poetry)? Who is the philosopher (what is philosophy)?—together? What do poetry and philosophy have to do with each other? We shall see that Wordsworth was inspired by the confidence that his friend and colleague, Coleridge, had in him that he would and could write the first great philosophical poem. In other words, we generally have no difficulty in thinking of major poems by, in addition to Wordsworth, poets such as Shelley, Keats, Tennyson, Whitman, Stevens, or T. S. Eliot as philosophic or even religious. But we do not normally call major works of philosophy, such as those by Kant, poetic. Yet, it is also true that the term "poetic" can simply mean fanciful or merely playful or artificial, just as two of the adjectives relating to "fiction" are fictive and fictitious (meaning made up or not true). When Kant asks what, for him, is the most fundamental of all philosophical questions—"How are synthetic judgments *a priori* possible?"—or when he undertakes, in *The Critique of Pure Reason*, what he calls "the transcendental deduction of the categories of possible experience"—readers hardly feel that they are in the presence of poetry. We may aptly call poetry (individual poems) "philosophic," but we do not normally call philosophy (individual works of philosophy) "poetic." Indeed, we have no philosophic equivalent of the word "poem" as an individual work of philosophy (except for generic terms like "essay" or "treatise"). There is also the question of the relationship between poetry (as metrical and, at times, rhyming verse) and prose (whether that of philosophy or that of the fictional art that we associate with novels, novellas, and short stories). Indeed, we have the term "prosaic"—meaning dull, banal, pedestrian. . . . But the question of the relationship of poetry and prose we shall defer until later in our study.

But why, I repeat, take up these two questions—What is poetry? What is philosophy?—together? The rationale, the (poetic, the transcendental!) justification of discussing poetry and philosophy in relationship to each other takes us back to Kierkegaard's observation that, precisely because all spiritual language is metaphoric, it involves and expresses the transfer from sensible nature to transcendental spirit, to what both Wordsworth and Kant, as we shall see, call mind, reason, will, desire . . . , and thus what signifies the realm of human dignity, freedom, equality, and social commonality (fraternity/sorority). The aim that I have in my study, consequently, is to show that, whatever the differences between poetry and philosophy, or between verse and prose, true poetry and true philosophy are each grounded in spirit, in the critical spirit of metaphor and in the metaphor of critical spirit. There is, it is evident, much poetry in the world that is mere verse and much philosophy in the world that is simply prosaic. But the point that I want to stress, above all, in my book is that it is only in learning to overcome the traditional opposition between philosophy as abstract, or rational, and poetry (together with all the arts) as concrete, or affective that we can properly come to terms with the critical content that each contains and expresses. In order, then, to deconstruct (overcome) the standard opposition between poetry and philosophy we must learn to see that they are each grounded in the language of spirit the origin of which, at once historical and ontological, is biblical. Indeed, it is precisely in light of modern poetry and philosophy, as they are represented by, for example, Wordsworth and Kant, that we come to realize that the Bible, both Hebrew and Christian (what Christians call the Old and New Testaments) is, as religious, at once poetic and philosophic.

It is evident, then, that in my study I shall be involved in a sustained, ongoing examination of, in addition to philosophy and poetry, religion as constituting their common grounding in the spirit of metaphor and the metaphor of spirit. This analysis will, in principle, be at once ontological and historical. For, indeed, as we learn from Hegel, together with Kierkegaard, history is the story of human beings coming freely and infinitely into existence and trailing clouds of glory, as Wordsworth puts it. Let us recall what Kierkegaard writes in the passage from *Works of Love* that provides the leitmotif of our study. In the beginning we are born spirit. Yet, our life, insofar as we are worthy of it, is the story of our critically metaphorical progress from spirit through spirit to spirit. In the beginning human beings exist as spirit. Yet, their existence, their being, their perfection, as Spinoza puts it, is the transition to ever more ample existence, to ever greater perfection of spirit (when it is not the transition to less perfect existence). It is little wonder, then, that we conventionally (and fittingly!) understand what we call modern philosophy to have begun with Descartes in the early seventeenth century: I think, *ergo* I am. What Kierkegaard calls spirit, in the tradition of biblical theology, constitutes the ontological, and the historical, relationship between thinking, or self-consciousness, and existence. That we are in the presence here of what, since Kant, has been called the ontological argument for existence—for the existence of God, of the other—in the presence, in other words, of that relationship of self and other that is at once historical and ontological is another of the grand topics that is central to our study.

Indeed, one of the most delicious of all philosophical ironies—should we call it poetic justice?—is that Kant, while he justly demolished in *The Critique of Pure Reason* what he calls there the ontological argument for the existence of God, makes what is properly to be understood as the ontological argument, as first formulated by in St. Anselm (in the late eleventh century) and then reformulated by Descartes and yet again by Spinoza in the seventeenth century, the very foundation of that least of all poetic-sounding concepts, the *Ding an sich*, the thing in itself, or, in other words, the spirit, the human person.

One of the enormous implications of working through, in comprehensive, systematic terms, the relationship between ontology (existence) and history (the human story of spirit) is the realization of the fundamental difference between, on the one hand, poetry and philosophy in the biblical (modern) tradition and, on the other hand, *poesis* and *philosophia* in the ancient Greek (pagan) tradition. As I indicated above, there is no concept of spirit (as distinct from what we saw Kierkegaard call the sensate-psychical) in the ancient Greek world of Homer and Socrates. Or, in the terms of Kierkegaard's *Fear and Trembling*, there is a fundamental difference between the aesthetic and the ethical, body and soul, on the one hand, and the religious when understood as the absolute relationship to the absolute, on the other. In the strictest terms, which we shall unpack as we proceed in our study, Greek poetry and philosophy contain no metaphor, no history as the never-ending transfer of spirit to what we shall see Kant call the transcendental kingdom of practical reason.

But it is now time for me to explain why I have chosen Wordsworth and Kant to represent in my study the poet and the philosopher. The reasons for my choice are at once simple and complex. While other figures might well be selected by different scholars and readers as the most outstanding or representative philosopher or poet, still, it is evident that Wordsworth and Kant are universally recognized as supremely important in their individual fields. Indeed, I could have selected other poets and philosophers from the period of the later sixteenth and earlier seventeenth centuries down to the present, as I indicated earlier. But I wanted to focus on a poet and a philosopher who not only were "modern" but also, in fundamental ways, created the very revolution in thinking, at once poetic and philosophic, that we call modern. Wordsworth, whose great period of poetic creativity belongs to the decade beginning in the later 1790s, is normally associated with the first generation of the so-called Romantic period of English (and German[3]) poetry (and also German philosophy). Kant, who wrote his major "critical" works in the fifteen or so years beginning with the publication of the first edition of *The Critique of Pure Reason* in 1781, is by and large identified with the Enlightenment, German, French, and British (i.e., both English and Scottish). Not only, however, are the terms "Romanticism" and "Enlightenment" notoriously difficult to pin down, like the term "modernity" itself, but also they are often misleadingly opposed to each other. In any case, my study is not historical in the conventional sense. I shall not be concerned with the history of poetry or philosophy, and thus I shall discuss neither the influence that earlier poets or philosophers had on Wordsworth or Kant nor their impact on later poets or philosophers. While Kant slightly precedes Wordsworth in time, there is no direct evidence that Wordsworth, by the later eighteenth century, was reading the German works of philosophy that were beginning to trickle by way of translation into England in the last decade of the eighteenth century. Still, we can assume that, as his intellectual friendship with Coleridge, beginning in 1795 when they first met, continued to develop and deepen, he would have learned about Kant through Coleridge, who specifically went to the continent to learn German so that he could read the works of Kant, Fichte, Schelling, and other German philosophers in their original language.

The reader may well ask at this point why I did not choose to focus on Coleridge, who is generally regarded not only as a great Romantic poet but also as the philosophic thinker who served as the major conduit of (romantic) German philosophy to the British Isles in the first decades of the nineteenth century. I shall return to Coleridge in the context of my discussion of Wordsworth. But I want now to proceed with my elaboration of why I chose to focus on the poet Wordsworth and the philosopher Kant in my study. First, Wordsworth as poet. There is broad agreement on the part of both contemporary commentators and scholars down to the present that it was the publication of the *Lyrical Ballads* in 1798, jointly planned by Wordsworth and Coleridge (although by far most of the poetry in the volume was written by Wordsworth), that launched the Romantic revolution in English poetry, as distinct from the neo-classical poetry of the later seventeenth and the eighteenth centuries. In the subsequent half-dozen or so years Wordsworth wrote *The Prelude*, which is arguably the greatest English poem of the nineteenth century and which, in my judgment, has but one rival, Whitman's "Song of

Myself" (in *Leaves of Grass*). I want to add here that I felt it important, when dealing with "my" poet, to confine myself to English poetry (since my knowledge of French, German, and Italian is not sufficient to plumb poems in those languages in depth; and I do not know Russian, etc.) However, since I find that the close reading of a poetic text is, in some ways, significantly different from the comprehensive reading of a philosophic text—an issue to which I shall return!—I felt prepared to choose as "my" philosopher one who wrote in German. (I shall rely on English translations of Kant's works, while making use of the original German texts when and as necessary.)

But to continue with Wordsworth. While calling upon some of his lyrical (shorter) poems, I shall concentrate in my book on his big poem of some thirteen books (in the 1805 version) and containing some nearly ten thousand lines, which we today know as *The Prelude or, Growth of a Poet's Mind; An Autobiographical Poem*. I shall deal with the salient, textual details of the poem, including why it is called *The Prelude*, in my next chapter. But here I want to point out that the passage from the Christian deliberation "Love Builds Up," in which Kierkegaard observes, as we have seen (in writing a commentary on 1 Corinthians 8:1), that all human speech, together with the divine speech of the Bible, involves and expresses the transfer, the metaphor, of spirit provides an uncanny account of what Wordsworth effects in his poem. The poet—William Wordsworth—is born spirit, like every human being. Yet, his life is the story of his becoming spirit, of spirit becoming spirit, and, in his case, the story of this particular man becoming worthy in adulthood of being a poet of the human spirit. At the conclusion of the final Book 13 of *The Prelude* (in the 1805 edition), the poet declares that he, together with Coleridge, whom he addresses throughout the poem, will, as "Prophets of Nature," speak to their readers

> A lasting inspiration, sanctified
> By reason and by truth; what we have loved
> Others will love, and we may teach them how;
> Instruct them how the mind of man becomes
> A thousand times more beautiful than the earth
> On which he dwells.

I shall not presently undertake a detailed exegesis of this passage. But I cite it here in order to signal key features of the poem as central to my choice of Wordsworth as my exemplary poet. The most important feature of the poem, perhaps, and doubtlessly its most subtle, is that, while it is forward looking—the past is prologue—it is a complete, finished, accomplished poem (work of art). What Wordsworth means by his use of the theological language of inspiration and sanctification, of the philosophic language of reason and truth, and of the poetic language of love the reader can understand only in terms of reading and thinking through the entire poem, from beginning to end. The poem's end is in the beginning. It begins and ends with the reader (with the universality of its readership, past, present, and future). It is, then, eternally a prelude to yet deeper, richer, more ample human experience.

I have not yet, however, commented on what is surely the most challenging element of the passage from *The Prelude* that I cited in the previous paragraph. How are we to understand the oxymoronic sobriquet "prophet of nature?" What, indeed, is the relationship, for Wordsworth in his poem, between nature and "the mind of man" or spirit, which, he declares, is infinitely, as it were, more beautiful than the earth (or nature). I call the self-designation "prophet of nature" an oxymoron since it brings together, we may say, religion and nature. The biblical prophets were prophets of God, not of nature. Does Wordsworth view nature, as distinct from the earth, as divine? Again, rather than explicating at this point how Wordsworth in his poem conceives of nature—a truly challenging question for all his readers—I want now to connect Wordsworth, the poet, with Kant, the philosopher. I chose Kant as "my" philosopher because it was he who, in the most elemental and fundamental terms, revolutionized philosophy in the modern world with his demonstration, in his two principal works, *The Critique of Pure Reason* (1781; second edition 1787) and *The Critique of Practical Reason* (1788), that reason (*Vernunft*) is, first and last, practice. With reason properly and truly understood as practice, as action, we see, then, that it is inseparable from will, desire, mind (spirit), and thinking—as distinct from knowledge, the province of the understanding (*Verstand*). The critical point to grasp at this point is that reason dwells, not in nature when understood as the world of objects, but in the world of what Kant calls the kingdom of ends, where we are commanded by the categorical imperative of reason to treat all human beings with dignity, as ends in themselves, not as means outside of themselves. Reason belongs to morality, to human subjects in their mutual relationships with each other, not to the scientific study of natural objects.

All of this will become clear, I trust—in showing that what we have loved others will love, if I may here recall Wordsworth! It is thus ironic, or paradoxical, that for Kant, as I indicated earlier, the transcendental realm (the human kingdom of mind, spirit, or reason) is the practical. We shall see that, Wordsworth, in, as it were, deifying nature (but he is no deist), uses the concept of nature, in whose name he speaks as a prophet, in a way opposite from Kant. For Kant, as I have indicated, sharply distinguishes in his two *Critiques* between natural objects (things) and rational (or moral) subjects. Still, they altogether agree on that distinction, although Wordsworth, as we saw in the passage from *The Prelude* that I cited above, unites nature with reason, truth, and mind, as distinct from the (natural) earth. Indeed, we shall see that Wordsworth and Kant, both the poet and the philosopher, adhere to the prophetic tradition of revelatory proclamation that, while we fittingly live on the earth, we do not live by the earth (the earth is not our fitting home).[4]

In concluding my introductory remarks, I shall now briefly outline the five chapters that lie ahead of us. In Chapters 2 and 3 I take up Wordsworth. In addition to providing in Chapter 2, as briefly as possible, the historical context in which Wordsworth established himself as the great poet he is, I shall introduce his poetic practice by way of considering some of his smaller, lyrical poems. I shall also summarize the views on poetry that he articulated in the various prefaces to the major collections of poetry that he published up to 1815 (one of which is in verse!). I shall also discuss his quite complex relationship to Coleridge, including the critique of Wordsworth's poetry that Coleridge, in calling upon German philosophers from Lessing and Kant to Schelling, made central to his *Biographia Literaria* (1817). There is present here the uncanny fact that in this work Coleridge also portrays the growth of the mind of the poet, yet of one who has become a writer of philosophic prose. Additionally, it will be my scholarly duty, in a book on poetry and philosophy, to make evident that Coleridge, notwithstanding his estimable standing as a poet, shows himself to be an altogether inadequate reader (interpreter) of Wordsworth's poetry and also at the same time a wholly inadequate philosophical thinker. While Coleridge has the highest praise for Kant as the venerable sage of Königsberg, in reality, since he provides no significant evidence that he in any fundament sense understands the revolutionary importance of Kant's demonstration that reason is practice, he makes little if any significant use of Kantian philosophy in his literary biography.

I shall also discuss in Chapter 2 the ideas that Shelley made central to his *A Defense of Poetry* (written in 1820 but published posthumously in 1840). In conflating Plato and Jesus (ancient Greek philosophy and Christianity) Shelley critically undermines what insight he has into the relationship between (modern) poetry and religion (Christianity). I emphasize this point since it is religion, that is, Christianity (or, more generally, the Judaeo-Christian tradition of theology), that provides the common framework for modern poetry and philosophy (although it is true, as it is also my duty to report, that Kant, in his discussion of biblical religion, reflects the anti-Judaism so deeply embedded in Christendom from the very beginning of the Common Era). Neither Wordsworth nor Kant falls into the error, still so very common today among thinkers and scholars of divers fields and intellectual orientations, of falsely conflating the worlds of the Bible and of ancient Greece (although we shall see that from time to time Wordsworth in *The Prelude* does refer to ancient versifiers as true poets). In Chapter 3 I shall provide a comprehensive reading of *The Prelude* in showing that the growth of the poet's mind embodies the metaphor of nature as the critical transfer from nature to spirit.

Chapters 4 and 5 on Kant, like Chapters 2 and 3 on Wordsworth, will be, respectively, introductory and comprehensively exegetical. In Chapter 4 I shall introduce Kant in focusing on the philosophical implications of the question that, as I indicated earlier, he asks as the most fundamental question of critical reason: How are synthetic *a priori* principles possible? We shall see that Kant, in posing the question of how the principles of critical reason, of rational critique, can and must be comprehended as at once deductive (i.e., analytic *a priori*) and inductive (i.e., synthetic *a posteriori*) is supremely conscious of founding the philosophy of modernity on a critical logic, on a logic of critique, that is fundamentally different from the logic of Aristotle and thus of all Greek metaphysics. Whereas the philosophers and poets of ancient Greece thought in terms of the unending opposition between appearance and reality, matter and forms, as based on the law of contradiction, on what Kant calls general logic, he shows that our modern (biblical) thinking—our will, our moral lives of communal practice—embodies what he calls transcendental logic. The Greeks can tell us that something either exists or does not exist (following the law of identity, the sister of the law of contradiction). But they cannot tell us whether it exists or not. But Kant, seemingly not altogether (or truly) self-conscious of the ontological (and historical) implications of his logic, demonstrates, to recall Kierkegaard, that we are born spirit. In the beginning we cannot even begin thinking without (outside of) the self-realization that to think is to exist. Or, we can say that to pose the question of the beginning (the principle, the origin) of reality (of being, life, existence) involves and expresses the existence of the very one who poses the question.

Thus, we see that Heidegger, in grounding his concept of being in the metaphysics of the ancient Greeks, is altogether wrong in claiming that the fundamental question of philosophy is why there is something and not nothing. What Kant demonstrates, in contrast, is that the fundamental question of philosophy is: Given that I exist (i.e., since I have received, like Adam and Eve, the actual gift of existence), I then can and must ask: How is it possible? What are the possibilities, the potentialities, the *potentiae* (the potencies or powers) of existence? In simple terms, then, Kant shows us that the fundamental question of life is: Given that something exists, how is it possible? Given that I exist, how is my existence possible? Or, in other words: How do I think my existence, will my existence, live my existence, practice my existence? In reversing the Greek logic of contradiction, according to which possibility takes precedence over actuality, theory over practice, Kant shows us that the actual (i.e., existence) precedes (grounds) the possible. Consequently, Kant asks as his fundamental question: How is metaphysics possible? Again, in simple terms, he thus asks: Given that metaphysics exists, how is it possible? In answering this question Kant demonstrates that what he calls the three fundamental principles or postulates of metaphysics— freedom, immortality, and God—are grounded in practical reason (in the will, in practice), not in theoretical reason (the understanding). Yet, again, in like terms, we cannot pose the question of the origin of freedom (whether ontologically or historically) without being conscious that we can and must pose this question solely because are free to ask it.

Before concluding these introductory remarks on Kant, I want to raise the following question. Given that he revolutionizes philosophy by founding it on the transcendental logic of rational practice, as embodying synthetic *a priori* propositions, and not on the Greek logic of contradiction as based on the interminable opposition between deductive (*a priori*) and inductive (*a posteriori*) propositions, what is the origin, historical and ontological, of the concept of reason as transcendental practice? It is evident that the metaphysics of modern poetry and philosophy does not and cannot have its origin, whether historical or ontological, in ancient

Greek poetry and philosophy. Kant, however, unlike Hegel, never directly poses the question of the origin of metaphysics, just as he also does not directly acknowledge that the "existential" proof involved in posing the question—How is metaphysics possible?—actually replicates the ontological argument proving the existence of God. But what a comprehensive reading of Kant does show us is that the metaphysics of practical reason, of rational practice, has its historical and ontological origins in the Bible. Indeed, as I am sure is becoming evident to the reader, the very idea that ontology begins historically and that history begins ontologically is epitomized by Kierkegaard in his observation that, while we are born spirit, our existence is actually constituted by historically working out and through the ontological possibilities (powers) of spirit. In short, in preparation for our in depth study of Kant's transcendental metaphysics in Chapter 5, I shall, in Chapter 4, outline the key ideas that are central to the two major works that Kant wrote on religion, *Religion within the Bounds of Mere Reason* (1793; second edition 1794)[5] and *The Conflict of the Faculties* (published in 1798). In Part I of the second work (written in 1794) Kant discusses the "conflict" between the (lower university) Faculty of Philosophy and the (higher university) Faculty of Theology. In his analysis of the relationship between philosophy and religion Kant repeatedly uses the phrase "the religion of reason" in order to make clear that, just as practical reason is embodied in the moral law of treating all human beings as ends in themselves, so religion is constituted by practice, the practice that is involved in loving your neighbor as yourself.

I want to add here that it is important to keep in mind that in Kant's time all publications in the Kingdom of Prussia were subject to censorship and that, with the radical impact of the French Revolution of 1789 and its aftermath, including the execution of the French queen and king, the Reign of Terror under Robespierre, and the territorial ambitions of what would become the French Empire under Napoleon reverberating throughout Europe, the Prussian censors became increasingly concerned with the public discussion of sensitive topics such as the critique of religion (as distinct from scholarly debate that was confined to the closed world of the university).[6]

I shall also discuss in Chapter 4 the altogether extraordinary essay that Kant wrote as a commentary on the story of Adam and Eve entitled "Conjectural Beginning of Human History." In undertaking to show in his essay how human beings, in and from the beginning, freely constitute their existence through and as rational practice, Kant sets forth on what he calls "a mere pleasure trip . . . on the wings of the imagination," since, as he tells us, we "must start out with something which human reason cannot derive from prior natural causes— . . . the existence of man." It is hard to resist asking whether we should consider this imaginative conjecture poetic or philosophic!

In my exegetical Chapter 5 on Kant I shall concentrate on the fundamental ideas of his two principal works: *The Critique of Pure Reason* and *The Critique of Practical Reason*. The first critique is nothing less (or more!) than a gigantesque preface in which its author clears the critical path to the second critique, which, while a much shorter work, constitutes the very heart of his philosophy. It is in these two works that he revolutionizes philosophy with his ground-breaking demonstration that it is solely on the basis of the transcendental reason of practice, of mind or spirit, that we can confidently (in good faith!) possess, at one and the same time, moral truth (as involving subjects) and scientific knowledge of nature (as involving objects). We shall see that Kant dramatically articulates in philosophical terms the proverbial truth of the Bible that we live in the world but not of the world with his statement that *that* by which (reason, spirit, mind, the thing in itself) we subjects know objects we cannot know as we know those objects. Kierkegaard rendered the critical truth of this radical insight in inimitable terms: truth is subjectivity.[7] Truth inheres in subjects, in the truth of their subjectivity and in the subjectivity of their truth, not in the objects of the natural world.

In summary, what I undertake to elaborate in the chapters that follow is the fundamental reason that it is so truly instructive, what Kierkegaard calls upbuilding or edifying, to consider the poetry of Wordsworth and the philosophy of Kant within the common framework of metaphor and critique. Each of our authors, both the poet and the philosopher, begins with the phenomenal world of natural objects. Yet, what each shows us, in his distinctively poetic or philosophic style, is that we truly begin as spirit, as rational or transcendental subjects. The infinite, divine, and eternal task of existence, each of them demonstrates, one poetically, the other philosophically, is, with the foresight of history, that is, providentially, to bring spirit into existence. All human beings have the duty, Wordsworth and Kant each maintain, to regard their life as always and forever the prelude to a yet fuller, more meaningful human practice as upbuilt by and through the metaphor of critique and the critique of metaphor. Still, there is no question but that the critical distinctions that Kant makes fundamental to his philosophy—between freedom and nature, subject and object, practice and theory, thought (will/desire) and knowledge, morality and science, and so between the transcendental world of practical reason and the phenomenal world of theoretical knowledge—helps us penetrate Wordsworth's use of terms, above all, nature and imagination, which can so often appear abstruse to the reader. But it is no less the case that what Wordsworth, in writing in the name of everyman, of Kierkegaard's single individual, shows us in his poetry, above all, in *The Prelude*, is that the poet, in beginning in and with the world of nature, which is both within and without all human beings, embarks on the critical path of metaphor conscious of living in but not of the world of nature. The story of the historical growth of the poet's mind, at once uniquely personal and universally human, makes practically vivid—metaphorical!—Kant's philosophical critique of pure reason as practice. Our consciousness of the awesomeness (awfulness) of nature embodies our self-consciousness that we begin freely as spirit, as moral subjects, not as natural objects. We do not and cannot live without (outside of) nature, for we are embodied objects of nature. Still, our existence as human subjects is constituted in and by the infinitely ceaseless effort of learning, with ever-increasing amplitude, to behold nature as the transfer to spirit that involves the metaphor of critique. Outside of metaphor, nature does not exist—for us. We do not exist—outside of nature—without critique.

CHAPTER 2

Thinking Poetically with Wordsworth

INTRODUCTORY

ABOUT MIDWAY INTO THE "Ode: Intimations of Immortality from Recollections of Early Childhood" the speaker in Wordsworth's poem of some two hundred lines addresses

> *Thou*, whose exterior semblance / doth belie
> Thy Soul's immensity;
> *Thou* best Philosopher . . .
> Haunted for ever by the eternal mind,—
> Mighty Prophet! Seer blest,
> On whom those truths do rest,
> Which we are toiling all our lives to find, . . .
> *Thou*, over whom thy Immortality
> Broods like the Day.

"*Thou* little Child. . . . Why . . . dost *thou* provoke / The years to bring the inevitable yoke" with the result that "thy Soul" bears "a weight" of "her earthly freight" and "custom . . . / Heavy as frost, and deep almost as life!"[8] I initiate the first of my two chapters on Wordsworth with a passage from one of his most famous poems since it introduces us to issues that are central to all of his critically important poetry. These issues are at once textual, historical, and interpretive and so no less philosophic (religious) than they are poetic (literary/aesthetic). I would be confident that not only readers who are new to the "Immortality Ode" are perplexed regarding how and why it is that "thou little Child" is or, indeed, can possibly be addressed as the "best Philosopher, "mighty Prophet," and "Seer blest" but also readers who have studied the poem carefully continue to find this passage challenging to understand. What does it mean? Indeed, this is the very question that, as we shall see, Coleridge raises when he discusses what he calls "the characteristic defects" and "beauties" of Wordsworth's poetry in Chapter 22 of his *Biographia Literaria*.

I begin my second chapter on the poetry of Wordsworth with consideration of his "Immortality Ode," together with a few of his other poems, in order to clear the critical, interpretive path to an in-depth engagement with *The Prelude* in Chapter Three. This will allow me to show not only how meaning (what a poem means) depends on close attention to key textual details but equally how textual details—e.g., who is "thou little child"?—depends on placing them within the overall meaning (or structure) of a poem. We shall continually move between part and whole, beginning and end. Along the way it will be important for us to take account of literary scholarship regarding, in particular, the fact that Wordsworth, together with Coleridge, but also Shelley, typically announced works or additions to works that were, in fact, never written. The issue of which version or versions of Wordsworth's poems—early (at times, unpublished and available only in manuscript), revised, final (sometimes posthumous)—it is best to consider, to adhere to the confines of this study, remains an unsettled, scholarly question. Readers will find, consequently, that they have not only copious citations of poetic passages to work through but also abundant notes regarding textual details to take into account.

As I indicated in Chapter One, I shall also discuss in this chapter the *Literaria Biographia* of Coleridge, together with a few of his poems, and *A Defense of Poetry* of Shelley. The purpose of discussing Coleridge is twofold, the first poetical and the second philosophical-theological. We shall see that in his poem "To William Wordsworth" (published in 1817) Coleridge provides a moving tribute to his poet friend. But in the *Biographia Literaria* (also published in 1817), whether praising "the beauties" or criticizing "the defects" of Wordsworth's poetry, he cites only individual lines or passages of particular poems in support of his claims. It will become evident that his rejection of the idea that a "little Child" could be the "best philosopher" as jejune and in violation of all common sense reflects his failure to consider this passage in the context of the whole poem. It will also, consequently, become evident that Coleridge, although at times he pronounces philosophical principles that are sound, fails to propound a philosophical (theological) position in adequate terms precisely because he does not think through, in comprehensive, systematic terms, the very ground (or structure) of his principles. His failure to account for how and why Kant was, as he called him, the venerable sage of Koenigberg, or, in my terms, the revolutionary founder of modern philosophy, is at once the cause and the effect of his lack of hermeneutical insight. As for Shelley, since in his *A Defense of Poetry* he does not discuss the poetry of his contemporaries but rather formulates what he views as the principles, at once historical and ontological, of poetry (together with the fine arts, in general), I shall discuss the *Defense* in the context of analyzing Coleridge's philosophical ideas. All of this, the reader will understand, is to help us see more amply how and why Wordsworth and Kant are our exemplary poet and philosopher. Or we could say that, as true poetry presupposes philosophical (and theological) truth, so true philosophy (theology) is enriched in and through the truth of poetry. To paraphrase Kant, poetry without philosophy is blind. Philosophy without poetry is empty.

But let us now undertake to explore how and why Wordsworth in his "Ode: Intimations of Immortality from Recollections of Early Childhood" avers that the little child is the best philosopher. What does he mean? We shall find, as we proceed in our two chapters on Wordsworth, that the structure, the shape, of the "Ode" prefigures (or indeed reflects) the structure of *The Prelude*. For, indeed, just as the child is the prelude that constitutes the overture to the symphony (the blending of tones) or the concerto (the concerted effort of life), so Wordsworth writes the prelude from the point of view of the conclusion (of the work as a whole). But it is here that I have the opportunity of indicating, in the most compressed terms possible, the textual problems with which the writings of Wordsworth, together with those of Coleridge and also Shelley, confront us. I begin with the *Prelude*. We have two "completed" versions of the poem, neither of which Wordsworth published in his lifetime: the thirteen book version of 1805 (today printed from manuscript) and the fourteen book version that was published, shortly after his death in 1850, by his widow Mary and executors. The title of the poem—*The Prelude or Growth of a Poet's Mind*—is known only from the posthumous 1850 version of the poem. Still, Coleridge's poem "To William Wordsworth," written in 1806 and published in 1817, contains the following sub-title: "Composed on the Night after his Recitation of a Poem on the Growth of an Individual Mind."[9] I shall shortly examine what Coleridge in his poem calls "that prophetic lay" of Wordsworth. But the point that I want to make here is that the first readers of Coleridge's poem would have had no access to the poem of Wordsworth that it celebrates.[10] It is yet more peculiar that, when Coleridge in his *Biographia Literaria*, in addition to specifying what he calls the defects and beauties of his friend's poems, criticizes key elements of the views on poetry that Wordsworth expresses in various prefatory pieces that he included with the several editions of his poetry from 1798 to 1815, he does not mention "a Poem on the Growth of an Individual Mind," although he does cite a few lines from the poem (which, to repeat, existed only in manuscript) without attribution.

The challenge, then, that both the general reader and the scholarly student of Wordsworth's poetry face, especially with regard to *The Prelude* (again recalling that neither Wordsworth nor Coleridge used this title in their lifetimes), is that Wordsworth continued to revise many of his poems, including *The Prelude*, into his final years. As regards my approach to his poems, and, above all, *The Prelude*, I shall make use of both their earlier ("original") and their later, revised ("definitive") versions. While the 1850 (posthumous) version of *The Prelude* contains copious revisions of the manuscript version of 1805—involving individual words and syntax, lines both single and multiple, and excisions of complete (although relatively short) passages—still, the poem remains fundamentally unchanged in terms of its overall structure and meaning from 1805 to 1850. At times, Wordsworth, in his revisions, especially when they involve syntax and word-choice, clarifies the meaning of dense passages. Why not, then, simply adhere to the 1850 (final, revised) version of *The Prelude*? What, in other words, is the original poem? Is it the poem that Wordsworth originally (first) wrote in the period from 1798 to 1805, when it was completed (in manuscript)? Or is it the poem that was originally (first) published in 1850 after the poet's death? There is, in my judgment, no definitive answer to this question. I do not myself have such an answer. Still, because *The Prelude* does belong to the relatively short time span of Wordsworth's truly creative life, from the last years of the eighteenth century to 1815, I think it is appropriate to view as original the poem that the poet made central to his artistic life during this period of time. An elemental way of putting this same point is that, if we possessed nothing written by Wordsworth after 1815, his poetic stature would remain unchanged.[11]

The "Immortality Ode" provides an apt example of the changes that Wordsworth effected in his poems. While Wordsworth wrote the "Ode" in the first years of the nineteenth century, he published it only in 1807. But it was only with its publication in Wordsworth's 1815 collection of poetry that the poem bears the title by which it is commonly known today and that I have cited. Additionally, it is also only beginning in 1815 that the "Immortality Ode" is introduced by way of citing the last three lines, with their double oxymoron, of the untitled poem of nine lines that was first published in 1807 and that begins: "My heart leaps up when I behold / A Rainbow in the sky.":

> The Child is father of the Man;
> And I could wish my days to be
> Bound each to each by natural piety.

I say double oxymoron in wanting to draw attention both to the idea that the child fathers (begets) the (adult) human being and to the phrase "natural piety." In the first instance Wordsworth reverses the "natural" relationship between father (parent) and child and in the second binds together two realms that we typically view as distinct from if not, indeed, opposed to each other: nature and religion (morality). Each of these reversals, or paradoxes, represents, as we shall repeatedly see, a critically metaphorical stance that Wordsworth makes central to his major poems and, above all, in *The Prelude*. Indeed, what is especially characteristic of his poetry is how he binds these two reversals into single, philosophic worldview.

It is clearly apparent that the declaration that the child is father of the man can provide the reader of the "Immortality Ode" with a sense of how to respond to its proclamation that "thou little Child" art the "best Philosopher." So, let us now undertake to discern how Wordsworth makes poetry out of this paradoxical claim in his "Immortality Ode." While citing key lines of the poem, I shall, insofar as I can, paraphrase and summarize its crucial moments (movements). The poem opens:

> There was a time when meadow, grove, and stream,
> The earth, and every common sight,
>   To me did seem
>   Apparelled in celestial light.

But then the speaker proceeds to observe that what was then like the "glory and the freshness of a dream" is "not now as it has been of yore. . . . / The things which I have seen I now can see no more." This contrast between past and present, then and now, typically characterizes Wordsworth's poetry. While the speaker observes yet again that lovely are the rainbow, the rose, the moon, and the sun, he adds once more: "But yet

I know, where'er I go, / That there has passed away a glory from the earth." He details more of nature's glories, including "the Babe" that "leaps up on his mother's arm." Still, everything on which he looks

> Doth the same tale repeat:
> Whither is fled the visionary gleam?
> When is now, the glory and the dream?

At this point in the poem Wordsworth articulates the logic underlying the idea of immortality:

> Our birth is but a sleep and a forgetting:
> The soul that rises with us . . .
>   Hath had elsewhere its setting
>   And cometh from afar:
>   Not in entire forgetfulness,
>   And not in utter nakedness,
> But trailing clouds of glory do we come
>   From God, who is our home:
> Heaven lies about us in our infancy!
> Shades of the prison-house begin to close
>   Upon the growing Boy.
> Although attended "as Nature's Priest . . . / by the vision splendid"
> At length the Man perceives it die away,
> And fade into the light of common day.

I shall not undertake to examine the metaphysics of immortality, as expressed in the above lines, until we reach the end of the poem. After further contrast between "then" (the celestial glory of the earth) and now (when the "vision splendid" fades "into the light of common day"), we encounter the lines with which I introduced this chapter, those addressing "thou little Child" as "Thou best Philosopher . . . over whom thy Immortality/ Broods like the Day . . . / A presence which is not to be put by." Yet again, however, do the years "bring the inevitable yoke."

At this point, however, in the poem Wordsworth begins to transform its motion of "then" (glory) and "now" (prison-house) into that of "now" and "then." We read:

> O joy! that in our embers
> Is something that doth live,
> That nature yet remembers
> What was so fugitive!

While yet it is the fire of childhood that paradoxically begets the embers of adulthood, the speaker now proclaims that "The thought of our past years in me doth breed / Perpetual benedictions." He continues: *Not for* the simple life of childhood "Delight and liberty . . . / *But for* those obstinate questionings / Of sense and outward things."[12]

> But for those first affections,
> Those shadowy recollections,
> Which, be they what they may,
> Are yet the fountain light of all our day,
> Are yet a master light of all our seeing.
>
> For, however "inland far we be,"
>
> Our souls have sight of that immortal sea
>   Which brought us hither,
>   Can in a moment travel thither,
> And see the Children sport upon the shore,
> And hear the mighty waters rolling evermore.

May now the birds sing and the lambs bound, and "We in thought will join your throng," the speaker in the poem proclaims:

> What though the radiance which was once so bright
> Be now for ever taken from my sight . . .
>   We will grieve not, rather find
>   Strength in what remains behind,
>   *In the* primal sympathy,
>   Which having been must ever be,
>   *In the* soothing thoughts that spring
>   Out of human suffering,
>   *In the* faith that looks through death,
> *In* years that bring the philosophic mind.

We have now reached the crux, the paradoxical center, of the poem. Earlier in the poem (*then*) "thou little Child" was addressed as "thou best Philosopher," as "Mighty Prophet! Seer blest!" But (*now*) we learn that it is only with the years that bring suffering and death that we gain the strength, the primal sympathy, the soothing thoughts, the faith, and consequently "the philosophic mind" capable of comprehending that the past is prelude, that whatever has been "must ever be" immortal. That the child is the best, the first philosopher we only know in and through the years that bring us "the philosophic mind," that primal sympathy with life that the end is in the beginning. The shadowy recollections and remembrances of life, while merely the embers of the original fire of our life that is now so fugitive, so fleeting, "Are yet the fountain light of all our day . . . [and] a master light of all our seeing."

Wordsworth then initiates the sixteen-line conclusion of the "Immortality Ode" in recalling the poem's opening line. However, whereas *then* "there was a time" that is gone, *now* the speaker addresses "oh ye Fountains, Mountains, Hills, and Groves" in the present imperative:

> Think not of any severing of our loves!
> Yet in my heart of hearts I feel your might;
> I only have relinquished one delight
> To live beneath your more habitual sway.
> I love the Brooks which down their channels fret,
> Even more than when I tripped [as a child] lightly as they.

The speaker goes on to observe that, while "an eye / That hath kept watch o'er man's mortality" bestows "a sober colouring" on "The clouds that gather round the setting sun" of childhood, he yet gives "Thanks to the human heart by which we live, . . . its tenderness, its joys, and fears." For now

> To me the meanest [humblest] flower that blows [dies] can give
> Thoughts that do often lie too deep for tears.

So Wordsworth concludes his "Ode: Intimations of Immortality from Recollections of Early Childhood." The poem, we see, centers on, is shaped by, the paradox that we can recollect the fugitive intimations of childhood immortality only insofar as we have attained the philosophic mind whose eye keeps sober watch over our mortality. Immortality thus gives birth to our mortality, just as the child is father of the man and as the original fire of our being constitutes the embers of our life. It is critically important to see that what is to be understood by immortality in Wordsworth's "Ode" is fundamentally different from the Platonic conception of the immortality of the soul, together with the doctrine of recollection.[13] For Plato (as also for Aristotle, the amalgam of whose thought we know historically as Neoplatonism) the soul is finite, unchanging, immortal (like the immortal gods), and knowable solely in itself (and not by mortal man). For, as Socrates teaches, what the philosophic mind brings to us is ignorance of the good. Socrates is deemed the wisest of all men, according to the Delphic Oracle of Apollo, precisely because he knows that, as a mortal, he is ignorant (of the good). However, as Hegel points out, while Socrates knows *that* he is ignorant, he does not know *what* he is ignorant of. Socrates, unlike Adam, does not possess, in being like God (in being made in the divine image), knowledge of good and evil. He is ignorant of what Kant critically shows in the following formulation to be, as we have seen, the critical paradox of knowledge: *That* by which human beings (as subjects) know things (as objects) they do not and cannot know as they know those things, whence the distinction, not between ignorance (appearance) and knowledge (being), but between, on the one hand, transcendental (noumenal and subjective) reason as practical and categorical and, on the other hand, empirical (phenomenal and objective) understanding as theoretical and hypothetical, between, in elemental terms, subject and object, person and thing, freedom and nature, the thing in itself and appearances (as the objects of phenomenal nature).

What Wordsworth shows us in his "Immortality Ode," together with his strongest poems, and in *The Prelude*, above all, as we shall see in the next chapter, is that we begin in nature, in our unconscious love of meadows, groves, and streams. But what we discover, as he writes in that section of Part 1 of Book I of *The Recluse*, entitled *Home in Grasmere*, that serves as a verse "Prospectus" to *The Excursion*, which was published in 1814 (but written in 1800), is that there is nothing in the universe that

> can breed such fear and awe
> As fall upon us often when we look
> Into our minds, into the Mind of Man—
> My haunt and the main region of my song. . . .
> How exquisitely the individual Mind
> (And the progressive powers perhaps no less
> Of this whole species) to the external World
> Is fitted:—and how exquisitely, too—
> Theme this but little heard of among men—
> The external World is fitted to the Mind;
> And the creation (by no lower name
> Can it be called) which they with blended might
> Accomplish: —this is our high argument.[14]

Still, before we continue with Wordsworth's "high argument" on how exquisitely the human mind is fitted to the world of nature and the natural world is fitted to the mind of human beings—doubtlessly, we are here in the presence of the "natural piety" that is embodied in the avowal that the child is father of the man—it is important, first, to recall the perplexing historical details that surround the two epic poems with which Wordsworth identified his poetic destiny. We remember that the poem that we know as *The Prelude* was only published after the poet's death in 1850 under a title that was never used by either its author or Coleridge, his poetical friend and philosophic companion. Wordsworth intended *The Prelude* to serve as the introduction to *The Recluse*, which he was inspired by Coleridge to believe would be his truly significant philosophical achievement in verse. *The Recluse* was to contain three books. Book II of *The Recluse*, entitled *The Excursion*, was published in 1814. In the Preface to *The Excursion* Wordsworth writes that the poem (the unnamed *Prelude*), in which "he undertook to record, in verse, the origin and progress of his own powers" and which he "addressed to a dear Friend [Coleridge], most distinguished for his knowledge and genius, and to whom the Author's Intellect is deeply indebted, has long been finished [since 1805]." He writes further that "the result of the investigation which gave rise to it [*The Prelude*] was a determination to compose a philosophical poem containing views of Man, Nature, and Society; and to be entitled, 'The Recluse;' as having for its principal subject the sensations and opinions of a poet living in retirement." He observes yet further that the "preparatory poem [*The Prelude*] is biographical and conducts the history of the Author's mind to the point when he was emboldened to hope that his faculties were sufficiently matured for entering upon the arduous labour which he had proposed to himself" in *The Recluse*. Wordsworth adds that the two works can be understood to be related to each other as "the ante-chapel" (*The Prelude*) "to the body of a gothic church" (*The Recluse*). As for *The Recluse*, while Book II of the poem was published in 1814 as *The Excursion*, Book III of the poem was never written. Of Book I Wordsworth wrote only Part 1, entitled *Home at Grasmere*, which, written in 1800, was first published in 1888, except for its last section of about hundred lines that, as noted above, was included in the Preface to *The Excursion* as a *Prospectus* to the poem.

Thus, we see that the untitled poem that we know as *The Prelude*, the ante-chapel to the Gothic Church of *The Recluse*, was not known to the public during Wordsworth's lifetime. While Coleridge, as I pointed out earlier, cites a couple of two-line passages from *The Prelude* in the *Biographia Literaria*, he does not identify them; and, more significantly, he does not discuss in his work what today we view as Wordsworth's greatest poem. However, as I also noted earlier, the silence on the part of Coleridge in the *Biographia Literaria* regarding *The Prelude* appears bizarre in light of the fact that he focuses on it in his poem "To William

Wordsworth" and that both his literary biography and his poem were published in the same year (1817). As for *The Recluse*, the principal edifice in Wordsworth's poetic enterprise, it exists, as we have seen, only in two large fragments: Book II, *The Excursion*, published in 1814; and Part 1 of Book I, *Home at Grasmere*, published posthumously, except for its final section, which was published as the Prospectus to *The Excursion*.[15]

Let me add that Wordsworth moved to Grasmere in the central Lake District of England in 1799 with his much beloved sister Dorothy, of whom we shall hear more in *The Prelude*. After marrying in 1802, he and his wife Mary lived there until 1820. It was in his dearly loved Grasmere that Wordsworth, in addition to the early poems of the *Lyrical Ballads*, wrote what we view today as his critically important body of poetry, together with his prefaces.

I shall also take the opportunity here of summarizing the basic details, historical and biographical, of the *Lyrical Ballads*. Wordsworth and Coleridge, having first met and initiated their mutually enriching friendship as poets in 1795, to which Wordsworth bears testimony in the Preface to *The Excursion*, as we saw above, jointly planned together the publication of the *Lyrical Ballads*, which appeared in 1798. The poems contained in the *Lyrical Ballads* revolutionized English poetry and, together with the contemporary writings, literary and philosophical, of German thinkers, brought about the movement in the arts (including music) and philosophy, that we call Romanticism. But it is important to keep in mind that the edition of the *Lyrical Ballads* that was published in 1798 appeared anonymously. It did not bear the names of their authors, Wordsworth and Coleridge. Additionally, most of the poems in the *Lyrical Ballads*, together with the "Advertisement" to the volume, were written by Wordsworth, although it did include among the few poems by Coleridge in the volume "The Rime of the Ancient Mariner."[16]

A second edition of the *Lyrical Ballads* was published in 1800 with the names of the two authors attached and with new poems included in the volume. However, the new poems that were added to the 1800 edition were all written by Wordsworth except for one new poem written by Coleridge (while the few poems by Coleridge that were published in the first edition of 1798 now appeared in versions revised by their author). Wordsworth also added a Preface to the 1800 edition of the *Lyrical Ballads*. A third edition of the *Lyrical Ballads* was published in 1802. It included a revised version of the 1800 Preface, plus an "Appendix to the Preface." It was the views on poetry that Wordsworth expressed in his prefaces, including the "Essay Supplementary to the Preface" to the edition of his poetry that he brought out in 1815, of which Coleridge in the *Biographia Literaria* (1817), as we shall see, was so critical.

Having now summarized the salient historical and biographical facts surrounding the key publications of Wordsworth (together with those of Coleridge), we return to the thematic center of the "Immortality Ode." In the years that bring us the philosophic mind what we human beings discover is that the faith that looks through death is the acknowledgement that what has been "must ever be." This is a statement, not of fatal necessitarianism but of the "natural piety" whose primal sympathy reflects the creative fit of mind and nature, of internal and external, of subject and object. The paradox here is that this fit or creative relationship exists only in and through the mind. It is the relationship of which nature knows nothing. Yes, mind is dependent on nature. But it is precisely our conscious awareness of this dependence in and by which we recognize how fittingly we live in the world of nature, yet not by the natural world, that reveals the independence of mind from nature. For, and here we anticipate Kant, whose ontological position is, as we shall see in future chapters, identical with that of Wordsworth, human beings are subjects (persons), not objects (things). The mind of human beings comes into existence "philosophically" in and through the recognition that we can know nature and so render nature creative only because, in the beginning, we human beings are subjects who, made in the image of God, are created from nothing, from nothing natural. The creation of poetry, the poetry of creation embodies (reveals) the paradox that the child is the father of man. In the beginning, from the beginning what has been "must" be immortal. The progress from childhood to adulthood, from one generation to another, involves change (development, growth, advance) that, while natural, is at the same time "spiritual." We do not change in kind. We amplify, deepen, realize, reveal the potentiality (the power) of the kind we actually are. It is precisely this idea of self-realization, of self-actualization (self-revelation) that allows Wordsworth to find in sorrow, pain, loss, death, what we could call, recalling Shakespeare, the tragedy of life, the very meaning or significance of life. We look through or beyond death, not to some future immortal state but to a mortal life on earth eternally composed of faith, hope, and love. But here I presently stop. For these are the big themes of *The Prelude*.

It is now time for me to take up here, in what is my introductory chapter on Wordsworth, the basic ideas on poetry that he expressed in the various writings attached to his (and Coleridge's) poetry, mainly in prose but also, as we have seen, in verse, whether advertisement, preface, prospectus, or appendix. I shall, additionally, examine the assessment that Coleridge provides in his *Biographia Literaria* of Wordsworth, both his writings on poetry and his actual poetry, and the conception of poetry that Shelley articulates in *A Defense of Poetry*. My aim in discussing the ideas on poetics that are found in the writings of Wordsworth's famous contemporaries, first, Coleridge, in the context of discussing Wordsworth, and, second, Shelley, independent of Wordsworth, is, as I indicated earlier, to show how fundamentally flawed their conception of poetry is and thus to deepen our understanding of Wordsworth's uniquely poetic achievement.

The prefatory materials of critically lasting significance in which Wordsworth outlined his conception of poetry begin with the brief Advertisement that he attached to the first edition of the *Lyrical Ballads*, which, we remember, appeared anonymously in 1798, and continue through the Preface to the 1800 edition, revised in 1802, together with the Appendix to the 1802 edition, and conclude with the Preface to the 1815 edition of his poems, plus the Essay Supplementary to the Preface of 1815. I shall make no attempt here to provide a systematic account of the contents of these prefatory materials. Indeed, in concentrating on their key ideas, I shall call upon them collectively, without, for the most part, being concerned to distinguish one piece from another. Overall, Wordsworth's conception of poetics, whether expressed in practice, in actual poems, or formulated critically in theoretical terms, in his prefatory materials, did not fundamentally change during the seventeen-year period of his major poetic production.

I begin with the opening sentence of the brief Advertisement to the *Lyrical Ballads* (1798): "It is the honourable characteristic of Poetry that its materials are to be found in every subject which can interest the human mind."[17] Wordsworth notes that, while the meaning of the word "poetry" is much disputed, he understands it to contain "a natural delineation of human passions, human characters, and human incidents." Indeed, he observes that, because the majority of the poems that are found in the volume to follow were written "to ascertain how far the language of conversation in the middle and lower classes of society is adopted to the purposes of poetic pleasure," they "are to be considered as experiments." Acknowledging that what he calls "readers of superior judgment" may disapprove of the style in which many of the poems in the volume were written, he points out, invoking the authority of Sir Joshua Reynolds, that "an accurate taste in poetry, and in all the other arts, . . . is an acquired talent, which can only be produced by severe thought and a long continued intercourse with the best models of composition"[18] (Gill, 591). In the opening paragraph of the Preface to the *Lyrical Ballads* (1800), Wordsworth repeats that the poems in the previous and present volumes were published as an experiment but then proceeds, in characterizing them, to add further details. His aim had been, he tells us (Wordsworth, in speaking in his own voice, makes no reference to Coleridge), "to ascertain how far, by fitting to metrical arrangement a selection of the real language of men in a state of vivid sensation, that sort of pleasure and that quantity of pleasure may be imparted which a poet may rationally endeavor to impart" (Baker, 1).

The claims with which Wordsworth initiates his discussion of poetry in his earliest prefatory pieces raise evident questions for us. I shall address only two of them at this point. First, how are we to understand the tension that exists between, on the one hand, the conception of poetry as written in the "real language of men" from the middle and lower classes and, on the other hand, the acknowledgement that accurate taste in poetry demands "severe thought" and a thorough education in the best poems ever written? The authority whom Wordsworth invokes here, the celebrated painter and theorist of art, Sir Joshua Reynolds, can hardly be understood to represent the middle and lower classes of society! Second, what is the sort and quantity of *pleasure* that the poet *rationally* endeavors to impart. Pleasure and rationality (reason) are typically viewed in opposition to each other, as they are, for example, in the philosophy of Kant, as we shall see. My point in raising these questions, among the many that the texts of all great thinkers, whether poetic or philosophic, raise for their readers who are committed to severe thinking about and an education (upbuilding) in and through their works, is to alert us to how Wordsworth addresses them, together with others, in both his poetry, above all, *The Prelude*, and in his prefatory pieces on poetics. Before, however, undertaking to address these questions, I want to proceed yet further in Wordsworth's prefatory materials in order to amplify and deepen our appreciation of them in and through the additional claims and observations that the poet makes.

While Wordsworth acknowledges that he does not undertake in his preface of 1800 to provide "a systematic defence of the theory upon which the poems were written," still he accepts the obligation of offering to his readers "a few words of introduction . . . [to] poems so materially different from those upon which general approbation is at present bestowed" (Baker, 2). Indeed, because, he continues, those "who have been accustomed to the gaudinesss and inane phraseology of many modern writers" will, in reading his poems, "frequently have to struggle with feelings of strangeness and awkwardness," he will undertake "to state what I have proposed to myself to perform [in them]" (Baker, 3). We are already familiar with his "principal object," that of choosing "incidents and situations from common life" and of relating them in the "language really used by men." But now Wordsworth adds two additional points: (1) "to throw over" the incidents and situations of common life, as related in language that people really use, "a certain coloring of the imagination, whereby ordinary things should be presented to the mind in an unusual aspect;" and, consequently, (2) to make them "interesting by tracing in them . . . the primary laws of our nature: chiefly, as far as regards the manner in which we associate ideas in a state of excitement" (Baker, 4).

Here we encounter the imagination, which, as we shall find, Wordsworth continuously invokes as the feature that, in truly characterizing the human mind, fundamentally shapes "the primary laws of our nature" such that we are aroused to "associate ideas in a state of excitement" (Baker, 4). Wordsworth presses on, without clarifying what he means by imagination, the primary laws of our nature, or the ideas whose relations arouse excitement in us. He tells us that his poetry generally features "humble and rustic life . . . because in that condition the essential passions of the heart find a better soil in which they attain their maturity," given that they are under less restraint, "speak a plainer and more emphatic language," exist "in a state of greater simplicity, may be more accurately contemplated and more forcibly communicated," are "more easily comprehended and are more durable; and, lastly, . . . are incorporated with the beautiful and permanent forms of nature" (Baker, 4). But then Wordsworth adds that the language "of these men has been adopted (purified indeed from what appear to be its real defects) . . . because such men hourly communicate with the best objects from which the best part of language is originally derived" and also because, given their humble status, they are "less under the influence of social vanity" with the result that their language, based on "repeated experience and regular feelings, is a more permanent and far more philosophical language than that which is frequently substituted for it by poets" (Baker, 4–5). Wordsworth observes yet further that, while "all good poetry is the spontaneous outflow of powerful feelings," still poems of value are produced only by writers who, "being possessed of more than usual organic sensibility, had also thought long and deeply. For our continued influxes of feelings are modified and directed by our thoughts," whereby they express "what is really important to men" (Baker, 5–6). He remarks yet further that "the subject is indeed important! For the human mind is capable of being excited without the application of gross and violent stimulants; . . . and one being is elevated above another in proportion as he possesses this capability. It has therefore appeared to me that to endeavor to produce or enlarge this capacity is one of the best services in which . . . a writer can be engaged" (Baker, 6–7).

Indeed, already earlier Wordsworth had noted that what distinguishes his "poems from the popular poetry of the day . . . is . . . that the feeling therein developed gives importance to the action and situation, and not the action and situation to the feeling" (Baker, 6). In other words, while the content of poem is important, what really counts is our capacity to respond to (in providing a critical and metaphorical evaluation of) it. It is precisely this capacity whose task, we saw Wordsworth write, it is the poet's to amplify. It will become evident, above all, in *The Prelude*, that, although without (outside) the world of nature there would be no poem, what makes the poem is not the natural object but the poet's response to it. "My heart leaps up, when I behold / A rainbow in the sky; / So be it is now I am a Man; / So be it when I shall grow old. . . . / The child is Father of the Man; / and I could wish my days to be / Bound each to each by natural piety." For, as we have seen yet again, Wordsworth emphasizes that what he calls our continued influxes of feelings are "modified and directed by our thoughts." It is evident, then, that when, as shall soon see, he invokes passion, he is concerned, not with raw feeling but with feeling disciplined and guided by thought (reason).

In addition to passion, central topics that Wordsworth will next take up in his Preface of 1800 include the relationship between poetry and prose and what he understands by the pleasure that poetry brings its readers. Since he holds that it is the subject (the individual human being), not the object, that makes the poem; that poetry expresses the excitement, the passion that beholding or contemplating the object creates in the subject; and that the language of poetry is the real language of our everyday lives, it is not surprising that Wordsworth holds that "every good poem . . . must necessarily, except with reference to the meter, in no respect differ from that of good prose" (Baker, 10).[19] He adds that, if "the language really spoken by men [is selected] with true taste and feeling, [it] will entirely separate the composition from the vulgarity and meanness of ordinary life, and [that], if meter be superadded thereto, I believe that a dissimilitude will be produced altogether sufficient for the gratification of a rational mind" (Baker 12).[20]

While thus distinguishing between what is real and common, on the one hand, and what is vulgar, mean, and ordinary, on the other hand, in the lives of human beings and claiming that good poetry and good prose are fundamentally identical in their embodiment of human nature, Wordsworth segues back to a discussion of what for him truly constitutes poetry. In noting that he has been told that Aristotle "has said that poetry is the most philosophic of all writings," he writes: "it is so: its object is truth, not individual and local, but general and operative; [truth] not standing upon external authority but carried alive into the heart by passion; truth which is its own testimony. . . . Poetry is the image of man and nature" (Baker, 15–16). The only restriction under which the poet operates, Wordsworth continues, is "the necessity of giving immediate pleasure to a human being possessed of that information which may be expected from him," not as a physician or a scientist, etc., "but as a man" (Baker, 16). While Wordsworth does not directly tell us how he conceives of "that information" that is expected of all human beings, he does then observe that the poet's art involves looking "at the world in the spirit of love" and paying "homage . . . to the native and naked dignity of man, to the grand elementary principle of pleasure, by which he knows, and feels, and lives, and moves. We have no sympathy but [through] what is propagated by pleasure" (Baker, 16). Wordsworth is quick to point out, however, that the sympathy that we have for pain no less involves pleasure. All knowledge, including the general principles of science, is pleasure. Consequently, "the poet principally directs his attention" to the "knowledge which all men carry about with them and to these sympathies in which, without any other discipline than that of our daily life, we are fitted to take delight" (Baker, 17).

Wordsworth now waxes poetic, as if he anticipated the discovery on the part of his readers that there is no real difference between the prose of his Preface and the verse of *The Prelude*. The poet, he writes, in

> singing a song in which all human beings join with him, rejoices in the presence of truth as our visible friend and hourly companion. Poetry is the breath and finer spirit of all knowledge. . . . He is the rock of defence for human nature, an upholder

and preserver, carrying everywhere with him relationship and love. In spite of [the] difference[s] of . . . language and manners, of laws and customs . . . , the poet binds together by passion and knowledge the vast empire of human society as it is spread over the whole earth and over all time. The objects of the poet's thoughts are everywhere. . . . Poetry is the first and last of all knowledge—it is as immortal as the heart of man. (Baker, 18)[21]

After this paean to poetry, whose content we shall be discussing throughout our study, Wordsworth now points out that, because poets write in the language common to all human beings, they differ only in degree, and not in kind from them. The poet, he observes, is to be "chiefly distinguished from other men" by two elements: (1) "a greater promptness to think and feel without immediate external excitement" and (2) "a greater power in expressing . . . [the] thoughts and feelings" so produced in him. "But these passions and thoughts and feelings," he yet repeats, "are the general passions and thoughts and feelings of men. And with what are they connected"? he asks. He answers in the style of repetition reminiscent of the poetry of the Hebrew Bible, which Robert Lowth had characterized as parallelism:[22] *with* "our moral sentiment and animal [bodily] sensations and *with* the causes which excite" them; *with* the revolutions of the natural elements of the visible universe; *with* "loss of friends and kindred, . . . injuries and resentments, gratitude and hope, . . . fear and sorrow" (Baker, 20).[23] So it is, then, that the poet describes "the sensations of other men and the objects which interests them. The poet thinks and feels in the spirit of human passions." How, then, Wordsworth asks, can the poet's language differ significantly "from that of all other men who feel vividly and clearly?" Indeed, since "poets do not write for poets alone, but for men" and because they write "to excite rational sympathy," they must express themselves "as other men express themselves" (Baker, 21).

Just as readers can expect the poet to address them in their common language, Wordsworth continues, so it is, too, with verse as characterized by meter that "is regular and uniform and not like that which is produced by what is usually called POETIC DICTION, arbitrary, and subject to infinite caprices upon which no calculation whatever can be made." Both poet and reader, he observes, "willingly submit" to the meter that "obeys certain laws" since these laws do not interfere "with the passion but serve only "to heighten and improve the pleasure which coexists with it" (Baker, 21–22). At this point in his discussion Wordsworth acknowledges that, since he has argued for the fundamental identity of poetry and prose, readers will ask why he has written in verse. His basic answer to this question is, although it is not, I think, a model of clarity, that, because "the end of poetry is to produce excitement in co-existence with an overbalance of pleasure . . . , the co-presence of something regular" helps temper the passion aroused by the verse (Baker, 23). Wordsworth acknowledges that the claim that meter in some sense artificially divests language of its reality will "appear paradoxical" (Baker, 24). But he adds that the pleasure received from "metrical language . . . derives from the perception of similitude in dissimilitude. This principle," he tells us, "is the great spring of the activity of our minds and their chief feeder." On this principle rests "the direction of the sexual appetite and all the passions connected with it, . . . the life of our ordinary conversation, . . . and our taste and our moral feelings" (Baker, 25). Wordsworth then reiterates his paradoxical claim that it is the combination of using "language closely resembling that of real life" and "meter differing from it so widely" that results in "a complex feeling of delight, which is of the most important use in tempering the painful feeling always found intermingled with powerful descriptions of the deeper passions" (Baker, 26). It is, consequently, his conclusion that "few persons will deny that, of two descriptions . . . of passions, manners, or characters, each of them equally well executed, the one in prose and the other in verse, the verse will be read a hundred times where the prose is read once"[24] (Baker, 27).

The tension in how Wordsworth conceives of the relationship between poetry and prose continues. There is essentially no difference between them, yet poetry trumps prose. But then Wordsworth provides two examples of four-line verse stanzas, by Dr. Johnson, one "admirable" and the other "superlatively contemptible." The difference between them is to be found, he tells us, not in their language, meter, or word order but in their "matter." Our proper response to the contemptible stanza is not to say, he continues, that it is poor poetry or even that it is not poetry at all but rather that it "wants [lacks] sense; it is neither interesting in itself" nor can it "*lead* to anything interesting." Its content does not "originate in that sane state of feeling which arises out of thought nor can [it] excite thought or feeling in the reader" (Baker, 29). So now we find that it is not meter that distinguishes poetry from prose. For what counts in poetry, and also in prose we may suppose, is the significance of the content; and we know that, according to the passage cited earlier from the verse Prospectus to the *Excursion*, what for Wordsworth constitutes his "high argument" is the Mind of Man and its creative relationship to (its fit with) the external world, at once human and natural, both subjective and objective.

Central to the mind of man, which, as is now evident to us, constitutes the true matter or content of significant poetry (and prose), are the three concepts of imagination, passion, and pleasure, whose critical role in poetics we have already seen Wordsworth emphasize in his prefatory pieces. I shall conclude my discussion of his poetic reflections by concentrating on these three ideas, together with their relations both with one another and with other closely linked ideas. In discussing imagination, Wordsworth emphasizes its difference from both fancy and taste. I want to point out here that his account of the difference between these two powers of mind, including his criticism of Coleridge's account of that difference, is, in being at once prolix and stilted, no model of lucidity. We shall also find that the account that Coleridge in his *Biographia Literaria* gives of imagination and its relationship to fancy, including his criticism of Wordsworth's treatment of this topic, is no standard of limpidity. Since Kant, as we shall see, no less fails to account for the imaginative powers of practical (moral, passionate, poetic . . .) reason, perhaps it is apposite for me at this point to ask my reader if he or she can instantly provide a simple definition of imagination that takes into account the essential complexity of the relationship between idea and image, in other words, of metaphor as the transfer from the world of sensible nature to the world of transcendental mind.

In the Preface to his collection of poems published in 1815 Wordsworth points out that imagination does not refer "to images that are merely a faithful copy, existing in the mind, of absent external objects but is a word of higher import, denoting operations of the mind upon these objects and processes of creation or of composition [that are] governed by certain fixed laws" (Gill, 631). Thus, the imagination is not merely "a[n] endowing or modifying power," but it "also shapes and *creates* . . . by innumerable processes" (Gill, 633). While Wordsworth yet again does not tell his reader, in concrete terms, what is to be understood by the "certain fixed laws" or the "innumerable processes" that are central to the power of the imagination, although he does invoke Shakespeare, Spenser, and Milton as exemplifying this power, he then criticizes Coleridge for failing to distinguish adequately between "the aggregative and associative Power" that fancy and imagination each possess (Gill, 635). While fancy does not substantially transform the materials of which it makes use, Wordsworth observes, the imagination, in contrast, "recoils from everything but the plastic [malleable], the pliant, and the indefinite." The processes of fancy are capricious in the sense of being accidental, playful, ludicrous, tender or pathetic. . . . She can win you over to her purposes. But she does not care "how unstable or transitory may be her influence, knowing that it will not be out of her power to resume it upon an apt occasion. But the Imagination," Wordsworth continues, "is conscious of an indestructible dominion." While our mind may not be "able to sustain its grandeur, but if [it is] once felt and acknowledged, by no act of any other faculty of the mind can it be relaxed, impaired, or diminished" (Gill, 636). In sum: "Fancy is given to quicken and to beguile the temporal part of our Nature, Imagination to incite and to support the eternal" (636).

It is little wonder, then, as Wordsworth explains to us in his "Essay, Supplementary to the Preface" (1815), that imagination has always to contend with the prevailing taste of the age. He is confident, he tells us, that the "discerning Reader," who is old enough to recall the first publication of some of these poems seventeen years ago in the *Lyrical Ballads*, "will remember the taste that [then] was prevalent . . . [and] to what degree the Poetry of this Island has since that period been coloured by them." Such a reader will also be "further aware of the unremitting hostility with which, upon some principle or other, they have each and all been opposed" (Gill 657.) The inescapable conclusion, consequently, is that "every Author, as far as he is great and at the same time *original*, has had the task of *creating* the taste by which he is to be enjoyed: so has it been, so will it continue to be" (Gill 657–58). For "the real difficulty of creating that taste by which a truly original Poet is to be relished," Wordsworth observes, lies "in breaking the bonds of custom, in overcoming the prejudices of false refinement, and in displacing the aversions of inexperience." Additionally, the poet is confronted with the task of "divesting the Reader of the pride that induces him to dwell" on the differences that separate human beings from each other "to the exclusion of those in which all Men are alike" and, additionally, of "making him ashamed of the vanity that renders him insensible" to the excellence that "civil arrangements . . . . and Nature illimitable in her bounty have conferred on Men who stand below him in the scale of society" (Gill, 658).

Wordsworth argues further that today taste, "a passive faculty, is made paramount among the faculties conversant with the fine arts." While it properly deals with "proportion" and "congruity," when supported by "the requisite knowledge, . . . in its intercourse with these the mind is *passive* and is affected painfully or pleasurably as by an instinct" (Gill, 658–59). Taste, consequently, is not the faculty that engages "the profound and the exquisite in feeling, the lofty and universal in thought and imagination, or in ordinary language the pathetic and the sublime. . . . And why? Because without the exertion of a co-operating *power* in the mind of the Reader, there can be no adequate sympathy with either of these emotions: without this auxiliary impulse elevated or profound passion cannot exist" (Gill, 659).

So Wordsworth thus segues to a discussion of how "passion," notwithstanding the fact that it derives from a word that signifies suffering, is not "passive" like taste but active. The "connection which suffering has with effort, with exertion and *action*," he declares, "is immediate and inseparable. To be moved, then, by a passion is to be excited often to external and always to internal effort—for either its strengthening or its suppression, the first painful and the second pleasurable. "If the latter, the soul must contribute to its support, or it never becomes vivid and soon languishes and dies" (Gill, 659). What this means, Wordsworth continues, is that, before we can enjoy a "great Poet in the highest exercise of his genius, . . . he has to call forth and to communicate *power*." This is even more true, he observes, in the case of "an original Writer, at his first appearance in the world." The only proof of genius "is the act of doing well what is worthy to be done and what was never done before." For "the only infallible sign" of genius in the fine arts

> is the widening [of] the sphere of human sensibility for the delight, honor, and benefit of human nature. Genius is the introduction of a new element into the intellectual universe; or, if that be not allowed, it is the application of powers to objects on which they had not before been exercised or the employment of them in such a manner as to produce effects hitherto unknown. What is all this but an advance, or a conquest, made by the soul of the Poet? (Gill, 659)

We are not to suppose, Wordsworth continues, that "the Reader can make progress of this kind like an Indian Prince or General—stretched [out] on his Palanquin and borne by his Slaves." Rather, we are to view the reader as "invigorated and inspirited by his Leader in order that he may exert himself, for he cannot proceed in quiescence, he cannot be carried like dead weight. Therefore, to create taste is to call forth and bestow power, of which knowledge is the effect; and *there* lies the true difficulty" (Gill, 659–60). Some passions are simple and direct, and others are "complex and revolutionary: some—to which the heart yields with gentleness; others—against which it struggles with pride." Additionally, the very medium of poetry, language itself, is "subject to endless fluctuations and arbitrary associations." Still, further, we have both a "meditative" and a "human" pathos, "an enthusiastic" as well as an ordinary sorrow—a sadness that has its seat in the depths of reason, to which the mind cannot sink gently of itself, but to which it must descend by treading the steps of thought." Then there is the sublime! If we consider how remote "are the cares that occupy the passing day . . . from the sources of sublimity in the soul of man, can it be wondered that there is little existing preparation for a Poet charged with a new mission to extend its kingdom and to augment and spread its enjoyments?"

Away, then, Wordsworth declares, with the *popular* when "applied to new works in Poetry as if there were no test of excellence in this first of all the fine arts." For the "writing[s] best fitted for eager reception" are those that either "startle the world" with their "audacity and extravagance" or superficially describe "the surfaces of manners" and relate "incidents by which the mind is kept upon the stretch of curiosity and the fancy amused without the trouble of thought. But," and here Wordsworth propounds what for him essentially constitutes poetic genius,

> in everything which is to send the soul into herself, to be admonished of her weakness or to be made conscious of her powers—*wherever* life and nature are described as operated upon by the creative or abstracting virtue [power] of the imagination; *wherever* the instinctive wisdom of antiquity and her heroic passions, uniting in the heart of the Poet with the meditative wisdom of later ages, have produced that accord of sublimated humanity, which is at once a history of the remote past and a prophetic annunciation of the remotest future—*there* the Poet must reconcile himself for a season to few and scattered hearers. (Gill, 660–61[25])

All you have to do, Wordsworth continues, is to go "to a silent exhibition of the productions of the Sister Art" (the visual arts) and you will "be convinced that the qualities which dazzle at first sight and kindle the admiration of the multitude are essentially different from those by which permanent influence is secured" (Gill, 661).

But does this mean, Wordsworth then asks, that "the judgment of the People is not to be respected?" Far from it, he answers. For the Spirit, which is both individual and species (humankind), "is that Vox populi which the Deity inspires." What he opposes, he observes, is the factitious imposition of the PUBLIC upon the PEOPLE. While he shows such deference to the Public "as it is entitled to," it is "to the People, philosophically characterized, and to the embodied spirit of their knowledge, so far as it exists and moves, at the present, faithfully supported by its two wings, the past and the future, [that] his devout respect, his reverence, is due" (Gill, 662). Wordsworth then takes leave of his readers in assuring them that, if they are not persuaded that his poems "evinced something of the 'Vision and the Faculty divine' and that, both in words and things, they will operate . . . to extend the domain of sensibility for the delight, the honor, and the benefit of human nature, . . . he would not, if a wish could do it, save them from immediate destruction . . . as a thing that had never been" (Gill, 662).

So Wordsworth brings to a conclusion the account of his conception of poetics that he gave in the prefatory pieces that accompanied the poems that he wrote and published from 1798 to 1815, the major period of his creative genius. While I would hope that it has become reasonably clear to readers what Wordsworth understands by the imagination, at least insofar as it is distinguished from both fancy and taste, and also by passion, as involving active, effective agency, I suspect that such may not be the case with regard to what Wordsworth understands by pleasure, to his idea that true poetry brings its readers an over-abundance of pleasure. We may well wonder how a poem that sends the soul of its reader "into herself," in order "to be admonished of her weakness or to be made conscious of her powers," as we saw Wordsworth write above, brings an overflow of pleasure to that reader. We might, indeed, ask: Did Adam and Eve receive superabundant pleasure in learning that it was precisely their expulsion from deathless, but also from lifeless, paradise for the covenantal life of loving conception, at once natural and spiritual, labor, and death, that revealed them to be like God in knowing good and evil? Still, it is important to remember that it is only because human beings are made in the image of Adam and Eve that they live by the paradox of *felix culpa* (which, incidentally, Wordsworth does not mention): the happy sin that it is only the fallen, the sinful, who are saved or redeemed. Or, to consider the *felix culpa* of humankind in more secular terms, the good of life exists only in and through confronting and overcoming life's evils. The immortal good of Adam and Eve in deathless paradise is an idolatrous mirage. In the terms of Rousseau: Man is born free and now he is in chains. How, Rousseau asks, did this change (fall) come about?

He responds: I do not know. How, he asks yet again, can the bonds of enslavement be transformed into the bonds of freedom? That, he responds, is what I now undertake to show in the treatise that follows (*The Social Contract*).

It is evident, I think, that the pleasure that Wordsworth views as the aim of poetry, of the fine arts, generally, and indeed of life, is centered in the mind, the soul, the Spirit, the heart, in the covenantal life of human dignity. While in no sense is the life of the spirit to be opposed to bodily (including sexual) pleasure, still, it is fundamentally to be identified with selflessness, with loving commitment to others, not with self-interest or self-gratification[26] but with what we have seen Wordsworth call, in often quite elusive terms, the self-knowledge on the part of readers that is presupposed by the poet and what he also in similarly vague terms refers to as rationality. More generally, he indicates that the pleasure of the arts, of life, is founded on the power of what we perhaps may call self-realization: the amplification on the part of readers of their capacity for insight and understanding, which Wordsworth associates with both sympathy and imagination. In anticipating our reading not only of *The Prelude* but also of Kant's works, we may say that the pleasure that we find in self-knowledge involves both the metaphor of critique (we are thrown into crisis by all meaningful encounters) and the critique of metaphor (do the images that we encounter in poetry transfer us to the spiritual life of covenantal bonds or do they leave us chained to the sensible world of idolatrous bondage?).

The language of spirit and idolatry, together with Wordsworth's invocation of the divine, albeit, as we have seen, not frequent and rather, perhaps, more philosophic than religious, brings me to the last major topic raised by Wordsworth in his prefatory pieces that I want to discuss here: the relationship between poetry and religion. It is interesting to note that the only time in which he discusses religion at any length in his prefatory pieces is in the context of berating his critics in the opening section of his Supplementary Preface of 1815 and so in the last of his significant prefatory pieces. Wordsworth initiates the Supplementary Preface in writing that he trusts that the "judicious Reader, who has now first become acquainted with these poems, is persuaded that a very senseless outcry has been raised against them and their Author." He writes that he is particularly incensed that "the ignorance of those who have chosen to stand forth as my enemies . . . has unfortunately been still more gross than their disingenuousness and their incompetence more flagrant than their malice" (Gill, 640). When men of mature age, he continues, find "it proper that their understandings should enjoy a holiday, while they are unbending their minds with verse," not only will they "be thus easily beguiled into admiration of absurdities, extravagances, and misplaced ornaments." But also, because of their prejudice and inaptitude, they will be unable "to be moved by the unostentatious beauties of a pure style." He adds yet further: "In the higher poetry, an enlightened Critic chiefly looks for a reflexion of the wisdom of the heart and the grandeur of the imagination." But, insofar as readers are "accustomed to the glaring hues of diction," is it not inevitable for them, he asks, to be rather repelled than attracted by an original Work the colouring of which is disposed according to a pure and refined scheme of harmony? It is in the fine arts as in the affairs of life [that] no man can *serve* (i.e., obey with zeal and fidelity) two masters" (Gill, 642).

Having thus invoked the Sermon on the Mount, in which Jesus reminds his listeners that they cannot in truth serve two masters, God and mammon (Matt 6:24), Wordsworth proceeds to observe that "Poetry is most just to its own divine origin when it administers the comforts and breathes the spirit of religion" (Gill, 642). But the point that he at once undertakes to stress is that readers who "perceive this truth and who betake themselves to reading verse for sacred purposes must be preserved from numerous illusions to which the[y] . . . are liable" (Gill, 642–43). He mentions two such illusions. On the one hand, readers who are deeply committed to the truths of religion "are prone to overrate the Authors by whom these truths are expressed and enforced. They come prepared to impart so much passion to the Poet's language that they remain unconscious how little, in fact, they receive from it." On the other hand, there are readers so zealous in their belief that they condemn out of hand a poet for holding seemingly different beliefs. What else can be expected but "contradictions," Wordsworth asks, "when Christianity, the religion of humility, is founded [by such readers] upon the proudest quality of our nature?" (Gill, 643).

Wordsworth explains yet further that it is precisely because poetry administers the comforts and breathes the spirit of religion, in being most true to its divine origin, that it is most subject to distortion on the part of its readers. Since faith leads "the religious man" to elevate his nature above "the treasures of time" and thus to settle "upon those of eternity . . . [as] presumptive evidence of a future state of existence and . . . a title to partake of its holiness," he "values what he sees chiefly as an 'imperfect shadowing forth; of what he is incapable of seeing." In other words, Wordsworth continues, since religion rests on "indefinite objects" as expressed in "words and symbols," the "commerce between Man and his Maker . . . [involves] a process where much is represented in little and the infinite Being accommodates himself to a finite capacity. In all this may be perceived the affinities between religion and poetry [and here I arrange Wordsworth's knotty presentation in schematic form so as to facilitate comprehension of it]:

> *between religion*—making up the deficiencies of reason by faith,
> *and poetry*—passionate for the instruction of reason;
> *between religion*—whose element is infinitude and whose ultimate trust is [in] the supreme of things, submitting herself to circumscription [limitation] and reconciled to substitutions;
> *and poetry*—etherial [*sic*] and transcendent, yet incapable to sustain her existence without sensuous incarnation.

In light, then, of the affinities between poetry and religion, Wordsworth outlines the qualifications that critics must possess if their "decisions" are to possess "absolute value." In addition to having "a mind at once poetical and philosophical," critics are to possess "affections . . . as free and kindly as the spirit of society and [an] understanding [that] is [as] severe as that of dispassionate government"; a composed mind that "no selfishness can disturb"; "a natural sensibility" both tutored and quick; and "active faculties capable of answering the demands which an Author of original imagination shall make upon them—associated with a judgment that cannot be duped into admiration by aught [anything] that is unworthy of it" (Gill, 644). But, then, Wordsworth arrives at what is surely an unexpected conclusion on the part of his readers. The class of critics that he has just described includes not only, he tells us, those whose judgments are "trustworthy" but also those whose judgments are "the most erroneous and perverse. For to be mis-taught is worse than to be untaught; and no perverseness equals that which is supported by system, no errors are so difficult to root out as those which the understanding has pledged its credit to uphold. . . . In this Class meet together the two extremes of best and worst" (Gill, 644–45).

What counts for us in this study is not so much *that*, according to Wordsworth, poetry is subject to the same uses and abuses as religion but, rather, *what* it is for him about poetry and religion that brings them together yet, also, it would appear, holds them apart from each other.

Still, when he writes that poetry is properly true to its divine origin in administering the comforts and breathing the spirit of religion it is not at all evident how we would distinguish poetry from religion. It is, however, the case that, although Wordsworth in the passage that we are presently examining emphasizes the affinities between poetry and religion, he does not directly identify religion with poetry. Indeed, he stresses, while using quite traditional terminology, the difference between "the supreme of things" as infinite Being and human beings as finite, between Maker (much) and Man (little). He views religion as the imperfect shadowing forth of indefinite objects by making use of words and symbols, which he also identifies with circumscription and substitutions. Finally, when Wordsworth states that religion makes up for the deficiencies of reason while poetry is passionate for the instruction of reason, it is not at all clear how he understands the relationship between religion and poetry. Still, in writing that poetry, although ethereal and transcendent, exists solely in and through sensuous incarnation, he adopts language that had traditionally been applied to the God-man of Christianity, the incarnation of God in and as the man Jesus.

Such are the issues that we shall continue to explore in our study. The reader will surely have noted that they bear significantly on Kierkegaard's observation that serves as our leitmotiv—that all language about the Spirit, including the divine language of Scripture, is transferred or metaphoric language. Reality, being, the supreme of things, the infinite, God . . . do not exist outside of or apart from what we have seen Wordsworth calls "words and symbols." In elemental terms, metaphor is incarnational, just as the incarnation is metaphorical. Metaphor does not exist outside of the Spirit of incarnation. The incarnation does not exist outside of the Spirit of metaphor. But it is no less important to see that the tantalizing[27] issues that Wordsworth raises in and through his discussion of the uses and abuses that commonly haunt both poetry and religion, given their metamorphic identity, their common dependence on words and symbols, also presage our discussion of metaphor as critique that is central to Kant's demonstration that we cannot know the thing itself except as an object of possible (empirical) appearance. For we human persons, as subjects, are the thing in itself whose representation is transcendental, not phenomenal; practical, not theoretical; spiritual, not natural; subjective, not objective; moral, not empirical . . . .

It is evident, then, that what Wordsworth undertakes to demonstrate to us is that, because the incarnational language of metaphor is common to both poetry and religion in their depiction of spirit, each of them is equally subject to the same abuses. But it is important to recall that the abuse of the language of spirit, in the history of Christianity, has traditionally been called idolatry. In falsely reducing God to man or falsely elevating man to God, idolatry involves the reduction both of the image of God—man—and of the image of man—God—to an immediately sensuous image of nature, to an object or thing. We see, then, that metaphor is nothing other than the critique of idols, of false images. It is fitting, consequently, that in the second of the two prefatory passages in which Wordsworth discusses religion he raises the issue of idolatry. Indeed, we can say: Where there is metaphor, there idolatry lurks in its shadow. Where there is idolatry, there critique exists to shine light on idols as false metaphors.

This second passage on religion as involving idolatry emerges out of Wordsworth's discussion of imagination, in the Preface of 1815, as a creative faculty that is to be distinguished from taste, which we considered earlier. In the context of citing Horace (in Latin) and then *Paradise Lost* (without directly naming either source), Wordsworth writes that the "grand store-house of enthusiastic and meditative Imagination, of poetical, as contradistinguished from human and dramatic Imagination, is the prophetic and lyrical parts of the holy Scriptures and the works of Milton" (Gill, 634).[28] In distinguishing poetic (enthusiastic[29] and meditative) imagination from human and dramatic imagination, Wordsworth writes that he chooses Milton, above all, in preference to the writers of "ancient Greece and Rome because the anthropomorphism [*sic*] of the Pagan religion subjected the minds of the greatest poets in those countries too much to the bondage of definite form, from which the Hebrews were preserved by their abhorrence of idolatry." He writes yet further that the abhorrence of idolatry "was almost as strong in "our great epic Poet," Milton, given both the "circumstances of his life [the English civil wars of the 1640s and 1650s, which resulted in the execution of King Charles I, followed by the restoration of the Stuart monarchy with King Charles II in 1660] and . . . the constitution of his mind. However imbued the surface might be with classical literature, he was a Hebrew in soul, and all things tended in him towards the sublime" (Gill, 634). As for "the human and dramatic Imagination," Wordsworth writes that "the works of Shakespeare are an inexhaustible source" (Gill, 635).

Before commenting on the complex relationship not only of ancient and Hebrew (and so also "modern" as represented by Milton) but also of the poetical (enthusiastic and meditative) imagination and the dramatic (and human) imagination, it is important to note, first, that Wordsworth at this point in his 1815 Preface seizes the opportunity of addressing "the insults which the Ignorant, the Incapable, and the Presumptuous have heaped upon these and my other writings." He avows:

> I may be permitted to anticipate the judgment of posterity upon myself; I shall declare ... that I have given, in these unfavorable times [of the Napoleonic Wars], evidence of exertions of this faculty [the imagination] upon its worthiest objects, the external universe, and the moral and religious sentiments of Man, his natural affections, and his acquired passions; which have the same ennobling tendency as the productions of men, in this kind, worthy to be holden in undying remembrance. (Gill, 635)

I seize here upon the opportunity of holding in undying memory or, in other words, of focusing on the three ideas that, in my judgment, are central to Wordsworth's by no means pellucid yet critically important reflections and that "have the same ennobling tendency as the—artistic, philosophic, and religious—productions of this—imaginative—kind." They are central to my choice of Wordsworth and Kant as my representative poet and philosopher. However, since these ideas are central to my concepts of metaphor and critique and will, therefore, seldom be absent from my ongoing discussion, I shall at present outline them solely in introductory fashion.

In focusing on the three ideas that are, in my view, central to the account that Wordsworth gives of the affinity between poetry and religion, I want to make clear that, while I believe my interpretation of them to be true to his poetics, their meaning is by no means self-evident. First, the distinction that he makes between, on the one hand, meditative and enthusiastic imagination and, on the other hand, dramatic and human imagination involves a difference in content, not in creative power. It is as the author of *Paradise Lost* that Wordsworth situates Milton among the "prophetic and the lyric" poets of Hebrew Scripture, i.e., as explicitly addressing the divine story of creation and fall.[30] It is manifest that Wordsworth in his own poetry, above all, in *The Prelude*, does not directly engage the biblical story of fall and redemption. Still, we shall see that he doubtlessly conceived of his "epic" poem as meditatively enthused. Second, Wordsworth does not differ fundamentally from his contemporaries—and it is here that Coleridge and Shelley will be particularly important for us—in generally failing to distinguish, in clear, systematic terms, between the poetry of the ancient Greeks and Romans and modern poetry (as expressing biblical, not classical, values). Still, he does situate Milton in the Hebrew tradition of the critique of idolatry in opposition to what he calls the bondage of the classical world to the anthropomorphism of "definite form." What Wordsworth, however, does not clearly see is that metaphor, as the transferred image of spirit, is not found in the ancient world, just as critique as the practice of reason (following the demonstration of Kant) is absent from world of antiquity. What this means, third, is that, since the critique of metaphor and the metaphor of critique are unknown to in the ancient world, it is not the Greeks and Romans of antiquity but the Hebrews and their Jewish and Christian (together with their Muslim) successors, along with all the rest of us who are their modern heirs, who must always contend with idolatry. Only those who are created from nothing—from nothing but the image of God (and not from the similitudes of finite nature)—can enslave themselves to false images by worshipping sham idols. Only those who are like God in knowing good and evil can sin in reducing good to evil. Only believers, not pagans, can fall into idolatry. Idolatry, like metaphor and critique, is unknown in the world of the ancients.

COLERIDGE ON WORDSWORTH

Having surveyed the conception of poetics that Wordsworth articulates in the prefatory pieces that he wrote in support of the poetry and that he (together, in the beginning, with Coleridge) published between 1798 and 1815, I shall now turn to the critique of Wordsworth's poetics that Coleridge made central to his *Biographia Literaria; or Biographical Sketches of My Literary Life and Opinions*, to give the full title of the work that he published in 1817. But, first, I shall begin with the moving tribute that Coleridge paid to his friend and fellow poet in his poem (of 112 lines), "To William Wordsworth: Composed on the Night after his Recitation of a Poem on the Growth of an Individual Mind." Coleridge wrote his poem in 1806 after hearing Wordsworth recite the poem that we know as *The Prelude* in the then-finished but never-published version of thirteen books (and possessing some ten thousand lines). Coleridge first published his poem in 1817, in the same year as the *Biographia Literaria*, in which he cites an eleven-line passage from his poem.[31] (Although

Coleridge does not identify the poem by name, he does identify the author of it.)

I shall make no attempt here to do justice to the poem that Coleridge addresses to Wordsworth. Rather, in concentrating on his conception of Wordsworth's poetic mission and not on his own (Coleridge's) account of his psychological-biographical recovery from deep despair in response to his friend's poem, I shall highlight key passages and ideas in it as introductory to the conception of Wordsworth's poetics, in both theory and practice, that Coleridge expresses in his *Biographia Literaria*. In his poem Coleridge addresses Wordsworth as "Great Bard" and "sage Bard," "Friend of the Wise! And teacher of the Good!"

> Into my heart I received that lay [song]
> More than historic, that prophetic lay
> Wherein (high theme by thee first sung aright)
> Of the foundations and the building up
> Of a Human Spirit thou has dared to tell.

Coleridge continues: You told of "fancies fair" but then "Of more than Fancy, of the Social Sense" when you found in France (following the Revolution of 1789) "man beloved by man . . . / When from the general heart of human kind / hope sprang forth like a full-born Deity." But after that hope was "afflicted and struck down," you returned home

>   thenceforth calm and sure
> From the dread watch-tower of man's absolute self . . .
>   to look
> Far on . . . An Orphic song indeed,
> A song divine of high and passionate thoughts
> To their own music chanted!
>   O great Bard!
> Ere yet that last strain dying awed the air,
> With steadfast eye I viewed thee in the choir
> Of ever-enduring men. The truly great
> Have all one age . . . They, both in power and act,
> Are permanent, and Time is not with them
> Save as it worketh for them, they in it.

Coleridge concludes his poem in writing:

> And when—O Friend! My comforter and guide!
> Strong in thyself, and powerful to give strength!—
> Thy long-sustained Song finally closed . . .
> Scarce conscious, yet conscious of its close, I

Sate, my being blended in one thought
(Thought was it? or aspiration? Or resolve?) . . .
And when I rose, I found myself in prayer.

Coleridge makes eloquently clear in "To Wordsworth" the elevated regard in which he holds the poet of the more than historic, the prophetic lay that its author read to him. Wordsworth belongs to the choir of ever-enduring, ageless, and timeless artists whose permanence in both power and act means that time does not exist for them save insofar as time serves them and they serve time. The time they serve, not as its slave but as its true laborer, is the eternity of historically unfolding creativity that they behold from the dread, the awful, the prophetic watchtower of humankind's absolute self. Such are the foundation and the upbuilding of a human spirit, of the growth of a poet's mind, that you, my comforter and guide, both powerful in yourself and powerful in giving strength to others, have dared to tell. In bringing together "man's absolute self," as the prophetic watchtower, with time as providing the very matter of human creativity wherein and whereby we humans found and upbuild the human spirit through the metaphor of critique and the critique of metaphor, Coleridge readies us for the time in which, I trust, we may thankfully arise from our reading of *The Prelude* truly grateful, as we remember that, as St. Benedict taught his monks: *orare est laborare*: to pray is to work.

But now it is time for us to take on the mighty labor of praying with Coleridge, of working through his laborious *Biographia Literaria* with the aim of learning how, or in what sense, it upbuilds our spirit in preparing us to encounter the more than historic lay that Wordsworth dared to relate in *The Prelude* from the prophetic watchtower of his absolute self. Coleridge writes that the reason for giving a biographical sketch of his own literary life and opinions was primarily "as introductory to the statement of my principles in Politics, Religion, and Philosophy, and the application of the rules, deduced from philosophical principles, to poetry and criticism" (1, 5). Since the poetic life of Coleridge was so closely bound up with that of Wordsworth in the fifteen or so years following their joint (but anonymous) publication of the *Lyrical Ballads* in 1798, the very structure and the content of the *Biographia Literaria* reflect the account that its author gives (1) of his philosophical-critical views together with (2) their application to the poetics of Wordsworth as found both in his theoretical statements (his prefatory pieces) and in his actual poetry. I cannot in any sense undertake here to provide a comprehensive survey (or summary) of the diverse content of the *Biographia Literaria*, which, in its sheer length, rivals *The Prelude* in its grandeur. Still, if its readers are to be in the position of properly evaluating its significance, at once historically and ontologically, especially in regard to Wordsworth, it is critically important for them to have in mind the uniquely peculiar characteristics of the structure (or shape) of Coleridge's argumentation in the work.

I shall outline here, in brusque terms, what I view to be the unique characteristics of the *Biographia Literaria* and then elucidate (defend) them in the context of discussing the two main points with which we are concerned: the overall conception of philosophy that Coleridge advances together with his application of what he calls true philosophical principles to poetics and, above all, to Wordsworth's poetic theory and practice. We shall see that, with the *Biographia Literaria* divided into two volumes, Coleridge broadly advances his own philosophic views in the first volume and his critical estimation of Wordsworth as a badly flawed theorist of poetics but as, with a few glaring exceptions, a great poet, consistent with the views that he expressed in his poem "To Wordsworth," in the second volume. But we shall find that the account that Coleridge gives of his own philosophical principles is inconsistent, incomplete, contradictory, misleading (deceptive), and so, ultimately, thoroughly confused (muddled) and confusing. These are highly charged accusations regarding a famous poet who, as philosophical critic is, in my judgment, often highly overrated by scholars. The proof, as always, is in the pudding. The question then becomes how or in what sense Coleridge, as we saw him write at the very beginning of the *Biographia Literaria*, applies "the rules, deduced from philosophical principles, to poetry and criticism."

Since Coleridge's account of his coming of age as a philosophic thinker and critic is largely biographical (historical), I am not concerned here with his conversion from what we may call his early commitment to the English empirical tradition of Locke and Hartley to German idealism. He went to the continent to study German in order to be able to read the original texts of Kant and his philosophic successors. He tells us that the "writings of the illustrious sage of Königsberg [Kant], the founder of the Critical Philosophy, more than any other work, at once [i.e., at one and the same time] invigorated and disciplined my understanding." He observes that "the originality, the depth, and the . . . , adamantine chain of the logic . . . of the" works of Kant, and here Coleridge provides the titles of several of the major works of Kant, "took possession of me as with a giant's hand. After fifteen years familiarity with them, I still read these and all his other productions with undiminished delight and increasing admiration" (9, 153).

The only problem with the claim on the part of Coleridge that Kant's philosophy fundamentally shaped his own philosophic understanding is that in the *Biographia Literaria* he provides little substantial evidence for it and much counter evidence against it. He never cites any of the major works of Kant or discusses any of the major ideas that constitute Kant's critical philosophy, beginning with the *Critique of Pure Reason*, which was published in 1781 when its author was in his late fifties. Indeed, the only texts of Kant that Coleridge occasionally cites come from his pre-critical period (which Kant largely repudiated and which philosophers and scholars today largely ignore as lacking critical importance). Moreover, Coleridge does not include among the major texts of Kant that he mentions the most important of all, the *Critique of Practical Reason*, which I shall make the basis of my exposition of Kantian philosophy in Chapter 5. Yet more important is the fact that, as we shall see, Coleridge advances philosophical claims that are altogether misleading or, indeed, fallacious when viewed in the light of Kant's principal ideas.

But the most important feature of the account that Coleridge gives of his own philosophic principles is that it is nothing less than disingenuous, misleading, and deceptive. I refer to the fact that, for the most part (and this means for page after page), the exposition that Coleridge gives of his philosophy is composed of passages that are lifted directly from the works of Schelling (and also at times of Fichte and Lessing, etc.,) without acknowledgment.[32] Plagiarism is always a serious issue (and scholars debate today how properly to adjudge Coleridge's unacknowledged use of the writings of others for his own ends). Much more serious, however, is the fact that Coleridge remains silent regarding the reasons why he puts a philosopher like Schelling, who derived his ideas, inconsistently, from his great predecessors (Kant and Hegel), above those truly original philosophers.[33] He never tells us why (silently and blindly) he follows Schelling instead of showing us (with his eyes wide open) what it meant for him to have the sage giant of Königsberg take philosophic possession of him. In other words, it is characteristic of Coleridge as a philosophic thinker, from what we shall now see, to declare (assert) his principles, often in inconsistent, contradictory terms, without providing thoughtfully sustained argumentation in support of them.

Coleridge sets forth what he views as his philosophical principles in Chapter 12 of Volume I of the *Biographia Literaria* in the form of ten Theses.[34] While some of these theses or philosophical premises are intelligent, in principle, Coleridge in no sense renders them intelligible, especially since he supports them, not with argumentation but with citations from and references to a dizzying array of sources. But, before he begins to outline his philosophical theses, Coleridge declares: "The postulate of philosophy, and at the same time the test of philosophical capacity, is no other than the heaven-descended KNOW THYSELF!" (12, 252).[35] In the Conclusion to the *Biographia Literaria* Coleridge repeats a complaint, which he makes throughout his work, that he has been attacked for adhering to a metaphysics "nearer to the visionary flights of Plato, and even to the jargon of the mystics, than to the established tenets of Locke." And "what," he asks, is "poor, unlucky Metaphysics . . . ?" He answers: "A single sentence expresses the object and thereby the contents of this science. '*Know thyself* [cited in Greek]: and so shalt thou know God, as far as is permitted to a creature, and in God all things [cited in Latin]': Surely, there is a strange—nay, rather a too natural—aversion in many to know themselves" (24, 240).

While it is easy to agree with Coleridge that the aversion shared by many to know themselves is strange in being all too natural, it is also important observe that it is no less unnaturally strange that Coleridge shares the aversion, which is widely shared by modern philosophers and scholars, to making a properly decisive distinction, at once historical and ontological, between "know yourself" as oracular in the Greek tradition" and "know yourself" as taking responsibility for knowing, like God, good and evil, in the biblical tradition. When Judge William, in Kierkegaard's *Either/Or*, Part II, undertakes to distinguish the ethical individual from the aesthetic individual, consistent, we may say, with Kierkegaard's distinction between the metaphorical transfer to Spirit and the merely sensate, he writes that "the crux of the matter . . . is that the ethical individual is transparent to himself. . . . The person who lives ethically has seen himself, knows himself, penetrates his whole concretion with this consciousness. . . . He knows himself. The phrase *know yourself* [given in Greek] is a stock phrase, . . . but . . . it cannot be the goal if it not also the beginning. The ethical individual knows himself, but this knowing is not simply contemplation, for . . . it is a collecting of oneself, which itself is an action, and this is why I have . . . used the expression 'to choose oneself' instead of 'to know oneself'"[36] (258).

When the imperative—know yourself—is understood to signify, not the unknown goal or telos of life in the Socratic tradition of oracular ignorance but the choice of self that the ethical individual makes in the beginning, from the beginning, in the prophetic tradition of self-revelation, we are in the presence of the concept of will as embodying the action of practical reason, to anticipate our discussion of Kant in later chapters. Coleridge, however, never sees or in any sense grasps the distinction between the Socratic (oracular) and the biblical (prophetic). Indeed, immediately after stating that the heaven-descended "know thyself!" is no less the postulate of philosophy than "the test of philosophical capacity, . . . at once practically and speculatively . . . ," he proceeds to state (while continuing to quote Schelling without acknowledgment) that (and I paraphrase) philosophy is a science not only of reason, or of the understanding, or of morals but of Being. "All knowledge rests on the coincidence of an object with a subject" (12, 252). After Coleridge continues to expiate in no less vague terms on the relation of subject and object, while yet quoting Schelling (without telling us), he writes that we have to acknowledge the truth, however much it is denied by the "philosophers of the schools, . . . that we are all collectively born idealists, and therefore and only therefore are at the same time realists." He then brings to a close what we might call his introduction to the ten theses of his philosophy, which he will proceed to articulate in the following section of Chapter 12, with the declaration that "in the third treatise of my *Logosophia* [combining the two Greek terms "logic/word" and "wisdom"], announced at the end of this volume, I shall give (deo volente [God willing]) the demonstrations and constructions of the Dynamic Philosophy scientifically arranged. It is . . . no other than the system of Pythagoras and Plato revived and purified from impure mixtures" (12, 263).

The misrepresentation (fabrication) that is present in what I called in the previous paragraph the introduction that Coleridge provides for his ten philosophical theses is surely unprecedented for a figure who is, at one and the same time, to be truly respected as a significant poet but to be falsely viewed as a significant, philosophical thinker. The misrepresentation on the part of Coleridge is of two sorts, philosophical and biographical. Philosophically, Coleridge shows that he has no substantial understanding of Kant in utterly failing to see any fundamental difference between ancient philosophy (in the tradition of Plato and Aristotle) and modern philosophy (in the biblical tradition of Kant, Hegel, and Kierkegaard . . .). To assert that in his forthcoming *logosophia* he will provide a scientific philosophy that is nothing other than a revived and purified version of the system of Pythagoras and Plato is to show that he has no critical understanding of Kantian philosophy whatsoever. Kant is profoundly aware, as we shall see, that the concept of reason as practice, as willing the good, has no basis whatsoever in ancient Greek philosophy. Yes, we can concede that the question of the relationship of subject and object, of idealism and realism, of the transcendental and the phenomenal, of freedom and nature is central to the philosophy of Kant and so to the philosophy of modernity, more generally. Still, when Coleridge simply mouths vague claims (in words taken blindly from Schelling) about the relationship of subject and object, he evinces no understanding whatsoever of the issues involved. Indeed, for him to state, as we saw above—"All knowledge rests on the coincidence of an object with a subject."—and not to provide an analysis of the complexity that is involved in the coincidence of object and subject, the explanation of which we could say occupied Kant throughout the whole of his two great critiques of pure and practical reason, is simply to indulge in fanciful thinking. But there is also biographical fabrication. First, Coleridge does not provide an announcement of the third treatise of his *Logosophia* at the end of Volume I of the *Biographia Literaria*. Second, and more important, he never did write (or publish) the so-called *Logosophia* either in part or in whole.

We now come to the ten theses in which Coleridge outlines his philosophical principles. In form, they are simple, brief declarations (assertions) that are accompanied by little or no explanation. In content, while they at times reflect important issues, they remain vague, abstract, formulations that are not fundamentally different from the claims that we have already seen him make. Just prior to Thesis I Coleridge tells us that the ten theses will provide him with the basis for his analysis of the imagination, together with the fine arts, in the following Chapter 13. I shall summarize Coleridge's theses in the most elemental terms possible. "Truth is correlative to being." To know is to know something (Thesis I). Truth is either mediate (derived/conditional) or immediate (original/unconditional) (Thesis II). We seek an absolute truth that is "self-grounded, unconditional, and known by its own light" (Thesis III). "There can be but one such principle" (Thesis IV). Because such a principle cannot be either any object (thing) or any subject, "it must be . . . the identity of both" (Thesis V). This principle is found in the "Sum or I am" as expressed by the words "spirit, self, and self-consciousness." Here "object and subject, being and knowing, are identical." If an individual is asked how he knows that he is, his only answer is: sum quia sum: I am because I am. But if he is asked how he came to be, he answers: "sum quia in deo sum: I am because I am in God." Coleridge continues:

> But if we elevate our conception to the absolute self, the great eternal I AM, then the principle of being and of knowledge, of idea and of reality, the ground of existence and the ground of the knowledge of existence are absolutely identical. Sum quia sum; I am because I affirm myself to be; I affirm myself to be because I am.

At this point Coleridge adds a note in which he writes that Jehovah "in the very first revelation of his absolute being . . . at the same time revealed the fundamental truth of all philosophy"—that it "must either commence with the absolute or have no fixed commencement, i.e., cease to be philosophy" (Thesis VI).[37]

Coleridge then proceeds to write that the identity of object and representation is found only "in the self-consciousness of a spirit." At this point he qualifies (explains) his earlier claim that knowledge and being are correlative in pointing out that a spirit is not originally an object "but an absolute subject for which all, itself included, may become an object. It must therefore be an Act," as distinct from an object, which is "dead, fixed, incapable in itself of any action, and necessarily finite." Indeed, spirit, as the identity of object and subject, can be conscious of this identity only in dissolving it. "But this implies an act, and it follows therefore that intelligence or self-consciousness is impossible, except by and in a will. The self-conscious spirit therefore is a will; and freedom must be assumed as a *ground* of philosophy and can never be deduced from it" (Thesis VII). While the object is originally finite, the spirit, because it is not originally an object, cannot originally be finite. Still, because the spirit cannot be a subject without becoming an object and so is "originally the identity of both, it can be conceived neither as infinite nor as finite exclusively but as the most original union of both." Indeed, Coleridge writes, "the process and mystery of production and life consist in the reconciling and recurrence of this contradiction" (Thesis VIII).[38] It is at this point, Coleridge indicates, with reference to Thesis VI, that "philosophy would pass into religion and religion become inclusive of philosophy." We begin with "I know myself" and end with "the absolute I AM. We proceed from the self in order to lose and find all self in God" (Thesis IX). The final Thesis X morphs, then, into a meandering discussion of the idea that we "can never pass beyond the principle of self-consciousness" since the principles of being and of knowledge "are co-inherent and identical" (12, 185). Having thus enunciated his ten theses Coleridge concludes Chapter 12 in taking notice of the objection that Wordsworth raised in his 1815 Preface to his definition of imagination as if in preparation for the succeeding Chapter 13 on the imagination.

My aim in taking account of the ten theses in which Coleridge expounds the basic principles of his philosophy is twofold. First, insofar as he brings together the subject, self-consciousness, spirit, will, freedom, action, and the infinite, as distinguished from the object as finite, he can be said to have conceived of his philosophy in the spirit of Kant's critique of reason as practice (will), as we shall find in subsequent chapters. But, second, insofar as he views the relationship of subject and object (freedom and nature) in terms of the original but contradictory identity of knowledge and being, Coleridge evinces little or no substantial understanding of Kantian philosophy. Furthermore, in remaining, it appears, altogether blind to the gross contradiction that is contained in his claim that the divine revelation of Jehovah: I AM simply revives and purifies the logosophia of Pythagoras and Plato, Coleridge exposes to us his substantial inadequacy as a thinker, whether philosophical or religious.

It perhaps does not bode well for us that Coleridge wrote that he views his ten philosophical theses as providing for him the basis of his discussion of the imagination in Chapter 13. In any case, he initiates that chapter by citing lengthy passages from *Paradise Lost* and Leibniz (the second in Latin), plus a hymn (in Greek) by Synesius (a bishop of the Eastern Church, c. 400, who fused Christian doctrine with Neo-Platonism). Next, after paraphrasing, in largely incomprehensible terms, a pre-critical work of Kant (1763) on the interaction of opposite forces, he suddenly informs the reader that he received a letter from a friend, who, unnamed but whose "practical judgment I have had ample reason to estimate and revere," advised him not to publish his chapter on the imagination but to save it for publication "in your announced treatises on the Logos or communicative intellect in Man and Deity." Coleridge tells us that, in agreeing with "this very judicious letter, . . . I shall content myself for the present with stating the main result of the Chapter, which I have reserved for that future publication, a detailed prospectus of which the reader will find at the close of the second volume [of the *Biographia Literaria*]" (13, 304). Consequently, the account that Coleridge gives of the imagination in Chapter 13 amounts to less than one page. Furthermore, it was actually Coleridge who wrote the letter that he claims to have received from an esteemed and revered friend. Not only that, but, again, no detailed prospectus on his announced treatises is to be found at the close of the second volume of the *Biographia Literaria*.[39]

In two brief paragraphs Coleridge provides definitions of imagination as primary and secondary and of fancy, which, however, are scarcely intelligible in themselves. He calls primary imagination "the living Power and prime Agent of all human Perception" and "the repetition in the finite mind of the eternal act of creation in the infinite I AM." He identifies secondary imagination as an echo of the former and so, because it is "identical with the primary in the *kind* of agency," it differs "only in *degree* and in the *mode* of its operation." As regards fancy, since it but plays with "fixities and definites," it is "a mode of Memory" that involves "that empirical phenomenon of the will, which we express by the word CHOICE" (13, 305). I am not concerned here with tracing the origins of the recondite definitions of imagination and fancy that Coleridge offers.[40] Since, however, he makes a fundamental error in identifying will and choice with the empirical and not with the rational, i.e., not with practical reason in the tradition of Kant, it appears that he had been befuddled in not seeing through the one, singular failure that the sage philosopher of Königsberg himself made. In uncritically adhering to the tradition of earlier eighteenth century German aesthetic philosophy, as I indicated in Chapter 1 (see n. 4), Kant continued to identify imagination with the understanding (*Verstand*) and not with reason (*Vernunft*), i.e., with empirical knowledge (sensation) and not with rational practice (thought and will). In any case, all that really counts for us at present is Coleridge's basic distinction between imagination as creative (divine, infinite) practice and fancy as inventive (human, finite) play, between the imaginative and the fanciful.

Thus ends Volume I of the *Biographia Literaria*, in which Coleridge, as we have seen, undertakes to provide for his readers the principles that, in his view, must be understood to underlie a true critique of poetry. Wordsworth is then central to Volume II. On the one hand, Coleridge discusses their personal relationship to each other as fellow poets whose jointly conceived *Lyrical Ballads* transformed English poetry. On the other hand, he takes issue with the theory of poetics that Wordsworth outlines in his prefatory materials while offering, at the same time, a critical assessment of his friend's poetry in terms of what he calls both its defects and its beauties. In the Conclusion of the *Biographia Literaria* Coleridge gives a final accounting of his own Christian faith in defense of his metaphysics against its harsh critics. In providing the most succinct account possible of Coleridge's views, my aim here, as always, is to enlarge and deepen the critical understanding that we bring to our reading of *The Prelude* in the next chapter.

Coleridge opens Chapter 14, initiating Volume II of the *Biographia Literaria*, with the observation that during the first year, when he and Wordsworth were neighbors (1797–98), "our conversations turned frequently on the two cardinal points of poetry, the power of exciting the sympathy of the reader by a faithful adherence to the truth of nature and the power of giving the interest of novelty by the modifying colours of imagination" (14, 5). He observes further that, in planning the *Lyrical Ballads*, "it was agreed that my endeavours should be directed to persons and characters supernatural, or at least romantic [as found, for example, in "The Rhyme of the Ancient Mariner"]. . . . Mr. Wordsworth, on the other hand, was to propose to himself as his object to give the charm of novelty to things of every day and to excite a feeling analogous to the supernatural by awakening the mind's attention from the lethargy of custom and directing it to the loveliness and the wonders of the world before us" (14, 6–7). It is useful to recall that among the twenty-three poems that constitute the first edition of the *Lyrical Ballads* only four were by Coleridge and that in the second edition (1800) he contributed only one additional poem. Coleridge also points out that he questioned the opinion expressed by Wordsworth in the Preface to the second edition (1800) that in his poetry he made use of "the language of *real* life" (14, 8). He adds that, in the Preface to the edition of his poetry that Wordsworth has recently published (1815), he continues to make the same claim. In order, however, to show where he agrees and disagrees with Wordsworth, it is necessary for him, he observes, to "explain my ideas, first, of a POEM, and, secondly, of POETRY itself, in *kind* and in *essence*" (14, 11).

A long-winded discussion brings Coleridge to what he calls "the final definition" of a poem as "that species of composition which is opposed to works of science by proposing for its *immediate* object pleasure, not truth" (14, 13). As he continues on his rambling way, he invokes Plato, together with earlier English theorists, as furnishing "undeniable proofs that poetry of the highest kind may exist without metre and even without the contradistinguishing objects of a poem." For proof of this claim he invokes the prophet Isaiah in telling us that "a very large proportion" of his book "is poetry in the most emphatic sense" (14, 14). But he immediately adds that it would be "no less irrational than strange to assert that pleasure, and not truth, was the immediate project of the prophet" (14,15). Coleridge does not, then, however, address the overt contradiction in his claim that the aim of poetry, unlike the aim of "science," is not truth, but pleasure, since, as he himself points out, it irrationally and strangely fails to take biblical poetry into consideration. Instead, he simply proceeds to write that the poet, "described in *ideal* perfection, brings the whole soul of man into activity, with the subordination of its faculties to each other, according to their relative worth and dignity" (14, 15–16). He then concludes Chapter 14 with the declaration that "good sense is the body of poetic genius, fancy its drapery, motion its life, and imagination the soul," all formed "into one graceful and intelligent whole" (14, 18).[41]

After discussing earlier English poetry in Chapters 15 and 16, Coleridge arrives at Wordsworth in Chapter 17. He praises Wordsworth for undertaking "in his preface [of 1800?] . . . a reformation in our poetic diction as far as he evinced the truth of passion and the *dramatic* propriety of those figures and metaphor in the original poets, which, stripped of their justifying reason and converted into mere artifices of connection or ornament, constitute the characteristic falsity in the poetic style of the moderns [post Milton]" (17, 40). But in the "title" of Chapter 17, which, like most of the chapter titles in the *Biographia Literaria*, simply provides a list of the topics to be discussed in the chapter to follow, Coleridge summarizes his critique of Wordsworth's poetic theory. After first indicating that the chapter to follow contains an "examination of the tenets peculiar to Mr. Wordsworth," the chapter title (heading) continues with a list of Coleridge's own views:

- Rustic life (above all, low and rustic life) [is] especially unfavorable to the formation of a human diction.
- The best parts of language [are] the products of philosophers, not [of] clowns or shepherds.
- Poetry [is] essentially ideal and generic.
- The language of Milton [is] as much the language of *real* life, yea, incomparably more so than that of the cottager.

Coleridge's principal objection in this chapter is the claim made by Wordsworth in his Preface (1800) that he undertook "to imitate the real language of men and, as far as possible, to adopt the language of men"

(17, 55).⁴² Indeed, Coleridge observes that, when Wordsworth in his Preface made clear that he purified this language of "its real defects" (as we noted earlier in discussing his prefatory materials), what this means is that "a rustic's language," once it is "purified from all provincialism and grossness" and "reconstructed as to be made consistent with the rules of grammar (which are in essence no other than the laws of universal logic applied to Psychological materials), will not differ from the language of any other man of common sense" (17, 52). Coleridge additionally points out that "the thoughts, feelings, language, and manners of the shepherd-farmers in the vales of Cumberland and Westmoreland . . . may be accounted for from causes which will and do produce the same results in *every* state of life, whether in town or country." He gives two principal causes for his observation. First is "that independence, which raises a man above servitude or daily toil for the profit of others, yet not above the necessity of industry and a frugal simplicity of domestic life." Second is a "solid and religious education" as based on the Bible "and the liturgy or hymn book" (17, 44). What Wordsworth calls "real" language, Coleridge observes, we should rather call "*ordinary* or *lingua communis* . . . [that] is no more to be found in the phraseology of low and rustic life than in that of any other class. Omit the peculiarities of each, and the result of course may be common to all" (17, 56).

But let us remember that in the heading (title) of Chapter 17, as we saw above, Coleridge indicates that poetry is "essentially ideal and generic." Indeed, he states in Chapter 17: "I adopt with full faith the principle of Aristotle that poetry as poetry is essentially *ideal*, that it avoids and excludes all *accident*" (17, 45–46). In other words, the persons described in poetry "must be representative of a class . . . and clothed with *generic* attributes, with the *common* attributes of the class" (17, 46). We may suppose that the passage of Aristotle that Coleridge has in the mind is to be found in that section of the *Poetics* where Aristotle writes that poetry is more philosophical than history since poetry expresses the universal and history the particular.⁴³ But what Coleridge, like so many readers of the *Poetics*, fails to grasp is that for Aristotle poetry, like practical wisdom, reflects the world of the *polis* in which knowledge of the good is unknowable and the philosopher (the one who knows the good in itself) is unknown. Because the *polis* represents the body, it is not the home of the soul. Furthermore, the distinction between philosophy as universal and history as particular (individual) is like Aristotle's golden mean: it is purely relative as the "inbetween" whose extremes are never known (as what is good and what is evil). Aristotle's golden mean bears no relationship whatsoever to the golden rule of the Bible: treat all individual human beings (universally, not in terms of their race, class, gender . . .) as you want to be universally treated by them as an individual. It is critically important to remember that Hegel shows that it is the individual (human being) who is truly universal and that it is universality that is truly embodied in the individual (human being). But Hegel here is but following Kant, the moral principle of whose categorical imperative—treat all human beings as persons, as ends in themselves, and not simply as things or means—brings together individual and universality. It is also important to note that, when Hegel shows us that history is the story of freedom (or in the words of Kierkegaard, the coming into existence of the single individual), this story is at once universal and individual, the story of "everyman."

It is no less worth pausing to ask how we view the significant figures in the plays of, say, Shakespeare, whether his so-called comedies, histories, tragedies, or romances. Is Rosalind or Prince Hal or Hamlet or Prospero . . . individual or universal? The answer, in elemental terms, is both. The figures in significant modern drama and fiction are at once unique and universal. In and through their unique individuality they embody, they address issues that are universally meaningful for all of us. To be or not to be is the universal question that Hamlet has personally to face in the uniqueness of the situation in which he has so unexpectedly found himself. Once again, then, Coleridge fails to grasp the fundamental difference between, in this case, Greek tragedy and Shakespearian tragedy. In the context of crediting Lessing for the discovery of the true Shakespeare, Coleridge praises him for having "proved that in all the essentials of art, no less than in the truth of nature, the Plays of Shakespeare were incomparably more coincident with the principles of Aristotle than [were] the productions of Corneille and Racine, notwithstanding the boasted regularity of the latter" (23, 210).[44] While most readers today would, I think, not hesitate to rank Shakespeare above his French compeers, it is not because he in any sense embodies the principles of Aristotle in his plays. It is, frankly, characteristic of the ineptitude of Coleridge as a reader of texts and so also as a critical thinker that he is unable to discern how fundamentally different is the interminable opposition in Greek tragedy between individual luck (*tyche*) and universal fate (*moira*) from the principle of Shakespearian drama (together with all significant modern fiction) that love—respect for the dignity and worth of all human beings in being like God in bearing the responsibility for knowing good and evil—conquers all.

In Chapter 18 of the *Biographia Literaria* Coleridge addresses the second of the two major claims made in Wordsworth's prefatory materials with which he fundamentally disagrees—that there is no essential difference between verse and prose. But he immediately comments: "I reflect with delight how little a mere theory . . . interferes with the processes of genuine imagination in a man of true poetic genius who possesses—as Mr. Wordsworth, if ever man did, most assuredly does possess—'The Vision and the Faculty Divine' [cited from Wordsworth's *The Excursion*]" (18, 59–60). Since the reasons that Coleridge gives for rejecting Wordsworth's position amount to little more than telling us that metrical arrangement in verse heightens the pleasure and deepens the excitement that readers experience in poetry (without distinguishing between, let's say, descriptive and fictional prose), I shall not review them. For what is of proper interest in this chapter is that Coleridge reiterates yet again how important it is for the poet to abide "by principles, the ignorance or neglect of which would convict him of being no *poet* but a silly or presumptuous usurper of the name! By the principles of grammar, logic, and psychology! In one word, by such knowledge of the facts, material and spiritual . . . as . . . governed by *good sense* and rendered instinctive by habit . . . [so as to acquire] the name of TASTE" (18, 81). Coleridge reiterates his position in the last sentence of Chapter 18 when he writes that what counts in judging a poem is whether it conforms with "grammar, logic, and the truth and nature of things confirmed by the authority of works, whose fame is not of ONE country or of one age" (18, 88).

Coleridge carries over the discussion of the principles of criticism into Chapter 21, which he devotes to "the present mode of conducting critical journals," whose writers frequently stung both Wordsworth and him with their harsh attacks on their poetry. He opens the chapter in remarking: "Long have I wished to see a fair and philosophical inquisition into the character of Wordsworth, as a poet, on the evidence of his published works." He notes further that he would "call that investigation fair and philosophical in which the critic announces and endeavors to establish the principles which he holds for the foundation of poetry in general. . . . Then, if his premises be rational, his deductions legitimate, and his conclusions justly applied," we are in the position of being able to evaluate the truth or the falsity of his judgment (21, 107).

It is, then, in Chapter 22 that Coleridge takes up, according to the chapter heading,

- The characteristic defects of Wordsworth's poetry, with the principles from which the judgement that they are defects is deduced;
- Their proportion to the beauties;
- For the greatest part characteristic of his theory only.

Up to now we have seen that, while Coleridge repeatedly calls for an articulation of the principles of critique, he simply proffers abstract concepts empty of significant content that are rendered yet further meaningless in being conflated with totally alien ideas taken from Plato and Aristotle. His criticism of what he considers to be the two principal defects of Wordsworth's theory is of greater interest. Still, in showing, first, that the "real" language used by Wordsworth in his poetry is not the rustic language of shepherds but the language commonly used by all educated human beings, he shows no appreciation of the fact that Wordsworth makes this irony central to his strong poems, as we saw in our discussion earlier of his immortality Ode. We shall be returning to this point shortly. Regarding, second, Wordsworth's claim that there is no essential difference in principle between poetry and prose, Coleridge again fails to render intelligible how it is that meter makes verse different from prose in the content of its meaning.

In reviewing, now, the five defects that Coleridge finds in Wordsworth's poetry, I shall make no attempt to examine in detail his elaboration of them all. Regarding the first defect, an inconstancy in style, Coleridge makes it clear that it occurs only in the occasional poem. The second defect is "not seldom a *matter-of-factness*" involving minute detail and the use of "accidental circumstances." Again, Coleridge appeals to Aristotle's *Poetics* as the basis for his claim that accidentality contravenes the essence of poetry, which Aristotle pronounces to be "the most intense, weighty and philosophical product of human art" since it is the most universal and the most abstract (22, 126). He adds that the "Poet should paint to the imagination, not to the fancy" (22, 127). Yet again he also writes that the failure to see that the immediate end of poetry is pleasure and not truth destroys "the main fundamental distinction, not only between a *poem* and *prose* but even between philosophy and works of fiction" (22, 130).

Coleridge next tells us that the third and fourth defects that are to be found in Wordsworth's poems are closely related to each other. The poet's reliance on "the *dramatic* form" results in two opposite results: undue incongruity or undue similarity between the figure dramatized and the poet. Additionally, incongruity between intensity of feeling and knowledge leads to "prolixity, repetition, and an eddying" (22, 136).[45] It is the fifth and last defect that Coleridge discusses that is of real interest to us, as I indicated in my introductory comments to the *Biographia Literaria*. Here we find "*mental* bombast" involving "thoughts and images too great for the subject." Still, Coleridge points out that this "is a fault of which none but a man of genius is capable" (22, 136). Exemplary here for Coleridge is the "Immortality Ode" in which the child is addressed as "Thou best philosopher . . . ."

We pass on, then, to the six excellences that Coleridge associates with Wordsworth's poetry. The first five involve:

(1) "an austere purity of language both grammatically and logically; in short, a perfect appropriateness of the words to the meaning" (22, 142)/

(2) "a correspondent weight and sanity of the Thoughts and Sentiments" (22, 144).

(3) "the sinewy strength and originality of single lines and paragraphs" (22, 148).

(4) "the perfect truth of nature in his images and descriptions as taken immediately from nature" (22, 148).

(5) "a meditative pathos, a union of deep and subtle thought with sensibility, a sympathy with man as man; the sympathy indeed of a contemplator rather than a fellow-sufferer or co-mate . . . but of a contemplator, from whose view no difference of rank conceals the sameness of the nature . . . [or] wholly disguise[s] the human face divine. The superscription and the image of the Creator still remain legible to *him* under the dark lines with which guilt or calamity had cancelled or cross-barred it. In this mild and philosophic pathos Wordsworth appears to me without a compeer" (22, 150).

In taking up the sixth and last excellence that he finds in Wordsworth's poetry, Coleridge writes: "Last, and pre-eminently, I challenge for this poet the gift of IMAGINATION in the highest and strictest sense of the world." While in his use of "the play of *Fancy*" he finds that Wordsworth is not always "graceful" and is sometimes "recondite," "in imaginative power he stands nearest of all modern writers to Shakespeare and Milton and yet in a kind perfectly unborrowed and his own." In preparing to provide a few select examples of Wordsworth's poetry "as most obviously manifesting this faculty," Coleridge adds that "if I should ever be fortunate enough to render my analysis of imagination . . . thoroughly intelligible to the reader, he will scarcely open on a page of this poet's works without recognizing . . . the presence and the influences of this faculty" (22, 151). This leads Coleridge to write that, while it would not be for him to prophesy what Wordsworth "*will* produce, . . . I could pronounce with the liveliest conviction what he is capable of producing. It is the FIRST GENUINE PHILOSOPHIC POEM [*The Recluse*]" (22, 156).

Coleridge concludes Chapter 22 in reiterating that most of the defects that he finds in Wordsworth involve his theory. "How small the proportion of the defects are to the beauties [of his poetry] I have repeatedly declared, and that no one of them originates in deficiency of poetic genius" (22, 158). He observes further that "I am not half as much irritated by hearing his enemies abuse him for vulgarity of style, subject, and conception, as I am disgusted with the gilded side of the same meaning, as displayed by some affected admirers with whom he is, forsooth, a *sweet, simple poet!* and *so* natural" with the result that their children "are *so* charmed with them [Wordsworth's poems] that they play at" figures taken from them (22, 158–59).

In the final Chapter 24 of the *Biographia Literaria*, simply entitled "Conclusion," Coleridge takes the opportunity of defending himself one last time against the accusation that his philosophy is incompatible with Christian doctrine by outlining what he calls "the true evidences of Christianity" of which for him there are four:

1. Its "consistency with right reason" is "the outer Court of the Temple, the common area within which it stands."
2. "The miracles with and through which the Religion was first revealed and attested I regard as the steps, the vestibule, and the portal of the Temple."
3. "The inward feeling in the soul of each Believer that he needs something, joined with the strong Foretokening that the Redemption and the Graces propounded to us in Christ are *what* he needs—this I hold to be the FOUNDATION of the spiritual Edifice."

4. With "the strong *a priori* probability" found in evidences 1 and 3, combined with "the historical evidence of 2, no man can refuse or neglect to make the experiment without guilt." "But it is the experience derived from a practical conformity to the conditions of the Gospel . . .—in a word, it is the actual *Trial* of the Faith in Christ . . . that must form the arched ROOF, and the Faith itself is the completing KEY-STONE." We "can only *know* by the act of *becoming*. 'Do the will of my father, and ye shall KNOW whether I am of God.'" (See John 7:17)

Without in any sense making clear to us how reason, miracles, the inner need on the part of individuals (for salvation), and doing the will of the Father (in living by the command of the golden rule?) together form the church (the city) of God on earth, Coleridge then writes that "the dictate" of *Credidi ideóque intellexi* (I believed and therefore I understood) is true "equally of Philosophy and Religion." It is not less true, he continues, that all "spiritual predicates" may be equally construed in terms of "modes of Action or as states of Being," of act and existence. Then, in recalling that the slander he has suffered for his ideas reflects in part his interest in Spinoza—given that the Jewish philosopher, since his death in 1677, had generally been condemned as a pantheist and/or an atheist—Coleridge writes that he wishes he "could find in the books of philosophy, theoretical or moral, which are alone recommended to the present students of Theology in our established schools, a few passages as thoroughly *Pauline*, as completely accordant with the doctrines of the established Church, as the following sentences in the concluding page of Spinoza's Ethics" (24, 245). Coleridge then cites a passage from the final proposition of the *Ethics*, as written in the original Latin (Part V, Prop. 42), without further comment.[46]

Coleridge is altogether right in his view that Spinoza concludes his *Ethics* with a passage that is thoroughly Pauline and so in accord with Christian doctrine in expressing ideas that are profoundly biblical (as true to both Hebrew and Christian Scripture). But, as is so sadly typical of Coleridge, he does not provide us with any insight into what it is that is contained in this concluding passage of the *Ethics* that leads him to make it central to his own conclusion. Indeed, it is no easy task to summarize what Spinoza says in summary of his own philosophy. But, in identifying blessedness with the love of God and so with the mind as the principle of human action, his basic point is that blessedness is not the reward of virtue (human strength), but virtue itself. "So because the Mind enjoys this divine Love or blessedness, . . . no one enjoys blessedness because he has restrained his affects [lusts]. Instead, the power to restrain lusts arises from blessedness itself." In short, love as action is virtue itself. Still, in order not to confuse the position that blessedness is not the reward of virtue but virtue itself with the Stoic doctrine that virtue is its own reward, it is important to see that the idea that blessedness as love of God is itself virtuous action presupposes two critically important principles that Spinoza articulates earlier in the *Ethics*. The first is found in his statement that we do not desire something because it is the good (itself) but rather that what we desire is the good (Part III, Prop. 9, Scholium). The second involves Spinoza's demonstration that desire, when articulated in and through what he calls the dictates of reason, is founded on the principle of not doing to others what you do not want others to do to you (i.e., on the principle of the golden rule) (Part IV, Prop. 18, Scholium).

Coleridge then concludes the *Biographia Literaria* with the statement that what he calls "the Scheme of Christianity, as taught in the Liturgy and Homilies of our Church, though not discoverable by human Reason, is yet in accordance with it" (24, 247). Without, however, telling us whether the accord between Christianity and reason is a religious or a philosophical truth, Coleridge proceeds to pursue his poetical way of faith from the Day of reason into the "sacred Night" when "the upraised Eye views only the starry Heaven . . . and the outward Beholding is fixed on the sparks twinkling in the aweful depth . . . only to preserve the Soul steady and collected in its pure *Act* of inward Adoration to the great I AM and to the filial Word that re-affirmeth it from Eternity to Eternity, whose choral Echo is the Universe. THEO, MONO, DOXA [in Greek letters]: Faith in the One God ("Glory to God alone" in the standard doxology).

So ends *the Biographia Literaria* with Coleridge affirming his Christian faith as consistent with reason yet a faith that, proceeding beyond nature, holds the soul steady in its pure act of inward adoration to the great I AM. But does, then, we ask, the "Know thyself" that descended from the sky into ancient Greek philosophy lead to the I AM of biblical affirmation? When Coleridge wrote earlier that he is confident that Wordsworth is capable of writing "the first genuine philosophical poem," are we to understand that this poem will remain outside of the Temple of religious truth? I trust that our review of the *Biographia Literaria*, in which both the potential strengths and the actual weaknesses of the account that Coleridge gives of the philosophic principles that he views as necessary for providing a true critique of poetics, will deepen our capacity to engage *The Prelude* of Wordsworth. It is now time, then, for us to see how or in what sense Shelley's *Defense of Poetry* serves the same end.

But, first, I want to conclude my account of Coleridge with consideration of his brief, ten-line poem, "Know Thyself," which was published in 1834, the year of his death. We shall we find that this poem serves as a repudiation of his literary biography and so, also, reveals that the conviction expressed in it—that his erstwhile friend Wordsworth was capable of producing the first genuine *philosophical* poem—is devoid of significance. For what, indeed, is the worth of philosophy or, indeed, of the mind of the poet in light of Coleridge's poem? Still, if a poem is to be successful in repudiating as worthless the life of the poet, must it not itself be worthy as a poem? In prefacing his poem with the epigram of Juvenal, the satiric poet of ancient Rome—"And from heaven descended KNOW THYSELF" (cited in Latin and Greek)—Coleridge begins his poem: "Know thyself" (in Greek) and then asks rhetorically (in ending his sentence, not with a question mark but with an explanation mark!) if "this is not the prime / And heaven-sprung adage of the olden time!" If thou canst make thyself, Coleridge continues, learn, first, what thou hast made.

> What hast thou, Man, that thou dar'st call thine own?
> What is there in thee, Man, that can be known?—
> Dark fluxion, all unfixable by thought,
> A phantom dim of past and future wrought,
> Vain sister of the worm, —life, death, soul, clod—
> Ignore thyself, and strive to know thy God!

Is it not ironic, as I intimated above, that Coleridge, in undertaking in his poem to sever the bond between Greek philosophy and Christianity, which earlier in the *Biographia Literaria* he had championed, now espouses a conception of Christianity that Kierkegaard calls Christendom as based on the baptism of paganism, i.e., as involving the rationalization of pagan values in Christian dress? The dualistic opposition between ignorance of self and knowledge of God that Coleridge now expresses in his poem "Know Thyself" is actually a version of Neoplatonism that is completely contradictory. For, as Descartes demonstrates, to doubt (to claim to be ignorant of) yourself is itself the revelation that all doubting, all denial of the self presupposes knowledge of the self. Rousseau, indeed, observes that you cannot alienate (be alien to) your own self. For the very act of self-alienation presupposes the self as the principle of alienation. We are not free to be unfree, i.e., to renounce our freedom.[47] We cannot choose to be slaves. Right does not derive from fact. Might is not right. The fact that slavery exists does not prove that it is right. History is the story of freedom, of liberation from slavery to the might of others.

What we see, then, in his poem "Know thyself" is that Coleridge is correct to repudiate the position, which he had previously upheld in the *Biographia Literaria*, that the ancients' oracular exhortation "know yourself" contains the truth of Christianity. But now, in his poem, he falls into the very opposite position that knowledge of God presupposes ignorance of the self. He never truly comes to understand that, as we shall see so clearly in Kant, to know God is to adhere to the command of the moral law, as based on knowledge of good and evil: will to do unto others what you want others to will to do unto you. In other words, Coleridge never evinces any understanding whatsoever of Kant's demonstration in the *Critique of Practical Reason* that God, together with freedom and immortality, is a postulate of practical reason. To know God within a progressively historical framework that is infinitely eternal (and so not finitely eternal and at an end as in the Greek world) is to act freely in your relationships to both self and other.

SHELLEY'S *A DEFENSE OF POETRY*

Now, I want to consider how Shelley, in his *A Defense of Poetry*, conceives of modern poetry, of the artistically creative imagination, in light of not only the poetry but also the philosophy and religion of the ancient Greeks and Romans, on the one hand, and of the ancient Jews (including Jesus and Paul), on the other. Our end, as the reader knows, is always that of enlarging our capacity to adjudge how or in what sense *The Prelude* fulfills Coleridge's pronouncement that Wordsworth had the capacity to write the first genuinely philosophic poem. For the question, at once historical and ontological, remains for us: What is philosophy? But the question that, as the reader also knows, is no less central to my book is whether this is not as well to ask: What is poetry?

What we find is that Shelley in *A Defense of Poetry*, which he wrote in 1820 (but which was published posthumously only in 1840, some eighteen years after his death in 1822 when he was not yet thirty years old), proclaims, in effusive terms, the identity of poetry and philosophy. The poet is the true philosopher, while true philosophers are poets. But since he identifies poetry with the origins of civilization and so with the savage, primitive, childlike beginnings of humankind and views Homer, together with his contemporaries "of infant Greece," as "the column upon which all succeeding civilization has reposed," the true test of his conception of both poetry and philosophy is, as always, how he understands religion, the religion of the Bible, in relationship to the poetic and to the philosophic (979/col 1). In undertaking to highlight the ideas that Shelley makes central to his conception of the poet as the true, philosophic teacher of humanity, I shall omit consideration of many of the details of his essay. But this does not spare us—author and reader—from having to wade into the depths of the torrential effusion of words that typify the essay's style of presentation and so, in effect, defies any straightforward summary or simple paraphrase of Shelley's overall point of view.

Shelley initiates his *Defense* in distinguishing between what he calls "two classes of mental action," imagination and reason. He associates imagination with *the poetic* and reason with *the logical* (both terms given in Greek), i.e., with the principles of, respectively, synthesis and analysis, of the similitudes and the differences of things. "Reason is to imagination," Shelley writes, "as the instrument to the agent, as the body to the spirit, as the shadow to the substance" (975, col. 1). But we see already that Shelley, in distinguishing between reason and imagination, simply repeats the contradictory logic of opposites that is found in ancient, Greek philosophy, as distinct from the new, revolutionary logic proclaimed by Kant as transcendental, wherein reason as practice is at once analytic (*a priori*) and synthetic (*a posteriori*).

Shelley proceeds to tell us that, since poetry "may be defined to be 'the expression of the imagination,'" it is "connate with the origin of man" (975, col. 2). "In the infancy of society," he writes further, "every author is necessarily a poet, because language is poetry itself; and to be a poet is to apprehend the true and the beautiful, in a word, the good which exists in the relation subsisting, first between existence and perception, and secondly between perception and expression" (976, col. 2). Thus it is that poets, in imagining and expressing "this indestructible order," are the authors of language and all the arts. But they are also "the institutors of laws, and the founders of civil society, and the inventors of the arts of life, and the teachers" who bring into relationship "with the beautiful and true that partial apprehension of the agencies of the invisible world which is called religion. Hence all originals religions are allegorical" (976, col. 2). Whence it is, Shelley tells us, that poets "were called, in the earlier epochs of the world, legislators or prophets.... A poet participates in the eternal, the infinite, and the one" (977, col. 1). At this point in his essay Shelley evokes the Greek tragedian Aeschylus, the biblical Job, and Dante as the author of *Paradiso* (Part III of the *Divine Comedy*) to exemplify his claim.[48]

In next calling the "distinction between poets and prose writers a vulgar error," Shelley thus prepares us for how he understands the relationship between "philosophers and poets.... Plato was essentially a poet" as was Lord Bacon. "All the authors of revolutions in opinions," Shelley proclaims, "are ... necessarily poets." Indeed, he continues, the "supreme poets" who write in verse are no "less capable of perceiving and teaching the truth of things than those who have omitted that form. Shakespeare, Dante, and Milton (to confine ourselves to modern writers) are philosophers of the very loftiest power. A poem is the very image of life expressed in its eternal truth" (978, col. 1). In continuation of this train of thought Shelley proceeds to write that the "poems of Homer and his contemporaries were the delight of infant Greece: they were the elements of that social system which is the column upon which all succeeding civilization has reposed. Homer embodied the ideal perfection of his age in human character." Everyone who read his verses was "awakened to an ambition of becoming like to Achilles, Hector, and Ulysses ... [in] the truth and beauty of friendship, patriotism, and persevering devotion to an object" (978, col. 1—979, col. 1).

While Shelley has hardly paused in the onward surge of his writing to provide his readers with any substantial basis for his claims, he does at this point slow down long enough to address the issue between poetry and morality, i.e., between what is traditionally called form and content. Let it not "be objected," he states, "that these characters [as found in Homer's epics] are remote from moral perfection, and that they are by no means to be considered as edifying patterns for general imitation." Every epoch, he declares, "has deified its peculiar errors." While *revenge* "is the naked idol of the worship of a semi-barbarous age," *self-deceit* (in modernity?) "is the veiled image of unknown evil, before which luxury and satiety lie prostate" (979, col. 1). For what the poet of any epoch does is to array "the vices of his contemporaries" in "temporary dress" that covers "without concealing the eternal proportions of their beauty. ... The beauty of the internal nature can not be so far concealed by its accidental vesture" that its spirit is hidden. The whole objection to the immorality of poetry rests, Shelley observes, on "a misconception of the manner in which poetry acts to produce the moral improvement of man" (979, col. 1). Unlike "ethical science" (philosophy?), which "propounds schemes and proposes examples of civil and domestic life . . . , poetry acts in another and diviner manner" (979, col. 2). Notwithstanding the fact that we have already seen Shelley call Plato and Bacon poets, he now waxes eloquent in elaborating how poetry, unlike "ethical science,"

> acts in another and diviner manner. It awakens and enlarges the mind itself by rendering it the receptacle of a thousand unapprehended combinations of thought. Poetry lifts the veil from the hidden beauty of the world, and makes familiar objects be as if they were not familiar; it reproduces all that it represents, and the impersonations clothed in its Elysian light stand thenceforth in the minds of those who have once contemplated them, as memorials of that gentle and exalted content which extends itself over all thoughts and actions with which it co-exists.

Shelley continues (I condense his effusive claims when and as possible):

> The great secret of morals is love; or a going out of our own nature, and an identification of ourselves with the beautiful which exists in thoughts, action, or person, not our own. A man, to be greatly good, must imagine intensely and comprehensively; he must put himself in the place of another and of many others; the pains and pleasures of his species must become his own. The great instrument of moral good is the imagination. . . . Poetry strengthens the faculty which is the organ of the moral nature of man in the same manner as exercise strengthens a limb. A poet therefore would do ill to embody his own conceptions of right and wrong, which are usually of his place and time, in his poetic creations, which participate in neither.

It is only lesser poets who, in affecting "a moral aim," diminish "the effect of their poetry . . . in exact proportion to the degree in which they compel us to advert to this purpose" (979, col. 1).

Without pausing to explain how love, when understood as regard for the other (and thus consistent with the moral law as commanded by the prophets and Jesus), was expressed by the heroes of Homeric epic, Shelley next tells us that "the dramatic and lyrical poets of Athens . . .

flourished contemporaneously with all that is most perfect in the kindred expressions of the poetical faculty: architecture, painting, music, the dance, sculpture, philosophy, and . . . the forms of civil life." Yet, he immediately adds that, although "Athenian society was deformed by many imperfections" that the poetry of chivalry (the Troubadours) and Christianity "has erased from the habits and institutions of modern Europe," yet no other period has ever shown "so much energy, beauty and virtue. . . . Of no other epoch in the history of our species have we records and fragments stamped so visibly with the image of the divinity of man." But it was poetry, he continues, that "rendered this epoch memorable above all others and the storehouse of examples to everlasting time." While next Shelley momentarily stops to point out that *King Lear* "may be judged to be the most perfect specimen of the dramatic art existing in the world," he reverts again to praising ancient Athenian tragedy for having co-existed "with the moral and intellectual greatness of the age." "In a drama of the highest order," he observes, "there is little food for censure or hatred; it teaches self-knowledge and self-respect" (979, col. 1).

But there did come a time, Shelley next observes, when "the ancient system of religion and manners had fulfilled the circle of its evolutions." The world, he notes, would have "fallen into utter anarchy and darkness" had it not been for the poets who were found "among the authors of the Christian and chivalric systems of manners and religion, who created forms of opinion and action never before conceived." While it is not his present aim, he continues, "to touch upon the evil produced by these systems," he does maintain, "on the ground of the principles already established, that no portion of it can be attributed to the poetry they contain" (983, col. 1). Not only does Shelley not tell us what the original "forms of opinion and action" were that were created by Christianity and chivalry. But also he does not tell us what evils they brought into the world (but we may assume that, as one who was critical of Christianity, he had in mind the association of sin with sexuality and woman that was central to the Christendom as founded on the Neoplatonic dualism between body and soul, which was a complete falsification of the ethos of both the Hebrew and the Christian Bibles).

What is then no less bizarre is that in the very next sentence of his *Defense* Shelley writes that it "is probable that the poetry of Moses, Job, David [in the Psalms?], Solomon, and Isaiah had produced a great effect upon the mind of Jesus and his disciples" (983, col. 1). The fragments that "the biographers of this extraordinary person" (i.e., Jesus) have preserved for us (in the New Testament!) "are all instinct with the most vivid poetry. But his doctrines seem to have been quickly distorted" (983, col. 1). Still, the "poetry in the doctrines of Jesus Christ, and the mythology and institutions of the Celtic conquerors of the Roman empire outlived the darkness" that ensued. "It is an error," Shelley declares, "to impute the ignorance of the dark ages to the Christian doctrines or [to] the predominance of the Celtic nations." For we find that it was in the eleventh century that

> the effects of the poetry of the Christian and chivalric systems began to manifest themselves. The principle of equality has been discovered and applied by Plato in his *Republic*, as the theoretical rule of the mode in which the materials of pleasure and of power, produced by the common skill and labor of human beings, ought to be distributed among them.... Plato, following the doctrines of Timaeus and Pythagoras, taught also a moral and intellectual system of doctrine, comprehending at once the past, present, and the future condition of man. (983, col. 2—984, col. 1)

Not only does the claim on the part of Shelley that Plato discovered and applied the principle of equality reflect total ignorance of Platonic works like the *Republic*, in which the philosopher-king is contradictorily said (by Socrates) to unite the opposites of right and might. But also he then proceeds to write that

> Jesus Christ divulged the sacred and eternal truths in these views to mankind, and Christianity, in its abstract purity, became the exoteric expression of the esoteric doctrines of the poetry and wisdom of antiquity.

What all of this shows, Shelley continues, is

> that no nation or religion can supersede any other without incorporating into itself a portion of what which it supersedes. The abolition of personal and domestic slavery, and the emancipation of women from a great part of the degrading restraints of antiquity were among the consequences of these events. The abolition of personal domestic slavery is the basis of the highest political hope that it can enter into the mind of man to conceive. The freedom of women produced the poetry of sexual love. Love became a religion, the idols whose worship were ever present. It was as if the statues of Apollo and the Muses had been endowed with life and motion and had walked

forth among their worshippers; so that earth became peopled by the inhabitants of a diviner world. The familiar appearance and proceedings of life became wonderful and heavenly, and a paradise was created as out of the wrecks of Eden. (984, col. 1)

Shelley then comments at some length on the Provençal Troubadours, Petrarch, and Dante as poets who celebrated love in their poetry. He continues:

> Love, which found a worthy poet in Plato alone of all the ancients, has been celebrated by a chorus of the greatest writers of the renovated world. . . . Ariosto, Tasso, Shakespeare, Spenser, Calderon, Rousseau, and the great writers of our own age, have celebrated the dominion of love, planting as it were trophies in the human mind of the sublimest victory over sensuality and force. The true relation borne to each other by the sexes into which human kind is distributed, has become less misunderstood; and if the error which confounded diversity with inequality of the powers of the two sexes has been partially recognized in the opinions and institutions of modern Europe, we owe this great benefit to the worship of which chivalry was the law and poets the prophets. . . . All high poetry is infinite. . . . A great poem is a fountain for ever overflowing with the waters of wisdom and delight. (984, col. 2—985, col. 2)

At this point in his *Defense* Shelley takes up again the issue with which he initiates his work, the relationship between reason and imagination but here in the context of discussing the relationship between utility and pleasure or the good. He tells us that today "poets have been challenged to resign the civic crown to reasoners and mechanists" (986, col. 1). While it is admitted that the exercise of imagination is delightful, the exercise of reason is now viewed as more useful. What is then required, Shelley continues, is to distinguish between two kinds of pleasure and also between two kinds of utility. The first kind of pleasure is "durable, universal, and permanent," while the second kind of pleasure is "transitory and particular" (986, col. 1). Utility can also be understood as "the means of producing the former or the later. In the former sense, whatever strengthens and purifies the affections, enlarges the imagination, and adds spirit to sense, is useful." But utility in the narrower sense (and here I paraphrase what is an exceeding obscure passage) is concerned with alleviating our animals wants, helping to make men secure in society, dispersing gross superstitions, and reconciling mutual relations "with the motives of personal advantage." But Shelley then warns that utilitarian speculations, "for want [lack] of correspondence with those first principles which belong to the imagination" may "tend, as they have in modern England, to exasperate at once the extreme of luxury and want. They have exemplified the saying, 'To him that hath, more shall be given; and from him that hath not, the little that he hath shall be taken away.'" The rich become richer and the poor become poorer. The state vacillates between "anarchy and despotism. Such are the effects which must ever flow from an unmitigated exercise of the calculating faculty" (986, cols. 1–2).

Shelley next acknowledges that it "is difficult to define pleasure in its higher sense" since it involves a number of paradoxes that reflect the "inexplicable defect of harmony in the constitution of human nature" in which "the pain of the inferior is frequently connected with the pleasures of the superior portions of our being." But it does not appear that Shelley understands inferior and superior in terms of body and mind given that he then observes: "Sorrow, terror, anguish, despair itself, are often the chosen expressions of an approximation to the highest good." He mentions, as examples, the pleasure that we take in "tragic fiction" and "the melancholy which is inseparable from the sweetest melody. The pleasure that is in sorrow is sweeter than the pleasure of pleasure itself." But Shelley also points out that we can enjoy "wholly unalloyed" pleasure in "the delight of love and friendship, the ecstasy of the admiration of nature, the joy of the perception, and still more of the creation of poetry. . . . The production and assurance of pleasure in this highest sense is true utility. Those who produce and preserve this pleasure are poets or poetic philosophers" (986, col. 2).

Shelley concedes that modern thinkers who have written "in favor of oppressed and deluded humanity are entitled to the gratitude of mankind." He refers to Locke, Hume, Gibbon, Voltaire, and Rousseau together with their (unnamed) disciples. He adds, however, that, if they had never lived, "moral and intellectual improvement" would still have taken place in our lives, even if more slowly. But "it exceeds all imagination," he continues, "to conceive what would have been the moral condition of the world" if the great writers from Dante to Milton and artists like Raphael and Michelangelo had not existed, "if the Hebrew poetry had never been translated, if a revival of the study of Greek literature had never taken place, if no monuments of ancient sculpture had been handed down to us, and if the poetry of the religion of the ancient world had been extinguished together with its belief." It is "the intervention of these excitements" that has led in the modern world "to the invention of the grosser sciences and that application of analytical reasoning to the aberrations of society," the success of which now leads analytical reasoning to attempt "to exalt over the direct expression of the inventive and creative faculty itself" (986, col. 2—987, col. 1). Today we have more moral, political, historical, scientific, and economic knowledge "than we know how to reduce into practice. . . . The poetry in these systems of thought is concealed by the accumulation of facts and calculating processes. There is no want [lack] of knowledge respecting what is wisest and best in morals, government, and political economy, or, at least, what is wiser and better than what men now practice and endure . . . We want" (and here I schematize Shelley's prose):

- the creative faculty to imagine that which we know;
- the generous impulse to act that which we imagine;
- the poetry of life.

"Our calculations have outrun conception; we have eaten more than we can digest." We have "enlarged the limits of the empire of man over the external world" as we have "proportionally circumscribed those of the internal world, and man, having enslaved the elements, remains himself a slave." Our discoveries, instead of lightening "have added a weight to the curse imposed on Adam. . . . Poetry, and the principle of Self, of which money is the visible incarnation, are the God and Mammon of the world."

Having identified the human self with Mammon as the incarnation of Adam's sin in the world, Shelley continues to exalt the deification of poetry. The "poetical faculty," he tells us, possesses two functions: (1) "it creates new materials of knowledge, and power, and pleasure," and (2) "it engenders in the mind a desire to reproduce and arrange them according to a certain rhythm and order which may be called the beautiful and the good" (987, col. 1). Indeed, he proceeds further in telling us that "the cultivation of poetry" is especially important in those times when, because of the "excess of the selfish and calculating principle, the accumulation of the materials of external life exceed the quantity of the power of assimilating them to the internal laws of human nature." Poetry, Shelley proclaims, is divine. "It is at once the center and the circumference of knowledge." It comprehends all science. "It is at the same time the root and blossom of all other systems of thought." Without the eternal light of poetry where would we find, he asks (and again I schematize Shelley's prose),

- virtue, love, patriotism, friendship;
- the scenery of this beautiful universe which we inhabit;
- our consolations on this side of the grave; and
- our aspirations beyond it?

"Poetry is not, like reasoning, a power to be exerted according to the determinations of the will." No man, not even the greatest poet can say: I will compose poetry. It is "an error to assert that the finest passages of poetry are produced by labor and study." Milton himself conceived of the *Paradise Lost* as a whole before he executed it in portions. "We have his own authority also for the muse having 'dictated' to him the 'unpremeditated song'" (988, col. 1). Shelley reiterates his claim that will belongs to analytical reason or logic in writing that poetry "differs in this respect from logic [in] that it is not subject to the control of the active powers of the mind and that its birth and recurrence have no necessary connection with the consciousness or will" (989, col. 1). Indeed, "in the intervals of inspiration . . . a poet becomes a man and is abandoned to the . . . influences under which others habitually live" (989, cols. 1–2).

After remarking that "the instinct and intuition of the poetical faculty is still more observable in the plastic and pictorial arts," Shelley declares:

> Poetry is the record of the best and happiest moments of the happiest and best minds. . . . It is, as it were, the interpenetration of a diviner nature through our own. . . . Poets are not only subject to these experiences as spirits of the most refined organization, but they can color all that they combine with the evanescent hues of this ethereal world. Poetry thus makes immortal all that is best and most beautiful in the world. . . . Poetry redeems from decay the visitations of the divinity in man. Poetry turns all things to loveliness; it exalts the beauty of that which is most beautiful, and it adds beauty to that which is most deformed; it marries exultation and horror, grief and pleasure, eternity and change. . . . It transforms all that it touches, and . . . its secret alchemy turns to potable gold the poisonous waters which flow from death through life; it strips the veil of familiarity from the world and lays bare the naked and sleeping beauty which is the spirit and its forms. All things exist as they are perceived. . . . But

poetry defeats the curse which binds us to be subjected to the accident of surrounding impressions.... It compels us to feel that which we perceive and to imagine that which we know. It creates anew the universe, after it has been annihilated in our minds by the recurrence of impressions blinded by reiteration. (988, cols. 1–2)

Shelley then concludes his eulogy of (i.e., his "good word" for!) poetry with a citation (in Italian) attributed to Torquato Tasso, the author of the epic poem *Jerusalem Delivered* (by Christians during the First Crusade) of 1581: "No one merits the name of creator except God and the Poet" (988, col. 2).

Shelley has now reached the end of his *A Defense of Poetry*. Before concluding it, however, he takes up two formal aspects of his essay. First, he tells us that he organized it following his own views of poetry "instead of observing the formality of a polemical reply." If his views are just, they will constitute "a refutation of the arguers against poetry, so far at least as regards the first division of the subject" (989, col. 2). Shelley refers here to the essay entitled *The Four Ages of Poetry*, and published in 1820, in which his friend, Thomas Love Peacock, satirist, novelist, and poet, had launched a vitriolic attack on modern poets and poetry. Although Shelley does not name either the author or his piece, it was Peacock's essay that aroused him to write his own essay in defense of poetry.[49] The second formal aspect of his essay involves its division into two parts. The first part is that which he has now written as

> related to poetry in its elements and principles ... in a universal sense. The second part will have for its object an application of these principles to the present state of the cultivation of poetry ... [including the] subordination [of] the modern forms of manners and opinions to the imaginative and creative faculty.[50] For the literature of England ... has arisen as it were from a new birth.... We live among such philosophers and poets as surpass beyond comparison any who have appeared since the last national struggle for civil and religious liberty [in the seventeenth century]. The most unfailing herald, companion, and follower of the awakening of a great people to work a beneficial change in opinion or institution is poetry. It is impossible to read the compositions of the most celebrated writers of the present day without being startled with the electric life which burns within their words. (989, col. 2—990, col. 1)

In the penultimate sentence of his essay Shelley piles up yet again multiple phrases in providing us with his final salute to poets. "Poets are

- the hierophants of an unapprehended inspiration;
- the mirrors of the gigantic shadows which futurity casts upon the present;
- the words which express what they understand not;
- the trumpets which sing to battle and feel not what they inspire;
- the influence which is moved not but moves.

Then comes the final, famous sentence of *A Defense of Poetry*: "Poets are the unacknowledged legislators of the world" (990, col. 2).

CONCLUSION

In now undertaking to provide an overall appraisal of the conception of poetry that Shelley advances in his essay, my aim is always that of assessing how or in what sense his *Defense*, together with Coleridge's *Biographia Literaria*, can aid us in responding to "the electric life that burns within" the words of Wordsworth, as found both in his prefatory materials and in his poetry, including, above all, *The Prelude*. But, first, I must point out that Shelley did not write the second division or part of his *Defense of Poetry* on the "philosophers and poets" who today "surpass beyond comparison any who have appeared" in the past nearly two hundred years.

I suggested, when initiating my discussion of the *Defense of Poetry*, that the true test of the validity of what Shelley in his essay calls the principles of poetry was how he understood the relationship of poetry to religion, to Christianity and so, in more general terms, to the Bible, both Hebrew and Christian. But since, as we have seen, Shelley closely identifies poetry with philosophy, we are no less asking how he conceives of the relationship of both poetry and philosophy to religion (when understood, at once historically and ontologically, as biblical). Shelley, as we have seen, celebrates poetry (together with philosophy) as divine, infinite, inspired, and so as possessing the creative power of God. At the same time, however, he tells us that Plato was a poet who made love and equality the very basis of his philosophy. Additionally, he holds that Jesus revealed to mankind "the sacred and eternals truths" that were contained in the doctrines of Plato (following Timaeus and Pythagoras) as teaching "a moral and intellectual system of doctrine, comprehending at once the past, present, and the future condition of man." Thus, Christianity became, through the teaching of Christ, "the exoteric [or public] expression of the esoteric [or hidden] doctrines of the poetry and wisdom of antiquity." This claim on the part of Shelley is at one with his avowal that Homer built "the social system" on whose column "all succeeding civilization has reposed." Still, Shelley does acknowledge that the social system of the ancients embraced the errors of both slavery and the subordination of women, which the poetry of chivalry and Christianity subsequently showed to be false. At the same time, however, he also claims that all cultures have their errors and corruptions and that true poets, while reflecting the errors of their times and places, do not themselves as such endorse them. True poets (and philosophers) do not express (or hold?) a moral point of view.

Consistent, then, with his claim that poetry, unlike ethics (as if ethics were foreign to philosophy!), is not concerned with teaching good and evil, Shelley also associates reason, together with will and work (effort), with mechanistic, utilitarian means (not with human beings as ends in themselves, to recall Kant). But what, then, for Shelley are poetry, philosophy, the imagination, creation, the good, the true, and the beautiful . . . ? When we return to the penultimate sentence of the *Defense of Poetry*, as cited above, we see that the poet is the hierophant (the ancient one who brings the select few into the presence of the esoteric mysteries) who does not comprehend that by which he is inspired. The poet is the one who does not understand the words that he uses. The poet is the one who blows the trumpet, not of prophetic revelation but of battle hymns of which he is not himself inspired. Finally, the poet is the one who, like Aristotle's god, the unmoved mover, influences (moves) others while remaining uninfluenced (unmoved) by others, which altogether contradicts Shelley's understanding of (the biblical concept of) love as concern for others. Indeed, nothing is more foreign to the God of the Bible, the God of creation and covenant, than the Aristotelian idea of God as the one who, in moving (ruling over) others, is unmoved (unruled) by others. The covenant that the God of the Bible establishes with the ancient Israelites and then, through Jesus as the Christ, with all human beings constitutes, in stark contrast with the ancients, equal, just, compassionate, loving, and free relationships among all.[51]

As Hegel makes clear in his *Lectures on the Philosophy of Religion*, the revolution in world culture that Christianity (and I would say the Bible) initiated is embodied (incarnate) in the revelation that the God of Holy Scripture is universally known to every human being as the truth for all. Hegel is here but following Paul who, in his Letter to the Romans (Chapters 1 and 2), writes, consistent with the prophets, that before God no human beings have excuses for the evil that they do. God is not hierophantic and so mysteriously revealed solely to the special few (the philosopher-kings). All human beings know, all human beings must know that how they judge others so are they judged by others. To know God is to know, poetically and philosophically—to adapt Shelley to our purposes!—that you are responsible, *in saecula saeculorum*, i.e., in and through all the ages unto eternity, for all the good as for all the evil that you do.

What, then, do we learn from Shelley's *Defense of Poetry*? Why read it? Why discuss it—in a book on poetry and philosophy? There is no simple answer to these questions. But my hope is that the contradictory confusions, as once historical and ontological, regarding the relationship of poetry and philosophy to religion, in which Shelley, even more dramatically than Coleridge, loses himself, will help prepare us for what lies ahead in our study: what it means to read the *Prelude* as a truly philosophic poem whose principal ideas are truly religious and to read Kant's *Critique of Practical Reason* as a philosophical account of moral life whose rational practice is truly poetic because truly religious.

CHAPTER 3

Reading Wordsworth's *The Prelude*

WORDSWORTH OPENS THE FINAL Book 13 of *The Prelude*—keeping in mind, as I explained in the previous chapter, that I primarily follow here the original (unpublished) version of the poem that he completed in 1805—with an account of the ascent of Mount Snowdon (in northern Wales) that he made at night with a friend, together with a shepherd as their guide and the shepherd's dog, in order to see the sun rise from atop the mountain. He made the trip in the summer of 1791 (again recalling that Wordsworth was born in 1770). To the astonishment of the poet the moon suddenly arose above the ocean of midst by which he was surrounded, while from the shore of a nearby lake appeared

> a blue chasm; a fracture in the vapour,
> A deep and gloomy breathing-place, through which
> Mounted the roar of waters, torrents, streams
> Innumerable, roaring with one voice.
> The universal spectacle throughout
> Was shaped for admiration and delight,
> Grand in itself along, but in that breach
> Through which the homeless voice of waters rose,
> That dark deep thoroughfare, had Nature lodged
> The Soul, the Imagination of the whole.

Wordsworth then proceeds to tell us that "A meditation rose in me that night" and

> it appeared to me
> The perfect image of a mighty Mind,
> Of one that feeds upon infinity, . . .
> The sense of God . . . , above all

> One function of such mind that Nature there
> Exhibited by putting forth, and that
> With circumstance most awful and sublime,
> That domination which she oftentimes
> Exerts upon the outward face of things,
> So moulds them, and endues, abstracts, combines . . .
> That even the grossest minds must see and hear
> And cannot chuse but feel. The Power which these
> Acknowledge when thus moved, which Nature thus
> Thrusts forth upon the sense, is the express
> Resemblance, in the fullness of its strength
> Made visible, a genuine Counterpart
> And Brother of the glorious faculty
> Which higher minds bear with them as their own.

He yet continues. Such is the spirit with which higher minds

> deal
> With all the objects of the universe;
> They from their native selves can send abroad
> Like transformations, for themselves create
> A like existence . . . .
> Them the enduring and the transient both
> Serve to exalt; they build up greatest things
> From least suggestions, ever on the watch,
> Willing to work and to be wrought upon.

Wordsworth tells us still further that such higher minds "need not extraordinary calls" to rouse them, for they are "not enthralled" but rather quickened and roused by "sensible impressions" and so "made thereby more fit / To hold communion with the invisible world.

> Such minds are truly from the Deity,
> For they are Powers; and hence the highest bliss
> That can be known is theirs, the consciousness
> Of whom they are, habitually infused
> Through every image, and through every thought,
> And all impressions.

Hence "religion, faith, / And endless occupation for the soul."

Hence "sovereignty within and peace at will, / Emotion which best foresight need not fear / Most worthy then of trust when most intense."

Hence "chearfulness in every act of life."

Hence "truth in moral judgements and delight / That fails not, in the external universe" (13.56–119).⁵²

I pause here to take stock, although Wordsworth, as we shall subsequently see, maintains his fervent pace onward for nearly another one hundred lines. I have begun with the Conclusion of *The Prelude* in order to signal from the beginning of our initial engagement with it that in his immense poem Wordsworth is, above all else, concerned with showing that what makes the story of the growth of a poet's mind of abiding (eternal, divine, infinite) significance is that through and by it he discloses that paradoxical relationship of beginning and end, of earth (world) and mind, of visible and invisible . . . . The poet climbs Mount Snowdon in the dark of night only to have the light of the moon dawn on him that, just as nature possesses the divine power of impressing itself upon the mind as "the imagination of the whole," so the mind is disclosed to be the direct counterpart of nature in possessing the power of transforming the semblances of the natural world into the resemblances, the metaphors, of spirit. To behold nature in truth poetically—metaphorically, critically, divinely—is to behold the mind enjoying, in highest bliss, "the consciousness" of being infused through every image, every thought, every impression. Where nature is there, truly, is the spirit (the mind, the soul) of human beings. Without (outside of) nature (earth, the world) the mind ("the soul," "the imagination of the whole") does not exist. But it is no less true that nature (as the infinite power of creation) does not "exist" outside of (without) the mind. Nature comes into existence solely in and through metaphor. It is the transfer from the sensible world of nature to the spiritual world of human beings that embodies the transformative, the creative, the divine, the infinite power of spirit.

We shall find, subsequently, that the very shape or structure of *The Prelude*, as relating the history of the growth of a poet's mind, is at once historical and ontological (metaphysical). Wordsworth tells the story, to recall the paradox that shapes the "Ode on Immortality" that, while the babe is the true philosopher, it is only in maturity (in historical retrospect) that this truth is philosophically realized and so made historical real (practical). In Book 1 of *The Prelude* Wordsworth begins with what, in the book's title, he calls "Introduction—Childhood and School-time." But the irony (paradox) here is that it is not the child but the mature adult who recalls (makes memorable) his beginning (as a babe). While, in what is in fact quite a loose sense, the poem moves from earlier to later, from *then* (earlier) to *now* (at the time of the actual composition of the poem), it is no less true that the poem moves from *now* to *then*, as the poet, in recalling his earlier experiences, establishes (poeticizes) their present significance. Indeed, we may note that the ascent of Mount Snowdon took place when Wordsworth was only coming of age as a young man and so a number of years before he first revealed his true genius as a poet in the *Lyrical Ballads*. Consequently, we may safely assume that the meditation he recalls having while atop the mountain did not occur, self-consciously and explicitly, that very same evening. Indeed, the meditation described there is actually the poetic account that he later gives of it (as the beginning of Book 13 of *The Prelude*). In other words, we arrive at the end of the poem (at the beginning of its final Book 13) only to discover that, at the same time, we have been transported to a critically important moment that occurred much earlier in the poet's life.

But such is the shape or structure of *The Prelude* not only historically but also, and equally no less, ontologically. We begin in nature (as natural beings) only to discover (trusting that we mature, as we shall see Wordsworth emphasize, as human beings who are at once loved and respected) that we begin as spirit (i.e., as created in the image of God, knowing good and evil, not in the image of nature). But that we make the ontological, the metaphorical transfer from nature to spirit we know only retrospectively (although, insofar as we are loved and respected by those who surround us, that is the prospect that they hold open to us).

We shall see that it is the intersection, the interweaving of these two motifs, historical (biographical) and ontological (metaphysical), that gives *The Prelude* its distinctive character, its unique expressiveness. As the poet attains "the highest bliss" of knowing that his self-consciousness as an artist is reflected in (and so revealed through) all his images, thoughts, and impressions of nature, he discovers at the same time, to recall the verse Prospectus of 1815 that we considered in Chapter 2, not only that his mind is exquisitely fitted to the external world but also

> how exquisitely too—
> Theme this but little heard of among men—
> The external world is fitted to the mind;
> And the creation ... which they with blended might
> Accomplish: this is my great argument.
> ("Home at Grasmere," 1009–14)

The creation of the historical self is no less than the creation of the imaginative (the poetic) self. The metaphorical passage from nature to mind, or spirit, embodies, and so reveals, the critically historical passage from the unconscious awareness that the babe is the true philosopher to the philosophical awareness on the part of the poet that, to recall Kierkegaard, truth is subjectivity. We begin as objects of natures only to learn that it is solely as subjects, as spirits of divinity, that we can know ourselves as natural objects. Indeed, can we not say that what Wordsworth shows us in *The Prelude*, together with all of his significant poetry, is that every human being is in spirit a poet? Still, the paradox here is that, while all language of the spirit is transferred or metaphorical language, it is only poets (together, I also argue, with philosophers) who embody this truth in their works. We (non-poets and non-philosophers) read, study, engage, reflect on . . . the works of great poets (and great philosophers) in order to see ourselves as others see us, to learn truly who we are. And to make this discovery is to take the journey of reading *The Prelude* in which we find that our end or goal is, yet again, in the beginning but now with enhanced (spiritualized, divinized, infinitized) consciousness of the end to which the prelude is prologue.

But with our prologue now completed, it is appropriate for us to return to the beginning of *The Prelude* where, early in Book 1 of the poem, the poet declares that "The earth is all before me" and observes, then, in concluding Book 1, that, with his plan to "bring down, / Through later years, the story of my life . . . / The road lies plain before me." Thus, Wordsworth recalls the final lines of *Paradise Lost* where Milton writes of Adam and Eve that, with their way back to the Garden of Eden and its Tree of immortal Life blocked forever, "The world was all before them, . . . and providence their guide." (12.646–47). The world that lay before our forebears, who, God has just indicated, are like him in knowing good and evil, was the covenantal world of creation involving conception (at once natural and spiritual), labor (effort, what Spinoza calls *conatus* or will), and death. This is what the archangel Michael, earlier in Book 12, tells Adam is "A paradise within thee, happier far" than the immortal paradise of the natural Garden of Eden (12.587). The paradise within us "happier far," as constituted by our mind, is the eternal (divine, spiritual, infinite) transfer from nature to spirit that is embodied in the story of the life of the poet for whom the earth represents the stage where the creative drama of nature and spirit, of givenness and gift, is historically played out by all human beings. The life of each human being is yet the prelude to the lives of all human beings in the eternal covenant of history where the earth lies all before us.

The Prelude overall is constituted by three elements (motifs): self-reflections on the part of the poet (on which I concentrate here in my study); tales of the poet's encounters with nature (such as that involving the ascent of Mount Snowdon at night); and narrative tales and tributes to key individuals in Wordsworth's life, above all, Coleridge, as we shall see. As always, I shall make no attempt to summarize in detail the content of the poem. Rather, I shall concentrate on its dual thematic (dialectic): the twofold beginning in childhood and in nature as the prelude to the life whose self-conscious end in spirit is metaphorically (providentially) the road that historically lies plain before us. I shall also not be punctilious in relating the biography of Wordsworth, since his poem, while rooted in his own experiences, at once natural and historical, is in no sense a factual autobiography. (I take the opportunity of noting here that Wordsworth does not include in the story of the growth of a poet's mind either the love affair that he had with Annette Vallon, in France, in 1791, including the birth of their daughter Caroline whom he first saw only a number of years later, or his marriage with Mary Hutchenson in 1802, together with the subsequent birth of their children, two of whom died while still children.) What counts is having a general sense of the timeline of Wordsworth's life, which I outline here:

- 1770   birth (to a well-off and well-connected family if not rich family; his parents both die while he is young);
- 1787–89 three years at Cambridge University;
- 1790   hiking trip with a friend through the Alps (in the year following the French Revolution);
- 1791   return to France (as a "patriot" in support of the revolutionary ideals and his love affair with Annette, whose family was royalist);
- 1790s   years in London (with financial support supplied by a deceased patron);
- 1795   meets Coleridge (their close relationship as creative poets results in the publication of the *Lyrical Ballads* in 1798, to which Wordsworth only alludes in *The Prelude*);
- 1799   Wordsworth takes up residence, with his beloved sister, Dorothy, in Grasmere, in the Lake District, in northern England (where he will live, together with his wife, after their marriage in 1802, for the remainder of his period of true creativity that lasts to c. 1815);
- 1805   completion of *The Prelude* in thirteen books (which was never published and, while known to Coleridge, remained unknown to the public and only became known in the

revised, fourteen-book version of the poem that was published in 1850, following the poet's death, under the title by which it is known today but which was then used for the first time).

In Book 1 of *The Prelude* Wordsworth celebrates the freedom that he now experiences (in Grasmere in 1799), with the earth all before him, as he assumes with self-conscious joy the task of poet. He writes of "a gift that consecrates my joy" as he feels "the sweet breath of Heaven . . . / blowing on my body, felt within / A corresponding mild creative breeze" that "is become / a tempest, a redundant [overflowing] energy / Vexing its own creation." With this promise of accomplishment comes "the hope / Of active days, of dignity and thought . . . / Pure passions, virtue, knowledge, and delight, / The holy life of music and of verse." The poet invokes the idea of prophecy in finding his spirit, "in priestly robe . . . singled out . . . / For holy services." Indeed, he now has before him the "assurance of some work / Of glory" (1.40–86). But, as always, we readers then face the paradox that is central to *The Prelude*: the poet expresses the hope that his work will in the future be worthy of glory in and through the very work in which he expresses that hope!

It is no heroic tale of the ancients or "Romantic tale, by Milton left unsung" that Wordsworth aspires to write, he tells us. Rather, what "suits me better" is

> Some Tale from my own heart, more near akin
> To my own passions and habitual thoughts . . .
> Lofty, with interchange of gentler things. . . .
> I yearn towards some philosophic Song
> Of Truth that cherishes our daily life;
> With meditations passionate from deep
> Recesses in man's heart.

After then relating stories in which he experiences as a child the awful power of nature, the poet reflects:

> The mind of Man is framed even like the breath
> And harmony of music. There is a dark
> Invisible workmanship that reconciles
> Discordant elements, and makes them move
> In one society.

What he finds astonishing is that "the terrors" of the miseries, regrets, vexations, and lassitudes of his life

> should ever have made up
> The calm existence that is mine when I
> Am worthy of myself. Praise to the end!
> Thanks likewise for the means!

Just as Nature, he continues, seeks out "A favored Being, from his earliest dawn / Of infancy. . . . / With gentlest visitations," so at times does Nature also use "Severer interventions, ministry / More palpable, and so she dealt with me." Wordsworth then addresses the "Wisdom and Spirit of the universe"—"Thou Soul that art the Eternity of Thought"—who

> from my first dawn
> Of Childhood didst . . . built up our human Soul,
> Not with the mean and vulgar works of Man,
> But with high objects, with enduring things,
> With life and nature, purifying thus
> The elements of feeling and of thought,
> And sanctifying, by such discipline,
> Both pain and fear, until we recognize
> A grandeur in the beatings of the heart.

Still, while "The earth / And common face of Nature spake to me / Rememberable things," they were "doomed to sleep / Until maturer seasons called them forth / To impregnate and to elevate the mind." So Wordsworth concludes Book 1 of *The Prelude* having attained, he tells us, his end in reaffirming his commitment to

> bring down
> Through later years, the story of my life.
> The road lies plain before me. . . .
> And certain hopes are with me, that to thee
> This labour will be welcome, honored Friend. (1.180–674)

Again, it is plain: the paradox lies before us readers. The road that is *The Prelude* lies plainly before us, with providence our guide, we may hope! But we are already on the road, which lies at once before and after, just as in the poem that we read its author relates his beginning having already attained his end (in completing his poem). A philosophic song that cherishes our daily life is built up, not with the mean and vulgar works of human beings but with high objects and enduring things. Yet it is only in retrospect, after we have attained the philosophical, the spiritual maturity that is required to distinguish enduring from passing things, that we know that Nature has truly spoken to us or, in other words, that we have learned to view Nature as our teacher. For it is, indeed, in traveling the road that leads from the sensuous to the spiritual, from objects passively observed to the subjective spirit of self-critical metaphor, that we discover that the paradise of nature lies within our mind, within the creative mind of human beings.

Wordsworth concludes Book 1 of his poem, as we saw above, with an address to his "honored Friend," Samuel Taylor Coleridge, who, as such, is not here identified. Coleridge is the constant addressee in *The Prelude*. Still, while it is evident that Wordsworth felt profoundly indebted to his friend and colleague Coleridge for his intellectual mentorship—for, indeed, they jointly planned and together launched the *Lyrical Ballads* in 1798—it is Wordsworth, as I indicated in the previous chapter, who composed by far the majority of the poems that are found in the three editions of their revolutionary work and who wrote all of the critical, prefatory materials that appear in them. Certainly, Coleridge in his poem, "To William Wordsworth," which I also discussed in the previous chapter, pays profound tribute to his friend and colleague, the great Bard, the sage Bard, who "first sung aright" in his "prophetic lay" the "high theme . . . of the foundations and the building up of a Human Spirit." Still, Coleridge wrote his poem in 1806, after the completion of *The Prelude* in 1805, and did not publish it until 1817. While Coleridge thus bestows lavish praise on Wordsworth for a poem that was unknown (and remained unknown) to the public, so Wordsworth bestows on Coleridge his future hope for glory as a poet in and through the very poem in which we readers see that hope fulfilled.

In the succeeding books of *The Prelude* Wordsworth continues on the plain road that, while leading to the future, makes it possible for him to relate the story of the poet's life wherein and whereby the poet transforms his past history into the very content of the poem that we readers presently have before us. I shall pick up that story at the end of Book 7, entitled "Residence in London" (in the 1790s), following his childhood, school-time, and residence at Cambridge University. While he initiates *The Prelude* in Book 1 with the celebration of his return to the pastoral world of Grasmere as a liberation from "a house / Of bondage, from yon City's walls set free, / A prison where he has been long immured," (1.6–8) we shall find that Wordsworth, in relating the growth of his mind as a poet, does not countenance any kind of simplistic (romantic, poetic, or even philosophic!) opposition between country (pastoral) and city (urban) life. He knows that he would not (have) become the poet that he is without either London (an enlarged world) or Cambridge (an enlarged mind). He begins life unconsciously moved by the world of nature only to discover that he becomes conscious of the role that nature played in shaping his future in and through his learning to be concerned, as we saw him tell us, with higher things and with higher minds.

Yes, it is true that Wordsworth records what was for him the confusion that he experienced as a young man in London with its multi-layered displays of interminable, human bustle. "Above all," he writes,

> one thought
> Baffled my understanding, how men lived
> Even next-door neighbours, as we say, yet still
> Strangers and knowing not each other's names.

Still, in the very next two lines Wordsworth writes:

> Oh wond'rous power of words, how sweet they are
> According to the meaning which they bring!

The poet knows, perhaps like few others, that the wonder expressed in and through the power of words—in verse and in prose (both poetic and philosophic)— is that they make us neighbors. In the beginning—of community—is the word (*logos*)—of communication. Still, later in Book 7 Wordsworth recalls the "one feeling" that summed up for him life in "this great City . . . [of] overflowing Streets." For, indeed, what he found, in going "forward with the Crowd," was that "the face of every one / That passes by me is a mystery. / Thus have I looked, nor ceased to look, oppressed / By thoughts of what, and whither, when, and how." Still, it was once his "chance / Abruptly to be smitten with the view / Of a blind Beggar, who, with upright face, / Stood propped against a Wall." He wore "upon his Chest"

> a written paper, to explain
> The story of the Man, and who he was.
> My mind did at this spectacle turn round
> As with the might of waters, and it seemed
> To me that in this Label was a type,
> Or emblem, of the utmost that we know,
> Both of ourselves and of the universe;
> And, on the shape of the unmoving man,
> His fixèd face and sightless eyes, I looked
> As if admonished from another world. (7.117–623)

It is striking that it is a city beggar, one who is dependent on the good works of others, not a country shepherd, who independently does his own good works, who here provides Wordsworth with what he calls the type or emblem both of ourselves and of the universe. Whereas the poet had earlier been troubled by the anonymity of the city's crowds whose individual faces and names are unknown to us, now he finds his own self-identity expressed in the fixèd face and sightless eyes of a blind beggar. Indeed, the identity of poet and beggar is further deepened paradoxically in and through the poet's acknowledgement that they are equally dependent on the "wond'rous power of words." The poet is blind outside of his capacity to tell his story as the growth of poet's mind, while the blind beggar can reach out to others only in and through the written paper on his chest that tells his story. We see ourselves as others see us. We can overcome our blindness solely in and through our recognition of others and their recognition of us.

In concluding Book 7 of *The Prelude* Wordsworth explicitly formulates the paradox that is implicitly contained in the emblem of the blind beggar. He observes that "the mighty City" remains a "blank confusion . . . / To the whole swarm of its inhabitants" except to "a Straggler here and there." It is an "indistinguishable world" in which men are "slaves . . . [to] low pursuits" and "Living amid the same perpetual flow / Of trivial objects, melted and reduced / To one identity, by differences / That have no law, no meaning and no end." Still, while this picture of city life wearies out "the eye" and is

> By nature an unmanageable sight,
> It is not wholly so to him who looks
> In steadiness, who hath among least things
> An under-sense of greatest; sees the parts
> As parts, but with a feeling of the whole. . . .
> This did I feel in that vast receptacle.
> The Spirit of Nature was upon me here;
> The Soul of Beauty and enduring life
> Was present as a habit and diffused,
> Through meager lines and colours, and the press
> Of self-destroying, transitory things,
> Composure and ennobling harmony. (7.696–741)

So it is in Book 8 of *The Prelude*, entitled "Retrospect—Love of Nature Leading to Love of Mankind," where Wordsworth tells us how it came about that his early love of the independent life of country shepherds led him to find in the blind beggar of the city the true emblem of humanity. Indeed, he now addresses Nature in writing that what he felt in "that great City" he "owed to thee":

> High thoughts of God and Man, and love of Man,
> Triumphant over all those loathsome sights
> Of wretchedness and vice; a watchful eye,
> Which with the outside of our human life
> Not satisfied, must read the inner mind.

He goes on to observe that he had already "been taught to love / My Fellow-beings," having been trained "Among the woods and mountains, where I found / In Thee a gracious Guide" to lead him forth beyond the "bosom" of his family and friends. It was "thy power" that filled his heart with "Love human to the Creature in himself / As he appeared, a Stranger in my path, / Before my eyes a Brother of this world." Indeed, simple, pastoral life, a shepherd with his dog and flock among the mountains, was a paradise fairer than that found in tales of ancient wonders. Here he found the "heart of man,"

> Man free, man working for himself, with choice
> Of time, and place, and object; by his wants,
> His comforts, native occupations, cares,
> Conducted on to individual ends
> Or social, and still followed by a train
> Unwooed, unthought-of even, simplicity,
> And beauty, and inevitable grace.

It is "the common haunts of the green earth, / With the ordinary human interests" that fasten

> on the heart
> Insensibly, each with the other's help,
> So that we love, not knowing that we love,
> And feel, not knowing whence our feeling comes. (8.63–172)

Again, Wordsworth emphasizes that the shepherd life that he grew to love was not that sung either by the ancient poets or by Shakespeare when in the "Wood of Arden . . . Phoebe sighed for the false Ganymede" or when "Florizel and Perdita [actually prince and princess] / Together danced, Queen of the Feast and King" (in *The Winter's Tale*). Nor did he learn from the "Smooth life" of "Flock and Shepherd" that was sung "in old time" by Virgil and Horace. Rather, it was the life of a shepherd who, in his service as a "Freeman," lived a

>   life of hope
> And hazard, and hard labour interchanged
> With that majestic indolence so dear
> To native Man. A rambling school-boy, thus
> Have I beheld him; without knowing why,
> Have felt his presence in his own domain
> As of a Lord and Master; or a Power
> Or Genius, under Nature, under God,
> Presiding. . . .
>   Thus was Man
> Ennobled outwardly before my eyes,
> And thus my heart at first was introduced
> To an unconscious love and reverence
> Of human nature; hence the human form
> To me was like an index of delight,
> Of grace and honour, power, and worthiness.

Such a man, Wordsworth continues, was

>   the most common; Husband, Father; learned,
> Could teach, admonish, suffered with the rest
> From vice and folly, wretchedness and fear;
> Of this I little saw, cared less for it,
> But something must have felt.

He thanks "the God / Of Nature and of Man" that to his "untaught eyes" he first beheld men "thus purified," and so it is, he continues, that "all of us in some degree / Are led to knowledge, whencesoever led, / And howsoever." How, he asks, could we bear up in our first years if we experienced evil and not good? For only thus was he protected "Against the weight of meanness, selfish cares, / Coarse manners, vulgar passions, that beat in / On all sides from the ordinary world." In thus having "my face towards the truth" from the beginning, he was

>   furnished with that kind
> Of prepossession without which the soul
> Receives no knowledge that can bring forth good, [and]
> No genuine insight ever comes to her.

Happy he was, Wordsworth reiterates,

>   that I with nature walked,

> Not having a too early intercourse
> With the deformities of crowed life,
> And those ensuing laughters and contempts . . .
>   [that do not permit us] to think
> With admiration and respect of man. (8. 187–468)

But at this point Wordsworth reminds "my friend" (Coleridge) that it was not really so that Man had taken such a preeminent place in his mind. Indeed,

> Nature herself was at this unripe time,
> But secondary to my own pursuits
> And animal activities, and all
> Their trivial pleasures.

Indeed, even when "Nature did / For her own sake become my joy," still, into his early 20s did "man in my affections and regards [remain] / subordinate to her." Further, "when that first poetic Faculty / Of plain imagination and severe" was "No longer a mute influence of the soul" as an "Element of the nature's inner self," he still found that it was "A wilfulness of fancy and conceit / Which gave . . . new importance to the mind" with the result that from the "touch of this new power/ Nothing was safe." However, since his "present Theme / Is to retrace the way that led me on / Through nature to the love of human Kind," he adds that then

>   rose
> Man, inwardly contemplated and present
> In my own being, to a loftier height;
> As of all visible natures crown; and first
> In capability of feeling what
> Was to be felt; in being rapt away
> By the divine effect of power and love,
> As, more than anything we know, instinct
> With Godhead, and by reason and by will
> Acknowledging dependency sublime. (8.472–640)

Wordsworth then recalls that it was London that next served as his "Preceptress stern . . . ."

> Thus here imagination also found
> An element that pleased her, tried her strength
> Among new objects simplified, arranged,
> Impregnated my knowledge, made it live,
> And the result was elevating thoughts

> Of human nature. Neither guilt nor vice,
> Debasement of the body or the mind,
> Nor all the misery forced upon my sight,
> Which was not lightly passed, but often scanned
> Most feelingly, could overthrow my trust
> In what we may become, induce belief
> That I was ignorant, had been falsely taught.

Indeed, when the poet's meditations turned away "from that awful prospect,"

> Lo! Everything that was indeed divine
> Retained its purity inviolate
> And unencroached upon, nay, seemed brighter far
> For this deep shade in counterview, that gloom
> Of opposition, such as shewed itself
> To the eyes of Adam, yet in Paradise,
> Though fallen from bliss, when in the East he saw
> Darkness ere day's mid course, and morning light
> More orient [i.e., bright/eastern] in the western cloud, that drew
> "O'er the blue firmament a radiant white,
> Descending slow with something heavenly fraught." (8.678–823)

Thus, Wordsworth cites a multi-layered passage from *Paradise Lost* (11.205f), without specifying his source as such, in which Adam indicates to Eve that the promise of their future brightness is to be understood solely in "counterview" with their loss of immortal paradise and so with the dust of their being, death, and sin. Still, it is only as sinners that they can know God. For it is solely in knowing good and evil that they are like their Lord. Without the counterview of sin, of evil, there is no good. *O felix culpa*! I want to note here how important it is not to view the "relationship" of good and evil that Wordsworth, like Milton, configures in the story of Adam and Eve in Platonist terms. For Plato to know the good is to be the good, consistent with Socrates' observation that all evil is done in ignorance of the good and with Aristotle's concept of God as thought thinking itself. For those, however, who write in the biblical tradition to know the good is to acknowledge, as Wordsworth makes clear to us in *The Prelude*, as we continue to discover, that it is precisely good that brings evil into the world as that which we have the responsibility of eternally overcoming.

Accordingly, Wordsworth proceeds to bring Book 8 of *The Prelude* to a close by following up his invocation of the fallen, yet also newly risen Adam with the observation

> that among the multitudes
> Of that great City, oftentimes was seen
> Affectingly set forth, more than elsewhere
> Is possible, the unity of man,
> One spirit over ignorance and vice
> Predominant, in good and evil hearts
> One sense for moral judgments. . . .
> When strongly breathed upon
> By this sensation, whencesoe'er it comes
> Of union or communion, doth the soul
> Rejoice as in her highest joy: for there,
> There chiefly, hath she feeling whence she is,
> And passing through all Nature rests with God.

Indeed, the poet continues, we find

> that vast Abiding-place
> Of human creatures, turn where'er we may.
> Profusely sown with individual sights
> Of courage, and integrity, and truth,
> And tenderness, which, here set off by foil [i.e., a contrasting counterview]
> Appears more touching.

It was tender scenes, Wordsworth tells us, that chiefly were his delight, "and one of these / Never will be forgotten. 'Twas a Man"—whom he saw sitting in an open square

> with a sickly Babe
> Upon his knee, whom he had thither brought
> For sunshine, and to breathe the fresher air.

The man, clearly a laborer who was "to the elbow bare," took no note of those who passed.

> He held the Child, and, bending over it
> As if he were afraid both of the sun
> And of the air which he had come to seek,
> He eyed it with unutterable love.

Wordsworth proceeds, then, to conclude Book 8 of *The Prelude* with the observation that his thoughts were

>   attracted more and more
> By slow gradations towards human Kind
> And to the good and ill of human life;
> Nature had led me on, and now I seemed
> To travel independent of her help,
> As if I had forgotten her; but no,
> My Fellow beings still were unto me
> Far less than she was; though the scale of love
> Were filling fast, 'twas light, as yet, compared
> With that in which her mighty objects lay. (8.824–69)

It is evident that the poetic road yet lies plain before Wordsworth, as also before us readers. We reach its end only to learn, once again, that, while the beginning of our excursion is, in the end, love of humankind, we can properly weigh humankind on the scale of love solely insofar as we continue to account for the weight that Nature, as the scale's standard, bears in our lives. Wordsworth dedicates Books 9 and 10 of *The Prelude* to the time that he spent in France in 1791–92, immediately following the Revolution, and then to the troubled times that he experienced after his return to England, as France passed from the Terror to the imperialist ambitions of Napoleon, who, to Wordsworth's deep disgust and distress, was crowned emperor by the pope in 1804, with the result that England, in its prolonged war with France, became the champion of human freedom in Europe. In the following two books he reflects on, to give the title of Book 11, as continued in Book 12, "Imagination, How Impaired and Restored." I shall hurry along the road that lies before us to the Conclusion in Book 13, pausing only to take note of key passages in Books 9 to 12 in which our understanding of how it is that our road continues to pass from nature to spirit, at once historically and ontologically, is deepened.

Wordsworth recalls in Book 9 that "I owed / To Cambridge and an academic life" the idea "Of a Republic, where all stood thus far / Upon equal ground, that they were brothers all / In honour, as in one community" with distinction dependent, not on "wealth and titles" but on "talents and successful industry," whence our "subservience from the first / To God and Nature's single sovereignty" with the result that we "hail / As best the government of equal rights / And individual worth." Thus it was that, when he returned to France in the years following the French Revolution, he befriended a military officer who, while a noble by birth, was a Patriot:

> unto the poor
> Among mankind he was in service bound
> As by some tie invisible, oaths professed
> To a religious Order. Man he loved
> As Man, and to the mean and the obscure,
> And all the homely in their homely works,
> Transferred a courtesy which had no air
> Of condescension.
>
> In their conversations together they painted to themselves
>   the miseries
> Of royal Courts, and that voluptuous life
> Unfeeling, where the Man who is of soul
> The meanest thrives the most, where dignity,
> True personal dignity, abideth not,
> A light and cruel world, cut off from all
> The natural inlets of just sentiment,
> From lowly sympathy, and chastening truth,
> Where good and evil never have that name,
> That which they ought to have, but wrong prevails,
> And vice at home. We added dearest themes,
> Man and his noble nature, as it is
> The gift of God and lies in his own power . . .
>   to build liberty
> On firm foundations, making social life,
> Through knowledge spreading and imperishable,
> As just in regulation, and as pure
> As individual in the wise and good.[53] (9.227–371)

In Book 10 Wordsworth recalls that he reluctantly returned to England (in late 1792), as war between England and France threatened to break out: "A Poet only to myself, to Men / Useless, and even, beloved Friend! [i.e., Coleridge] a soul / To thee unknown." Still, he recalls that the ancient prophets did not lack in

>   consolations . . .
> And majesty of mind, when they denounced . . .
> [their] Towns and Cities, wallowing in the abyss
> Of their offences, punishment to come. . . .
> So did some portion of that spirit fall
> On me, to uphold me through those evil times. . . .
> Then was the truth received into my heart,
> That under heaviest sorrow earth can bring,

> Griefs bitterest of ourselves or of our [human] Kind,
> If from the affliction somewhere do not grow
> Honour which could not else have been, a faith,
> An elevation, and a sanctity,
> If new strength be not given, or old restored,
> The blame is ours, not Nature's. When a taunt
> Was taken up by scoffers in their pride,
> Saying, "Behold the harvest which we reap
> From popular Government and Equality,"
> I saw that it was neither these, nor aught [i.e., anything]
> Of wild belief engrafted on their names
> By false philosophy, that caused their woe,
> But that it was a reservoir of guilt
> And ignorance, filled up from age to age,
> That could no longer hold its loathsome charge,
> But burst and spread in deluge through the Land. (10.199–439)

But Wordsworth now recalls that "from these bitter truths I must return / To my own History." Even though he found himself immersed in matters not yet "thoroughly understood / By Reason," still

> Bliss was it in that dawn to be alive,
> But to be young was very heaven!

This was a time when Fancy, a "prime Enchanter," could wield its plastic powers as it wished,

> Not in Utopia [literally, no place], subterraneous Fields,
> Or some secreted Island, Heaven knows where,
> But in the very world which is the world
> Of all of us, the place in which, in the end,
> We find our happiness, or not at all.

Wordsworth further recalls that it was then (in 1795) that he first met Coleridge and was reunited with his beloved sister, Dorothy (from whom he had been separated since the death of their mother years earlier). Thus was

> Maintained for me a saving intercourse
> With my true self; for, though impaired and changed
> Much, as it seemed, I was no further changed
> Than as a clouded, not a waning moon:
> She, in the mist of all, preserved me still
> A Poet, made me seek beneath that name
> My office upon earth, and nowhere else;

> And lastly, Nature's self, by human love
> Assisted, through the weary labyrinth
> Conducted me again to open day,
> Revived the feelings of my earlier life. (10.657–924)

In concluding Book 10 of *The Prelude* Wordsworth devotes its last nearly one hundred lines to Coleridge. He is ever grateful to Coleridge for the unconditional support that he received from his friend that he would become *then* (in the years following their first meeting in 1795) the poet that he is *now* (in 1805). But he also bemoans the absence of his friend (who left England in 1804 for Sicily and Malta to gain respite from his severe sickness of both mind and body, acutely exacerbated by his nearly uncontrolled dependence on laudanum as a pain reliever).[54] It is after the return of Coleridge (still quite ill) to England in 1806 that Wordsworth will read to him *The Prelude*, which he completed in the previous year and which Coleridge will celebrate in his poem, "To William Wordsworth, Composed on the Night after his Recitation of a Poem on the Growth of an Individual Mind" (but first published in 1817), as we saw in the previous chapter. "Thus, O Friend!", so Wordsworth addresses Coleridge,

> Through times of honour, and through times of shame,
> Have I descended, tracing faithfully
> The workings of a youthful mind, beneath
> The breath of great events, its hopes no less
> Than universal, and its boundless love;
> A story destined for thy ear.

but for one who now finds himself living in Sicily "Among the basest and the lowest fallen / Of all the race of men" (10.947–48). If today, Wordsworth continues, we bemoan what France has become, still more sorrowful is the land where you today find yourself. Once the glory of the ancient world, Sicily is today

> Strewed with the wreck of loftiest years. . . .[55]
> But indignation works where hope is not,
> And thou, O Friend, wilt be refreshed. There is
> One great Society alone on earth
> The noble Living and the noble Dead. (10.940–69)

In Book 11 of *The Prelude* Words yet again acknowledges the struggles that he, a youthful poet finding his artistic way, continued to face. Once more he addresses Coleridge:

> This History, my Friend, hath chiefly told
> Of intellectual power, from stage to stage
> Advancing, hand in hand with love and joy,
> And of imagination teaching truth
> Until that natural graciousness of mind
> Gave way to over-pressures of the times
> And their disastrous issues.

What light, he asks, "remained in such eclipse?" He answers:

> The laws of things which lie
> Beyond the reach of human will or power;
> The life of nature, by the God of love
> Inspired, celestial presence ever pure....
> This feeling, which howe'er impaired or damped,
> Yet having been once born can never die....
> Oh! Soul of Nature! that dost overflow
> With passion and with life, what feeble men
> Walk on this earth! how feeble have I been
> When thou wert in thy strength!...
>   [But] I had felt
> Too forcibly, too early in my life,
> Visitings of imaginative power
> For this to last: I shook the habit off
> Entirely and for ever, and again
> In Nature's presence stood, as I stand now,
> A sensitive, and a creative soul. (11.42–257)

It is precisely the "visitings" of imaginative power in our early life that become, Wordsworth continues, "in our existence spots of time" by and through which we renew our lives. An

> efficacious spirit chiefly lurks
> Among those passages of life in which
> We have had deepest feeling that the mind
> Is lord and master, and that outward sense
> Is but the obedient servant of her will.

Present from earliest childhood these spots of time represent "moments worthy of all gratitude.... Life with me, / As far as memory can look back, is full / Of this beneficent influence.... / Oh! mystery of man," Wordsworth exclaims, "from what a depth / Proceed thy honours!" Still, while I "see / In simple childhood something of the base / On which thy greatness stands," I also find "That from thyself it is that thou must give, / Else never canst receive." Indeed, Wordsworth continues, just when it seems that the hiding places of his power—his childhood, the dawn of life, the days gone by—are open to him, "then they close":

> I see by glimpses now; when age comes on,
> May scarcely see at all, and I would give,
> While yet we may, as far as words can give,
> A substance and a life to what I feel:
> I would enshrine the spirit of the past
> For future restoration. (11.258–343)

Wordsworth has shown us yet again that it is only in looking back (remembering) that we can look forward, since to look forward is to draw upon one's past history. We cannot receive from the past except insofar, as poets, we revive, relive, re-imagine our past in and through our compositions of words in which we "give a substance and a life to what we feel." Thus, he tells us in Book 12 of *The Prelude* that

> Thus moderated, thus composed, I found
> Once more in Man an object of delight,
> Of pure imagination, and of love;
> And, as the horizon of mind enlarged,
> Again I took the intellectual eye
> For my instructor, studious more to see
> Great Truths, than touch and handle little ones.
> Knowledge was given accordingly; my trust
> Was firmer in the feelings which had stood
> The test of such a trial. . . . I sought
> For good in the familiar face of life
> And built thereon my hopes of good to come.

Wordsworth proceeds then to probe the by-no-means evident relationship between "great truths" and "the familiar face of life." He tells us that, "having gained / A more judicious knowledge of what makes / The dignity of individual Man," it had become clear to him that "man" was no mere "composition of the thought," no

> Abstraction, shadow, image, but the man
> Of whom we read, the man whom we behold
> With our own eyes; I could not but inquire,
> Not with less interest than heretofore,
> But greater, though in spirit more subdued,
> Why is this glorious Creature to be found
> One only in ten thousand? What one is,
> Why may not many be? (12.53–92)

In undertaking to answer this question Wordsworth tells us that he "chiefly looked"

> Among the natural abodes of men,
> Fields with their rural works, recalled to mind
> My earliest notices, with these compared
> The observations of my later youth,
> Continued downwards to that very day. . . .
> therefore did I turn
> To you, ye Pathways and ye lonely Roads,
> Sought you enriched with everything I prized,
> With human kindness and with Nature's joy.

He tells us further that "I love a public road" with its "power / O'er my imagination." Disappearing out of sight it was "like a guide into eternity, / At least to things unknown and without bound."

> When I began to inquire,
> To watch and question those I met, and held
> Familiar talk with them, the lonely roads
> Were schools to me in which I daily read
> With most delight the passions of mankind,
> There saw into the depths of human souls,
> Souls that appear to have no depth at all
> To vulgar eyes. (12.107–68)

Just as education,[56] Wordsworth continues, seldom embodies "real feeling and just sense," so to "the talking world" toil is linked with ignorance. But what he, wandering on rural roads, heard from the mouths of lowly and obscure men were tales "of honour; sounds in unison / With loftiest promises of good and fair." Thus recalling what he saw when

> A youthful Traveler, and see daily now
> Before me in my rural neighbourhood,
> Here might I pause, and bend in reverence
> To Nature, and the power of human minds,
> To men as they are men within themselves. . . .
> Of these, said I, shall be my Song; of these,
> If future years mature me for the task,
> Will I record the praises, making Verse
> Deal boldly with substantial things, in truth
> And sanctity of passion, speak of these
> That justice may be done, obeisance paid
> Where it is due.

Thus "haply" may I teach and inspire and "through unadulterated ears / Pour rapture, tenderness, and hope, my theme / No other than the very heart of man / As found among the best of those who live / in Nature's presence" while at the same time "Not unexalted by religious hope" or "uninformed by . . . good books, though few." Telling us that he has "dared to tread this holy ground" in "Speaking no dream but things oracular." Wordsworth acknowledges that he writes, not for those who are "most elevated when admired most" but for those "of other mold" who, "their own upholders," express "liveliest thoughts in lively words / As native passion dictates." There are yet higher men "among the walks of homely life" who, while "for contemplation framed," are shy, meek, and "unpracticed in the strife of phrase," whose "very souls perhaps would sink / Beneath them" if they "were summoned to such intercourse: / Theirs is the language of the heavens, the power, / The thought, the image, and the silent joy." It is "the genius of the Poet," Wordsworth continues, "boldly [to] take his way among mankind / Wherever Nature leads." Just as the poet "has stood / by Nature's side among the men of old," so shall he "stand for ever." Then, he asks forgiveness of his "Dearest Friend" (Coleridge) if, in viewing poets as prophets who, "Connected in a mighty scheme of truth," have been "enabled to perceive /Something unseen before,"

> I, the meanest of this Band, had hope . . .
> that a work of mine,
> Proceeding from the depth of untaught things,
> Enduring and creative, might become
> A power like one of Nature's. . . .
> I remember well
> That in life's every-day appearances
> I seemed about this period to have sight
> Of a new world, a world, too, that was fit
> To be transmitted and made visible
> To other eyes, as having for its base
> That which our dignity originates,
> That which both gives it being and maintains
> A balance, an ennobling interchange
> Of action from within and from without:
> The excellence, pure spirit, and best power
> Both of the object seen, and the eye that sees. (12.171–379)

Always yet pursuing his ennobling theme that our human dignity rests in our capacity to see in life's everyday appearances a new world, "something unseen before," Wordsworth concludes Book 12 of *The Prelude*. Indeed, it is precisely insofar as the poet brings the power of his imagination to play upon the earth that his works may, to other eyes, possess the prophetic power like one of Nature's. The balance between the object seen and the eye that sees, the interchange from within and from without, represents at the same time the relationship between the poet and the reader, between the reader and the poem being read. Creation is active. What the poet sees outside of himself is what he writes, seeing: he creates what he sees in and through an act of imaginative power. What the reader sees in the poem that he is reading is an image of his mind as actively engaged in imaginatively seeing (in thinking through) what it sees in the poem as an image of his own mind.

It is appropriate, then, that, in now taking up the concluding Book 13 of *The Prelude*, we recall that, at the beginning of this chapter, we initiated our discussion of the poem with its opening section in which Wordsworth describes "one of these excursions" in which he finds himself meditating on the "ennobling interchange / Of action from within and from without," in this instance, his ascent of Mount Snowdon at night to behold the sunrise from atop the mountain. As Nature, awful and sublime, demonstrates its dominion through the power it "exerts upon the outward face of things," so what the poet sees (in his mind's eye) is the perfect image of a mighty, infinite, and divine mind. Indeed, because, as we noted, Wordsworth writes that "higher minds" have the power of transforming, of creating the earth on which they dwell in their own image, such minds are truly divine in possessing "the highest bliss that can be known": the consciousness of whom they are habitually infused through every image, through every thought, and through every impression.

But it turns out that another name for the blissful consciousness of beholding in the outward appearances of nature the true image of ourselves—for there is no receiving without giving—is love. In love "we begin and end," Wordsworth writes.

> From love . . . all grandeur comes,
> All truth and beauty, from pervading love.
> That gone, we are as dust.

He calls upon us
to *behold* "the fields / In balmy spring-time, full of rising flowers."

to *see* "that Pair, the Lamb / And Lamb's mother, and their tender ways /Shall touch thee to the heart."

to *rest* "in some green bower . . . / and be not alone but have thou there / The One who is thy choice of all the world, / There linger, lulled and lost, and rapt away, / Be happy to thy fill."[57]

However, Wordsworth continues:

> thou call'st this love
> And so it is, but there is higher love
> Than this, a love that comes into the heart
> With awe and a diffusive sentiment;
> *Thy* love is human merely; *this* proceeds
> More from the brooding Soul, and is divine.[58]

How Wordsworth expects us to understand the sharp contrast that he introduces here between "this" higher, divine love, which comes into the heart and proceeds from the soul, and "thy" merely human love of a fellow human being is, in my judgment, by no means immediately evident. Indeed, readers will recall the loving devotion that he expresses in *The Prelude* for his friend Coleridge and his sister Dorothy, among others, not to mention the tender scenes of love that he describes in his poem. (13.149–60)

But let us see, then, what he intends as he proceeds to write that "this" love is "more intellectual" since it

> cannot be
> Without Imagination, which, in truth,
> Is but another name for absolute strength
> And clearest insight, amplitude of mind,
> And reason in her most exalted mood.

"This faculty" (imagination, mind, reason . . .), he continues, "hath been the moving soul / Of our long labour . . . / Among the ways of Nature"—from darkness to light. Although I often lost sight of it and was left "bewildered and engulphed," still

> it rose once more
> With strength, reflecting in its solemn breast
> The works of man and face of human life;
> And, lastly, from its progress have we drawn
> The feeling of life endless, the one thought
> By which we live, Infinity and God.
> Imagination having been our theme,

> So also hath that intellectual love,
> For they are each in each, and cannot stand
> Dividually.—Here must thou be, O Man!

Having been told by Wordsworth that imagination and intellectual love stand undividedly in each other, he then proceeds to explicate the imperative that immediately follows—"Here must thou be, O Man!"—by means of multiple epithets that, again, are surely not immediately self-evident:

- "Strength to thyself" without a "Helper";
- "No other can divide with thee this work" when thou here keepest "thy individual state."
- "No secondary hand can intervene / to fashion this ability."

> The prime and vital principle is thine
> In the recesses of thy nature, far
> From any reach of outward fellowship,
> Else 'tis not thine at all. But joy to him,
> Oh, joy to him who here hath sown, hath laid
> Here the foundations of his future years!
> For all that friendship, all that love can do,
> All that a darling countenance can look
> Or dear voice utter, to complete the man,
> Perfect him, made imperfect in himself,
> All shall be his. (p. 583)

But thus it transpires that the "man" who, strong in himself, is beyond the reach of outward fellowship in his individual state and, consequently, without a secondary hand to help him in the work that is his alone, is in himself incomplete and imperfect. He is no Stoic sage sufficient to himself, we might say. Rather, he is a sinner in the tradition of biblical theology whose (creative, imaginative, intellectual, divine, infinite . . .) foundation in love of others is his salvation. For all that friendship and love can do, that is, what friendship and love only wholly can do, in completing and perfecting us: all this shall be ours.

It is the very paradox of love, of the moral law as we shall see Kant show us in the next two succeeding chapters, that, as covenantal, eternally involves us in (multiple, infinitely varied) relationships with our neighbor (including our own very self). Nobody else, nothing else, not God, not man, not Nature . . . can *make* us love (or act ethically, i.e., responsibly). It is true that love is imperative (categorical: *love thy neighbor*)—from which there is no escape. But at the same time love is always a gracious invitation, a welcoming, a salutation (may you be well!), an acknowledgment (of our dignity, our personhood). It is surely because we are all, as individuals, responsible for becoming (historically) the loving person that we are (in the beginning)[59] that Wordsworth places such emphasis on our individuality and independence, on love as the prime and vital principle in the recesses of our nature. Love is the creative gift of existence. Love is not a given fact of history. It is our responsibility, in possessing the freedom, to receive the love that is offered us. Indeed, we have seen Wordsworth write that we cannot receive without giving. I shall defer further comment on love as the "all" that completes and perfects us (as) human beings until we reach the end of *The Prelude*. But I do want to point out here that, when Wordsworth writes above about "all that love can do" in completing and perfecting us, he does not call it "intellectual." Nor does he again characterize love as "intellectual" in completing his poem, as we shall now see.

Wordsworth once more addresses Coleridge in bringing *The Prelude* to an end. "And, now, O Friend! . . . having tracked the main essential Power, / Imagination, up her way sublime,"

> this History is brought
> To its appointed close: the discipline
> And consummation of the Poet's mind,
> In everything that stood most prominent,
> Have faithfully been pictured.

He has reached the time, he continues, when he may suppose, "not presumptuously, I hope," that his powers and knowledge show him "capable / Of building up a work that should endure." Even if the tides of history should turn against men and nations, he assures Coleridge, "we" shall be

> Blessed with true happiness if we may be
> United helpers forward of a day
> Of firmer trust, joint-labourers in the work
> (Should Providence such grace to us vouchsafe)
> Of their redemption, surely yet to come.
> Prophets of Nature, we to them will speak
> A lasting inspiration, sanctified
> By reason and by truth; what we have loved
> Others will love, and we may teach them how;

>   Instruct them how the mind of man becomes
>   A thousand times more beautiful than the earth
>   On which he dwells, above this Frame of things
>   (Which, 'mid all revolutions in the hopes
>   And fears of men, doth still remain unchanged)
>   In beauty exalted, as it is itself
>   Of substance and of fabric more divine. (13.269–452)

So we reach the conclusion of *The Prelude* only to have its author tell us that he has now arrived the beginning of his poetic task. Together with his poet friend Coleridge he finds himself in the blessed state of true happiness in having been empowered to teach others how to love "what we have loved." But the evident paradox here, as I continue to emphasize, is that Wordsworth expresses his future intention in the very poem whose conclusion we have now reached, in the poem, indeed, that bears the title of prelude. It is salutary to remember that the ancient prophets of the Bible, when prophesying the future, did not (like ancient seers) predict the future. Rather, they portrayed the future as the past yet to be fulfilled—as sanctified and redeemed and so to be made whole in all that love can do. It has, I am sure, become manifestly clear to the reader that, when Wordsworth writes that he and Coleridge will speak, as Prophets of Nature, to the dwellers upon the earth, "Nature" represents, not what we saw Kierkegaard call the sensate (objects of nature) but rather the world of spirit (heart, mind) as "transferred" or metaphoric nature. "Nature," in other words, represents for Wordsworth what we shall see Kant call the realm of transcendental reason and so also the kingdom of ends, where all human beings are to be loved as subjects and not be used (or abused) as objects.

Wordsworth indulges, then, in poetic license in telling us that the human mind is a thousand times more beautiful than the earth. There is no numerical comparison between mind (the spirit of metaphor) and body (the sensate), between (infinite) Nature and (finite) nature, between subject and object. For it is, indeed, the mind that beautifies nature, that sees in nature (atop Mount Snowdon) an image, a metaphor of its own divine, infinite powers of creative beauty, of Nature as mirroring the beauty of the mind.[60] Wordsworth can appear at times to use the terms Nature, Imagination, and Reason rather loosely, both independently of each other and also on occasion in close relationship with each other. But it is evident that together they embody (express) the power of the mind to create nature in its own image, in other words, to see in nature the

Nature (the "Being") of its own powers of imagination, consistent, as we shall see, with Kant's concept of reason as practice, will, desire, action....

But we have also seen Wordsworth declare that the human mind is at one and the same time changing and unchanging. The very title of the poem (as given solely in the 1850 edition, we recall) implies that the actual composition of the poem is yet to follow upon its prelude. Furthermore, the subtitle of the poem, like the subtitle of Coleridge's poem "To William Wordsworth," signals to the reader that in his poem Wordsworth focuses on the growth of a poet's mind. Even more significant is our experience in reading *The Prelude*. For in it we find that Wordsworth views his poem as the story or history of his mind as a poet from childhood to maturity, from his recollections, in later life, of what we may call the immortal mind of the babe as the true father of man, as the true philosopher. As I have emphasized, the two themes that fundamentally shape *The Prelude* and constitute its true stature as a poem are the dual beginnings in nature (unconscious of itself as Nature) and in childhood (unconscious that its mind is a thousand times more beautiful than nature). In his poem Words depicts the critical transfer, we may say, from sensate nature to metaphoric Nature, from the mind unconscious of its creative powers to the mind in conscious possession of its poetic powers of teaching others what it has come to love: all that love can do. At the same time, however, we have also seen that Wordsworth, after writing that we poets will teach others how their mind *becomes* infinitely more beautiful than the earth on which they dwell, concludes his poem in writing that, amid all the "*revolutions* in the hopes and fears of men," their mind "doth still remain *unchanged.*" For in substance and in fabric the mind "is [in] itself more divine" than the earth.

I have taken the liberty of giving Wordsworth's concept of the mind as unchanging a Kantian flavor. Kant holds, as is famously known and as we shall soon see, that, while we can know the thing in itself (*das Ding an sich*) as an object of possible experience (in the world of sensible nature), we (subjects) cannot *know* what the thing is in itself as a subject that exists in the kingdom of ends, in the transcendental realm of thinking, action, will, desire.... Kant uses the term "transcendental" to describe the mind in itself. But Wordsworth, in adhering to a more traditionally religious vocabulary, calls the mind divine (and also, as we have seen, infinite, eternal...). The mind is unchanging. Yet, in *The Prelude* Wordsworth tells the story, the history of a poet's mind in its growth (development, advance, progress) from childhood to adulthood, from nature to spirit with its concept of Nature representing the metaphoric transfer from natural objects to the self-conscious realization (revelation) on the part of the human subject that, as it is (in) itself divine, it constitutes the creative foundation of nature. The mind is unchanging in the beginning, from the beginning, as it is unto the end divine and eternal in itself. Yet, the mind is historical: it has a story, at once individual (personal) and universal (communal). What we learn, then, is that it is only in relating our story as the history of our mind that we realize, make real, and so bring into existence our mind as the unchanging foundation of history, as the unchanging and so as the ever-changing story of human life. In the spirit of Hegel, we have the eternal task of making the actual rational and of making the rational actual, of critically judging who we actually are (now, today) in light of the universal standards of rationality that are true for all human beings but also, and equally, of ensuring that our highest standards of rational truth are grounded in what is humanly actual (and are not merely abstractions or, indeed, idols). It is evident that, as we make the critical transfer from the sensate to the spiritual, from the actual to the rational (from the real to the ideal), so we, at the same time, grow in spirit in and through our realization that our concept of spirit (of the rational, of the ideal) has grown in depth and amplitude. «Plus ça change, plus c'est la même chose." Truth or cliché? Insight or excuse?

Does God change? While this is not a question that Wordsworth poses, it does allow us to focus on the critical difference between natural change and historical change. It also allows us to reflect on the significance of Wordsworth's continuous use of religious (biblical, Christian) language in describing the mind. The God of the Bible is typically viewed as unchanging, as abiding forever, as eternal, infinite, omnipotent (all-powerful), and omniscient (all-knowing): the rock of ages. Indeed, it is in the image of God that human beings—in their infinite difference, in their infinite likeness—are created. As Kierkegaard emphasizes at the close of *Works of Love*: like for like. Like God, like human beings. Like human beings, like God. Human beings are made in the image of God. Is God not, consequently, made in the image of humankind? It is evident that this likeness is metaphoric, not naturalistic. It is no less evident, consequently, that, just as human beings cannot be known outside of (without) God, so God cannot be known outside of (without) human beings. In the beginning is relationship Martin Buber tells us in articulating, in elemental terms, the biblical truth of the covenant. It is only in light of the covenant, which God made with his holy people, the ancient Israelites, that they can reflect on their pre-history. Indeed, we may call the story of Adam and Eve (prior to their having become conscious of being made in the image of their Lord God in knowing good and evil) the Prelude, whose composition—poetic? philosophic?—is conceivable solely in light of the story of creation as the history of covenantal relationship. It follows, then, that, as our human mind grows historically in amplitude and depth, so the more ample and profound also becomes our idea of God or whatever it is, in today's secular world, that we understand, in response to Montaigne's searching question—*What* do I know?—as that than which we cannot conceive (imagine) anything greater. I recall here the "rational" proof of the existence of God that St. Anselm formulated, in the late eleventh century for the first time in history, in response to the request on the part of his pious monks that their religious mentor supply them with a non-biblical proof of the existence of God, which, since Kant, we know as the ontological argument.

The basic point that I want to emphasize here, in reflecting on the continuous use that Wordsworth makes of traditionally theological language in describing the mind of man as at once unchanging in itself and, yet, as always finding itself historically *still* at the point of writing the prelude to the composition of its life story, is that, unlike Coleridge and Shelley, whose reflections on poetry I discussed in the previous chapter, his poetry, together with his poetic prefaces, is profoundly consistent with the biblical conception of humankind as at once creative and covenantal. In contrast to Coleridge Wordsworth shows no interest in proclaiming his own Christian faith. Yet, the "philosophic mind" that is at work in *The Prelude*, which is presently my focus here, is profoundly religious (theological, spiritual . . .). Indeed, what is particularly significant is that we have seen Wordsworth indicate that, and I render in prose the passage that I cited earlier from Book 10 of *The Prelude*, it is "in the very world, which is the world of all of us, that is the place in which, in the end, we find happiness or not at all." Again, as distinct from Coleridge, Wordsworth sets up no artificial and (ultimately Platonist) dualism between mortal and immortal, earth and heaven, body and spirit, nature and Nature, man and God, human and divine. . . . The poet of *The Prelude* freely, and creatively, makes use of this distinction as fundamental. At the same time, however, he shows us that it embodies (incarnates) the critical transfer from nature to spirit. We may say, paraphrasing Jesus, whom, by the way, Wordsworth never mentions in *The Prelude*, that, while we live on the earth, we live by the metaphorical critique of pure (transcendental) reason, which, as practice, embodies the golden rule as all that love can do. The paradox, as always, is that, while we find happiness only on earth and not in some future place as a return to unhistorical nature whose story is not prelude but mere postlude devoid of story, the earth is prefigured in the image of mind as metaphorical critique.

We also see that, in contrast with Shelley, Wordsworth does not conflate the human story as at once creative and covenantal with Plato (the ancient Greeks). Again, what is so interesting is that, while Wordsworth does not present himself in his poetry (or in his poetic theory as found in his various prefaces) as one who is an overtly Christian believer, the values that he espouses are profoundly biblical. It is true that Wordsworth at times makes loose reference to the poets of antiquity as belonging to the line of inspired versifiers to which he himself belongs. Still, he does not, like either Coleridge or Shelley, conflate the values of the ancients with his own (in conveying the modernity of Spirit and Nature as the truth that is at once religious and secular, both human and divine).[61]

It is especially important to remark that Wordsworth, in making the growth of a poet's mind the theme that structures *The Prelude*, evinces a profound grasp of history as the metaphorical critique of nature. The mind of man is forever (eternally) unchanging. Yet, the mind of man is ever bound to grow and develop historically in the amplitude of its self-conscious recognition that its life's story is but the prelude to its next stage of development. In portraying the unchanging mind of man as embodying, as incarnating and revealing, its story as one of historical growth, Wordsworth evinces an understanding of temporality as history that is fundamentally biblical and without precedence (prelude!) in the world of the ancient Greeks. It is here that he absolutely distances himself from the platitudinous claims of Coleridge and Shelley regarding the ancients.

Indeed, what is especially ironic is that, as will become manifest in the following two chapters on Kant, it is Wordsworth, with his grasp of the historicity of metaphorical critique as truly the domain of practical reason, who is truly Kantian, not Coleridge. We saw Coleridge claim, as we found in the previous chapter, that it was the "writings of the illustrious sage of Königsberg, . . . more than any other work, [that] at once invigorated and disciplined my understanding." It became evident to us, however, that his grasp of Kant was largely dissipated in the dualism between earth and heaven, between the mortal and the immortal, between man and God that he deemed Christian but that was fundamentally based on the

Platonic opposition between changing appearances and unchanging forms (being in itself). It is yet additionally ironic that Wordsworth concludes *The Prelude*, as we have seen, in addressing Coleridge as a fellow helper and joint-laborer in telling him that together, as prophets of Nature, they will inspire and sanctify others through reason and truth to love what they have loved. We may be sure that Wordsworth found himself inspired and sanctified by the trust that Coleridge placed in him in prophesying that, with the earth all before him along the road that lay plain ahead of him, he was destined to become the greatest philosophical poet of all time. Wordsworth, however, unlike Coleridge, claimed no special knowledge of philosophy. Yet, he shows us in his poetry and, above all, in *The Prelude* that he is a truly philosophical poet precisely because he knows that the poet, the prophet, and the philosopher are one and the same being who, each and all, is called to the common, spiritual task of showing others that what they have loved—the earth sanctified in and by metaphor—they, too, will love. Unlike Coleridge and Shelley, Wordsworth possesses a critical grasp of metaphor as the transcendental domain of practical reason. So, now I turn to Kant to show, consistent with the aim of my study, that philosophy, like poetry, is grounded in all that love can historically do on earth.

CHAPTER 4

Thinking Philosophically with Kant

INTRODUCTORY

I CONTINUE HERE MY inquiry into the common framework of ideas that in truth shapes both poetry and philosophy. To think poetically with Wordsworth and to think philosophically with Kant is, I argue, to find ourselves thinking at once metaphorically and critically. All the works of the spirit—and here I paraphrase Kierkegaard, whose concept of transition from nature to spirit I have made fundamental to my study—all the works of human beings that truly embody their spirit are at one and the same time metaphorical and critical. They demand that we think, and rethink, our beginnings, our principles, and our end, our purpose. In our two previous chapters we saw Wordsworth create poetry out of the story of the growth of a poet's mind. We human beings begin unconscious of our beginnings in nature and, yet, as the babe who, the true philosopher of life, provides (providentially/provisionally foresees) our conception of life as always a prelude to a yet more ample grasp of spirit. We could thus paraphrase Kierkegaard: all language of the spirit, whether poetic or philosophic, is transferred and so is at once critically metaphorical and metaphorically critical language. It is solely in and through our critical transfer from the sensuous world of nature to the metaphorical world of spirit that we are enabled and so, indeed, commanded, to realize and thus make real what Kant, as we shall now see, calls the domain of human practice when poetically made the blessed kingdom of ends.

That all language of the spirit, including the language of Scripture, is metaphor is the blessed word of Kierkegaard that I have made the logos of my study. I have shown in my two previous chapters on Wordsworth how it is realized poetically. Now I shall proceed to argue in my two chapters on Kant that the revolution he effected in modernity with his demonstration that reason is, in the beginning as in the end, practical no less embodies the critical logos of metaphor as the transfer from the sensuous world of nature to the metaphorical world of spirit. Does it not, then, follow from our Kierkegaardian *logos*, as made living by Wordsworth, that God is a metaphor, indeed, that it is precisely God as metaphor, as spiritual critique, that throws our life into crisis in asking with Montaigne: What do I know? The question is not: Do I know anything? not: Do I exist? The question is not hypothetical, theoretical, or speculative, but categorical. I could not ask the question without knowing that I am responsible for knowing—for doubting, for questioning, for thinking through—what it means for me to exist. In elemental terms what Kant demonstrates in his philosophy is that I cannot know what nature is as the very possibility of life (we are all natural beings) without knowing what I actually am, the thing in itself, which I cannot know as an object of nature (a thing) but can only will (live) as a subject in the kingdom of ends.

As we come to understand, with and through Kant, how and in what precise sense nature is hypothetical and theoretical and that spirit, as practical reason, is actual in and through categorical duty, we shall find that he makes the discussion of the relationship between reason and religion, and so between the human and the divine, central to his philosophical critique. In this chapter I shall provide an introduction to the overall philosophical orientation of Kant, just as the first of my two chapters on Wordsworth served as an introduction to his poetics. Here, I shall concentrate on several of Kant's lesser works as the way of preparing us, in the succeeding Chapter 5, for our encounter with his two extraordinary critiques of pure and practical reason. It is of particular interest that in the key works that I shall discuss in this chapter Kant makes the critique of religion, the religion of the Bible, fundamental to advancing his conception of reason as the practice of bringing into existence the kingdom of ends. Central, then, to this chapter are Kant's two major works on religion, *Religion within the Boundaries of Mere Reason* and *The Conflict of the Faculties*, Part 1: "The Conflict of the Philosophy Faculty with the Theology Faculty." I shall also call upon Kant's *Groundwork of the Metaphysics of Morals* and three of his essays: "What Is Enlightenment?," "Conjectural Beginning of Human History," and "Perpetual Peace." I want to indicate here that I shall make no attempt to provide an historical or, in that sense, a scholarly account of Kant. Suffice it to say that he deserves the accolade of the Sage of Köningsberg that Coleridge bestowed upon him for the extraordinary suite of writings that began with *The Critique of Pure Reason* in 1781. Although Kant, unlike Wordsworth, embarked on his remarkable, philosophical journey as an older, not a younger, man (he was fifty-seven in 1781), our philosopher wrote his truly creative works, as our poet wrote his, in a period of some fifteen years. (Kant died in his 80th year in 1804.)

I shall initiate my presentation of Kant with a quartet of his fundamental propositions as a means of introducing us to the extraordinary range and depth of his thinking. They will allow us to begin to address the critical questions that the metaphorical transition from nature to freedom, from the sensuous to spirit raises. What is the prelude to life? How do we begin? Where do we begin? We know that Descartes begins with "I think, *ergo* I am." It is evident, however, that thinking does not lead to being but is contained within being. To think is to exist. To exist is to think. But it is also evident, Descartes undertakes to prove, that to begin thinking, to begin as a thinking being, is to think of that which cannot be thought without necessarily existing (to think of that than which nothing greater can be thought). *Ergo*, I have an idea of a perfect being, in light of which it is evident to me that I am not perfect. Yet, Descartes opens his *Discourse on Method* with the observation that what he calls "good sense" or "reason," i.e., "the ability to judge correctly and to distinguish the true from the false—which is really what is meant by good sense or reason—is the same by nature in all men." It follows, then, that "differences of opinions are not due to differences in intelligence, but merely to the fact that we use different approaches and consider different things. For it is not enough to have a good mind; one must use it well. The greatest souls are capable of the greatest vices as well as of the greatest virtues." Whence it follows, Descartes writes, that reason or good sense, because "it is the only thing which makes us men and distinguishes us from the animals, . . . is fully present in each one of us" (3–4). Since the minds of all human beings are naturally and so equally whole and entire and since all human beings equally have the power of distinguishing between truth and falsehood, between virtue and vice, in what sense, then, we may ask, is the mind of human beings to be understood as imperfect when compared with their Idea of God as perfect?

I begin with Descartes as the father of modern philosophy or, perhaps I should write, as the babe who, the original philosopher, was the father of man whose immortal mind exists whole and entire, in order to problematize issues that since Descartes remain fundamental to philosophy and, I would add, to poetics, to our human lives. Kant in no fundamental way deviates from Descartes' insight that all human beings, in equally possessing wholly complete (perfect) minds, exist as things in themselves, as persons.

But, yes, Kant (like Spinoza before him) does overcome the seeming dualism in Descartes' separation of the mind, as thinking substance (spirit), from the body, as extended (quantifiable) substance (nature). We may say that Kant saves (liberates), not the mind from the body but nature (the earth) for the mind. But that is the fundamental aim of the *Critique of Pure Reason*, as we shall see in the next chapter. Still, what Kant demonstrates in all of his critical writings[62] is that metaphysics, i.e., how we are understand ourselves as thinking beings whose mind is whole and complete, is practical, not theoretical, moral and not scientific. Mind is will. To think is to will the good. Yet, this is in the spirit of Descartes who, as I indicated above, conceives of mind as our power of distinguishing truth from falsehood, virtue from vice.[63] Before taking up Kant I also want to take special note of Descartes' observation that it is because all human beings are thinking beings, i.e., because they each possess a mind that is complete, whole, and perfect, that they are to be (can be, must be) distinguished from animals. The point that Descartes makes here is simple and would appear to be held as self-evidently true by many (if not all) of the world's cultures. It was a truism, for instance, in ancient Greek culture. Still, when Descartes writes that it is in possessing a mind that is whole and complete that makes us human and distinguishes us from the animals, what are we to think about those cultures in which it is denied that all human beings equally possess whole, complete, and perfect minds? Were those human beings whose minds were held to be imperfect, partial, and incomplete wholly and properly human? Plato's philosopher-king (whose perfect mind, as found solely in the mere words of metaphysics and not, it appears, in existence, is constituted in and through the contradictory identity of right and might) is superior in mind to all others. We may recall that Aristotle looked upon slaves as those who by nature lacked a rational soul. If slaves were not truly human beings, were they but animals (to be used and abused by others for their own rational ends)? We may also remember that Aristotle defines man as a political animal, i.e., as an animal that lives in a *polis*. Aristotle categorizes the *polis* in terms of those who rule over others: the rule of one (monarchy), the rule of some (aristocracy), and the rule of many (democracy[64]). In holding, consistent with the whole of ancient Greek culture, that all power (natural and human) reflects the hierarchical, cosmic order of ruler and ruled (master and slave), Aristotle had no conception of the rule of all over all. The civil state, whose every individual member is a free, sovereign citizen, is that *civitas* (*polis*) and only that *civitas*, which, as Spinoza demonstrates in his *Theologico-Political Treatise*, is the true and proper democracy.

Democracy is not partial, not partially the rule of one, some, or many minds over the minds of all others. The minds of its citizens are not partial but equally whole and wholly equal. This is what we shall see Kant call the metaphysics of morals or what we could also call the morality of metaphysics. Metaphysics is practice, action—as founded on the categorical imperative of willing to do unto others what you want others to do unto you. Kant, we shall find, is wholly in the tradition of the social contract (compact) as articulated, above all, by Hobbes, Spinoza, and Rousseau. In simple terms, he distinguishes between the state of nature and the civil state, between the natural war of all against all and the civil peace of all as found in the kingdom of ends in which all citizens treat each other as ends in themselves, not as a means, as persons, and not as things. In holding that it our unconditional duty to treat all human beings in terms of their dignity, of their unconditional (absolute) worth and not of their conditional (contingent or relative) price, what Kant shows us is that Descartes' principle that all human beings possess a wholly perfect mind is a moral and so, equally, a political principle.

In demonstrating that the metaphysics of mind is the metaphysics of morals, that the mind (as will and desire) is, as the principle of metaphysics, the principle of the moral law, Kant raises fundamental issues for us, above all, those arising from the distinction (which Kant shows us to be the transcendentally necessary) between mind (freedom) and nature. What, we may ask, is the origin, ontologically and historically, of the concept of mind as wholly complete and of absolute worth? What then are we to understand by history, by what Wordsworth in *The Prelude* shows to be the growth of a poet's mind—from and through nature to the absolute dignity of man in himself as worthy of God? Since the distinction between mind and nature involves the distinction between the civil state and the state of nature as the war of all against all, many additional questions follow. Is the "original" paradise of Adam and Eve, prior to their "fall" into the divine knowledge of good and evil, to be understood as the state of nature? Did the Greeks, in their ignorance of the good and also, consequently, of the evil, live in the state of nature? Is the concept of nature in itself as the war of all against all, as found in the social contract theorists, together with Kant, consistent with Wordsworth's account of the mind as finding its beauty and glory in the image of nature? How, indeed, are we to understand Kierkegaard's edict that all language about the spirit, including the language of Scripture, is metaphor? Kant, then, is of especial interest to us since he make the issue of Scripture, how we are to understand the Bible, and hence the issue of interpretation central to his metaphysics of morals.

Finally, then, I think we are ready to begin our discussion of Kant as a metaphysician of morality with consideration of his declaration of four basic principles. Kant opens (Section 1 of) the *Groundwork of the Metaphysics of Morals* with our first principle as follows: "It is impossible to think of anything at all in the world, or indeed even beyond it, that could be considered good without limitation except a good will" (49). The only thing that is absolutely, unconditionally, infinitely (without limit), and perfectly good, in itself, is, whether within or without the world, the will (as we remember that, for Kant, will, mind, desire, thinking, action all bear the meaning of conscious, responsible intent, consistent with Descartes and Spinoza). But whose will is this? It is, surely, the will of human beings. But in the tradition of biblical (Judaeo-Christian) thinking it was the will of God that was considered to be absolutely infinite in itself without conditions. Yet, since Kant states that the only thing good in itself, whether inside or outside the world, is the will, he must also include within his concept of the "good will" the will of God (together with the will of angels, including that of Satan?). Not only, however, do we come here face to face with the question of the relationship of the human and the divine, of philosophy and theology. But also we see raised here what is surely the most fundamental question of ethics. What is the good? In other words, what is the origin, the source, the principle of the good. If, as Kant writes, solely the will can be considered the good, or, rephrased, if the only thing good in itself, within or without the world, is the will, the will, consequently, must be the source, the principle, of the good. We are, it is evident, in the presence of the absolute reversal of the metaphysics of the Greek world. For we remember that, according to Plato, the good is identical with itself as the unchanging, immortal, finite end (*finis*), in opposition to the world of in-finite appearances (which lack their end, their *finis*). Since for Plato to know the good is to be the good, the good in itself cannot be thought by human beings. It is a logical (and metaphysical) impossibility for an ancient Greek to state: I think, *ergo* I am (the good in itself). Aristotle, we know, defines God as thought thinking itself and so also as that which, in moving others (as their unknown and unthinkable [thoughtless] end), is unmoved by others (as in-finite and so lacking their end).

Consistent with Kant's avowal that the only thing that is good in itself is the will is what I call here his second declaration, that morality (as based on the will as absolutely good in itself) leads to God, not God to morality. He writes in *Religion within the Boundaries of Mere Reason* that "each individual can recognize by himself, through his own reason, the will of God which lies at the basis of his religion; for the concept of the Divinity actually originates solely from the consciousness of these [moral] laws and from reason's need to assume a power capable of procuring for them the full effect possible in this world in conformity with the moral final end [which we remember is the good will]" (137). In elemental terms, human reason as practical (will) is the (moral) principle (the metaphysical origin) of God. God is not the (supernatural) cause (end) of human beings. What, then, is religion for Kant? Who is God for our philosopher? If religion and God are not to be found outside of the moral consciousness, the practical reason, of human beings, does it also follow that reason is to be found solely within the boundaries of pure (moral) religion—as the Word of God that we call Scripture? Indeed, Kant never hesitates in making use of the metaphor common to Christendom that the moral law is written in, is inscribed in, the human heart. It is little wonder, then, that Kant makes an incisive examination of the relationship between philosophy and theology, reason and faith, and so between man and God central to his philosophical critique. If religion and God are not found outside of the good will of human beings, does this also mean that the concept of the good will is not found outside of the Bible and its God? Is the Bible no less philosophical than it is theological?

In declaring the third of what I am calling the four basic principles of his philosophy Kant follows closely upon the first two. He writes in the *Groundwork* that, "unless we want to deny to the concept of morality any truth and any relation to some possible object, we cannot dispute that its law is so extensive in its import that it must hold not only for human beings but for all *rational beings as such*, not merely under contingent conditions and with exceptions but with *absolute necessity*" (62). To consider any human beings or even God to be exceptional does not mean that, as a rational being, i.e., as a being whose reason is the origin, the principle, of the moral law, they can make themselves an exception to the moral law. It is evident, then, that, as human beings are bound by and to the moral law, so equally is God. Our fourth and last declaration, as found in the "Conjectural Beginning of Human History," puts the nail into the coffin of any concept of God as supernatural and so as miraculously or mysteriously outside the bonds of pure reason. Kant writes that our forebears Adam and Eve, once they had been released from the Garden of Eden as "the womb of nature, . . . entered into a relation of equality with all rational beings, whatever their rank, with respect to the claim of being an end in themselves, respected as such by everyone, beings whom no one might treat as a mere means to ulterior ends."[65] There may be "other beings" whose "natural gifts" incomparably surpass those possessed by human beings. "Nevertheless, man is without qualification equal even to higher beings in that none has the right to use him according to pleasure. This is because of his reason—reason considered not insofar as it is a tool to the satisfaction of his inclinations, but insofar as it makes him an end in himself" (59).

We thus see that, as human beings are equally divine, so God is equally human. Still, this is not surprising when we recall that God is the holy One of the covenant and that the ancient Israelites are the holy people of the covenant. Can we (rationally, practically) covenant or enter into relationship with anyone other than our equal—without returning to the state of the natural warfare of ruler-ruled domination? Does not the very idea of the God-man represent a "metaphor" that expresses at once the incarnation of God in history and the divinization of his providentially chosen people as the transition to spirit? Big issues lie ahead of us, in particular, two questions, in addition to those already previously raised. First, if we are to understand the Garden of Eden as representing the state of nature in which good and evil are unknown, would not, then, the fall (sin) of man represent his rebirth as a new man, who, created in the image of God and so reborn a creature of reason, knows, like his Lord, good and evil? As we noted earlier, Kierkegaard postulates like for like: like God, like man/like man like God, each the metaphor of (the transition to) the other. The second question follows closely upon the first. Whereas good and evil are unknown in the natural garden of immortal (unchanging) paradise, still, strangely, yet providentially (and not naturally), a tree grows there whose fruit, knowledge of good and evil, is deadly mortal with the first bite. How else can we explain the original (the "first") transition from nature to spirit, from in-nocence (ignorance of what is noxious, i.e., of evil) to knowledge of good and evil, from the state of nature to the civil state of covenantal relationships? If we are all born in the state of nature, how is it that the babe is the philosophic father of man? Whence the second question. Since, according to what we have already learned from Kant, the only thing that is good in, and even outside, the world is the will, it must also follow that the only thing that is evil in, and even outside, the world is the will. In locating the good in human will as an end in itself, as the thing in itself, all hell breaks out. Since the will is the sole good within, and even without, the world, it follows, then, that my will is the sole and the universal good—for me. But since all other individuals make the same claim for their will, we return to the state of nature as the war of all against all. For, as we know, our covenantal history, beginning with the accounts of the prophets that are recorded in and as Hebrew Scripture, is replete with the endless story of human beings turning loving ends into selfish means, in treating others as they would not want to be treated by others. Not only do human beings reduce God to their own image in claiming divine power over others, but they also reduce themselves to the image of an omnipotent God in asserting their impotent dependence on divine grace. Idolatry is found, consequently, not in the state of nature (and so also not in the pagan world) but solely in the world that distinguishes between nature and spirit, means and ends, things and persons....

With the transition from the state of nature to the civil state—from, in my judgment, the ancient world of paganism to the biblical world of the will of man as the universal good of all (to remain with Kant)—history is the story of the good constantly overcome by evil yet winning out in the end. In the lyrics of a seventeenth century Baroque opera: suffer and hope, or do not love.[66] According to Croce, in his twentieth century version of Hegel, history is the story of liberty (liberation).[67]

It is not surprising, then, that Kant clearly and profoundly sees that philosophy, when understood as the critique of practical reason, must account for its relationship, both metaphysical and historical, to theology and thus to the religion of the Bible. He views his task as demonstrating that religion is purely bound to reason. But, in holding that the moral law is universally found in the hearts of all human beings, it is not so evident that he clearly sees that universality is not only a metaphysical but also a historical concept. In other words, what the ancient Hebrews found in their hearts—love of God and man—is not what the ancient Greeks and Romans (together with other pagans) found in their hearts, which was the chance (fortune) of fate: either rule (over others) or be ruled (by others). Like his great predecessors—Spinoza in the *Theologico-Political Treatise* (1670) and Vico in *The New Science* (2nd ed., 1730)—Kant is unerring in finding what he calls "the religion of reason" in the Bible (although he reflects the anti-Judaism[68] that pervaded Christendom for nearly two millennia in holding that the moral law of reason emerged only in the New Testament and is not to be found in Hebrew Scripture). While Kant asserts time and again that the moral law is universal, he never once claims that it is to be found in (or that it was foreseen by) Plato, Aristotle, or any other Greek philosopher, as was so common in earlier centuries. There is no hint in Kant that the birth of Christ was foretold by the sibyls.

It is striking that among the key works in which Kant discusses the relationship between philosophy and theology, between reason and religion, is his remarkable essay, "Conjectural Beginning of Human History," that he wrote as a commentary on the story of Adam and Eve. Kant's essay is unprecedented, so far as I know, in the history of philosophy.[69] He has two principal aims in his essay, each closely related to the other. First, since we do not and cannot "know" how the beginning of man as a rational being was possible, since, in other words, it is the actual existence of man for which we must account, all we have is a "conjecture" as to the beginning of human history. Whereas Kant makes central to the *Critique of Pure Reason*, as we shall see in the next chapter, what he calls the transcendental deduction (or justification) of the categories of possible experience (of the objects of nature)—on the basis of the actual existence of the human mind—the mind can be "deduced" or justified solely in beginning from itself alone. The mind, as the agent of freedom, freely begins willing from itself alone (it is what Spinoza calls the *causa sui*, the cause of itself). For, as we have already seen Kant indicate, the will is the only actual good that exists on earth or even outside the earth. All possibilities arise from what the mind, or will, is in itself. In yet another dramatic break with ancient philosophy, Kant demonstrates that actuality (what Spinoza calls the *potentia* of *conatus* or will) precedes possibilities. Possibilities (when they are not theoretically vain wishes or even ravings) express (represent) the actual power that is inherent in our will that is yet to be built up and upon. Aristotle, in contrast, holds, consistent with all the thinkers (philosophic and poetic) of antiquity, that (pure) possibility precedes (impure) actuality.

What Kant thus demonstrates, in sum, is that the mind can know objects as the possible appearances of the actual thing in itself. But the mind cannot know, theoretically (metaphysically), what it is in itself. For all that the mind can do, as "the all" that the mind actually does, is to will the good. In short, what Kant shows us, but does not tell us in explicitly, self-conscious, terms, is that "I think, *ergo* I exist." I "think," i.e., I explain (account for) existence solely in existing. I exist solely in thinking. Consistent, then, with Wordsworth in *The Prelude*, we begin our life rich in the possibilities of our human nature; yet, what we discover, in relating the story of our growth as a poet, is that, from the beginning, we have been called to be the poet that we actually are and must will to be.

Once again, we find ourselves in the midst of the most gripping philosophical issues. I shall, at this point, only invoke them, as they will, both indirectly and directly, constantly be with us. First, Kant assumes (presupposes), in making profound use of the ontological argument (proving the existence of God), that there is one thing that cannot be thought (by us human beings) without existing necessarily (freely), which is God. Thinking (will) and existence are given in and through each other. We cannot even ask—Does God exist?—or, in Descartes' version, I doubt that God or that even I exist, without already existing as a thinking (willing) human being. But neither Descartes nor Spinoza, our two great ontological thinkers of the seventeenth century, explicitly showed that the ontological argument proves the existence of the human being no less than of God. But, as the reader who is familiar with Kantian philosophy is aware, Kant shows (in the last major section of the *Critique of Pure Reason* called the "Transcendental Dialectic") that what he named there the ontological argument is fallacious. The irony, however, is that what he actually shows us there is that the ontological argument belongs to practical reason, to human will as the good, not to theoretical (metaphysical) reason as understanding. The second point to which I shall here refer is that the idea that reason is, first and last, actually practical will presupposes (is based on) the biblical doctrine of creation, that human beings are created by God from nothing, from nothing prior to the actual existence of thinking persons (or subjects). In simple terms, God is not "prior" to human beings in natural space and time. God, rather, is the priority for all human beings just as every human being is our priority. In principle, we are never to favor one person over another. As I say, these issues are with us always. It is now time to see how they play out in Kant's conjecture on the biblical story of humankind as the beginning of human history.

KANT AND RELIGION

Right from the beginning of his essay on the "Conjectural Beginning of Human History" (1786) Kant makes a critical distinction between, on the one hand, history as "the progression of the history of human actions," which he also calls "an account of the progression of freedom," and, on the other hand, the "first beginning" or, in other words, "the first development of freedom" (53). We begin as historical beings the history of whose actions is the story of the progress of our freedom. But what is the beginning of that beginning? How did our history as the liberating story of human progress begin? Where did it come from? How did it emerge (from nothing that was not historical, we might add)? In pondering these questions Kant proposes that we join him "on a mere pleasure trip" and take along as our map "a sacred document. . . . Let the reader consult it (Gen. 2–6) and check at every point whether the road which philosophy takes with the help of concepts coincides with the story told in Holy Writ" (54).

But Kant immediately tells us that we must start our journey "with something which human reason cannot derive from prior natural causes—in the present case, the existence of man." Without indicating to us that he thereby invokes the ontological argument for existence (I think, *ergo* I am), Kant adds that we must also conjecture that man exists as an adult, must be a pair (man and woman), and a single pair (for otherwise war would immediately break out) in order for us "to bring about the highest end intended for man, namely, sociability [*Geselligkeit*]." While my adult pair of human beings, Kant continues, is provided with natural necessities (food and shelter), "I begin with this pair, not in the natural state" but only once they have "already taken mighty steps in the skillful use" of their natural powers. They can walk upright, talk, "i.e., speak according to coherent concepts (Gen. 2:23), and hence think." Kant emphasizes that these are self-acquired skills that are not based on heredity. But once man had begun to think, indicating that he had been released from natural instinct, a strange thing happened. In following his imagination, man created "artificial desires which are not only unsupported by natural instinct but actually contrary to it." Such, then, was the result of "man's first attempt to become conscious of his reason as a power which can extend itself beyond the limits to which all animals are confined." So, tempted by attractive fruit, man's "first attempt at a free choice" did "violence to the voice of nature." Still, with his eyes now opened, man "discovered in himself a power of choosing for himself a way of life" that was infinitely beyond the way of animal instinct. He experienced delight but also anxiety and fear. "He stood . . . at the brink of an abyss." How was he to choose among the infinity of objects that now lay before him? Yet, "it was impossible for him to return to the state of servitude (i.e., subjection to instinct) from the state of freedom, once he had tasted the latter" (54–56).

Among the desires that imagination created for original man beyond those generated by natural instinct was "sexual attraction," which, among animals, "is merely a matter of transient, mostly periodic impulse. But man soon discovered that for him this attraction can be prolonged and even increased by means of the imagination." But thus it was that, in addition to choice, original man discovered that "refusal" was the act that allowed him to pass "from mere animal desire . . . to love . . . and to a taste for beauty" in both man and nature. "In addition, there came a first hint at the development of man as a moral creature . . . [which is] the real basis of all true sociability." What may appear to be only a "small beginning," Kant observes, is actually "epoch-making" in giving "a wholly new direction to thought. . . . It is then more important than the whole immeasurable series of expansions of culture which subsequently spring from it" (57).

In addition, then, to free choice and refusal reason took its third and most decisive step. "This was the conscious *expectation of the future*" (57). The capacity for what Kant calls "facing up in the present to the often very distant future, instead of being wholly absorbed by the enjoyment of the present, is the most decisive mark of the human's advantage" (57–58). Still, while human beings can thus prepare themselves for their properly human aims, the uncertainty of the future "is also the most inexhaustible source of their cares and troubles" (58). Man and woman were faced not only with labor, including the labor of bearing children, but also with death.

There is, however, "yet a fourth and final step which reason took, and this raised man altogether above community with the animals." Man came to realize, "however obscurely," Kant writes, "that he is the true end of nature, and that nothing that lives on earth can compete with him in this regard." It was thus that human beings because conscious of the fact that, while they can use an animal for their own human ends (for, e.g., wool and meat), they must view their fellow human being "as an equal participant in the gifts of nature. This idea was the first preparation of all those restraints in his relations with his fellow men which reason would in due course impose on man's will, restraints which are far more essential for the establishment of a civil society than inclination and [sensual] love." In observing that so it was, then, that man, in being an end in himself and not a mere means, "entered into a relation of equality with all rational beings, whatever their rank," Kant states that, as we saw earlier, "man is without qualification equal even to higher beings in that none has the right to use him according to pleasure. This is because . . . [reason is primarily not a tool for satisfying his inclinations but because] it makes him an end in itself." Thus we see, Kant writes, that the "last step of reason is at the same time man's *release* from the womb of nature," although at the same time man now finds himself exposed to dangers that were unknown to him in the natural garden of paradise. Still, "restless reason" left man with no choice but to choose the way of freedom in "irresistibly impelling him to develop the faculties implanted within him" (58–59). Man would rather endure toil, strife, and death than give up his reason.

Kant then expiates at some length on the evils that history as the story of reason's liberation from nature brings in its wake. But what counts, he tells us, in concluding his "conjecture" on the beginning of human history, is that, because man knows that he could not remain in, let alone return to, the original state of nature, "he must . . . ascribe his present troublesome condition to himself and to his own choice." He must neither "blame the evils which oppress him on Providence, nor attribute his own offense to an original sin committed by his first parents" since "free actions" are not "hereditary. . . . Such an exposition teaches man that, under like circumstances, he would act exactly like his first parents, that is, abuse reason in the very first use of reason. . . . Hence he must recognize what they have done as his own act and thus blame only himself for the evils which spring from the abuse of reason." Such, "then," Kant writes, in concluding his essay on the conjectural beginning of history,

> is the lesson taught by a philosophical attempt to write the most ancient part of human history: contentment with Providence and with the course of human affairs, considered as a whole. For this course is not a decline from good to evil, but rather a

gradual development from the worse to the better; and nature itself has given the vocation to everyone to contribute as much to this progress as may be within his power. (68)

Sin, we see, is original, to recall the orthodox Christian formulation. Sin begins first with our original forebears. But the concept here of an original or first beginning is not natural in the sense of things happening one after another in a temporal sequence. Rather, original or first characterizes that which begins from itself alone or, in other words, is an end in itself alone. Every human being, like original man and woman, is original. We repeat the actions of our forebears in beginning our life, historically, from the beginning. In the words of Marx, we are not only the products but also the producers of history. Yes, what we are, in the beginning, in terms of our natural endowments of mind and body, of gender, race, class, caste, etc., are crucial (they are the cross that we bear in life, its crux). But what we make of our natural endowments— the reason for our life that we find in and through them—this is what constitutes our history. To paraphrase Jesus: what counts, that for which we can account solely in rational, i.e., moral terms, is the recognition that, while we live in our body, in the state of nature, we do not live by the body but rather by our mind (spirit, will). To will the good is to make proper use of the body, of nature, in the spirit of love.

I want to point out here, if only briefly, that Kant in "Conjectural Beginning" adheres to the distinction that Kierkegaard will later make between Christianity, as true to the Bible, and Christendom, as baptized paganism, as the rationalization of pagan values in Christian terms. The most famous, indeed, the truly infamous example of the reduction of biblical to pagan values is to found in the treatment of the story of Adam and Eve over the centuries by Christian authors. Sin was typically associated with our sensuous nature (with what Kant in formal terms calls our sensible inclinations) and, in particular, with our sexuality, and thus, specifically, with woman (as the seducer of the innocent Adam). The mind (of Adam) was pure (without sin). The body (of Eve) was impure (and so the very origin, the principle of sin). Human beings are sinful because they have a body. The hierarchical subordination of the senses (sex, woman) to the mind (reason, man) has its origins, both ontological and historical, in the Neo-Platonic distinction between body and mind, matter and form, as originally formulated by Plato and Aristotle. (Still, it is important to remember that Christian commentators, when elaborating the Genesis story, inserted within it the story of the heavenly angels who, as immortal and supernatural, lacked a natural body. Still, some of these heavenly angels did sin—Satan and his evil crew. But this was simply another, in this case, perverse, "conjecture" conjured up to explain the beginning, the origin, of evil!)[70] Kant absolutely rejects, in refuting, any idea that sin or evil begins in nature. Sin is not a natural inheritance, for it is originally inherent, from the beginning unto the end, in our reason, in the practical relations, the social relationships that we constitute with our fellow human beings when and as we do not treat them, one and all, as truly and equally our brothers and sisters—as our neighbors; as ends in themselves; as persons to be respected and not as things to be used (and abused): in sum, when we do not treat others as we want to be treated by others.

What is particularly arresting, then, about "Conjectural Beginning of Human History" is that in his essay Kant makes it clear that the conjecture with which we have to begin—as our categorical imperative, as it were—is "the existence of man" (but also, it is surely evident, the existence of God, although it is true that Kant never directly refers to God in his essay). Human existence is conjectural. It is our best guess, our best bet, that on which we must wager in playing the game of life, as Pascal tells us in his *Pensées*. We do not choose either to play or not to play the game of life. For when we awaken with Adam and Eve from living in the dream world of natural paradise, we find that, like God, we are at the gaming table of life where we have already placed our wager on existence, whose consequences then lie ahead of us as our history, at once individual and social (universal). It is, consequently, daunting to learn, both humbling and exalting, that reason is always conjectural. This does not mean that reason lacks certitude (it is not simply relativity, indifference, probability, possibility . . .). But it does mean that reason is not certain as the facts of nature are certain. There is no immediate touchstone of reality. For what we actually are we must yet will (in the future) to become. It is only in becoming what we are that we are what we become. The more conventional concept for conjecture is faith, which is so easily confused with, in being reduced to, blind faith, just as we so often in our life make foolish or even bad guesses or conjectures (as mere illusions or pretentions). To have faith in life is to find reason in life and life in reason. We do not know our future, just as we do not know our past—as an object appearing naturally in nature. History is the story of—conjectural and subjective—reason (of faith, hope and love), not the story of—certifiable and objective—knowledge (as verified scientifically). Indeed, the ultimate paradox of the entire Kantian critique, as we shall continue to see, is that scientific knowledge rests on conjectural reason. Nature, as we have found in Wordsworth, comes into existence for us only in and through the reason of imagination.

But at this point in my study I want to emphasize how critically important it is for us to grasp the significance of how and why Kant locates the beginning of human existence as historical, rational, moral, free, social... in biblical story, consistent with Kierkegaard's observation that all writing (scripture) about the spirit, including Holy Scripture (the *logos* of God), is metaphoric (poetic, conjectural). The story of original man and woman is mere conjecture. Yet it reveals the truth of reason as created from nothing—from nothing that is natural (or objectively certain). But it equally follows, then, that religion and faith (together with the doctrines regarding God, grace, miracles, etc.) and so, too, Christianity itself are mere conjectures. For, as the Christian story as related in Christendom shows, reliance on the Bible as containing and conveying the truth of human being as the work of God has resulted more often than not in idols of false belief and superstition than in metaphors of rational belief and loving practice. But Kant sticks to his guns. He does not deviate from his perseverance in demonstrating that the existence of man can be understood only practically, rationally, morally, and freely when shown to be consistent with biblical conjecture and so neither scientifically, on the basis of nature, nor metaphysically, on the basis of Greek philosophy. But he knows, in facing, the risks that so very easily does theological conjecture regarding the mind (soul), freedom (free will), and God become what he calls transcendental illusion (or dialectic) in the *Critique of Pure Reason*. But we have no choice: I exist, *ergo* I think. It is little wonder, then, that Kant finds himself called to demonstrate, as we shall now see, that religion is only to be understood (as conjecture) within the bonds (limits) of mere reason. But the irony, the paradox, here, as surely is evident to the reader, is that Kant no less demonstrates (although never explicitly as such) that reason (as mere conjecture) is to be understood solely within the bonds (limits) of pure religion. Where there is false religion, there is false reason. But it is no less true that where there is false reason there is false religion.

In now taking up Kant's two major works on religion, *The Conflict of the Faculties*, Part 1: "The Conflict of the Philosophy Faculty with the Theology Faculty," and *Religion within the Boundaries of Mere Reason*,[71] I shall make no attempt to treat either work in exhaustive detail or even to provide a detailed summary of their content. My aim, simply, is to bring to light the significance of Kant's demonstration that to "think" or to will our existence as the good is to live by and through the values (principles) that are "originally" biblical, both ontologically and historically. We shall see, then, that Kant is especially committed to spelling out the criteria that guide (direct) biblical exegesis, that is, to enunciating the principles of interpretation that are true to (in being properly founded on) the biblical word. Since all language of the spirit, including the Word of God, is metaphor, the world is rife with false images, with illusory idols. Indeed, we shall see that interpretation is but another term for conjecture. I exist, *ergo* I interpret. I am faced, always, with thinking through, with interpreting what it means to exist. Indeed, what is the meaning of existence? How do I make existence—my existence and the existence of others—meaningful? All life is interpretation, but this does not mean that all interpretations are equal (or merely relative or probable). There are good (adequate) and bad (inadequate) interpretations, to recall Spinoza's dictum that truth is its own standard, the standard both of the true and of the false. For there is only one thing good in the world, or even outside of the world, and that is the will. We can equally say that there are good and there are bad conjectures, not relatively but absolutely. But yes, our conjectures, our interpretations are always yet to be perfected, to be expanded, to be amplified, to be made more inclusive. Yet, we must also remember that inclusivity always involves sacrifice in maintaining the absolute difference between good and evil, between loving your neighbor and doing harm to your neighbor (including yourself), between what Kant calls character (quality of spirit as the effect of will) and external attributes (whose quantity results from natural fortune).

I shall begin with Kant's essay on the conflict of the philosophical with the theological faculty (written in 1794 and published in 1798 along with the two additional essays on the conflict of the Faculty of Philosophy with the Faculties of Law and Medicine). I shall not be concerned here with examining, as such, Kant's response to the Prussian government's censorship policies. All that needs to be said is that Kant at all times defended, courageously and incisively, the free expression of thought in the public domain as the very embodiment of the moral law, of the critique of pure reason as practice. What makes his essay on the conflict between philosophers and theologians important for us is that, in setting forth what he calls the "philosophical principles of scriptural exegesis for settling the conflict," Kant continues to articulate his concept of reason as the very embodiment of the universally moral law—of treating all human beings as ends in themselves. He thus writes that if there are passages in Scripture that contain certain theoretical (supernatural) teachings that transcend rational and even moral concepts, they "*may* be interpreted in the interests of practical reason." But if there are scriptural passages that "contradict practical reason, . . . [they] *must* be interpreted in the interests of practical reason. . . . The only thing that matters in religion is *deeds*, and this final aim and, accordingly, a meaning appropriate to it, must be attributed to every biblical dogma. . . . Action must be represented as issuing from the human being's own use of his moral powers, not as an effect [resulting] from the influence of an external, higher [supernatural] cause" (264–67).

Kant writes further that "we must regard the credentials of the Bible as drawn from the pure spring of universal rational religion dwelling in every ordinary human being; and it is this very simplicity that accounts for the Bible's extremely widespread and powerful influence on the hearts of the people. . . . [T]he Bible was the vehicle of religion" (284). It thus follows, Kant states, that only "a moral interpretation [of Scripture] . . . is really an *authentic* one—that is, one given by the God within us; for, since we cannot understand anyone unless he speaks to us through our own . . . reason,"[72] it is only by concepts of *our* reason, insofar as they are pure moral concepts and hence infallible, that we can recognize the divinity of a teaching promulgated to us" (271–72). He repeats this claim in the following dramatic terms: "The God who speaks through our own (morally practical) reason is an infallible interpreter of His words in the Scripture, whom everyone can understand. And it is quite impossible for there to be any other accredited interpreter of his words (one, for example, who would interpret them in a historical way); for religion is a purely rational affair" (286–87). This is why, Kant points out, that, whatever historical inconsistencies are to be found in the Bible, the "*divinity* of its moral content adequately compensates reason for the *humanity* of its historical narrative which, like an old parchment that is illegible in places, has to be made intelligible by adjustments and conjectures [i.e., interpretations] consistent with the whole. And the divinity of its moral content justifies this statement: that the Bible deserves to be kept, put to moral use, and assigned to religion as its guide *just as if it is a divine revelation*" (284–85).

This is a rich brew of densely compacted ideas, which we shall find ourselves continuously having to confront and to unpack as we proceed.

Most striking, I believe, is the idea (the metaphor!) that "the pure spring of universal rational religion" is to be found infallibly in the heart and reason of "every ordinary human being" as "given by the God within us," when viewed in combination with the idea of reason as that in and through which all speech, or communication, takes place. Religion is universally, naturally, rationally, infallibly, divinely, and morally possessed, i.e., known, by all ordinary human beings, as given by the God within them or, indeed, as their very reason (heart, mind, spirit). Such, too, is the mind, the spirit, that we must bring to the Bible in order to understand and so to live by its moral dictate: go and do likewise. Do unto others what you want others to do unto you. How you reason—how you speak, act, and think—is how you are to be reasoned with. As you adjudge the rationality—the speech, action, and thought—of others, so, too, will you be judged. As you interpret others so you, too, will be interpreted. Interpretation is, we may say, recalling Spinoza, its own infallible standard, the standard both of true interpretation and of false interpretation. But my reader doubtlessly recalls that what here Kant calls universal, rational, moral, and infallible he calls conjectural in his essay on the story of Adam and Eve as embodying the beginning of human history.

Additionally, we marvel: why the Bible? In the first instance, the answer to this question is easy. Kant is profoundly aware that how you interpret, how you think about the Bible—within Christendom—is how you think about existence, in all of its infinite manifestations, both physical and spiritual. He defends the right of philosophers to interpret the Bible, over the protests of theologians as members of the "higher" university faculty that the Bible is their own exclusive domain, in claiming that the Bible was merely "the vehicle of religion" for the morally divine law that is found universally dwelling in the minds and hearts of all—ordinary—human beings. The Bible is to be interpreted from reason alone. It's as if Kant (always polite, always polished, always collected) is (resolutely) saying to the theologians, on behalf of all ordinary human beings who constitute the "public" domain of truth: I merely show, as a philosopher, that the Bible contains the truth universally known by all. The moral law leads to, i.e., precedes the Bible. The Bible does not lead to, or precede, the moral law. It is not, then, a big step that Benjamin Jowett took when, in 1860, he proclaimed that the Bible was to be interpreted like any other text.[73]

Still, the Bible is the sole text in which Kant found the true—conjectural and metaphorical—story of the beginning of human history as universally true for all human beings. Additionally, while Kant never tires of affirming the universality of what he calls "the reason of religion," he never once directly ascribes it to the philosophy of the ancients or, more broadly, to paganism. Thus, he writes in *Conflict* that the "tenets of faith," when "conceived as divine commands," are to be understood either as statuary doctrines, which are imposed on us (from outside by the "church" to which we belong as private members), or as moral doctrines, which are willed by us (from inside us as publically true for all citizens). We possess, then, what Kant calls a "touchstone" of interpretation: "to the extent that any dogma gives out merely statutory teachings of faith [regarding both ritual and belief] as essential religious teachings, it contains a certain *admixture of* paganism; for paganism consists in passing off the externals (non-essentials) of religion as essential" (273).[74] This is what we shall see Kant elsewhere call idolatry.

In the second, instance, however, it is not so evident why for Kant the Bible takes precedence, apparently, over all other texts, if not over the Word of God as universally written in the hearts of all human beings. If the moral law of practical reason is universal, why was it not known by (or revealed to) those peoples whom we have seen Kant call pagans, including the ancient philosophers? It is striking that Kant never raises this question, even though what he constantly (if not self-consciously) demonstrates in his work is that not only was (and is) the Bible first, both morally (ontologically) and historically, but also that there were times prior (historically) to the Bible in which it, together with its moral law, was unknown. Kant is clearly aware that the idea of moral development or progress (the growth of our mind) is historical: it involves time. But he does not explicitly recognize that history, as the story of freedom (moral development), is conjecture (which is infallible!): the recognition (the wager) on the part of human beings that their will is the sole good in and even outside the world, with the result that they are eternally faced with the task of becoming historically who they are ontologically.

Still, Kant does acknowledge that "there is something in us that we cannot cease to wonder at when we have once seen it." Indeed, it is "the same thing that raises *humanity* in its idea to a dignity we should never have suspected in the human being as an object of experience" and, we can add, that nobody outside of the Bible ever suspected or wondered at. It is not, he continues, that we wonder why we are "subject to moral laws and destined by our reason to obey them . . . ; for obedience to the moral laws lies objectively in the natural order of things as the object of pure reason, and it never occurs to ordinary, sound understanding to ask where these laws come from." But what "we do wonder at [is] our *ability* so to sacrifice our sensuous nature [our self-love or self-interest] to morality that we *can* do what we quite readily and clearly conceive we *ought* to do. This ascendancy of the *supersensible* human being in us over the *sensible*, such that (when it comes to a conflict between them) the sensible is *nothing*, though in its own eyes it is everything, is an object of the greatest *wonder*; and our wonder at this moral predisposition in us, inseparable from our humanity, only increases the longer we contemplate this true (not fabricated [yet metaphoric]) ideal." Kant proceeds to acknowledge that, since "the *supersensible* [what he calls the "transcendental" in the *Critique of Pure Reason*] in us in inconceivable [as an object of possible experience] and yet practical," we can well understand how easily the "supersensible" (as practical reason) is confused with the *supernatural*. But to hold that there is a "higher spirit, something not within our power and not belonging to us as our own," which causes us to act is to deny that the deed and the power are our own. The Bible, too, Kant writes, is concerned, not with "supernatural experiences and fantastic feelings which should take reason's place in bringing about this [wondrous] revolution" in becoming the "new man" in and from the beginning, but with "the spirit of Christ, which he manifested in teachings and examples so that we might make it our own—or rather, since it is already present in us by our moral predisposition, so that we might simply make room for it." The Bible, then, is concerned neither with "orthodoxy which has no soul" nor with "mysticism which kills reason" but with "teaching . . . a faith which our reason can develop out of itself. This teaching is the true religious doctrine based on the *criticism* of practical reason, that works with divine power on the hearts of all human beings toward their fundamental improvement and unites them in one universal (though invisible) church" (280). Kant's other term for the one, true, universal but invisible church is the kingdom of ends.

Once again we are brought face to face with the issue of how we are to understand the metaphysics not only of morality but also of history, the wonder (or miracle), we may say, that the morality of history is the history of morality. If we are properly to distinguish the "supersensible" (as the practical power that exists solely in and through the good of our own will) from the "supernatural" (as the end or *telos* that moves us and is not moved by us), then it follows, as Kant shows us, that *ought* wondrously (miraculously) entails *can* (capacity, *potentia*/power, ability, desire). I can will (I have the power) to do what I ought to do, as commanded to me by God, by my neighbor, by the Charter of Rights and Freedoms (in Canada), by the police in a democracy . . . because I judge the command to be right and so my duty to fulfill. Although, Kant observes, Jesus is known historically to have taught that the divine law of Scripture is contained in the command to love God above all others and your neighbor as yourself, what makes the command true (just) is not because Jesus said it. We have to find that he speaks to us through our reason (as persons who know in their hearts that to command others is to will to be commanded by others). We have to prove the truth of his saying—in our actions. But then the wonder of the teaching of Jesus (as it was increasingly spread abroad by his disciples, together with Paul) was that it was judged to be true by—that it was proved to be true in the lives of—not only (some but not most) Jews but also (many, yet, in fact, relatively few) Gentiles. So it is that Kant points out how easy it is to confuse the supersensible (as the self-imposed power of our will) with the supernatural (as the superimposed power of another will). In other words, history, as descriptive (empirical) fact, does not establish moral right, or, again, in the words of Rousseau: we argue not from fact to right but from right to fact. Still, as I have indicated before, what is lacking in Kant is an explicit understanding of action (human deeds) as historical and of history as the story of human actions, as the story of our liberation. . . . For history as the growth of our mind is the method of proving the truth of the commands that we receive.

I also want to point out that there is yet an additional item in the above passage on the true source of wonder that it is important for us to consider, that involving, yet again, the duplex sense in which Kant uses the term "nature" and thus what he means by the terms objective (object) and subjective (subject). He writes in that passage, as we saw, that "obedience to the moral laws lies objectively in the natural order of things as the object of pure reason." Here, "the natural order of things," when understood as "the object of pure reason," refers to the supersensible (transcendental) realm of the moral law, not to the sensible realm of the natural objects of possible appearance. The "object of pure reason," then, is to be understood in the sense of the aim, purpose, goal, or end of our life, as is evident if we ask someone: What is the object of your life? What is it that you intend (will) to concentrate on as central to fulfilling your life's objectives? Strangely, then, "objective" signifies the truth of our subjectivity (of our lives as subjects in which we are "subject" to the moral law), while "subjective" indicates that we have falsely turned our life into one in which we are guided solely by our (sensible) inclinations (feelings) or mere opinions, i.e., by the mere objects of sensuous desire.

We turn, now, to Kant's *Religion within the Boundaries of Mere Reason* (1793).[75] While a much grander work than the essay on the *Conflict* of the university faculties, it adds nothing fundamentally new to what we have learned from the smaller work on the relationship of philosophy (reason) and religion (revelation), together with what is called there the moral obligation of interpreting the Bible according to the principles of pure reason. Still, Kant, in elaborating in *Religion* how and in what sense religion is bound by "mere reason," truly enlarges our understanding of the issues that the relationship between reason and religion fundamentally involves. At the same time, however, as he continues to demonstrate why, in his view, it is so critically important to distinguish between rational (moral) religion and historical (dogmatic) religion, between what he calls "the philosophical doctrine of religion" and "learned religion," he provides us, yet again, with additional insight into how and why his work could equally be entitled "Reason within the Bounds of Pure Religion." The issue, here, as I indicated above, is that involving the relationship between the universality and the historicity of the moral law. As before, I shall make no attempt here to explore, or even to summarize in detail, the rich content of *Religion*. Rather, I shall concentrate on those passages of the work in which Kant truly allows us to enlarge our understanding of what he calls "the religion of reason."

But I do think readers will find it helpful to have before them an outline of the work. *Religion* contains, in addition to the prefaces of each of two major editions of the book (1793 and 1794), four parts, each of which is followed by a "Remark." It is also worth noting that each of the four parts bears the title "The Philosophical Doctrine of Religion."

> Preface to the First Edition (1793)
> Preface to the Second Edition (1794)
> Part 1: Concerning the Indwelling of the Evil Principle alongside the Good or Of the Radical Evil in Human Nature
>   General Remark: Effects of Grace
> Part 2: Concerning the Battle of the Good against the Evil Principle for Dominion over the Human Being
>   General Remark: Miracles

Part 3: The Victory of the Good Principle over the Evil Principle; and the Founding of a Kingdom of God on Earth
   General Remark: Mysteries
Part 4: Concerning Service and Counterfeit Service under the Dominion of the Good Principle, or, Of Religion and Priestcraft
   General Remark: Means of Grace

    Kant initiates the Preface to the first edition of *Religion within the Boundaries of Mere Reason* with the observation that, since morality is "based on the conception of the human being" as one who freely "binds himself through his reason to unconditional laws," it is evident that human beings depend solely on themselves, and not on a higher being above them, in recognizing their duty. Because "the free power of choice" is it own self-"determining ground," we see that "morality really has no need of an end for right conduct.... Yet an end proceeds from morality just the same ... [to] the idea of a highest good in the world, for whose possibility we must assume a higher, moral, most holy, and omnipotent being who alone can unite the two elements of this good": right conduct and happiness. Still, what counts, Kant emphasizes, "is that this idea rises out of morality and is not its foundation; that it is an end which to make one's own already presupposes ethical principles.... Morality thus inevitably leads to religion, and through religion it extends itself to the idea of a mighty moral lawgiver outside the human being, in whose will the final end (of the creation of the world) is what can and at the same time ought to be the final human end" (57–60). In summarizing, then, the spirit of his conception of religion as freely bound to the dictates of mere reason, Kant concludes *Religion* in writing that what he has shown in his work "proves that the right way to advance is not from grace to virtue but rather from virtue to grace" (215).

    In the Preface to the second edition of *Religion* Kant follows up on his argument in the first Preface that it is reason that leads to religion (as rational), and not religion to reason (as religious). He points that, while "*revelation* can at least comprise also the pure *religion of reason*," it is not the case that the pure religion of reason can "do the same for what is historical in revelation." He illustrates the relationship between revealed (historical) religion and rational (moral) religion with the image of two concentric circles. The "wider sphere of faith ... includes the other, a *narrower* one, within itself (not as two circles external to one another)." With reason thus constituting the inner core of religion, it follows, Kant observes, then we can "say that between reason and Scripture there is, not only compatibility but also unity, so that whoever follows the one (under the guidance of moral concepts) will not fail to come across the other as well" (64). In simple terms, while the religion of reason can do without revealed or historical religion, still, it can find itself enriched and amplified in and through all true religion. If revealed or historical religion, however, attempts to get along without reason (the moral law), then it will simply become superstition as based on self-deluding miracles and mysteries.

Kant devotes a significant portion of *Religion* to a discussion of the claim central to Christendom that man is sinful from birth, that the sin of man is original. In other words, because human beings are evil by nature, they are subject to radical evil (they are "rooted" in evil, they are evil at root). Kant's analysis of evil and its relationship to good is at once sophisticated and searching. But I shall make no attempt to examine here the details of that analysis. Rather, I shall concentrate our attention on the essential elements of what it is, according to Kant, that constitutes the "nature" of man as a moral being in possession of practical reason, consistent with what we have already learned from the *Critique of the Faculties*. He emphasizes two points. First, "the ground of this evil cannot be placed, as is commonly done, in the sensuous nature of the human being and in the natural inclinations originating from it" (81). We are not, as such, responsible for the existence of our sensuous being, for, "as connatural to us, natural inclinations do not have us for their author." We could say that, while our bodily nature is given to us, how we look upon it as our gift—well, that is where evil enters in.

Second, Kant also points out that the ground of evil "cannot "be placed in a *corruption* of the morally legislative reason, as if reason could extirpate within itself the dignity of the law itself, for this is absolutely impossible" (82). In simple terms, we are not free to be unfree. We are not free to renounce (alienate) our freedom. We may well act in a slavish and not in a free way. But we can only know this on the basis of freedom. This argument is but another version of the ontological argument (although Kant does not acknowledge this). I may doubt (deny) that I am a thinking being, but, in doing so, I affirm myself as a freely thinking person. Kant adds that we also must not view good and evil as merely relative to each other, as if we were at once both morally good and morally evil. Evil results, rather, from their reversal, in subordinating, we can say, love of neighbor to self-love, in treating others as means (objects/things) and not as ends (persons) in themselves. Kant later observes in *Religion* that it "is a peculiarity of Christian morality to represent the moral good as differing from the moral evil, not as heaven from *earth*, but as heaven from *hell*." He adds that, while this "figurative representation" is "stirring," it is "not any the less philosophically correct in meaning. For it serves to prevent us from thinking of good and evil, the realm of light and the realm of darkness, as bordering on each other and losing themselves into one another by gradual steps (of greater and lesser brightness); but rather to represent them as separated by an immeasurable gap." Because "this form of representation" (i.e., metaphor, in the terms of my study) depicts the "total dissimilarity of the basic principles" and so dispels the illusion that the two realms border on each other, it is, Kant avers, "though containing an element of horror, . . . nonetheless sublime" (103).

In his discussion of radical evil Kant points out that, when we say that a human being is by nature good or evil or that good and evil are innate, this "only means that he holds within himself a first ground (to us inscrutable) for the adoption of good or evil (unlawful) maxims and that he holds this ground *qua* human, universally," i.e., as true for all human beings. Because "the first ground of the adoption of our maxims . . . lie[s] in the free power of choice" and cannot be given to us in experience, it "is thus represented [metaphorically] as present in the human being at the moment of birth—not that birth itself is its cause" (71). This birth, which is not natural but represents, we may say, the transition from the sensuous to the spiritual, has traditionally in Christendom been called the second birth of the new man (as represented in baptism—of the spirit). It is important always to keep in mind, as Kant tirelessly repeats that our birth into the free human being of spirit is inscrutable, unknown, and so not derivable from experience, that what he means is that human nature (as the thing in itself) is not the effect of prior natural causes. Human beings are subjects, not objects. They are their own ground of morality, of the moral law. They are the cause of themselves. In the beginning, from the beginning, Kant writes, God "created human beings for freedom" (205). As we saw in "Conjectural Beginning of Human History," once Adam and Eve are reborn as created in the image of God in knowing good and evil, the life before them is a trial: how they are to make use of their good will in building the kingdom of ends while being eternally tempted by the infinite plenitude of objects that the world before them has to offer. The paradox, as always, is, as Kant makes clear, that, while evil does not have its ground (cause) in the world of nature (in our earthly life), still, if we were not natural, embodied beings, there would be no evil. Our unending task is, in living on the earth, not to live by the earth but by the moral law (of the city of God).

Another way of putting this paradox is that, if we were not temporal beings (in being subject to time), we would not be evil. Still, as Kant points out, the cause of evil is not temporal. We have, he reminds us, two different ideas of origin (beginning): "*origin according to reason*, or *origin according to time*" (85). This is the distinction that he famously characterizes, as we shall see in the next chapter, as the difference between nature (cause through another) and freedom (cause through itself: it begins from itself alone, originally . . .). The cause that is according to reason or freedom is equally the cause that is according to history, although, as I continue emphasize, Kant does not systematically distinguish between natural time and historical time, with the second involving progress, development, and thus the growth of the human mind. Strange as it may appear, freedom is at one and the same time the cause of evil and the cause of good. Indeed, Kant writes, we must view our evil action, when we seek its "rational origin, as if the human being had fallen into it directly from the state of innocence." Whatever the "natural causes," whether interior or exterior, that were influencing him, "his action is yet free and not determined through any of these causes; hence the action can and must always be judged as an *original* exercise of his power of choice." He should have withstood them "whatever his temporal circumstances and entanglements; for through no cause in the world can he cease to be a free agent. . . . Hence we cannot inquire into the origin in time" of human deeds but must seek their "origin in reason" (86–87).

Thus it is, Kant continues, that the Bible represents "the origin of evil" as having its beginning, not in a fundamental propensity to it, for otherwise its beginning would not result from freedom, but in "sin (by which is understood the transgression of the moral law as *divine command*)" (87). Still, the "rational origin . . . of . . . this propensity to evil . . . remains inexplicable to us. . . . Evil can have originated only from moral evil (not just from the limitations of our nature). . . . The Scriptures express this incomprehensibility in a historical narrative" by locating it "in a *spirit* of an originally more sublime destiny [i.e., the angelic Satan]. The absolutely *first* beginning of all evil is thereby represented as incomprehensible to us (for whence the evil in that spirit?); the human being, however, is represented as having lapsed into it only *through temptation*, hence not as corrupted *fundamentally* (in his very first predisposition to the good) but, on the contrary, as still capable of improvement. . . . And so for the human being, who despite a corrupted heart yet always possesses a good will, there still remains hope of a return to the good from which he has strayed." Kant adds in a note that what he has written here is not to "be regarded as though intended for Scriptural exegesis, which lies outside the boundaries of the competence of mere reason. We can explain how we put a historical account to our moral use without thereby deciding whether this is also the meaning of the writer or only our interpretation." What counts, he declares, is whether "this meaning is true in itself, apart from all historical proof," and also whether it is the only meaning that is "edifying" (upbuilding) in contributing "to our becoming a better human being" (89).

Kant continues his discussion of how it is that we are good yet originally evil with the observation that the "human being must make or have made *himself* into whatever he is or should become in a moral sense, good or evil." It is only thus that good and evil are "the effect of his free power of choice, for otherwise they could not be imputed to him, and, consequently, he could be neither morally good nor evil." The very idea that human beings are "created good" can only mean that they have been "created for the good and that their "original predisposition ... is good." Human beings are "not thereby good as such," for their good depends on whether they become (historically) either good or evil as based on the choices that they freely make. Kant grants "that some supernatural cooperation is also needed" for us to become good or better"—but only so long as we make ourselves "antecedently worthy of receiving it." For we must "*accept* this help." He asks yet again: "How it is possible that a naturally evil human being should make himself into a good human being surpasses every concept of ours. For how can an evil tree bear good fruit?" Still, just as the tree was originally good and just as the fall from good into evil shows us "that evil originates from freedom, ... the command that we *ought* to become better human beings still resounds unabated in our souls; consequently, we must also be capable of it," even if that means that "we only make ourselves receptive to a higher assistance inscrutable to us." But what "we must presuppose in all this," Kant explains further, "is that there is still a germ of goodness left in its entire purity [in us], a germ that cannot be extirpated or corrupted." We see, consequently, that the "restoration of the original predisposition to good in us is not therefore the acquisition of a *lost* incentive for the good." We are not able to lose "the respect for the moral law," for, if we ever did lose it, we would never regain it. "The restoration is therefore only the recovery of the *purity* of the law as the supreme ground of all our maxims.... The original good is holiness of maxims in the compliance to one's duty." Still, since there always remains a wide gap "between maxim and deed," the human being who wills to do his duty is, while not holy, yet set "upon the road of endless progress towards holiness" (89–91).

Kant proceeds, then, to distinguish between a revolution in and a reform of moral attitudes. A revolution, he writes, involves "a transition to the maxim of holiness of disposition" and so what in Christendom is called the rebirth of a new man, a new creation, and a change of heart.[76] A reform involves (what we can call) our obligation to become what we originally are: the true image of God on earth. Kant writes:

> If by a single and unalterable decision a human being reverses the supreme ground of his maxims by which he was an evil human being (and thereby puts on a "new man"), he is to this extent, by principle and attitude of mind, a subject receptive to the good; but he is a good human being only in incessant laboring and becoming; i.e., he can hope—in view of the purity of the principle which he has adopted as the supreme maxim of his power of choice ... —to find himself upon the good (though narrow) path of constant *progress* from bad to better. (92)

In light of what Kant writes here we may say that his "conjectural" account of the story of Adam and Eve, as representing the beginning (the origin, the principle) of history, shows us that history is at once creational and covenantal, to recall the two concepts on which, in my view, the Bible is fundamentally grounded. Creation is that revolution in world history whereby human beings are primordially and originally grounded, not in natural time and space but in covenantal history as resulting from their action to make real the good that can only be realized in overcoming the evil in which they have fallen. But the covenant, both the covenant that God makes with his holy people, in their recognition of the Lord God as their good shepherd, and the social contract that human beings make in willing to bring into historical existence the kingdom of ends, is itself at once original revolution and eternal reform. The passage from the state of nature, in which good and evil are unknown, to the civil state of covenantal existence is revolutionary. Because the transition from sensate nature to spirit as the metaphor of existence is from nothing, from nothing that is not covenantal, it is, as Kant continues to show us, inexplicable by and unknown to us—on the basis of natural causation. We only know this transition as our "conjecture" whose proof is our inalienable obligation to do the good. We are now subjects whose future, as spirit, is to make historically better our original good as we confront and so are inspirited to overcome the evil that we have brought into the world in departing from the state of nature. Historical time, as distinct from natural time, involves progress and so also eternal reform, but also, frequently, regression. But we can never relinquish our revolutionary beginning, just as we can never go beyond our original good, love of God and neighbor. Still, we can make our original good actual only in and through history. History, we see, is the very embodiment of, at once, creation and covenant.

As we have noted, Kant sharply distinguishes between, on the one hand, the religion of reason as universal, public, and known to and by all people and, on the other hand, revealed religion as historical, contingent, private, and known only to a special few (priests, monks, scriptural scholars). Thus, he denies that rational faith, as publically communicated and so subject to public scrutiny and criticism, can be based on mysteries and miracles, to the attestation of whose truth only a few privately bear witness. At the same time, however, he does call upon "revelation" and even refers to "history" in his unceasing effort to account for the inexplicable beginning that, as I indicated in the previous paragraph, embodies the transition from nature to spirit as constituted by the covenantal creation of human beings.

I shall, consequently, consider key passages in which Kant reveals to us (*sic!*)—not altogether self-consciously, yet again—that the concept of revelation is rooted in the concepts of creation and covenant and also of history. Thus, he writes, consistent with the above passage in which we saw him examine the revolution in human consciousness that resulted in a decisive reversal of history from nature to spirit:

> The basis for the transition to the new order of things must lie in the principle of the pure religion of reason, as a revelation (though not an empirical one) permanently taking place within all human beings, and this basis, once grasped after mature reflection [we remember that Adam and Eve "began" their lives as mature adults] will be carried to effect, inasmuch as it is to be a human work, through gradual reform. (152)

Kant also states that the "one and true religion contains nothing but laws, i.e., practical principles [principles to be put into practice], of whose unconditional necessity we can become conscious and which we therefore recognize as revealed through pure reason (not empirically)" (188). It is salient to remember that, in common parlance, when I say (to myself or to someone else)—"It was revealed to me that . . ."—I mean, simply: "I have suddenly become conscious of," unexpectedly, without, apparently, any rhyme or reason. But of course it is my responsibility to test my "revelation." Is it real insight (in making connections that I had not seen before), or is it mere day-dreaming or perhaps even illusory wish-fulfillment? The paradox of revelation, as of truth, generally, is that I can have revealed to me solely what I already know, in principle, but which, as Kant would say, I have constantly to put self-consciously into practice. The truth of the mysterious atom is not going to be revealed to me, as a scientist, without untoward previous study and labor on my part.

In bringing revelation together with the self-consciousness that is involved in our recognition of the truth (of, say, Scripture)—for us—Kant thus continues to stress that all judgment, all proof, all demonstration originates in practical reason: how do I act upon what I know? As we now take up the third and final passage on the revelation of reason as the reason of revelation, we shall see that in it Kant shows that history is also to be viewed as rational and practical and not as theoretical or hypothetical. It is a complex passage in and through the very density of which Kant lucidly embodies the distinctions that he shows to be the critical task that practical reason must ever undertake to make. It is in the context of discussing what he calls the supernatural "mysteries" of revealed religion that Kant in this passage calls upon revelation and also at the same time invokes the idea of history. When we consider these mysteries, in "so far as they touch upon the moral life-history of every human being," Kant writes, we must ask the following three questions:

1. Why do moral good and evil exist in the world?
2. How is it that, if evil is found in every human being at all times, "good will still originates from it and is restored in a human being"? and
3. Why does this happen in some people and not in others?

And what we find, he continues, is that "regarding this God has revealed nothing to us, nor can he reveal anything, for we would not *understand* it." Indeed, Kant further observes that "we can with right require of every mystery proposed for belief that we *understand* what is meant by it." It is evident that here "understand" signifies "meaning" in the sense of when we ask? What does it mean to me? How am I duty-bound to make it meaningful in my practice (in my thought, speech, and deeds)? Understanding here does not signify *Verstand* when, as merely speculative, theoretical, and hypothetical, it is distinguished from reason (*Vernunft*). Thus it is, Kant observes yet further, that "we understand perfectly well what freedom is"—in a practical context that involves our duty. "However, for theoretical purposes, as regards the causality of freedom (and equally its nature), we cannot even formulate without contradiction the wish to understand it" (169).[77]

Kant points out yet further what would happen if we failed to distinguish between practical (rational) understanding and theoretical (empirical) understanding, between meaning and mystery:

> It would be as if from the human being, through his freedom, we wanted to *explain* and *make comprehensible* to us what happens; regarding this God has indeed revealed his will through the moral law in us but has left the *causes* whereby a free action occurs or does not occur on earth in the same obscurity in which everything must remain for human investigation; all this ought to be conceived, as history, according to the law of cause and effect yet also from freedom. Regarding the objective rule of our conduct, however, all that we need is sufficiently revealed (through reason and Scripture), and this revelation is equally understandable to every human being. (169)

It is critically important to consider with care what Kant means here when he writes that it is history that we properly conceive or understand "according to the law of cause and effect yet also from freedom" and so as what it is that is "sufficiently revealed" to every human being through both reason and Scripture. But, first, we must see this dense passage through to its end. Kant proceeds to tell us

> "that the human being is called to a good life conduct through the moral law;
> "that, through an indelible [i.e., scripturally ineradicable] respect for the law which lies in him, he also finds in himself encouragement to trust in this good spirit and to hope that . . . he will be able to satisfy this spirit; [and] finally
> "that, comparing this expectation with the rigorous command of the law, he must constantly test himself as if summoned to accounts before a judge."

It is evident, consequently, Kant concludes, that "reason, heart, and conscience all teach this and drive us to it. It is thus presumptuous to require that more be made manifest to us." Still, he adds that, "although that great mystery, which encompasses in one single formula all those [mysteries] we have mentioned, can be made comprehensible to every human being through his reason as an idea necessary in practice, yet we can say that, to become the moral foundation of religion, and particularly of a public one, it was revealed at the time when it was *publically* taught for the first time and was made into the symbol of a totally new religious epoch" (169–70).

Kant also observes that, because a "rationalist," unlike a "naturalist," philosopher "must of his own accord hold himself within the limits of human insight . . . , [he will not] ever contest either the intrinsic possibility of revelation in general or the necessity of a revelation as divine means for the introduction of true religion; for no human being can determine anything through reason regarding these matters." He adds that "a religion can be *natural*, yet also *revealed*, if it is so constituted that human beings *could and ought to have* arrived at it on their own through the mere use of their reason, even though they *would* not have come to it as early or as extensively as is required, hence a revelation of it [historically] at a given time and a given place might be wise and very advantageous to the human race, for then, once the thereby introduced religion is at hand and has been made publicly known, everyone can henceforth convince himself of its truth by himself and his own reason." Thus we see, Kant writes in summary, that an "*objectively*" natural religion is consistent with a "*subjectively*" revealed religion (178).

In the above paragraph it is evident that Kant, while acknowledging that a religion that is natural and universal can also be revealed and historical, does not explicitly address the relationship between ontology and history. He does not see, in other words, the intrinsic bondedness of the concepts of universality, revelation, and history with "nature" when understood as a state, condition, quality, or property and so not as natural when understood as physical or phenomenal. Still, Kant does suggest that a revealed religion can prompt (move, inspire) human beings to discover in themselves what had remained unknown to them—consciousness of the moral law. Indeed, he further suggests that another advantage of revealed religion is that, because it is publicly known, all individuals are free to use their own reason to test its truth. It's as if revealed religion allows human beings to actualize the very possibilities that are originally inherent in their creation.

It is important to remember here that revealed religion is scriptural. Indeed, the very paradox of the Bible is that it is at once written and revealed, both writing and revelation. There is no revelation that is not written and no writing (scripture) that is not revealed. Scripture always tests me to find in it what for me is the revelation of the truth. That the written text is revealed tests me always to confirm the truth of revelation in and through the text. The letter of Scripture is the test of spirit just as the spirit of Scripture is the test of the letter. Fundamental, then, to the revealed spirit of Scripture's letter is what Kant calls publicity—that the Bible as *scriptura* is revealed, made public, to all people—in self-conscious possession of the critique of pure reason.

Although Kant does not explicitly comprehend the tight bondedness of revelation, scripture, and publicity (the public domain of the covenantal republic as founded on the universality of the moral law as true for all people), he does suggest that there is a fundamental difference between written religion as publicly revealed and oral religion as known only through diverse (contradictory) traditions of private opinion, between, in other words, the religion of the book (the Word of God, which, the rabbis fondly reminded us, we know solely in the words written by human beings!). Consistent, then, with the above observation on the part of Kant that a likely advantage of a revealed religion (as written historically) over a natural religion (as found universally in human reason) is that it was publicly accessible to all people, are two additional passages in *Religion within the Boundaries of Mere Reason* in which he comments, albeit briefly, on the uniqueness of religion as written. In the first passage, after stalwartly denying that what he calls "a *statutory ecclesiastical* faith," involving temples and priests, is to be seen as "added to the pure faith of religion as its vehicle and the means for the public union of human beings in promoting it," Kant then comments on what he views to be the advantage of scripture over tradition (139–40). He observes that "the preservation of this pure faith unchanged, its universal and uniform diffusion, and even the respect for the revelation assumed within it can hardly be adequately provided for through *tradition* but only through *scripture*." He continues:

> A holy book commands the greatest respect even among those (indeed, among these most of all) who do not read it, or are at least unable to form any coherent concept of religion from

> it; and no subtle argument can stand up to the knockdown [*niederschlagenden*] pronouncement, *Thus it is written*. Hence also the passages in it that are to lay down a point of faith are simply called *sayings* . . . ; and history proves that never could a faith based on scripture be eradicated by even the most devastating political revolutions, whereas a faith based on tradition and ancient public observances meets its downfall as soon as the state breaks down. How fortunate [Kant explains in a note that "fortunate" here means "providential"] when one such book, fallen into human hands, contains . . . the purest moral doctrine of religion. . . . [B]oth because of the end to be attained thereby and the difficulty of explaining by natural laws the origin of the enlightenment of the human race proceeding from it, the book can command an authority equal to that of revelation. (140)[78]

Once again, while Kant here offers us richly suggestive observations, he does not pursue them systematically. There is nothing, he tells us, like the "knockdown pronouncement": "Thus it is written." For, in principle, anyone has the right to locate the passage "thus written" and to submit it to rational critique. Indeed, it is because the moral law is written—in a book (plus endless commentaries, which are also published)—that it cannot be historically eradicated (torn up by its roots). For it is precisely history that preserves scripture as historically rooted. It is wondrously significant, then, that in this context Kant writes that, unlike natural laws, "history proves" how the enlightenment of the human race proceeded from "the purest moral doctrine of religion," that is, because this doctrine was written in and as the Book whose sayings knock us down on the spot. We recall here that another name for historical proof, which is superior to the demonstrations of natural law, is conjecture—regarding the biblical origin of human history. It is also important to note that, while Kant in the passage that we are discussing draws together revelation and Scripture (writing), he does not in precise terms show that they depend upon each other.

In the second passage regarding the uniqueness of scriptural faith as historically ineradicable, Kant observes that "a people in possession of a written religion (sacred books) never assimilates in faith with a people which (like the Roman Empire, i.e., the whole civilized world at the time) has nothing of the kind but only has customs; it [i.e., a written religion] rather soon or later makes proselytes [i.e., converts]." He points out that "the Jews too, after the Babylonian captivity [of the sixth century BCE] (when, as it appears, their sacred books were read publically for the first time), were no longer accused of their propensity to run after false gods, at the very time when the Alexandrian culture ... could have made it easy for them to give these gods a systematic form."[79] Furthermore, "what the Jews would not have achieved on their own" the Christian, together with the Mohammedan, religion, "did for them, since these religions presuppose the Jewish faith and the sacred books pertaining to it" (163).[80]

It is evident that Kant does not explain how Christianity, in presupposing the Hebrew Bible and its moral faith, is to be understood, at once historically and ontologically, as a completely new religion. But what counts here in this study is to take critical note of the significance that Kant ascribes to writing (scripture) as distinguishing Christianity (together with Judaism and Islam) as a religion of the book from religions that were not written. Again, he does not analyze in detail what it is about "writing" that sets Christianity apart from all those (pagan) religion that rest on tradition (and so on mere opinion). But he is clear that a Scripture is a public document (or record). It is accessible to all, not only to the scholars in theological faculties. It is open, always, to the critique of pure reason. Closely related to the publicity inherent in writing is the principle of interpretation, the distinction between the letter and the spirit. It is only in having the letter before me that I find that I have the duty to ask: What does it mean to me? What is its spirit? What is the relationship between history and ontology? Does the text mean the same to me that that it meant to Abraham, to the prophet Jeremiah, to Jesus, to countless readers, subsequently? The paradox here of course is that it is only when the text is written that we come to distinguish between its letter and its spirit.

I also want to mention one more point. It is surely only with the idea of Scripture as the written Word of God, which human beings are to make the word true for them in their own lives, that we have the idea that God's word is written (inscribed) on the human heart. The idea that the moral law is universally written in the heart, soul, and mind of every human being constitutes, then, the challenge for each and every individual: in deed, how do I live the word obliging me to love my neighbor as myself, to treat all human beings as ends in themselves? In the most elemental terms, it is my duty to make public the moral law that is written in my heart—hermeneutically, morally, politically, critically . . . .

Complexity leads to complexity, when we undertake, with Kant, in this instance, to comprehend, at once ontologically and historically, the relationship between religion and philosophy. The religion of reason, as grounded in the moral law, is found universally, Kant argues, in the reason, heart, and conscience of all human beings. Yet, not only is it revealed universally through reason, but also it was historically revealed through Scripture as a singular book. Indeed, in order for religion as the revelation of the moral law to become publically known by and so universally accessible to all human beings, it was (had to be) revealed at a particular moment in historical time and place.

But why, we ask, did the moral law, which is universally found in the reason, heart, and conscience of all human beings, not become publically known and accepted by all? Why did it require the revelation of the moral law, historically and so publically, to bring into existence "a totally new religious epoch"? What, indeed, is the relationship, at once ontological and historical, between revelation "through reason" and revelation "through Scripture"? Kant does not directly or explicitly address (in self-consciously comprehending) these questions, although it is evident, surely, that he acknowledges (in assuming) a fundamental relationship between what we may call ontological universality and historically singularity (in the sense that every human person is at once universal and individual). The task, always, is to understand how the universal is individualized (differentiated) and how what is individual (different) is made universal—without falling into what Kant calls the dualistic opposition between the abstractionism of dogmatism and the relativity of skepticism, each the mirror image of the other, that continues to prevail in our own day, as always.

We shall continue to ponder how we are (what it means) to grasp the relationship between revelation and both reason and Scripture or, how, in other words, revelation is to be understood as universally rational yet also as historically singular. Before concluding, however, with my final thoughts on these issues, I want to introduce several additional passages in which Kant continues to show us the importance of making key distinctions that help us amplify our understanding of the complexity of the relationship between the universality of rational revelation, which did not become historically public, and the historical particularity of scriptural revelation, which did become universally public. For, first, it is important for us to grasp what Kant intends us to understand in writing that, when "the moral foundation of religion" was revealed and publically taught for the first time historically, it was "made into the symbol of a totally new religious epoch." Consistent with what he writes elsewhere in

Religion, as we shall now see, he holds that a totally new period of history emerged in and through Christianity as the only true religion with the New Testament constituting the only true scripture.

Kant holds, consequently, that Christianity, being "grounded on an entirely new principle," completely abandoned "the Judaism in which it originated" by bringing about "a total revolution in doctrines of faith." Through "*introducing* a pure moral religion in place of an old cult . . . , Christianity suddenly, though not unprepared, arose. The teacher of the Gospel announced himself as one sent from heaven while at the same time declaring, as one worthy of this mission,

- "that servile faith (in . . . professions and practices) is inherently null" and
- "that moral faith, which alone makes human beings holy 'as my father in heaven is holy' [the translator here cites Matt 5:48 and 1 Pet 1:16] and proves its genuineness by a good life-conduct, is on the contrary the only one which sanctifies."

Once this heavenly-sent teacher had provided in his person, "through teaching and suffering even to undeserved yet meritorious death, an example conforming to the prototype of a humanity well-pleasing to God, he was represented as returning to the heaven from which he came." It is here, Kant tells us, that "the public record of his life (which can therefore also serve universally as an example for imitation) ends. The more esoteric story of his *resurrection* and *ascension* . . . , added as sequel and witnessed only by his intimates, cannot be used in the interest of religion within the boundaries of mere reason, whatever its historical standing." Thus it was, Kant observes, that "to this teaching there are nonetheless added in a holy book miracles and mysteries, and the propagation of these is itself a miracle requiring a historical faith which cannot be authenticated or secured in meaning and import except through [historical] scholarship." Still, however much ugly strife constituted the consequent history of Christendom (Kant does not use this term here), even up to our own present time, it is evident, he concludes, that "Christianity's true first purpose was none other than the introduction of a pure religious faith, over which there can be no dissension of opinions" (156–59).

In reducing Judaism to what he calls "a mechanical cult" (156), Kant reflects what I earlier called the anti-Judaism that persisted so insidiously in Christendom for some two millennia. Still, how it was that Christianity, unlike the Judaism in which, not unprepared, it originated, founded a totally new religious epoch, to recall Kant's own phraseology, remains much debated today by theologians, philosophers, historians, and biblical scholars. It is not my purpose to enter directly into that debate. What counts for us here is to take note of the issue that lies at the heart of that debate and that Kant himself brings to our attention. How can that which is new and original, at once historically and ontologically, have its preparation and origin in that which precedes it historically and ontologically? We are, yet again, in the presence of the miracle, the mystery that is history. Each of us as a human being begins life as the universal (generic) product of history, both natural and cultural. Yet, our task is to make new, to renew that history in and through the creation of our own individuality, of our own singularity or difference. Such is the covenantal vocation of having been created from nothing, from nothing outside of the gift of eternally transforming the givenness of our nature into the gift of which we are the unique recipient, to do with as is our moral duty in conformity, Kant tells us, "with this idea, 'God is love'" (as found in 1 John 4:8, 16) (170). History is at once old and new, past and future, givenness and gift, nature and freedom. We are eternally called to the task of ever renewing the critically metaphorical transition from the sensate to the spiritual.

How, then, history is to be understood as revelatory and revelation as historical, with both history and revelation grounded in creation, there is yet more to say. It is important, first, however to be sure that we grasp how and why it is that Kant writes that the Teacher of the Gospel exemplifies the prototype, the model, the metaphor, we could say, of "the idea of a human begin morally pleasing to God" (105) that is already present in our reason. He writes that "the person [Jesus] who can be revered" as the exemplary model of the moral good is not to be viewed "as the *founder* of the *religion* which, free from every dogma, is inscribed in the heart of all human beings . . . , but as the founder of the first true [and universal] *church*" (181). While again we see here the tension in Kant between rational revelation (as universal) and historical revelation (as particular), my emphasis here is on understanding why Kant is so insistent in distinguishing between them. It is in the *Groundwork of the Metaphysics of Morals* that Kant provides us with an especially lucid account of the importance of distinguishing, in his terms, between rational revelation and historical revelation. There is no worse advice, he writes there, than wanting to derive morality from examples, as if (and this is my extension of his thought) the one we view (or venerate) as our example of the moral law were the thing in itself, which could only be miraculously or mysteriously revealed to us supernaturally. The fundamental issue in question here is the very nature of authority. Who is the author of the moral law? What is the basis, the source, of the moral law? What we must see, Kant continues, is that every example of the moral law that "is represented to me must itself first be appraised [by me] in accordance with principles of morality, as to whether it is also worthy to serve as an original example, that is, as a model." No example of the moral law can "authoritatively provide the concept of morality. Even the Holy One of the Gospel must first be compared with our ideal of moral perfection before he is known as such.... But whence have we the concept of God as the highest good? Solely from the *idea* of moral perfection that reason frames a priori and connects inseparably with the concept of a free will. Imitation has no place at all in matters of morality" (63). In simple terms, every example of the moral law that we encounter in life, including our religious life and so life as described in the Bible, must be tested by and so proved through its compliance with our duty to treat all human beings as ends in themselves, not as means. As you judge, so are you judged. Authority, indeed authorship, is covenantal. Whatever the source of authority, whether person or institution, it is subject, always, to free, public, and communal critique.

Just as the author of the Letter of 1 John notes that, with the historical revelation of the Word of God to us, many false spirits have gone forth into the world in its name, so it is only with the revelation of God that we know historically in and through the Bible that idolatry as the worship of falsely authoritative gods also emerges. We remember that the Hebrew prophets incessantly condemned their people for whoring after false gods. It is important, consequently, to distinguish critically between idolatry and paganism. Since pagans have no knowledge of good and evil, no concepts of creation or covenant, they do not and cannot worship false gods as idols. It is precisely because the gods of the Greeks are equally reliable and unreliable that the heroes of ancient tragedy suffer, together with Socrates, the fate of having no knowledge of the good (with evil understood as resulting from ignorance of the good).[81] It is in this context that it is particularly interesting to see Kant observe, in *Religion*, that, while "it certainly sounds questionable, it is in no way reprehensible to say that every human being *makes a God* for himself." Indeed, he continues, "he must make one according to moral concepts ... in order to honor in him *the one who made him.*" But then Kant is careful to point out that "a human being must yet confront this representation with his ideal first in order to judge whether he is authorized [has the authority] to hold and revere this being as Divinity"—as that than which he can truly think nothing greater, to recall St. Anselm's formulation of the ontological argument. But Kant does not himself, yet again, acknowledge that he has here invoked the ontological argument—according to which God is the one thing that cannot be thought, by human beings, without necessarily existing (to recall Spinoza's formulation of the ontological argument). It is significant that Kant emphasizes the point that we human beings must create a god for ourselves according to our concept of the moral law, while also making it clear at the same time that we must subject our metaphor of that than which, we hold, nothing greater can be necessarily thought to exist to our ideal, i.e., to critical scrutiny. If, however, we rely "on the basis of revelation alone, without that concept being *previously* laid down in its purity at its foundation as touchstone, there can be no religion, and all reverence for God would be *idolatry*" (189). I think, *ergo* I am. I think, *ergo* God exists—as that than which I can think nothing greater to exist.

It is evident that what Kant understands here by relying "on the basis of revelation alone" signifies slavish dependence on supernatural dictate the authority of which is not subject to the public scrutiny of all. But is the idea of relying solely on supernatural revelation as externalized authority essentially different from relying solely on my own natural reason as internalized authority? How do I know that, how do I prove that the moral law that I claim is grounded in my reason, i.e., is the god within me, is not merely my illusory self-idol? All claims to authority, all claims to author the truth, whether interior or exterior to me, must be subject, always, to public critique, if we are going to be able to count on reason as the revelation of truth and on revelation as the truth of reason.

It is useful in this context to take up yet again how and why it is that Kant so urgently insists that we must distinguish between what we may call private and public mysteries or miracles. We do not know the cause of the moral law, when understood as founded on the freedom and equality of all persons, just as we do not know the cause of gravity the natural laws of which are universally accepted as true. What Kant thus emphasizes, in discussing what he calls the holy mysteries of Christianity, such as the resurrection and the ascension of Christ, is, as we have already seen, the critical difference between that which is known only privately and that which is known as publically communicated. While mysteries can be known, privately, by the individual, they cannot, he writes, "be professed publically, i.e., cannot be communicated universally." We are not, however, "to count among the holy mysteries the *grounds* of morality," even though they "are inscrutable to us" and their "cause is not given to us." This is why, Kant continues, that freedom, "which is made manifest [i.e., revealed!] to the human being through the determination of his power of choice by the unconditional moral law . . . is no mystery, since knowledge of it can be *communicated* to everyone; the ground of this property, which is inscrutable to us, is however a mystery, since it is *not given* to us in knowledge" (164).

This is also why, Kant additionally points out, as we noted above, that the "*cause* of the universal gravity of all matter in the world is equally unknown to us. . . . Yet gravity is not a mystery; it can be made manifest to everyone, since its *law* is sufficiently known." While, consequently, there "are mysteries that are hidden things of nature (*arcana*), and there are mysteries of politics (things kept secret, *secreta*); yet we *can* still become acquainted with either, inasmuch as they rest on empirical causes. With respect to that of which it is our universal duty to have knowledge of (namely anything moral) there can be no mystery" (165). Thus, Kant shows us that, notwithstanding the fact that science and politics contain hidden things and that the ground or cause of morality is unknown to us, still, we cannot and must not, therefore, claim that the holy mysteries of supernatural religion rest on equally valid grounds. For what counts is whether the claims of science or politics, like those of the moral law, meet the test of communicability, of public trust and respect.

That all moral truth is communal and that all true community is grounded on the moral law—in other words, that morality is political and that politics is moral Kant lays out with pellucid clarity in his essay on "Perpetual Peace" (1795), "A state," he writes there, "is not, like the ground which it occupies, a piece of property. . . . It is a society of men whom no one else has any right to command or to dispose [of] except the state itself. It is a trunk with its own roots." It follows, then, that to reduce the state "as a moral person . . . to a thing . . . thus contradicts the idea of the original contract without which no right over a people can be conceived" (86).[82]

It is important, consequently, to see how and why the moral law, which is universally found within all human beings, is at the same time the universal right of the state as originally found without (outside of) every individual in the social contract. The moral person is a state. The state is a moral person. In thus undertaking to show the importance of understanding how and why the interior (the individual) is truly—but, also, of course, often falsely—exterior (the social), and vice-versa —I shall not discuss as such Kant's purpose in writing "Perpetual Peace," which is to argue for the ultimate union of individual and social peace in and through an international league of nations, what he calls "the positive idea of a world republic" (as the kingdom of God on earth) (102). Kant observes that the "only constitution which derives from the idea of the original compact, and on which all juridical legislation of a people must be based, is the republic." For, he writes further, "the republican constitution is the only one entirely fitting to the rights of man" (111). In understanding republican government as representative government, Kant observes further that what constitutes the individual's "external (juridical) freedom" is the right "to lend obedience to no external laws except those to which I could have given consent." He observes yet further that, if I want to elevate the validity of my "inborn rights, which are inalienable and belong necessarily to humanity," by associating them with God, I must bear in mind that, in regard to "my freedom, I have no obligation with respect to divine law, which can be acknowledged by my reason alone, except in so far as I could have given my consent to it. Indeed, it only through the law of freedom of my own reason that I frame a concept of the divine will" (93).

Kant reminds us that the "state of peace among men living side by side is not the natural state (*status naturalis*); the natural state is one of war. . . . A state of peace, therefore, must be *established*" (92). The natural state, in other words, is the private condition in which self-love as self-interest rules. The civil state of peace is established only through the willed pledge of all to do unto to their neighbor what they want their neighbor to do unto them. In the civil state we are all neighbors: near ones. This is the state whose constitution, Kant writes, "is the act of the general will through which the many persons become one nation. In this respect government is either republican or despotic" (95–96). Only a republic government is representative. Otherwise, "government is despotic and arbitrary, whatever the constitution may be. None of the ancient so called 'republics' knew this system, and they all finally and inevitably degenerated into despotism under the sovereignty of one [e.g., the Caesars]" (97). Although Kant does not point it out, it is evident that, since all despotic, non-representative governments have no truly public law but only private law based on self-interest, all ancient "republics"—*res publicas* or "public things"—existed in and as the state of nature, i.e., of interminable, ruler/ruled (master/slave) relationships.

Because the civil state (the republic) exists only in and through the moral law and since, equally, the moral law exists only in and through the civil state, Kant argues that there is, in principle, "no conflict of practice with theory," of politics with the moral law. Even though politics advises— "Be ye wise as serpents"—morality puts in with: "and guileless as doves" (Matt 10:16). Kant acknowledges that, while "the proposition, 'Honesty is the best policy,' implies a [moral] theory which practice unfortunately often refutes, the equally theoretical 'Honesty is better than any policy' is beyond refutation and is indeed the indispensable condition of policy" (117). Thus, we see, he observes, that "objectively, or in theory, there is no conflict between morals and politics. Subjectively, however, in the selfish propensity of men (which should not be called 'practice,' as this would imply that it rested on rational maxims), this conflict will always remain. Indeed," Kant exclaims, "it should remain, because it serves as a whetstone of virtue, whose true courage (by the principle 'do not yield to evils but proceed more boldly against them')"[83] consists not so much in undertaking resolutely to oppose evils as "in detecting and conquering the crafty and far more dangerously deceitful and treasonable principle of evil in ourselves, which puts forward the weakness of human nature as justification for every transgression" (127). We see, then, that the conflict between theory and practice is not simply between morality and politics but also within morality itself. I am often in conflict with myself over what I have done or what I ought to have done.

Still, Kant argues that, because moral evil is "indiscerptibly [wholly] . . . opposed to[84] and destructive of its own purposes (especially in the relationships between evil men)" and so, we can add, always wholly in contradiction with itself, "it gives place to the moral principle of the good, though only through a slow progress" (127). Thus we see, he continues, that

> providence is justified in the history of the world, for the moral principle in man is never extinguished, while with advancing civilization reason grows pragmatically in its capacity to realize ideas of law. But at the same time the culpability for the transgressions also grows. If we assume that humanity never will or can be improved, the only thing which a theodicy seems unable to justify is creation itself, the fact that a race of such corrupt beings ever was on earth.

> To such dubious consequences we are inevitably driven if we do not assume that pure principles of right have objective reality, i.e., that they may be applied, and that the people in a state and, further, states themselves in their mutual relations should act according to them. . . . Thus true politics can never take a step without rendering homage to morality. Though politics by itself is a difficult art, its union with morality is no art at all, for this union cuts the knot which politics could not untie when they were in conflict. The rights of man must be held sacred, however much sacrifice it may cost the ruling power. One cannot compromise here and seek the middle course between the morally right and the expedient. All politics must bend its knee before the right. But by this it can hope slowly to reach the stage where it will shine with an immortal glory. (128)

Since Kant in the above passage does not identify the political with the state as the social contract, he would appear to subordinate politics to morality. Nevertheless, I do think that what he intends to show us overall in his discussion of the relationship between personal morality and the politics of the state, between reason and republic, is that they are indiscerptibly and thus indissolubly bound together in and through the rights of man.

What is especially important for us to see in the analysis of the relationship between morality and politics that Kant provides for us in "Perpetual Peace" is how closely he binds together the ultimate triumph of good over evil in and through the kingdom of ends with theodicy. If humanity, at once individual and communal, is not seen to realize its gloriously immortal end in and by the means of evil, if, in other words, the providential end of God does not justify the historical means of human beings, then theodicy will have altogether failed to account for creation. Theodicy has bedeviled biblical theology ever since the beginning of creation. For what else is the story of Adam and Eve but a theodicy in which biblical thinkers undertook to justify the ways of God to human beings (to recall Milton's words of justification for his poem on paradise lost as paradise regained) as the conjectural beginning of human history? How and in what sense does theology—the *logos* (the Word, the logic) of God—embody theodicy—the justice of God? If we do not see good emerging from evil, if evil means are not understood to serve the end of good, if good does not in the end triumph over evil, then, as Kant indicates, what "a theodicy seems unable to justify is creation itself, the fact that a race of such corrupt beings ever was on earth." Why is there evil if the Lord God is good? Why do human beings sin if they are created good by God? In what if in any sense can God be understood to be omniscient and omnipotent if he is unable to wipe evil off the face of the earth? What justice is there in God, how can God be understood to be just and so be justified by human beings, if, with their creation, their first act was to disobey their lord God in allowing themselves to be seduced, satanically (by the evil one), into savoring the sinful fruit of the tree of knowledge of good and evil? Indeed, if all creation is good and the angels are perfect, how did there emerge in heaven the evil angel Satan, together with his evil cohort? Is there, in fact, not one good God but two Gods, a God of good and a God of evil, as found in Manicheanism?

The answer to these questions rests on our concept of creation, as Kant pointed out to us in the above passage on theodicy. Kant, however, does not provide us with a systematic account of creation, except for a critically important if brief passage in the *Critique of Practical Reason*, as we shall see in the next chapter. Still, in his occasional references to creation in *Religion within the Boundaries of Mere Reason* he does makes it clear to us how the idea of creation is to be understood as the conjectural beginning of human history, which, as covenantal, remains to us for all time unknown, inscrutable, and incomprehensible. What it means, consequently, to comprehend creation as incomprehensible is to comprehend theodicy as incomprehensible, and what it means incomprehensibly to comprehend theology is to see the indiscerptible (unbreakable) bond (compact) between creation and freedom.

It has seldom, however, been understood that creation is the "conjecture" that we must make if we are to fathom, to plumb the depths of, the beginning and thus, also, the end, of human history as providential. In confirmation of this view Kant summarizes in *Religion* the report of a Jesuit missionary in Canada (as published in 1744) in which "he told his Iroquois catechumen the story of all the evil that the evil spirit wrought on a creation originally good and how this spirit is still constantly seeking to thwart the best divine arrangements." But when, then, the catechumen indignantly asked the father: "'But why does not God strike the Devil dead,'... he candidly admits that he was unable, on the spot, to find an answer" (118). We may also remember, on the opposing side of the theodicy question regarding the relationship of good and evil, Voltaire's *Candide*.[85] In his satire Voltaire unsparingly ridicules, in the person of the learned Professor Pangloss, the idea central to Leibniz' *Theodicy*[86] that this is the best of all possible worlds.

In his brief references to creation in *Religion*, together with the key passage in "Perpetual Peace" connecting creation with theodicy, which we have been discussing, Kant shows us that the critical way to understanding theodicy is at once creational and covenantal. We begin with his observation that when it is said—"The human being is created good"—this can only mean: "He has been created for the good," not that he is "good as such, but [that] he brings it about that he becomes either good or evil" according to whether he chooses to will good or to will evil (89). We see, then, Kant observes, that "evil originates from freedom" (90) precisely because God "created human beings for freedom" (205). While the first act of man was to fall into sin, still, the knowledge of the good, the knowledge that we ought and so are capable of freely willing the good is the "germ of goodness [that is] left in its entire purity, a germ that cannot be extirpated or corrupted" (90). We are born free, and what the realization of this freedom entails is our acknowledgment that now we are in chains. So it is that Kant, like Rousseau before him, shows us that to be created free is to be faced with the never-ending struggle, both individual and social, at once personal and covenantal, of transforming the state of nature into the kingdom of ends of republican freedom. It is for this reason, Kant writes, that he has always been suspicious of the common "way of speaking" that "even clever men are wont to use." To wit, they say that

- "A certain people (intent on establishing civil freedom) is not ripe for freedom."
- "The bondsmen of a landed proprietor are not yet ripe for freedom."
- "People are in general not yet ripe for freedom of belief."

With this assumption, Kant observes, "freedom will never come, since we cannot *ripen* to it if we are not already established in it." We must be free in order to use "our powers purposively in freedom." While our first attempts, he points out, will often be crude, still "we do not ripen to freedom otherwise than through *our* own attempts (and we must be free to be allowed to make them)" (204). Again, we see that we are born free, although freedom does not result from our birth but from our creation from nothing that is not in itself the good of freedom. We also see, yet again, that it is precisely because I cannot repudiate my freedom—I cannot alienate my self, in the words of Rousseau, because I cannot will evil or make evil my first principle—it is precisely against my evil heart that I must constantly struggle. In yet other words, with which we are familiar, I do not begin in nature. For I begin freely as one whose future is to become historically in the end the free, covenantal being that I am creatively in the beginning.

In the "Concluding Remark" of the *Groundwork of the Metaphysics of Morals* Kant articulates in dramatically antithetical language his conclusion that we human beings are able to come to sane terms with what I am here calling the challenge of theodicy solely in and through a metaphysics that is grounded in practical reason. We begin our lives with that which Hegel calls the absolute (infinite) knowledge of Spirit and which Kant call the unconditional conjecture that we must make if we are to comprehend the beginning of human history as the fall, not from but into the creative practice of covenantal relations. Because Kant's conjecture is grounded, not on (finite) conditions that result in, at one and the same time, skepticism (probabilism) and dogmatism (absolutism) but on the unconditional grounds of the absolute necessity of freedom as self-determination, we "know" our beginning only as that which grounds itself in the practice of the will. For it is solely the will, of all the things that exist within or even without the world, that we can consider absolutely good in itself without finite limitations. Thus it is, Kant writes in his "Concluding Remark," that the "absolute necessity," which grounds the freedom of the will in "the practical use of reason," has to do only with the "*laws of actions* of a rational being as such," not with the laws of natural causation. It follows, then, he continues, that "it is an essential *principle* of every use of our reason [which, we remember, is our will whose good is absolutely unlimited] to push its knowledge to consciousness of its *necessity*," which is its absolute freedom to think and to exist. But then Kant adds, and here it is important to engage directly the antithetical rhetoric that he employs:

> It is, however, an equally essential *limitation* of this same reason that it can see neither the *necessity* of what is and what happens [in the state of nature] nor the necessity of what ought to happen [in the civil state] unless a *condition* under which it is and happens or ought to happen is put at the basis of this. In this way, however, by constant inquiry after the condition, the satisfaction of reason is only further and further postponed. Hence it [i.e., reason] restlessly seeks the unconditionally necessary and sees itself constrained to assume it without any means of making it comprehensible to itself, [and thus it is] fortunate enough if it can discover only the concept that is compatible with this presupposition.

Because practical reason, as will, does not and cannot know, as a natural object of possible appearance, the "condition" under which it ought to act, it is (we may say) subjectively limited to assuming its compatibility with the presupposed concept of the infinite and absolute freedom of the subject. "And thus," Kant writes, in bringing the *Groundwork* to a close,

> we do not indeed comprehend the practical unconditional necessity of the moral imperative, but we nevertheless comprehend its *incomprehensibility*; and this is all that can fairly be required of a philosophy that strives in its principles to the very boundary of human reason. (108)

The will, which is good without limitation, is limited to the condition that constitutes the unconditional necessity of the freedom by which it is infinitely bound to the moral imperative of pushing its consciousness to the absolute limits of the self. While, consequently, we do not comprehend the unconditional freedom of the moral imperative as a necessary law of nature, we do, nonetheless, comprehend its incomprehensibility as that which is created, in the beginning, in beginning freely from itself alone as its own necessary cause. The condition that we must assume and so presuppose as the unconditionally necessary beginning of freedom is, it is evident, the conjecture by which we comprehend the incomprehensible story of the fall of man as the beginning of history whose story we restlessly advance in the progressive realization of the kingdom of ends on earth. While it is in the *Critique of Pure Reason*, which we shall take up in the next chapter, where Kant systematically demonstrates that, to recall his famous words, we have to negate and so appropriate and overcome the knowledge of objects in order to make room for faith in pure reason as the covenantal practice of subjects, our purpose here is to indicate that it is through making the incomprehensibility of creation comprehensible as the conjectural beginning of history that he addresses theodicy. In brief, the Bible is theodicy. How we interpret the Bible—as interpreting us—is how we understand the good of creation as the origin of the evil that constitutes the *felix culpa* without which the kingdom of God cannot be realized as the earthly kingdom of human beings.

The conundrum that is theodicy Kant also addresses, although still indirectly, when in *Religion* he takes up conscience as "the Guiding Thread in Matters of Faith." He observes that it is not conscience that needs a guide, but, rather, it is we human beings who need conscience as our guide "in the most perplexing moral decisions." For conscience is nothing other than the consciousness of our duty. But then Kant proceeds to make a distinction involving the relationship between good and evil, between right and wrong, the point of which is evident solely on the basis of the most conscientious scrutiny on our part. He observes that it is "a moral principle, requiring no proof," that we should undertake no action that "*might be wrong*: 'Do not do what you doubt,'" and here Kant cites Pliny, whom he names, in Latin. So, while "the *consciousness* that an action *which I want to undertake is right*, is unconditional duty, . . . it is understanding, not conscience, which judges whether an action is in general right or wrong." Indeed, Kant continues, it is "not absolutely necessary to know" whether "all possible actions . . . are right or wrong." Regarding, however, "the action that *I* want to undertake, I must not simply "be of the opinion that it is right; I must also be *certain* that it is." Thus, conscience is opposed to the mere probabilism of opinion. For conscience "calls upon the human being to [bear] witness *for* or *against* himself" (202–3).

What makes the above passage on conscience unsettling in the first instance is that, while Kant begins by calling Pliny's imperative—"Do not do what you doubt."—an indubitable moral principle, he then proceeds to connect it with the probabilism of mere opinion, which is never certain about right and wrong. Further, he goes on to argue that the action that I undertake as my duty I must know to be certainly right and not wrong. I must always will the good. I cannot will the evil. I cannot will to make lying into a universal principle, as he writes earlier in the *Groundwork*.[87] Still, I do wrong continuously. I continue to lie both to myself and to others. Indeed, what is so discomfiting about the moral law is that it is only in willing the good that I bring evil into the world and thus sin. Evil originates from freedom. It is, consequently, critically important to see that Pliny's "doubt" is absolutely unlike Cartesian doubt, by which I demonstrate the absolute certitude of the bond between my thinking (willing) and my existence. Pliny's imperative dictum bears witness to us, but not to the ancients to whom it was directed, that, because there was, for them, nothing in the world of appearance that was not to be doubted, the ancients had no concept of will, of action, of knowledge of good and evil. We remember that the reason that Socrates was called the wisest man in Greece was because he possessed the oracular knowledge that he was ignorant of the good.

It is evident, consequently, that theodicy is unthinkable to the ancients. Only those who know the absolute good of the will as having the unconditional duty of absolutely willing the good have to struggle eternally with the problem of evil. We have seen that Kant makes it clear in "Perpetual Peace" that the idea of the republican civil state, when understood to represent the rights of all human beings, was unknown to the ancients. But at times in *Religion within the Boundaries of Mere Reason*, as we have seen with regard to his invocation of Pliny, Kant can appear to call upon the ancients in support of his conception of the moral law. So it is, too, when, in initiating Part 2 of *Religion*, entitled "Concerning the Battle of the Good Against the Evil Principle for Dominion over the Human Being," he invokes the Stoic philosophers. Kant begins by writing here that, in order for human beings to become morally good, it is not sufficient for them "to let the germ of the good, which lies in our species, develop unhindered." For they must also combat "an active and opposing cause of evil" that is in them. "It was especially the Stoics," he declares, "who among the ancient moralists called attention to this through their watch word *virtue*." In signifying courage and valor, in both Greek and Latin, *virtus*, he tells us, "presupposes the presence of an enemy." How different this is, he continues, from the individual (Christian, we may suppose) who—lazy, timid, and so lacking in trust in himself that he waits upon external help—"unharnesses all the forces of a human being and renders him unworthy even of this help." But then Kant immediately adds that the valiant Stoics "mistook their enemy, who is not to be sought in the natural inclinations, which merely lack discipline and openly display themselves unconcealed to everyone's consciousness, but is rather, as it were, an invisible enemy, who hides behind reason and hence [is] the more dangerous." The Stoics, consequently, "send forth *wisdom* against *folly* ... instead of summoning it against the *malice* (of the human heart), which secretly undermines the disposition with soul-corrupting principles" (101).

Yet again, however, in a note Kant appears to hold the Stoics in high moral regard when he writes that they "derived their universal moral principles from the dignity of human nature," that is, "from its freedom . . . [and] independence from the power of the inclinations . . . , and they could not have laid down a better or nobler principle for foundation." Furthermore, they "drew the moral laws directly from reason, the sole legislator, commanding absolutely through its laws." All of this is quite correct, Kant observes, "provided that one attributes to the human being an uncorrupted will" that without hesitation incorporates "these laws into its maxims." But this is precisely the mistake that the Stoic philosophers made. "For no matter how far back we direct our attention to our moral state, we find that this state is no longer *res integra* [i.e., a pure thing or state] and that we must rather start by dislodging from its possession the evil that has already taken up position there.... That is, the first really good thing that a human being can do is to extricate himself from an evil which is to be sought, not in his inclinations but in his perverted maxims and hence in freedom itself." Indeed, Kant points out that, considered "*in themselves* natural inclinations are *good*,... and to want to extirpate them would not only be futile but harmful and blameworthy as well.... Only what is unlawful is evil in itself, absolutely reprehensible, and must be eradicated." He adds that it is not, therefore, surprising that the "*invisible* enemy," who corrupts from within our "basic principles," is represented by "an apostle" as being "an evil spirit" outside of us: "'We have to wrestle not against flesh and blood (the natural inclinations) but against principalities and powers, against evil spirits'" (See Eph 6:12). Kant adds yet further that the point of the apostle's words is not "to extend our knowledge beyond the world of the senses but only to make intuitive [metaphorical!], *for practical use*, the concept of something [that is] to us unfathomable." What counts is not whether we locate the tempter inside or outside us, for "we would not be tempted by him were we not in secret agreement with him" (101–3).[88]

Having seen now that Kant came, not to praise the Stoics as the true teachers of virtue but to bury them as ancient philosophers who were ignorant of good and evil and, further, to show that the apostolic author of Ephesians was the true philosopher—or perhaps we should say the true poet!—of morality, there is one more elusive element in the complex passage that we have been discussing that remains to be elucidated. Indeed, it is the very one that we have heretofore brought up as central to the issue of theodicy. I refer to what Kant in the above paragraph calls the unfathomability of the concept of the evil power that lurks as an invisible enemy in the shadow of our reason. It is precisely because the concept of evil, like the concept of good, is unfathomable, he points out, that "we can well understand how philosophers—to whom the basis of an explanation remains forever shrouded in darkness, and though absolutely necessary, is nonetheless unwelcome—could mistake the real opponent of goodness with whom they believed they had to stand in combat." Consequently, philosophers often think that they can easily explain moral evil by basing it either on the power of sensibility over us and/or on the weakness of our reason in resisting it. Since this would mean, however, Kant continues, that moral good was equally easy to explain, we would end up in an "unthinkable" (i.e., contradictory) position. Thus, he concludes:

> Now reason's ability to become master over all the inclinations striving against it through the mere idea of a law is absolutely inexplicable; hence it is also incomprehensible how the senses could have the ability to become master over a reason which commands with such authority on its side. For if all the world proceeded in accordance with the precept of the law, we would say that everything occurred according to the order of nature, and nobody would think even of inquiring after the cause. (102–3)

Once again, we see that the origin of moral evil and so also the origin of the moral law (of the good will, of practical reason, of freedom) is incomprehensible and inexplicable and, hence, unfathomable—in the precise sense that the origin, the principle, the historical beginning of the covenantal life of human beings cannot be viewed as the effect, as the product or result, of prior natural causes. Just as there are, for Kant, two concepts of law, moral (human) and natural (scientific), so there are also two concepts of necessity—(1) moral necessity (duty/self-determination): what I as a free human being must, ought, am obligated, bound to do; and (2) natural necessity: what I understand to happen scientifically according to the laws of natural cause and effect. The first is categorical (practical). The second is hypothetical (theoretical).

What is, then, comprehensibly incomprehensible, inexplicable, and unfathomable is the story of the fall of Adam and Eve into evil and their redemption (liberation) from the state of nature which, not evil but good in itself, we turn into evil if we choose—freely, rationally, and practically—to act on the basis of our natural and not of our moral incentives. For what the conjectural beginning of human history, as the transition from the sensible world of finite nature to the moral world of infinite spirit, shows us is that it is solely in the covenantal world of republican freedom that human beings creatively reveal themselves to be responsible for knowing good and evil. Like God, like man. To be created in the image of God, and not in the image of natural things, is to behold nature eternally as the metaphoric prelude to the ever-progressive growth of the human mind whose fulfillment in life, both philosophic and poetic, we know as the kingdom of God on earth.

We see, then, that creation resolves the problem of theodicy in showing us that how we justify evil is the insoluble (indiscerptible) predicament that we must always yet face *in saecula saeculorum*, unto the (eternity of the) ages of the ages. Creation makes theodicy comprehensible in showing us that our beginning in freedom is incomprehensible from the beginning unto the end. Why are we created? The biblical answer is that, in the beginning, God created man and woman, and lo! they were very good. But who is this God and what is creation? What Kant shows us, with incomparable insight, is that, since human beings are created—made!—in the image of God as self-determining, free creators, God is to be understood as the cause that human beings must make their cause, their object, in creating their covenantal existence as the republic of free and equal human beings. Kant tirelessly asserts, as we have seen, that the moral law is to be found universally in the reason of all human beings. At the same time, however, he makes it clear that it was only the Word of God as written in and as Scripture that historically bore witness to the universality of the Word of God as human *logos* or reason. Again, it is incomprehensible how or why the Bible, as the creative Word of God, came historically in existence. For, as Kant shows us, it is only on the basis of the moral law as the reason for God's creation that it is our duty, that we are obligated to confront, and so to think and work through, the challenge of theodicy. Without evil, no good. Without the state of nature, no covenant. Without bondage, no freedom. Without the earth, no human values. Without the laws of nature, no moral law. But the paradox, always, is that, in beginning with our creation from nothing—from nothing natural—we are born free and equal citizens in the kingdom of ends that are not given to us, either externally or internally, but that we must forever, and so unto eternity, will to become the ends of all human beings.

Creation, together with covenant, is profoundly intertwined with history and revelation. For creation is not something that happens just once, in a given time or place, although it is true that there was a period of time "before creation," which, on the basis of creation as historical, of historical time as creational, we call pre-history. The ancient Greeks and Romans, for example, lived in a pre-historical era. But, suddenly and unexpectedly—miraculously—they were brought to their knees in finding themselves exposed to the temporal demands no longer just of nature but now also of history. Creation is, we may say, the continuous and continuing revelation of history as the story of first beginnings that must always be created anew and afresh by each person and every generation of persons. Again, revelation is not to be understood as a supernatural (or as a merely subjective) dictate. Rather, revelation represents the recognition on my part that the truth that has been made known to me substantiates, gives life to, my own will and desires. In this sense, then, revelation is conjecture, metaphor, idea, ideal: that to which I give and that for which I must give my life. For I know, always, that I have to lose my life (of passive acceptance of idolatrous opinion) in order to regain it anew and so be rejuvenated in becoming, like a child, the poetic father of immortality.

CONCLUSION

What, then, I have undertaken to show in this chapter as introductory to the philosophy of Kant is the importance of learning both why and how he makes the explication of religion central to his critique of pure reason as philosophical practice. It is useful here to remember the call to arms that for Kant epitomizes the answer to the question that he raises in his essay "What Is Enlightenment?" (1784): *Sapere aude* (taken from Horace's *Ars poetica*!)—"dare to be wise" (unlike Socrates), "dare to know." For not only did Kant, as an Enlightenment thinker, consider it necessary to provide a searching critique of religion, given the role that religion and Christianity, above all, played and continued to play in both the intellectual and the political history of Europe. But also, and it is this which is of primary significance to us here, Kant daringly took on the fundamental task of demonstrating that the "reason of religion" is nothing other than the religion of reason. It is evident to us that Kant argues that religion can be, and so also must be, understood solely within the bounds of pure reason. Religion, the religion of Christianity (as found, according to Kant, in the New Testament), is rational to its very core. But I do hope that it has also become evident to the reader that Kant demonstrates, although only implicitly and indirectly, that philosophy, too, can and must be understood solely within the bounds of pure religion (as found in the Bible, Hebrew and Christian). For it is thanks to the biblical concepts of creation and covenant and so, too, of the concept of the moral law as the saving truth for all, that human beings are duty-bound to constitute the kingdom of ends as the truly creative republic of covenantal virtue. In short, to bind religion to the limits of infinitely pure reason is to bind reason to the infinite limits of pure religion. The Bible is the origin, at once historical and ontological, of not only religion but also philosophy as created from nothing—but the covenantal law of knowing good and evil in and through practicing the moral law. Dare to know it!

The task, then, that lies ahead of us in the next chapter is to work through Kant's two epic critiques of pure and practical reason. As I have indicated previously, it is through demonstrating that reason is practice that Kant truly brings about the revolution in modern philosophy. Central to our task, then, will be to savor the paradox that practical reason is incomprehensively comprehensible and so, in that sense, always a conjecture, although one that is morally and, at the same time, freely necessary for us to make. In contrast, our knowledge of nature, as constituted in and through the necessary laws of causation, is theoretical and hypothetical. Thus it is, as we shall now see, that Kant systematically demonstrates that the *logos* (reason, word) that underlies modern philosophy as practice is transcendental. Unlike the law of contradiction, on which ancient philosophy is based, the logic that constitutes (edifies or builds up) modernity is at once *a priori* and *a posteriori*, both before and after. We might call it the necessary conjecture that human beings will to verify in undertaking to prove, in and through their lives as thinking individuals, that it must be true, both historically and ontologically. I think, *ergo* I am.

CHAPTER 5

Reading Kant's Practical Philosophy

PRELIMINARIES

How are synthetic *a priori* principles possible? In making this question, whose key terms stand broadly for sensible (inductive) and analytic (deductive), as I shall explain later, the pivotal center of *The Critique of Pure Reason*, published in 1781, Kant launches the critical revolution in western (and so also world) philosophy. His answer, as elaborated in *The Critique of Pure Reason* (including the second edition of 1787), *On the Prolegomena of a Future Metaphysic* (1783), *The Groundwork of the Metaphysics of Morals* (1785), and, above all, *The Critique of Practical Reason* (1788), is that reason is practice and so to be comprehended as will, desire, action, thinking . . . . What Kant, then, proceeds to show us is that, because reason as practice embodies (incarnates) the principle of morality, the moral law, it is actually the moral practice of reason that makes synthetic *a priori* principles possible: treat all human beings as ends in themselves, as persons, and not simply as means or things, as (fellow) subjects and not as objects to be used. Thus, we have his famous claim that, while we can and do know the thing in itself (*das Ding an sich*) as an object of possible appearance, we do not and cannot know what the thing is in itself. But how, then, we ask, do we know the thing in itself as an object of possible appearance? Precisely because we do not know what the thing in itself—practical reason—actually is. The answer, then, to the question: How are synthetic *a priori* principles possible? is that because they are actual—always already, to recall Derrida; ontologically and historically, in my language—in and through the practice of reason.

While we shall be exploring what Kant understands by his terms "synthetic" and "*a priori*," as found in traditional logic since Plato and Aristotle, throughout this chapter, what I want, however, to emphasize here, at the beginning of our examination of Kant's two great critiques, is the radical import of the question itself. Kant does *not* ask: Are synthetic *a priori* principles possible? He does not ask, as the most fundamental question in metaphysics, why is there something and not nothing?[89] While it is doubtlessly not immediately evident, early on in *The Critique of Pure Reason*, that the possibility of (our knowledge of) nature rests on the practice of reason, on the thing in itself as that which we cannot know as an object of nature, still, as we shall see, Kant makes the distinction between the objects of possible appearance (the sensible world) and the thing in itself (practical reason) altogether evident in the Preface to the second edition of *Pure Reason*. But my point here, in beginning with the question on which Kant grounds his critique of reason, is that we can pose the question about how our knowledge of nature is possible precisely because (and only because) it is actual. To raise questions about reality, to provide a critique of pure reason (as practical), and so, consistent with Descartes, to doubt the existence (of myself, of God, of any thing) is to presuppose (to demonstrate) the existence both of the one who doubts and of the thing that is doubted (questioned, criticized). There is one thing that cannot be thought (criticized, doubted) by me without existing necessarily and that is the object of my thought. Here I paraphrase the ontological argument, demonstrating the existence of God (as necessarily found in human thought), with which Spinoza initiates his great work, the *Ethics* (1670). Overall, we may say that what Kant accomplishes in his critical philosophy is to show that the ontological argument proving the existence of God belongs to practical reason (thinking, will, desire) as the groundwork of the metaphysics of morals. Still, while Kant, in the last major section of *Pure Reason*, demolishes the ontological proof of the existence of God by showing that it is neither synthetic (based on experience) nor *a priori* (based on analytic reason), he never directly acknowledges that he saves (liberates) the ontological argument from both dogmatists and skeptics by showing (consistent with Spinoza) that it is at once synthetic and *a priori* and so grounded in the rational thinking of freely willing subjects.

We are here, yet again (as always), in the grips of the paradox, a term, by the way, that Kant himself not infrequently uses, the paradox that our knowledge of nature rests on that which we do not know—as an object of nature. Objective knowledge, knowledge of objects, rests on the practice (the reason) of subjects. The whole of *The Critique of Pure Reason* is, as we shall now see, taken up with, consequently, the demonstration that the possibility of our knowledge of nature depends on that which we do not know as subjects. What this means, consequently, as we saw in the previous chapter, especially in the context of the *Groundwork*, is that nature depends on (presupposes) freedom, objects on subjects, knowledge on reason (as will, thinking, desire), and so, ultimately, on an unceasing, critical drive on the part of human beings to determine how knowledge of nature is possible in their actual lives—without falling either into the dogmatism of holding that the empirical world of nature is knowable as a thing in itself or into the skepticism of denying that nature as a thing in itself is knowable. The paradox, then, is that Kant saves—liberates—knowledge of nature, as science, both from its dogmatic adherents as complete in itself and from its skeptical naysayers as incomplete in itself by grounding it on conjecture, to recall our discussion in the previous chapter. Conjecture is not merely a whim or a fantasy or simply a wild guess but, indeed, our self-conscious acknowledgement that, while nature is not complete in and of itself, our knowledge of it is made complete through and by that which is complete in itself and yet is always to be completed. In the elemental terms that Kant uses, the conditional world of nature (as phenomenal) is grounded in the unconditional world of freedom (as noumenal). In order, then, to show "how" synthetic *a priori* judgment are possible Kant makes it clear that we have to replace classical logic, with its dichotomy between appearance and reality, with a new, transcendental logic according to which existence (the will that is good in itself, as we learned in the previous chapter from the opening of *The Groundwork of the Metaphysics of Morals*) is given in and through our self-consciousness: I will, *ergo* I exist. Indeed, Kant views his groundbreaking question—How are synthetic *a priori* judgments possible?—as no less asking: How is metaphysics possible? He tells us that it is evident that metaphysics exists and that it will always be with us. The question, then, is: How is it possible? The answer, we shall see, is to be found, not in nature (i.e., not in the objects of possible appearance) but in practice, in the practice of reason (will, desire, thinking . . .) as the thing in itself.

It is, however, I suspect, not evident how and why Kant holds that metaphysics is actual or that, because metaphysics will always be with us (that it cannot and will not be done away with by natural science), we have to come to terms with what it is that makes it possible—without, falling, once again, into the dualistic opposites of (religious) dogmatism and (anti-religious) skepticism. We understand, then, the title of his book: *The Groundwork of the Metaphysics of Morals*. The metaphysics that is inseparable from us is the moral law: how we relate to our fellow human beings (and so, indirectly, also to our natural world) at once ethically (personally) and politically (socially). Still, we ask again, why are we subject to the moral law (why do we impose the moral law on ourselves)? Kant's response is unrelenting: that is the conjecture that we must make and that is incomprehensible in itself. Why was I born? To this question there is no natural (scientific) answer. I did not choose to be born or not to be born. But, once I am born, I have the obligation—at once moral and metaphysical—to choose having been born, to will the best life for myself (and for others) that is possible. My life, my existence, my will is actual. What then, are its possibilities? We see, then, that, having been born a natural creature (a creature of nature), I am full of unnatural possibilities. To make these possibilities actual, to actualize them in and through my life: that is my duty, my freedom. I am free solely to do my duty. I can in truth do my duty solely freely.

The paradox here is palpable. Scientific knowledge of nature depends on the conjecture that the beginning of human existence is inseparable from the metaphysics of the moral law. The paradox is doubtlessly intensified when we recall that Kant makes it clear in his works on religion, as we saw in the previous chapter, that the moral law, as embodied in reason, is that found in the Gospel (and, I would say, the Bible, at once Jewish and Christian). It thus turns out, as we shall see, that reason (I think, I will), in being distinct from the knowledge of objects of possible experience (I know), is inseparable (indistinguishable) from faith when understood as the action that it is my duty to undertake: the imperative to do unto others what I want others to do unto me. The paradox keeps recurring. Just as I am not originally a natural and only subsequently a moral (rational) being, for I am first and last (unconditionally, originally, creatively) a human person, not a natural thing, so, in living the life of the golden rule, I do not begin with my (natural) self-interest. For what is truly of interest to me (what truly engages, inspires, moves me) must be universally true for all persons. Yes, I do love a particular human being (and that person loves me as a particular human being). Still, love expresses universal worth (quality), not merely relative use (or quantity). I shall not, at present, pursue this topic further. For I present it here in providing an introduction to Kant's critical philosophy. Indeed, as I have already indicated, it is often not evident that the answer to the question about the possibility of synthetic *a priori* propositions is answered, ultimately, in and through the demonstration that reason is practice (will, desire, thinking . . .). Still, as we shall now see, Kant makes it pellucid, in the Preface to the second edition of *Pure Reason*, that what he demonstrates is that true philosophy constitutes (depends on) a twofold distinction between nature and freedom, between theoretical understanding (knowledge of nature) and practical reason (the moral law).

Before, however, undertaking to discuss the critiques of pure and practical reason, I want, first, to point out that, as with his works that I examined in the previous chapter, I shall in no sense undertake to provide a detailed (let alone exhaustive) treatment of them. I shall concentrate on the fundamental points that are central to grasping Kant's demonstration that reason is practice. This will often involve emphasizing key relationships among central points that can easily go unnoticed (or not be properly grasped). I also want to add that it is important not to gloss over difficult passages whose philosophical terminology can appear to us to be rebarbative. Kant's writing is dense, but it is not obscure. At its strongest (which is most of the time), it is profoundly discerning and thoughtful. It is humbling, and exalting, to be in the presence of such great texts as his two critiques of pure and practical reason. I want to note further that I shall not be concerned to distinguish between the first and the second editions of *The Critique of Pure Reason*. Kant was supremely confident of the absolute veracity of his philosophical claims, while, at the same time, acknowledging that he could and must improve their expression (articulation). Thus, he observes in the *Prolegomena* that a critique of pure reason "is never trustworthy except [that] it be perfectly complete, down to the most minute elements of pure reason. In the sphere of this faculty you can determine and define everything or nothing" (11).[90] Later in this same work he writes: either my system or another. You choose (128). Already in our previous chapter we have seen Kant make clear that human beings are not, in principle, partially free (and so not yet ripe for freedom as their masters often claim). Freedom is absolute (unconditional). We are either free, as citizens in the civil republic, or not free (in, for example, the republics of the ancient Greece and Rome as based on the state of nature: either rule or be ruled). The idea that metaphysical principles are partial (incomplete, conditional), like the idea of partial freedom, is unthinkable (it cannot be willed). It is only in absolutely willing the truth that I am able to confront the inadequacy (the incompleteness) of my principles. Our conjectural beginning, in and with practical reason, is the absolute, transcendental, and unconditional truth.

It follows, then, that Kant wholly embraces the idea of inevitable (infinite, providential . . .) progress as rational (moral and social) development. It is solely because our existence, our freedom, is complete (absolute, infinite) and so actual in itself that we can and must will to realize it ever more fully and richly. It is also the case, as we have seen, that Kant makes it absolutely clear that radical evil is central to (that evil is rooted in) human existence (consistent with the biblical doctrine of sin). It is precisely because the will is the sole thing that is good in, or even outside of, the world that evil (in its infinitely diverse manifestations) is central to our existence. Evil is the product of my good will, not the product of nature. Indeed, Kant stresses how important error is in making rational progress, at once morally and scientifically. Error can be committed only in the presence of the truth. Error is not ignorance of the truth. Education (edification) involves, and must involve, self-critique (self-examination, self-doubt, self-sacrifice), the humbling recognition on my part of the inadequacy (incompleteness) of my own concept (my own practice) of, for instance, freedom. The critique of pure reason as rational practice is an infinite process, always yet to be completed.

I shall conclude my preliminary remarks on what is involved in working through Kant's critiques of pure and practical reason with the observation that my reading of the two works will be largely sequential. I shall begin with the prefaces to the two editions of *Pure Reason*, together with the Introduction, followed by consideration of its three major sections: the Transcendental Aesthetic (sensibility), the Transcendental Analytic (understanding), and the Transcendental Dialectic (the errors that result when we claim to know what the thing is in itself), which is divided into psychology (the Paralogisms of the soul), cosmology (the Antinomies involving the world order, and so focusing on moral, natural, and divine necessity), and the Ideal of Pure Reason (on the three classical proofs of the existence of God). Kant holds that reason is naturally dialectical, i.e., that it unavoidably falls into illusion through its constant failure to restrict knowledge to objects of possible experience and thus its ceaseless effort to know the soul, the world, and God as things in themselves. But he also celebrates the fruitfulness of our errors insofar as we continue to struggle with and so never relinquish our effort to overcome them. There is no truth without error: error presupposes the truth. (There is no salvation without sin: sin presupposes salvation.) Still, we human beings have to work constantly not to rationalize our errors in either dogmatic or skeptical terms (that we either know or do not know the thing in itself).

Following our discussion of the first critique we shall continue to pursue our examination of how synthetic *a priori* judgments are possible in the second critique. What we shall find, however, is that our end is in our beginning. For reason is first and last practical, moral, free, self-determining, rational, categorical, immanent, noumenal, transcendental, and not (merely) theoretical, empirical, natural, determined, sensible, hypothetical, extrinsic, phenomenal, or temporal-spatial. The idea that reason is primarily (originally, in the beginning) practical is implicit throughout *The Critique of Pure Reason*. But it is only in the second *Critique* that Kant makes it explicitly clear that the answer to the question—How are synthetic *a priori* principles possible?—is that reason, in existing as the thing in itself, constitutes human beings as free, moral subjects whose vocation is critically active thinking as critically thoughtful action. It follows, then, that the answer to the question—How is metaphysics possible?—is that metaphysics is possible only because it is postulated by practical reason as actual. It is little wonder, then, as we shall now see, that Kant writes in the Preface to the second edition of *The Critique of Pure Reason* that he had to negate (overcome)[91] knowledge in order to make room for faith.

THE CRITIQUE OF PURE REASON

Kant opens the preface to the first edition of *The Critique of Pure Reason* with the observation that human reason is burdened with problems that it cannot dismiss and yet the solution to which exceeds all experience. The result is that reason finds itself on the battlefield of "endless controversies [that] is called *metaphysics*" (99). But today, he continues, we live "in the genuine age of *criticism*, to which everything must submit. *Religion* through its *holiness* and *legislation* through its *majesty* commonly seek to exempt themselves from it" (100–1). But thus they fail to see that abiding respect is granted "only to that which has been able to withstand its free and public examination" (101). In the *Prolegomena* Kant points out that it is critique alone that can "establish metaphysics as a science. . . . This much is certain, that whoever has once tasted critique will be ever after disgusted with all dogmatic twaddle" (114–15). For critique, he tells us, is "to the common metaphysics of the schools" what chemistry is to alchemy and astronomy to astrology (115).[92] In thus making it clear to us that critique is public, that it presupposes the republic of free citizens, as we saw Kant write in his essay on "Perpetual Peace," he indicates that ultimately both church and state, in all of their manifestations, are subject to public scrutiny. Yet, what are we to understand by "critique?" Chemistry and astronomy are sciences. Is critique a "science"? What Kant will ultimately show us is that, because the science of critique is metaphysics and the science of metaphysics is critique, metaphysical critique (the critique of metaphysics) rests on the concept of reason as practice (as that which cannot be known as a thing in itself). Indeed, we shall find that the sciences of nature themselves depend on answering, critically and metaphysically, the question that is central to metaphysical critique: How are synthetic *a priori* judgments possible?

In the Preface to the second edition of *Pure Reason* Kant observes that logic has always distinguished between the inductive (the *a posteriori* or synthetic) and the deductive (the *a priori* or analytic) sources of knowledge. But he then asserts what indeed it is that he undertakes to demonstrate in and through his two critiques: that, because all sciences must be *a priori* (and so not merely based on experience), they have knowledge of their object in two different respects: "either merely *determining* the object and its concept (which must be given from elsewhere), or else also *making* the object *actual*. The former is *theoretical* [scientific], the latter *practical* [moral] knowledge of reason" (107).[93]

Kant goes on to point out that we possess two species of theoretical knowledge, mathematics and physics (natural science). While mathematics, he writes, has long travelled "the highway of science," it is only since "a sudden revolution in the way of thinking" as initiated by such scientific thinkers as Copernicus, Bacon, and Galileo that we have a true science of nature (108).[94] When scientists like Galileo undertook to test (experiment with) nature scientifically, "a light dawned on those who study nature. They comprehended that reason has insight only into what it itself produces according to its own design; that it must take the lead . . . and compel nature to answer its questions." For merely "accidental observations, made according to no previously designed plan, can never connect up with a necessary law. . . . Reason, in order to be taught by nature, must approach nature with its principles" that it tests through experiments. Thus, reason discovers that, in order to learn from nature, "it has to seek in the latter (though not merely ascribe to it) in accordance with what reason itself puts into nature. This is how natural science was first brought to the secure course of a science after groping about for so many centuries" (109). What our scientists have shown us, consequently, is that we must "seek the elements of pure reason in that *which admits of being confirmed or refuted through an experiment*" (111). Thus it was that Copernicus initiated the scientific revolution, leading to Newton, by proceeding "in a manner contradictory to the senses yet true, to seek for the observed movements not in the objects of the heavens but in their observer" (113).

Since natural science has thus shown us that knowledge of empirical objects is not only synthetic (based on experience) but also *a priori* (based on prior principles), it is surely appropriate, Kant observes, to apply the analogy with science to metaphysics. "Up to now," he writes,

> it has been assumed that all our knowledge must conform to the objects; but all attempts to find out something about them *a priori* through concepts that would extend our knowledge have, on this presupposition, come to nothing. Hence let us once try whether we do not get farther with the problems of metaphysics by assuming that the objects must conform to our knowledge, which would agree better with the requested possibility of an *a priori* knowledge of them, which is to establish something about objects before they are given to us. (110)

According, then, to what Kant calls "the altered method of our way of thinking," our *a priori* knowledge of things consists of "only what we ourselves have put into them." But thus it follows, Kant continues, that we have knowledge of objects in two different respects: as objects of possible experience (nature) and as objects that we cannot know as things in themselves. Kant's point is that what he undertakes to demonstrate in *The Critique of Pure Reason* is that "the principle of pure reason" avoids conflict with itself only "when things are considered from this twofold standpoint but that an unavoidable conflict of reason with itself arises with a single standpoint [as either dogmatic or skeptical], [with the result that] then the experiment decides for the correctness of that distinction" (111). With this twofold standpoint, Kant observes further, it is evident that "the unconditioned must not be present in things" insofar as we know them but rather only insofar as we do not know them as things in themselves. It follows, then, that, since "speculative reason has been denied all advance in . . . the supersensible, what still remains for us is to try whether there are not data in reason's practical data for determining that transcendent rational concept of the unconditioned in such a way as to reach, beyond the boundaries of all possible experience, in accordance with the wishes of metaphysics, cognitions *a priori* that are possible, but only from a practical standpoint" (112). Kant acknowledges that a critique of reason that limits our understanding to the sensible world can appear to be metaphysically negative. But it becomes positive, he tells us, "as soon as we have convinced ourselves that there is an absolutely necessary practical use of pure reason (the moral use), in which reason unavoidably extends itself beyond the boundaries of sensibility, without needing any assistance from speculative reason, but in which it must also be made secure against any contradictions from the latter" (114).

Kant proceeds, then, to summarize the contents of his critique of speculative reason. In the Transcendental Aesthetic he shows that space and time are pure forms of sensible intuition (sense experience) and hence not things in themselves but "only conditions of the existence of the things as appearances." In the Transcendental Analytic he shows that the concepts of the understanding relate only to our sensible intuitions (sensible experience). Consequently, "we can have knowledge of no object as a thing in itself, but only insofar as it is an object of sensible intuition" (115). Still, while we cannot know objects as things in themselves, "we at least must be able to *think* them as things in themselves." It is thus evident, Kant reiterates, that, if we did not make our twofold distinction between speculative (theoretical) reason and practical (moral) reason, we would have no concept of freedom. For it is only with this twofold distinction that we, as natural objects of appearance, come under the sway of the mechanistic laws of nature, yet, as things in themselves, are free, moral subjects. It also follows, Kant continues, that I can have no true concepts of God, freedom, and immortality "for the sake of the necessary practical use of my reason unless I simultaneously *deprive* speculative reason of its pretension to extravagant insights. . . . Thus I had to deny *knowledge* in order to make room for *faith*." For it is, indeed, "the prejudice that without criticism reason can make progress in metaphysics . . . [that] is the true source of all unbelief conflicting with morality, which unbelief is always very dogmatic" (117). He adds that it is through "criticism alone [that] we can sever the very root of *materialism, fatalism, atheism*, of free thinking *unbelief*, of *enthusiasm* and *superstition*, . . . and finally also of *idealism* and *skepticism*" (119). It is in the Dialectic of *Pure Reason*, which is the last of the three major sections of the work, that Kant demonstrates the importance of limiting speculative (theoretical) reason to knowledge of objects of appearance. If, however, we extend speculative reason beyond experience to knowledge of things in themselves, then all we are left with are the extravagant contradictions of dialectical illusion.

Before he launches himself into the Transcendental Aesthetic on the pure (non-empirical) forms of sensible intuition, space and time, Kant yet again, in his Introduction, addresses the relationship between empirical (*a posteriori*) and analytical (*a priori*) knowledge, between experience and logic. He begins with the paradoxical observation that, "although all our knowledge commences *with* experience, yet it does not on that account all arise *from* experience" (136). We remember that, while all of us begin as natural beings, we are first and last moral beings. Kant's point is that our (scientific) knowledge of nature rests on both sensible experience and the concepts of necessity and universality. As Hume pointed out, while the sun has risen innumerable times in the past, we have no proof, either empirical (*a posteriori*) or logical (*a priori*), that it will rise tomorrow. Kant, indeed, saves the empirical science of nature, as requiring necessary and universal principles, from Hume (and also from scientific dogmatists who reduce human existence to sensible experience) by showing that, for example, the universal and necessary principle of causation (as found, for example, in gravity) is not empirical but *a priori*. But there are equally what Kant calls the "unavoidable problems of pure reason," those involving God, freedom, and immortality. These ideas cannot be based on either empirical knowledge or analytical logic. So how is metaphysics possible? How do we avoid getting lost in merely transcendent ideas? Kant points out that the

> light dove, in free flight cutting through the air that resistance of which it feels, could get the idea that it could do even better in airless space. Likewise, Plato abandoned the world of the senses because it set such narrow limits for the understanding and dared to go beyond it on the wings of the ideas, in the empty space of pure understanding. He did not notice that he made no headway by his efforts, for he had no resistance, no support. (140)

So it is, then, that "the real problem of pure reason is now contained in the question: *How are synthetic judgments a priori possible?*" (146). On the one hand, scientific knowledge (knowledge of nature) is at once synthetic (as based on experience) and *a priori* (as based on universal and necessary concepts, which Kant will subsequently call the categories of the understanding). On the other hand, moral practice (practical reason) is based on the universal and necessary principle of freedom, on the self-conscious relationship of will and existence: to exist is to will to exist; to will is to exist willingly. Thus, Kant writes that, while the principles of morality (moral existence) are *a priori*, they belong, not to the understanding, whose categories are of use only in knowing things of possible experience, but to reason, whose basis is the moral law (and so to be dealt with in *The Critique of Practical Reason*).

Having surveyed the prefatory and introductory sections of *The Critique of Pure Reason*, in which Kant outlines the issues that are central to responding to the question how our judgments are at once synthetic (as based on experience) and *a priori* (as found in necessary and universal principles that do not arise from nature), it is now time for us to consider the three major sections of his work. In the first two sections, the Transcendental Aesthetic and the Transcendental Analytic, Kant examines the structure of knowledge that is involved in our knowledge of things as objects of possible experience or, in simple terms, our knowledge of nature (the material, sensible world, the world of things or bodies as the objects studied by the natural sciences). His aim, in these two sections, is to show that our experiential knowledge is at once synthetic and *a priori*. Our knowledge of nature, as universal and necessary, involves the relationship between the aesthetic (sensibility) and the understanding (*Verstand*). Kant uses the term "aesthetic" in its pre-romantic (pre-nineteenth century) meaning and hence as traditionally (classically) understood as referring to the senses (sensibility). What is of particular importance is that Kant systematically distinguishes between understanding (*Verstand*), together with its categories of possible experience, and reason (*Vernunft*), together with its transcendental ideas (concepts). Thus, the human mind is constituted by a triad of functions: on the one hand, sensibility and understanding, which, united, constitute knowledge of objects of possible experience; and, on the other hand, reason, which, as the thing in itself, can be known, not in itself but solely as an object of possible experience, and which, in underlying objects of possible experience, constitutes practice (thinking, will). When the understanding attempts to go beyond sensible experience and to know the thing in itself, the result, as presented in the Transcendental Dialectic, which is the third principal section of *The Critique of Pure Reason*, is the illusory (dialectical) rationality of psychology (the soul), of cosmology (the world both natural and human), and of theology (God). We remember that Kant has indicated that we can grasp how metaphysics is possible only when its three principal ideas—the immortality of the soul, freedom, and God—are understood to be postulates as willed (thought) by practical reason and, consequently, not viewed as things that are knowable in themselves. But here we find ourselves, yet again, within the purview of *The Critique of Practical Reason*.

In undertaking to demonstrate to us how we know objects of possible experience *a priori*, Kant begins, in the Transcendental Aesthetic, with an explanation of the manner in which we receive sensations in and through what he calls the matter of sense experience. It is important to see that, in calling our sensations at once appearances and intuitions, he does not view either "appearance" in the Platonic sense as set in opposition to form (in representing what is true in itself) or "intuition" as special (intellectual) insight. But he does distinguish between the matter of our appearances or intuitions (our sensations) and their pure form—but, again, not in the sense of the Platonic opposition between them. His basic point is that the matter (the content) of our sensations (appearances or intuitions) is given to us *a posteriori* "while its form must lie ready for it in the mind *a priori*" (173). He thus holds that we have two kinds of *a priori*, pure, or transcendental forms of intuition, space and time. Space is the pure form of outer intuitions, and time is the pure form of inner intuitions. Thus, we see that space and time are not things (objects) in themselves but merely the subjective forms of our intuitions.

I shall follow the order of Kant's exposition in taking up, first, the pure form of outer intuition, space, and then, subsequently, the pure form of inner intuition, time. In regard to space, Kant's basic point is that space "is a necessary representation, *a priori*, that is the ground of all outer intuitions." While it is impossible to hold that there is no space, we can easily think of space without any particular objects. "It is therefore to be regarded as the condition of the possibility of appearances, not as a determination dependent on them, . . . [and so one that] is an *a priori* representation that necessarily grounds outer appearances" (175). It follows, then, that we can "speak of space, extended beings, and so on, only from the human standpoint," i.e., from one that is subjective, not objective. Space is thus real (objective) regarding the objects that it grounds. At the same time, however, space is ideal as the product of reason. "We therefore assert," Kant writes, "the *empirical reality* of space (with respect to all possible outer experience) though to be sure its *transcendental ideality*, i.e., that it is nothing [in itself] as soon as we leave aside the condition of the possibility of all experience and take it as something that grounds the things in themselves" (177). Kant summarizes his view of space as at one and the same time empirical and ideal (transcendental) in writing that the

> transcendental concept of appearances in space ... is a critical reminder that absolutely nothing that is intuited in space is a thing in itself and that space is not a form that is proper to anything in itself, but rather that objects in themselves are not known to us at all and that what we call outer objects are nothing other than mere representations of our sensibility, whose form is space but whose true correlate [or ground], i.e., the thing in itself, is not and cannot be known through them, but is also never asked after in experience. (178)

Having shown that space is the pure form of outer intuition that grounds objects as appearances, Kant proceeds to demonstrate that time as the pure form of inner intuition "is not an empirical concept that is somehow drawn from an experience" (178). We would not perceive simultaneity or succession (what we could call circular time and linear time) "if the representation of time [as the pure form of inner intuition] did not ground them *a priori*.... Different times are only parts of one and the same time" (178–79). Since time is not an objective but a subjective determination, it "is nothing other than the form of inner sense, i.e., of that intuition of our self and our inner state" (180). What this means, then, is that time is "merely a subjective condition of our (human) intuition (which is always sensible, i.e., insofar as we are affected by objects), and in itself, outside the subject, is nothing [in itself]'" (181). Because, then, time, like space, is at once empirically real and transcendental ideal, it applies only to objects of appearance, not to things in themselves. It follows, consequently, that the thing in itself, which can be known only as an object of appearance, does not "exist" in time and space. Kant points out that, while we do say that our representations succeed one another in time, this "only means that we are conscious of them as in a temporal sequence, i.e., according to the form of inner intuition. Time is not on that account something [absolute] in itself or any determination objectively adhering to things" (182). In other words, "time does not adhere to the objects themselves, rather merely to the subject that intuits them" (183).

Kant summarizes his exposition of space and time by reiterating the following two points. (1) The things (objects) that we intuit "are not in themselves what we intuit them to be, nor are their relations so constituted in themselves as they appear to us." (2) Without the subject intuiting, i.e., without "the subjective constitution of the senses," not only would the relations of objects in space and time but "indeed, space and time themselves would disappear. . . . [For] as appearances they cannot exist in themselves but only in us. What may be the case with objects in themselves [e.g., human beings] . . . [when] abstracted from all this receptivity of our sensibility remains entirely unknown to us" (185). It is thus always critically important to remember that, while we do not *know* what things are in themselves, what they are in themselves is precisely their existence as thinking, willing, desiring, active human beings: I think, *ergo* I exist as the thing in itself.

In light of his demonstration that space and time are pure forms of (sensible) intuition and not (rational) things in themselves, Kant proceeds to point out that the claim of idealist metaphysics (the school of Leibniz) that our appearances are but indistinct representations of things in themselves is utterly false. For what he has shown us is "that through sensibility we do not know the constitution of things in themselves merely indistinctly but rather not at all and [that], as soon as we take away our subjective constitution, the represented object with the properties that sensible intuition attributes to it is nowhere to be encountered, nor can it be encountered, for it is just this subjective constitution that determines its form as appearance" (186).

We recall, consequently, the observation on the part of Kant, which constitutes the basis of his revolution in modern philosophy—that we can proceed with a sound philosophy of both natural science and morality only in and through the recognition that knowledge of objects depends upon the mind (the subject), and not the mind (of the subject) on objects. He thus equally saves not only the natural science of objects but also the moral science of subjects from both the dogmatists (Leibniz) and the skeptics (Hume). The paradox, as always, is that we can possess systematic, necessary, comprehensive, and universal accounts of not only science but also morality solely if these accounts are at once actually real and transcendentally ideal, the first theoretical and the second practical. Thus, Kant stresses the importance of acknowledging that inner intuition (as the pure intuition of time) has nothing to do with knowing ourselves (as things in themselves). "Consciousness of itself (apperception)," he writes, "is the simple representation of the I." It does *not* represent self-activity (will or thought). "I do not say that bodies merely *seem* to exist outside me or that my soul only *seems* to be given" in my intuitions, for then my appearances would turn into mere illusion (189). "But this does not happen according to our principle of the ideality of all of our sensible intuitions; rather, if one ascribes *objective* [as distinct from empirical] *reality* to those forms of representations, then one cannot avoid thereby transforming everything into mere *illusion*" (190–91). Kant, consequently, concludes the Transcendental Aesthetic with the observation that we now possess the first of the two elements that are required to answer the question of how synthetic *a priori* propositions are possible. He has made clear to us that the only way in which to establish the reality (the reliability) of appearances (our sense experience of objects) is to show that our knowledge of objects as they appear to us is at once empirically real and transcendentally ideal and so presupposes the subject (who, as the thing in itself, to repeat yet again, can be *known*, not in itself but solely as an object of possible appearance).

Having shown in the Transcendental Aesthetic that the pure forms of intuition, space and time, ground (and so give coherence to) our sense experience, Kant next undertakes to demonstrate in the Transcendental Logic that our knowledge of nature is no less dependent on the concepts of the understanding. He points out that our knowledge of the natural world has two fundamental sources in the mind. They involve "the reception of representations (the receptivity of impressions)" and "the faculty for knowing an object by means of these representations (spontaneity of concepts)." Thus, an object of possible experience is at once "given" to us through the senses and "thought" by us through the understanding. "Intuition and concepts therefore constitute the elements of all our knowledge." Neither sensibility nor understanding "is to be preferred to the other. Without sensibility no object would be given to us, and without understanding none would be thought. Thoughts [concepts] without content are empty, intuitions without concepts are blind" (193–94).

Kant calls the logic in which the concepts of the understanding are grounded "transcendental" in order to distinguish it from the "general logic" of traditional metaphysics with its origins in the philosophy of Plato and Aristotle. General logic is based on the law of contradiction, which can tell us *that* a thing either exists or does not exist (something cannot both exist and not exist). But general logic cannot tell us that something exists, i.e., *what* its existence is. It is transcendental, as *a priori* synthetic, logic that allows us to determine that things exist and what they are—in the twofold sense of objects of possible (empirical) appearance and of things (rational) in themselves. We know the first but think (will/practice) the second. Transcendental logic is, we see, ultimately practical reason.

Kant thus prepares us for what he calls "the transcendental deduction of the categories of possible experience." Here, deduction is not analytic, as based on the law of contradiction, and so to be distinguished from induction as synthetic. Rather, transcendental deduction is the logic that we use in justifying our knowledge of possible experience as at once universal and necessary. For, as Kant proceeds to point out to us, jurists, when dealing with legal issues, distinguish between "what is lawful (*quid juris*) and that which concerns the fact (*quid facti*)" (219–20). Because jurists demand both legal proof and factual proof, they call legal claims deductions (or justifications). Thus it is, Kant writes, that "I . . . call the explanation of the way in which concepts can relate to objects *a priori* their *transcendental deduction* and distinguish this from the *empirical* deduction," since what it involved here is their "lawfulness." We see, then, that the pure forms of intuition and the concepts (categories) of the understanding, while distinct from each other, "both relate to objects completely *a priori*" (220). Kant provides us with the example of natural causation. That effects follow from a given cause, universally and necessarily (i.e., without exception or deviation), is not an empirical rule (indicating that things usually happen in this way) but a transcendental law. Yet, again, then, Kant declares that there are only two ways in which concepts and their objects can be brought together. "Either if the object alone makes the representation possible, or if the representation alone makes the object possible." Because the first way is empirical, it never yields universally necessary laws. Thus, it is only when we "justify" our knowledge of objects of possible experience transcendentally that we can possess knowledge that is universal and necessary. But Kant is careful to add that "we are not here talking about . . . causality by means of the will" since the concepts of the understanding do "not produce its object as far as its *existence* is concerned" (224). Our sensible experience is real but only in and through objects of possible experience. But I *exist* as a subject who wills to exist.

Kant points out yet further that our knowledge of objects, as based on both the pure forms of intuition and the categories of the understanding, presupposes the unity of consciousness, i.e., one consciousness that gives unity to our experience. He calls this unity of consciousness "the transcendental unity of apperception." Indeed, if we speak of having different experiences, this is only because "they belong to one and the same universal experience" (234). Without this unity of consciousness, Kant points out, our perceptions "would be nothing but a blind play of representations, i.e., less than a dream" (235). Indeed, he writes that it is "only because I ascribe all perceptions to one consciousness (of original apperception) can I say of all perceptions that I am conscious of them. . . . The objective unity of all (empirical) consciousness in one consciousness (of original apperception) is thus the necessary condition even of all possible perception" (240).

It is for this reason, then, Kant observes, that all "attempts to derive these pure concepts of the understanding from experience and to ascribe to them a merely empirical origin are therefore entirely vain and futile" (235). But he acknowledges that the idea that "nature should direct itself according to our subjective ground of apperception, indeed in regard to its lawfulness even depend on this, may well sound quite contradictory and strange." But his point, as always, is that "this nature is nothing in itself but a sum of appearances, hence not a thing in itself but merely a multitude of representations of the mind" (236). He writes additionally that "we ourselves bring into the appearances that order and regularity in them that we call *nature*, and [that] moreover we would not be able to find it there if we, or the nature of our mind, had not originally put it there. For this unity of nature should be a necessary, i.e., *a priori* certain unity of the connection of appearances" (241). It follows, he continues, that understanding legislates (provides the law) "for nature, i.e., without understanding there would not be any nature at all. . . . All appearances as possible experience, therefore, lie *a priori* in the understanding and receive their formal possibility from it, just as they lie in the sensibility as mere intuitions and are only possible through the latter as far as their form is concerned" (242). Kant repeats yet again that, while it sounds "exaggerated and contradictory . . . to say that the understanding is itself the source of the laws of nature," such, however, is the truth. But he is careful to remind us that, while merely empirical (as distinct from necessarily universal) laws do not have their origin in the pure understanding, they are, nevertheless, "only particular determinations of the pure laws of the understanding" (242–43). Kant provides a summary of his transcendental deduction of the categories of possible experience in writing that the pure concepts of the understanding are

> necessary *a priori* in relation to experience only because our knowledge has to do with nothing but appearances, whose possibility lies in ourselves, whose connection and unity (in the

representation of an object) are entirely encountered in us, and thus must precede all experience and first make it possible as far as its [universal and necessary] form is concerned. And from this ground, the only possible one among all, our deduction of the categories has been conducted. (244)

Still, Kant has important clarifications to add. He writes that it is important "to make intelligible the paradox that must have struck everyone in the exposition of the form of inner sense [the pure form of inner intuition]: namely how this presents even ourselves to consciousness only as we appear to ourselves, not as we are in ourselves" (257). In other words, it is critically important to acknowledge "that through inner sense we intuit ourselves only as we are internally affected *by our selves*, i.e., as far as inner intuition is concerned, we know our own subject only as appearance but not in accordance with what it is in itself. . . . I therefore have *no knowledge* of myself *as I am* but only as I *appear* to myself" (259–60). What follows, then, is that consciousness of self is not knowledge of self, for which intuition is required. It also follows that "I cannot determine my existence as that of a self-active being [i.e., as a thing in itself], rather I merely represent the spontaneity of my thought, i.e., of the determining, and my existence always remains only sensibly determinable, i.e., determinable as the existence of an appearance. Yet this spontaneity is the reason I call myself an *intelligence*" (260).

Kant repeats yet again that we *think* objects solely through the categories of the understanding and that we *know* objects solely through the sensible intuitions that are related to those categories. It follows, then, that we have *a priori* knowledge solely of objects of possible appearance. But Kant is careful to add that, in order to forestall what he calls any premature unease regarding the restriction of knowledge to sensible objects, our thinking is not bound to the knowledge of objects, for it "can still have its true and useful consequences for the *use* of the subject's *reason*, which, however, cannot be expounded here, for it is not always directed to the determination of the object, thus to knowledge, but rather also to that of the subject and its willing [i.e., to practical reason]" (264).

Having completed the transcendental deduction of the pure concepts (categories) of the understanding, Kant has now attained his goal of demonstrating how synthetic *a priori* judgments are possible. But he has also signaled to us that, while knowledge is limited to objects of sensible experience, thinking is not so limited. Thus, there lies ahead of us the Transcendental Dialectic, as the third principal section of *The*

Critique of Pure Reason, which results from the illusory attempt on the part of the understanding to surpass the limits of sensibility in claiming to know the thing in itself. Finally, of course, there is the critique of practical reason itself, wherein thought (as will) is directed, not to the natural determination of the object but to the free determination of the subject. Before, however, taking up the Transcendental Dialectic, I want, first, to consider several subsidiary passages in the Transcendental Logic in which Kant deepens our grasp of his accomplishment in demonstrating that, while our knowledge of objects of possible experience rests on the transcendental unity of subjective consciousness (apperception), we do not know what the subject is in itself. Indeed, he has shown us that we do not know what nature is in itself. For the unity of nature, i.e., the necessary universality of natural law, is subjective, not objective.

In the first passage to consider Kant refutes what he calls the material idealism of those metaphysicians who claim either dogmatically that knowledge of the existence of objects in space outside us is false and impossible (Berkeley) or skeptically that knowledge of the existence of objects in space outside us is doubtful and indemonstrable (Descartes). Having already demonstrated that space is not a thing in itself, Kant dismisses the dogmatic claim. Regarding the skeptics, he observes that, because the "I" as the unity of consciousness does not constitute knowledge of the self as a thing in itself, "the determination of my existence in time is possible only by means of the existence of actual things that I perceive outside myself" (327). In other words, "inner experience in general is possible only through outer experience in general. Whether this or that putative experience is not mere imagination must be ascertained according to its particular determinations and through its coherence with the criteria of all actual experience" (328–29). In thus restricting knowledge to objects of possible experience, Kant saves the reliability of our sense experience. Knowledge of our inner self, as an object of possible experience, presupposes knowledge of outer things (and vice versa).

In the second passage to consider Kant raises the question whether the field of possibility is greater than the field of actual things. His point in addressing this question is to remind us that transcendental logic deals with actual things. That something is possible which is not actual can be true only in analytical logic, while in transcendental logic only that which I know to be actual is possible. Possibility, consequently, does not extend the reach of actual experience. He adds, however, that the concept of "absolute possibility (which is valid in every respect) is no mere concept of the understanding and can in no way be of empirical use; rather it belongs solely to reason, which goes beyond all possible empirical use of the understanding" (332). Indeed, we shall find that absolute possibility characterizes the actuality of the will.

In the third and last passage to consider here Kant examines "the ground of the distinction of all objects in general into *phenomena* and *noumena*" (338). The phenomena-noumena distinction provides Kant with yet another way in which to spell out the difference between things as objects of possible appearance and things in themselves and so between understanding (nature) and reason (freedom). He opens this section—let us say, poetically!—with the observation that, having now surveyed "the land of pure understanding . . . and determined the place for each thing in it," it is but an island that is "surrounded by a broad and stormy ocean, the true seat of illusion," whose fog banks and rapidly melting icebergs "pretend to be new lands and, ceaselessly deceiving with empty the hopes the voyager [who is] looking around for new discoveries, entwine him in adventures from which he can never escape and yet also [can] never bring to an end" (338–39). The point that Kant wants to make in poetically designating understanding as occupying nature as an island that is surrounded by the illusory promises of new lands to conquer is that understanding "cannot accomplish one thing, namely, determining for itself the boundaries of its use and knowing what may lie within and what without its whole sphere." Since understanding, then, does not know the limits of its own horizons, "it continually oversteps the boundaries of its territory (as is unavoidable) and loses itself in delusion and deceptions." Thus, Kant proceeds to show that, in order for understanding to be limited to the fruitfulness of its unlimited use in the empirical sphere, we must presuppose the "transcendental use of a concept" that is "related to things *in general* and *in themselves*" (340). It is, consequently, only in and through the distinction between noumena and phenomena, between reason and understanding, that we can restrict knowledge to objects of possible appearance. Kant reminds us that he has already demonstrated that sensible appearances "do not pertain to things in themselves but only to the way in which, on account of our subjective constitution, things appear to us." Still, we have to consider what this subjective constitution is. In other words, it "follows naturally from the concept of an appearance in general that something must correspond to it which is not itself appearance . . . but which in itself . . . must be something, i.e., an object independent of sensibility" (348).

We arrive, consequently at the concept of a noumenon. But Kant takes care to add that its use is solely negative, in limiting understanding to its empirical use, and not positive in giving us knowledge of the thing in itself. "The concept of a noumenon," he writes, "is therefore merely a *boundary concept*, in order to limit the pretension of sensibility and therefore only of negative use" (350). He is careful, then, to emphasize that, since the noumenon is required in setting limits to sensibility, "it is not a special *intelligible object* for our understanding" (351). He thus concludes:

> The concept of the noumenon is therefore not the concept of an object but rather the problem, unavoidably connected with the limitation of our sensibility, of whether there may not be objects entirely exempt from the intuition of our sensibility, a question that can only be given the indeterminate answer that, since sensible intuition does not pertain to all things without distinction, room remains for more and other objects; they cannot therefore be absolutely denied, but in the absence of a determinate concept (for which no category [of the understanding] is serviceable) they also cannot be asserted as objects of our understanding. (380–81)

It is evident, yet again, that the objects that are not phenomenally determined as objects of the understanding but are noumenally determined are human beings who freely, and necessarily, determine themselves as active subjects through their use of practical reason. The paradox, as always, is that human beings can and do possess universal and systematic knowledge of nature solely because reason is, first and last practical (self-determining). Scientific knowledge of nature presupposes (rests) on human freedom. Phenomenal understanding is grounded on noumenal reason as practice.

Still, before taking up the critique of practical reason as the groundwork of the metaphysics of morals, it is important for us to see the contradictory consequences that follow when the understanding exceeds its phenomenal limits and falsely claims to know the noumenal thing in itself. In, then, the third (and last) principal section of *The Critique of Pure Reason*, the Transcendental Dialectic, Kant discusses the topics that have traditionally been central to metaphysics: the soul, the world (both natural and human), and God: psychology, cosmology, and theology. As always, his aim is to demonstrate that, if we do not limit knowledge to objects of possible appearance but, instead, claim to know the thing in itself, then we find ourselves bereft of both the universal and necessary laws of nature and the universal and necessary laws of morality. Both or neither. Reason thus becomes dialectical, i.e., illusory, when we fail to distinguish between understanding as serving a solely phenomenal (hypothetical or theoretical) end and reason as serving a solely noumenal (categorical or practical) end. In other words, we have to limit knowledge to objects of possible appearance in order to make room for faith as the critique of practical reason.

Kant introduces the Transcendental Dialectic as the "logic of illusion" by pointing out that illusion, i.e., error, is to be found neither in our senses (appearances) nor in our understanding but solely in our judgments. The senses do not and cannot err; and the understanding, insofar as it is consistent with itself, does not and cannot err. Kant also points out that he is concerned here, not with empirical (e.g., optical) illusion, which is self-correcting, but with transcendental illusion, i.e., when the understanding attempts to surpass the limits of sensibility whereby it becomes falsely "transcendent." He also distinguishes between logical illusion, which, again, is self-correcting, and transcendental illusion. Transcendental illusion occurs, consequently, when "the subjective necessity of a certain connection of our concepts on behalf of the understanding is taken for an objective necessity, the determination of things in themselves" (386). The paradox, as always, is that, since knowledge of objects is grounded in the subject (on subjective unconditionality), we constantly fall into the illusion of turning the subject into an object that is knowable as conditional things in nature are knowable.

Indeed, Kant points out that it is altogether impossible to avoid, i.e., to eliminate, transcendental illusion. We shall always be tempted to depart from the island of understanding and to sail forth into the fog and icebergs of illusory reality. His aim, then, in the Transcendental Dialectic is to uncover and thus to protect us from our dialectical illusion. He acknowledges that transcendental, unlike merely logical, illusion will never "disappear and cease to be an illusion. . . . Hence there is a natural and unavoidable dialectic of pure reason," which, unlike the errors committed by either an artless bungler or an artful sophist, "irremediably attaches to human reason, so that, even after we have exposed the mirage, it will still not cease to lead our reason on with false hopes, continually propelling it into momentary aberrations that always need to be removed" (386–87).

Kant calls the three species of dialectical illusion, corresponding to the three classical topics of metaphysics—the soul, the world, and

God—the paralogisms, the antinomy, and the ideal of pure reason. The paralogisms of pure reason result when the "I," which is "a mere consciousness that accompanies every concept," is turned into an object that is knowable in itself. In exposing the dialectical illusion of the paralogisms on the soul, Kant associates it with the metaphysics of what he calls "*transcendental realism*, which regards space and time as something given in themselves (independent of our sensibility)." He calls his own position "transcendental idealism," according to which appearances are "regarded as mere representations and not as things in themselves, and accordingly that space and time are only sensible forms of our intuition, but not determinations given for themselves or conditions of objects as things in themselves" (426). Thus, he writes that "external things exist as well as my self, and indeed both exist on the immediate testimony of my self-consciousness, only with this difference: the representation of my Self, as the thinking subject, is related merely to inner sense, but the representations that designate extended beings are also related to outer sense." It follows, then, that the transcendental idealist (Kant) is no less an empirical realist who "grants to matter, as appearance, a reality which need not be inferred but is immediately perceived" (427). In contrast, the transcendental realist (whether skeptic or dogmatist) is, consequently, also an empirical idealist who denies the reality of matter. Kant thus holds that matter (bodily nature) is mere appearance. Indeed, he writes that we "must note well this paradoxical but correct proposition, that nothing is in space except what is represented in it." He observes further that it will "sound peculiar" to claim "that a thing can exist only in the representation of it" solely if we forget that corporeal things "are not things in themselves but only appearances, i.e., representations" (429).

Why, then, Kant asks, "do we have need of a doctrine of the soul grounded merely on pure rational principles?" He answers: "chiefly with the intent of securing our thinking Self from the danger of materialism." In other words, it is not a question that, if matter were eliminated, "then all thinking and even the existence of thinking beings would be abolished." Indeed, the opposite is the case: "if I were to take away the thinking subject, the whole corporeal world would have to disappear, as this is nothing but the appearance in the sensibility of our subject and one mode of its representations" (433). Regarding the answers that have traditionally been given to the "metaphysical" questions about the soul—its relationship to the body and its existence both prior and subsequent to the body—they are mere hypostatizations of "what exists merely in thoughts." Then, in a truly extraordinary passage, Kant explains to us how matter is to be viewed as at once empirically real and transcendental ideal. It needs to be quoted at length:

> For matter, whose community with the soul excites such great reservations, is nothing other than a mere form, or a certain mode of representation of an unknown object, through that intuition that one calls outer sense. Thus, there may very well be something outside us, which we call matter, corresponding to this appearance; but in the same quality as appearance it is not outside us but is merely as a thought in us, even though this thought, through the sense just named, represents it as being found outside us. Matter thus signifies not a species of substance quite different and heterogeneous from the object of inner sense (the soul) but rather only the heterogeneity of the appearances of substances (which in themselves are unknown to us), whose representations we call external in comparison with those that we ascribe to inner sense, even though they belong as much to the thinking subject as other thoughts do; only they have in themselves this deceptive feature that, since they represent objects in space, they seem to cut themselves loose from the soul, as it were, and hover outside it, although space itself, in which they are intuited, is nothing but a representation, whose counterpart in the same quality outside the soul cannot be encountered at all. (434)

The issue, then, is not how the soul relates to an external substance different from itself but simply how our inner and outer representations "may be conjoined with one another according to constant laws so that they are connected into one experience" (434). Kant makes it clear that, if we ask *why* outer intuition (i.e., material space filled with motion) is possible in a thinking subject, we must answer that we do not know and will never know. Indeed, it is important to remember that the question that shapes the critique of pure reason is *how* synthetic *a priori* judgments are possible, not why they are possible. They are possible solely because they are actual. We do not and cannot know *why* they exist. I do not and cannot know "why" I exist. All I can and must say is: I think, *ergo* I exist. Thus, we see that the endlessly metaphysical debate about the nature of our soul as a thinking being and its relationship to the material world of the body "is merely a consequence of the fact that one fills the gaps regarding what one does not know with paralogisms of reason, making thoughts into things and hypostatizing them.... One can place all *illusion* in the taking of a *subjective* condition of thinking for the knowledge of an *object*" (439). There follows, then, what is surely the most extraordinary passage in all of Kant:

> Now it is indeed very illuminating that I cannot know as an object in itself that which I must presuppose in order to know an object at all and that the determining Self (the thinking) is different from the determinable Self (the thinking subject) as knowledge is different from its object. Nevertheless, nothing is more natural and seductive than the illusion of taking the unity in the synthesis of thoughts for a perceived unity in the subject of these thoughts. One could call it the subreption of hypostatized consciousness. (442)

In short: underlying the surreptitious arguments of classical metaphysicians is their failure to see that, if they hype and so hypostatize human consciousness (the "I") as an object that can be known in itself, they will fall into the endless contradictions of dialectical illusion. Only in and through what Kant calls our twofold point of view, according to which we distinguish nature from freedom, phenomena from noumena, and subjects from objects, do we secure universal and necessary laws of both science and morality. That by which I know an object I cannot know as an object but can and must solely will as a subject whose existence is grounded in practical reason.

In the second section of the Transcendental Dialectic, entitled "The Antinomy of Pure Reason," Kant takes up questions of cosmology. He examines, in four antinomies, the conflicting (contradictory) claims that are made about the world in traditional metaphysics. In the first two antinomies, metaphysicians claim that, on the one hand, the world is finite, has a beginning and an end in time, and consists of simple parts and that, on the other hand, the world is infinite and has no beginning or end and no simple parts. In the third antinomy we encounter the antinomian debate whether human beings are originally free or whether, like all natural beings, they are subject to the necessary laws of nature. Finally, in the fourth antinomy metaphysicians debate whether there is an original being or whether natural objects constitute their own being. These cosmological claims are antinomian in the sense that each of the two opposing sides in the four pairs of antinomies claims that the assertion advanced in the proposition that it opposes is false because it contradicts the law, i.e., it is *anti-nomos*. The approach that has traditionally been taken in addressing these four pairs of cosmological antinomies is that, following the law of contradiction, one of the propositions in each of the four pairs of antinomies must be true and one must be false. Thus, the antinomian debate has continued for centuries without resolution. Kant shows, however, that the four cosmological antinomies are all soluble—once we give up the law of contradiction as the basis of metaphysics and demonstrate how synthetic *a priori* propositions are possible. His solution, then, to the four antinomies is to show that each of the two opposing claims in both the first and the second antinomies is false and that each of the two opposing claims in both the third and the fourth antinomies is true. Since the first two antimonies involve the world as an object of possible appearance and not as a thing in itself, it is evident, Kant writes, that we do not know, cannot know, and shall never know *what* the cosmos is in itself, i.e., whether it is finite (it has an end) or infinite (it is endless), whether it is simple (indivisible) or infinitely divisible. The opposing propositions in each antinomy are equally false since neither of them has a basis in scientific demonstration. But the situation regarding the third and the fourth antinomies is completely different. For here we are concerned with, not only things of possible appearance but also things in themselves. Thus, Kant shows us that, in the third antinomy, there is no contradiction between human freedom (the moral law) and natural freedom (scientific law) and, in the fourth antinomy, no contradiction between the idea of a supreme (original) being and beings in the world, since neither the human being nor the original being, as a thing in itself, can be known as an object of possible appearance. Each of the two opposing propositions in both the third and the fourth antinomies can, consequently, be viewed as true.

Of the four antinomies it is, above all, the third that interests us here, for in it Kant provides a truly insightful discussion of freedom. In other words, in the third antinomy, as in no other section of *The Critique of Pure Reason*, he directly calls upon (presupposes) the concept of reason as practice. It is instructive to cite the complete title of the third antinomy: "Resolution of the Cosmological Idea of the Totality of the Derivation of Occurrences in the World from their Causes." Causation, Kant writes, involves two completely different notions of totality, one constitutive (of the thing in itself) and the other regulative in providing understanding with the rules to which it must adhere in determining things as object of possible appearance. He initiates his discussion of the third antinomy with the declaration that, regarding "what happens, one can think of causality in only two ways: either according to *nature* or from *freedom*" (532). On the one hand, since the causality of appearances rests on temporal and so always on preceding conditions, everything that occurs in nature has a prior cause. But freedom, he tells us, is "the faculty of beginning a state *from itself*," with the result that it is not determined in time according to the law of nature.[95] Thus, freedom is spontaneous (as we keep in mind that *spons* is a Latin word for will) in starting from itself alone. Indeed, he observes, this is the "*transcendental* idea of *freedom* on which the practical concept of freedom is grounded." What this means is that "in the human being there is a faculty of determining oneself from oneself, independently of necessitation by sensible [natural] impulses" (533). There would, consequently, be no power of choice if "appearance were things in themselves" (534). Thus, we distinguish between intelligible and sensible causes. Put differently, the human being is intelligible in his actions and sensible in belonging to the natural world of causal effects. Kant reminds us, then, of the significance of the distinction that he makes between transcendental idealism (involving the idea of freedom) and empirical realism (that we do belong to the world of sensible nature). If, however, we were to "give in to the deception of transcendental realism, then neither nature nor freedom would be left" (518). It is also instructive to recall that neither freedom as the totality of self-causing actions nor nature as the totality of causal effects was found in classical antiquity.

Kant points out yet further that the "ought" of moral imperatives "expresses a species of necessity and a connection with grounds which does not occur anywhere else in the whole of nature. . . . We cannot ask at all what ought to happen in nature, any more than we can ask what properties a circle ought to have" (540). However powerfully sensible stimuli may move me, "they cannot produce the *ought*" (541). Whatever contingent conditions may help us to explain why, for example, an individual told a malicious lie, "one nevertheless blames the agent." The agent's action is to be regarded as "entirely unconditioned in regard to the previous state, as though with that act the agent had started a series of consequences entirely from himself. This blame is grounded on the law of reason, which regards reason as a cause that, regardless of all the empirical conditions . . . , could have and ought to have determined the conduct of the person to be other than it is." Indeed, Kant continues, we regard the causality of reason as "complete in itself," and "the action is ascribed to the agent's intelligible character; . . . hence reason, regardless of all empirical conditions of the deed, is fully free, and this deed is to be attributed entirely to ... [the agent's] failure to act" (544). But Kant is careful to add that, while we know how rational human beings ought to act, we do not know "why" a particular person acts in a particular way. Still, he observes that this question does not touch upon his demonstration "that, since in freedom a relation is possible to conditions of a kind entirely different from those in natural necessity, the law of the latter does not affect the former; hence each is independent of the other and can take place without being disturbed by the other" (545).

Kant adds yet further that he has not been concerned here "to establish the *reality* of freedom" or even "to prove the *possibility* of freedom. . . . Freedom is treated here only as a transcendental idea, through which reason thinks of the series of conditions in appearance [as] starting absolutely through what is sensibly unconditioned." Thus, his sole aim in the third antinomy has been solely to show that it "rests on a mere illusion and that nature at least *does not conflict with* causality through freedom" (546). Kant's aim in the fourth antinomy is precisely the same, i.e., to show that the idea of the existence of sensible things does not prelude the existence of an original, necessary being, while also, at the same time, it does not lead to it. Empirically conditioned necessity, he writes, does not lead us to "deny that the entire series [of conditions] could be grounded in some intelligible being" (547–48). But again he stresses that his intent here is not "to prove the unconditionally necessary existence of any being" but just to show "that there is no true contradiction between these [two] assertions, hence they can *both be true*. . . . Reason goes its way in its empirical use and a special way in a transcendental use. . . . For here the intelligible cause . . . of the possibility of the sensible series, in general, whose existence, independent of all conditions of the latter and unconditionally necessary in regard to it, is not at all opposed to the unbounded contingency of the former" (548). Consequently, both of the opposing propositions of the fourth antinomy—that everything in the world of sense has an empirically conditioned existence and that there is an original, unconditioned existence—may be viewed as true.

In concluding his discussion of the fourth antinomy Kant observes that it quite naturally leads us to "look around us for something different from all appearances, hence for an intelligible object, with which this contingency would stop" (550). Thus, it is that, in the third and last part of the Transcendental Dialectic, entitled "The Ideal of Pure Reason," he examines the three arguments that have traditionally been advanced to prove the existence of God as the unconditioned, absolute, and infinite being that would bring contingency to its true end and that are known as the ontological, the cosmological and the teleological (called by Kant the "physico-theological) arguments proving the existence of God.

As a means of introducing the ideal of pure reason Kant observes that we do possess the transcendental idea of the sum total of all possibility. For, indeed, since all negation depends on affirmation, we possess the idea of "transcendental affirmation, which is a Something.... No one can think of a negation determinately without grounding it on the opposite affirmation.... The ignorant person has no concept of his ignorance.... All concepts of negations are thus derivative." We arrive, consequently, at "the idea of an All of reality.... All true negations are then nothing but *limits*, which they could not be called unless they were grounded in the unlimited (the All)," i.e., in the affirmation of reality (555). Since this is, however, simply the concept of the thing in itself and so the transcendental ideal, Kant is quick to add that we thus presuppose, not "the existence of a being, conforming to the ideal, but only the idea of such a being in order to derive from an unconditioned [infinite] totality of thoroughgoing determination the conditioned totality, i.e., that of the limited [the finite]" (557). This ideal of pure reason, in being viewed as the ground of the possibility of all things, can thus be called the original being, the highest being, and the being of all beings. But if we claim that this highest reality is given objectively and that it constitutes a thing, then we are in the realm of mere fiction in hypostatizing our idea through our transcendental subreption. Still, such, Kant reminds us, "is the natural course taken by every human reason.... If something, no matter what, exists, then it must also be conceded that something exists *necessarily*" (560). He acknowledges "that this concept has a certain cogency if it is a matter of making *decisions*," for, within the practical realm, we must take sides. But, in the theoretical realm (of the understanding), "nothing impels us to come to a decision" (561).[96] There is then no moral "ought" or obligation involved.

I shall summarize, in the simplest terms possible, Kant's critique of the three arguments, which were traditionally advanced to prove the existence of God, as dialectical (illusory). Two points are essential here. First, Kant demonstrates that both the cosmological argument (in arguing from existence in general to an originally existing thing) and the teleological argument (in arguing from existing things to their end or first cause) presuppose the ontological argument (in showing the necessary relationship between beings and the concept of being). Second, it is thus his denial of the cogency of what he calls and has been called ever since the ontological argument that is essential here. In order to be clear, I shall begin by citing the ontological argument as found in the opening proposition of Spinoza's *Ethics* (Kant does not as such refer to this formulation): there is one thing that cannot be thought (by human beings) without existing necessarily and that is God. Kant's basic point, in denying the cogency of the argument linking thought and existence (I think, *ergo* I exist), is that it involves either an analytic or a synthetic proposition. If I say that God exists, God is, or God is being, I provide merely an analytic definition that describes not the actual existence of anything but only its possibility. For it is no less true to state that God does not exist. . . . If, on the other hand, I say that I have one hundred thalers (dollars) in my pocket, my claim is purely hypothetical—until and unless I take the money out of my pocket and thus prove the empirical factuality of my claim. It would then be false to say that I do not have the money that I say I have. Kant writes, consequently, that the "entire problem of the transcendental ideal comes to this: either to find a concept for the absolute necessity or to find the absolute necessity for the concept of some thing. . . . But both entirely transcend all the utmost efforts to *satisfy* our understanding on this point but also all attempts to make it *content* with its incapacity. The unconditioned necessity, which we need so indispensably as the ultimate sustainer of all things, is for human reason the true abyss" (574).

Kant proceeds, however, to point out that he has been concerned, in the Ideal of Pure Reason, to define "theoretical knowledge" as regarding "*what* [sensibly] *exists*" and "practical knowledge" as regarding "*what ought* [actually] *to exist*." He observes further that, because

> there are practical laws that are absolutely necessary (the moral laws), then, if these necessarily presuppose any existence as the condition of the possibility of their *binding* force, this existence has to be *postulated*, because the conditioned from which the inference to this determinate condition proceeds is itself known *a priori* as absolutely necessary. In the future we will show about the moral laws that they not only presuppose the existence of a highest being but also, since in a different respect they are absolutely necessary, they postulate this existence rightfully, but, of course, only practically. (585)

Kant writes yet further that "all attempts of a merely speculative use of reason in regard to theology are entirely fruitless and by their internal constitution null and nugatory . . . [and] that the principles of reason's natural use do not lead at all to any theology; and, consequently, if one did not ground it on moral laws or use them as guides, there could be no theology of reason at all." It follows, then, that the synthetic *a priori* principles of the understanding have only an immanent (empirical), not a transcendent, use. Experience "never offers us the greatest of all possible effects" (586). Kant adds, nevertheless, that, while speculative reason thus has no positive use, it has an enormously significant negative use "since the same grounds for considering human reason [to be] incapable of asserting the existence of such a being ... also suffice to prove the unsuitability of all counter-assertions" as found in atheism, deism, and anthropomorphism (588). The highest being thus remains a "faultless ideal" whose objective reality cannot be proved by speculative reason "but also cannot be refuted; and, if there should be a moral theology that can make good this lack, then transcendental theology, up to now only problematic, will prove to be indispensable" (589). He continues:

> Necessity, infinity, unity, existence outside the world (not as soul of the world), eternity without all conditions of time, omnipresence without all conditions of space, omnipotence, etc.: these are purely transcendental predicates, and hence a purified concept of them, which every theology needs so very badly, can be drawn only from transcendental theology. (589)

In simple terms, theoretical reason properly regulates the empirical understanding of objects of possible experience. It does not constitute the objective existence of the thing in itself.

Kant summarizes what he calls "the result of the entire Transcendental Dialectic" in writing that "the final aim of the ideas of pure reason ... become dialectical only through misunderstanding and carelessness. ... The unity of reason is the unity of a system, and this systematic unity does not serve reason objectively as a principle, extending it over objects, but subjectively as a maxim, in order to extend it over all possible empirical knowledge of objects" (610). Thus, reason directs the understanding to open "up new paths into the infinite (the undetermined) with which the understanding is not acquainted, yet without ever being the least bit contrary to the laws of its empirical use." Because reason is "a mere idea ... it is therefore not assumed absolutely and *in itself* as something [empirically] actual" (611). Kant notes once again that to "take the regulative principle of the systematic unity of nature for a constitutive one and to presuppose hypostatically, as a cause, what is only in the idea as a ground for the harmonious use of reason is only to confuse reason" (617).

Still, Kant continues to make it clear to us that, if we ask "whether there is anything different from the world which contains the ground of the world order and its connection according to universal laws, then the answer is: *Without a doubt*. For the world is a sum of appearances, and so there has to be some transcendental ground for it, a ground thinkable merely by the pure understanding" (618–19). But if we ask whether this ground is an absolutely real and necessary being, then our question is entirely meaningless. Nevertheless, we may "think this being different from the world in accordance with an *analogy* with objects of appearance ... but only as object in the idea and not in reality" and so only as a thing in itself that is not known to us as an object of sensible experience. In other words, we "can allow certain anthropomorphisms" that are useful to reason in its regulative function (619). Thus, while we can and must presuppose such a being in seeking systematic unity in nature, still, we do not thereby extend our knowledge beyond the objects of possible experience. It is, consequently, evident, Kant concludes, that our critique of pure reason has demonstrated that speculative reason can "never get beyond the field of possible experience and that the proper vocation of this supreme faculty of knowledge is to employ all its methods and principles only in order to penetrate into the deepest inwardness of nature in accordance with all possible principles of unity" (622).

Kant has thus made it evident to us, in and through his critique of reason as limiting the understanding to knowledge of sensible objects in the natural world, that our answer to the question how synthetic *a priori* principles is possible is because they are in actuality practical. It is thanks only to the twofold standpoint of noumenal reason and phenomenal understanding, whereby we limit knowledge to objects of possible experience, that we can, on the one hand, secure systematic (scientific) knowledge of the natural world and, on the other hand, uphold human freedom as the domain of practical reason. We are thus eternally in the presence of the paradox that objects (as known) rest on subjects (as unknown), i.e., that the thing in itself can be known as an object of possible appearance only insofar as it is not knowable as a thing in itself but is solely willed or thought. It is because the pure forms of sensible intuition, natural space and time, and the rational categories of the understanding are both grounded in the transcendental apperception of the conscious "I" that they make possible our actual knowledge of nature. For nature, we saw Kant indicate to us, is not itself natural (phenomenal) but noumenal. Nature is not conscious of itself as natural. Nature is the product of the human mind conscious of itself as not only natural (sensible) but also rational (transcendental). But human beings constantly fall into the dialectical illusion of attempting to extend their knowledge beyond the limits of knowing *that* sensible things exist (as subject to natural law) to *what* their existence is in itself—as the soul, the world, and the ideal of pure (reason). The result is the subreption of the hypostatized consciousness, the surreptitious attempt on our part to know the knower (the knowing human subject) as an object. Thus, Kant dramatically reminds us: that by which we know an object (of nature) we cannot know as an object of nature but only practice freely as a rational human subject. Either/or. Either we absolutely distinguish between natural law and moral law. Or we absolutely lose both the laws of nature and the laws of morality.[97] We thus understand why the ancient Greeks possessed neither the universal laws of nature nor the universal laws of morality.

It is also instructive to recall why and how it was that Hume (in typifying Enlightenment thinkers) denied the possibility of either natural law or moral law, of either natural science or human freedom. In continuing to adhere to the logic of contradiction as the ground of truth, he distinguished between synthetic claims (as inductively based on experience) and analytic claims (as deductively based on logic). Thus, he asserts at the end of *An Enquiry Concerning Human Understanding* that, because metaphysics contains neither "*any abstract reasoning concerning quantity or number*" nor "*any experimental reasoning concerning matters of fact and existence*," I say—"Commit it then to the flames: for it can contain nothing but sophistry and illusion" (184). Indeed, just a page earlier in *An Enquiry* he writes that "the sciences of quantity and number ... may safely, I think, be pronounced the only proper objects of knowledge and demonstration. All other enquiries of men regard only matter of fact and existence; and these are evidently incapable of demonstration. Whatever *is* may *not be*. No negation of a fact can involve a contradiction. The non-existence of any being, without exception, is as clear and distinct an idea as its existence" (183). Still, in the Conclusion of Book I of *A Treatise of Human Nature*, Hume acknowledges that, having denied the possibility of experiential knowledge, he inescapably finds himself in express contradiction with himself. To rely on the understanding is to find that it entirely subverts itself. To give up the understanding is simply to follow fancy. "We have, therefore, no choice left but betwixt a false reason [understanding] and none at all [fancy]. For my part, I know not what ought to be done"—except, as he will proceed to show us, either to give up thinking altogether or to base all knowledge (both natural and moral) on habit and custom, i.e., on the thinking of others (and so, ultimately, on their fancies) (268).

What Hume failed to recognize is that there is one fact whose non-existence is contradictory, the fact of his own existence, together with the existence of that which he thinks. He cannot deny (doubt) the existence of either that which thinks or that which is thought without justifying (and so proving by transcendentally deducing) the necessary existence of both as freely determined. It is little wonder, then, that Kant famously acknowledged that Hume awakened him from his dogmatic slumbers in the bed of German metaphysics (as transmitted by what Kant calls the school tradition of Leibniz and Wolff). Kant rescued metaphysics from the flames of skepticism by submitting it to what we may call the fiery critique of pure reason. In asking how metaphysics—as based on the transcendental logic of synthetic *a priori* propositions and not on the law of logical contradiction, according to which there is no fact whose non-existence is contradictory—is possible, he shows us that metaphysics actually exists solely as postulated, necessarily, by self-determining human beings. The conventional content of metaphysics—soul (psychology), nature (cosmology), and God (theology)—can be liberated from the dialectical illusions of the paralogisms, the antinomies, and the ideal of pure reason (involving the proofs of the existence of God), all of which stem from the dualistic opposition between logical deduction and empirical induction, between the noumenal and the phenomenal, as found in the philosophy of Plato and Aristotle, solely by demonstrating that reason is, first, last, and always, transcendentally (noumenally) practical. Human beings, as self-determining, free agents, are obligated to view their existence as grounded in, not the general logic of contradiction but the transcendental logic of the necessary relationship between thinking (willing) and existence. There *is* one thing whose non-existence is contradictory, i.e., which cannot be thought without necessarily existing, and that is "I (who) am."

Kant, consequently, not only saves metaphysics from the dialectical illusions of both skeptical nihilism and dogmatic absolutism. But also he indicates, yet, only in general terms (except in the third antinomy), that we can demonstrate the necessary relationship between thinking (the *a priori*) and existence (the synthetic or the *a posteriori*), the very claim made in the ontological argument as formulated by Anselm, Descartes, and Spinoza, solely on the basis of the concept of reason as practical (transcendental). The paradox here, which is also the very epitome of irony, is that what Kant truly manages to accomplish in the Transcendental Dialectic is to save the ontological argument from the dialectical illusions of metaphysics, as based on general logic of contradiction. He shows us, but only indirectly, that the necessary relationship between thinking (will) and existence constitutes, not theoretical reason (the understanding) but practical reason. Having named "ontological" the argument underlying all proofs claiming to establish the necessary existence of God and having shown it to be false, Kant thus prepares the critical way for grasping the necessary relationship between thinking (will) and existence as constituting reason as practice. In the most basic terms his answer to the question—How are synthetic *a priori* judgments possible and so How is metaphysics possible?—is because metaphysical judgments are actual as constituted in and through the necessary existence of reason as practice. Indeed, we saw Kant make clear, in the fourth antinomy, that, when we limit the understanding to the phenomenal knowledge of objects of possible experience and so give up all claims to know God as an object, we in no sense eliminate the idea of the supreme cause (or end) of the world.

We are now ready, I think, to take up *The Critique of Practical Reason* in which Kant demonstrates that the groundwork of metaphysics is the moral law. Freedom, immortality of the soul, and God are postulates of practical reason and so not objects that can be known in themselves. They can and must be thought, willed, and so necessarily brought into existence by practical reason as grounded in the universal law of morality. We human beings constitute the necessary—the *a priori* synthetic—relationship between thought and existence in willing to bring the kingdom of ends into practical existence. It is evident, then, that reason is the revelation of religion, as we saw Kant write in his works on religion that we discussed in the previous chapter. What lies ahead of us, then, is the challenge of comprehending the critique of practical reason as constituting the truth of the ontological argument and so as proving the necessary existence of not only the thinker but also of that than which the thinker can think nothing greater in existence.

THE CRITIQUE OF PRACTICAL REASON

I begin with the Conclusion of *The Critique of Practical Reason*. Here, Kant articulates yet again, but now in strikingly poetic manner, the twofold position that, he continues to show us, characterizes our human world as at once sensible and intelligible, both theoretical and practical. He writes: "Two things fill the mind with ever new and increasing admiration and reverence, the more often and the more steadily one reflects on them: *the starry heavens above me and the moral law within me*." He continues: I don't have to search for and merely speculate about them as if they were veiled in a transcendent region beyond me. "I see them before me and connect them immediately with the consciousness of my existence." The first begins from my place in the visible world of sensibility and boundlessly extends in both space and time. "The second begins from my invisible self, my personality, and presents me in a world which has true infinity." Because this second world is intelligible it is evident to me that my connection with both the visible and the invisible worlds "is not merely contingent, as in the first case, but universal and necessary." What follows, then, is that my place in the visible world of contingent nature, with its "countless multitude of worlds, annihilates, as it were, my importance as an *animal creature*"—with the result that, soon after my visible self has been "provided with vital force (one knows not how) [it] must give back to the planet (a mere speck in the universe) the matter from which it came" (269). In contrast, however, my place in the invisible world

> infinitely raises my worth as an *intelligence* by my personality, in which the moral law reveals to me a life independent of animality and even of the whole sensible world, at least so far as this may be inferred from the purposive determination of my existence by this law, a determination not restricted to the condition and boundaries of this life but reaching into the infinite. (269–70)

Kant indicates to us in *The Critique of Pure Reason* that the answer to the question how synthetic *a priori* judgments are possible, in other words, how we justify the laws of nature as universal and necessary, was inextricably bound to the question how metaphysics is possible. He now proceeds in *The Critique of Practical Reason* to show us, in comprehensively systematic terms, that metaphysics is possible solely because it is actually founded on the moral law as practiced, universally and necessarily, by all human beings. The paradox here, as is evident in what we saw him write above in the Conclusion of *Practical Reason*, is that the visible world of nature is finite while the invisible world of personality, which is grounded in the moral law, is infinite. We justify our necessary and universal knowledge of the visible things of possible appearance on the basis of the invisible thing in itself, our personal self, which we do not know. But what Kant now proceeds to make clear to us is that there is no transcendental deduction (justification) of the universal and necessary existence of the self. For practical reason begins from itself alone in determining the infinite existence of the self as grounded in the moral law. I think, *ergo* I exist—in relationship to others. It is evident that Kant, in demonstrating that reason as practical necessarily brings into existence the universality of the moral law, goes beyond Descartes, but certainly not Spinoza (whose great work in philosophy is entitled *Ethics*!). But the irony here is that his demonstration that practical reason, as based on the moral law, is thus self-justifying simply represents a deeper grasp of the necessary and universal relationship between thought and existence as demonstrated earlier by Anselm, Descartes, and Spinoza. Having repudiated, in naming as ontological, the argument claiming to prove the necessary existence of God, in *The Critique of Pure Reason*, Kant demonstrates its absolute truthfulness in *The Critique of Practical Reason*. But he never acknowledges, in explicit terms, that the demonstration that reason is transcendentally practical and so constituted in and through the moral law as universally necessary is but to realize the truth of the ontological argument.

Metaphysics, Kant thus shows us, is possible because its three fundamental principles—freedom, the immortality of the soul, and God—are actually postulates of, i.e., the demands made by, reason in and through its practice of the moral law. He also shows us that the practical demands that reason makes upon us are nothing other than the moral law of the Bible: do unto others what you want others to do unto you.[98] In short, we may say that, from the beginning, metaphysics, in bringing into the existence the kingdom of ends, is moral practice, not dogmatic theology. We remember that Kant tells us in the Preface to the second edition of *The Critique of Pure Reason* that he had to limit knowledge to visible objects of possible experience—the starry heavens above us—in order to make room for faith—in the moral law within our invisible self as the thing in itself. The finite is what we know as a conditional, contingent object. The infinite is what we practice as an unconditionally absolute subject.[99]

In now undertaking to discuss *The Critique of Practical Reason* I shall, as always, confine my examination of Kant's revolutionary work to consideration of its most critically important ideas. Stripped, then, of its often merely formalistic details, the work is structured on what Kant views as the fundamental distinction between, on the one hand, the postulate of freedom, and, on the other hand, the postulates of the immortality of the soul and of the existence of God. Whereas the moral law presupposes, i.e., it is unthinkable outside of, the idea of freedom (of the freedom of the will), it is the moral law that leads to and so provides the grounds of the ideas of the immortality of the soul and of the existence of God. The immortality of the soul is postulated as the idea of infinite progress. The self, in being freely grounded on the moral law, is infinitely and absolute whole and one (it is not merely partly itself). Yet, we human beings must always contend with the (partial) demands of our inclinations (our flesh) and so with what it is that constitutes our happiness as a subject. There is no escaping our subjectivity. Freedom is an infinite project that is always yet to be wholly completed. Regarding the postulate of God, we human beings aspire to a life whose ultimate end, in conjoining freedom, as an infinite project, with the attainment of true happiness, is the realization of the highest good. Happiness does not lead to morality. Rather, the moral law, while it is not founded on, yet, at the same time, is not opposed to our sensual nature, postulates God as the highest good whereby the actual union of morality and happiness, of duty and pleasure, of mind and body is made possible.

In the very first paragraph of the Preface of *Practical Reason* Kant declares that, precisely because reason is practical, "it proves its reality and that of its concept by what it does, and all subtle reasoning against the possibility of its being practical is futile." Then, in the very next sentence he declares that with "this faculty transcendental *freedom* is also established." He immediately adds that freedom is "the *keystone* of the whole structure of a system of pure reason" and that the concepts of God and immortality, while finding no support in speculative reason, have "their *possibility* ... *proved* by this: that freedom is real, for this idea reveals itself through the moral law" (139). He adds further that, while freedom "is the condition of the moral law," the "ideas of *God* and *immortality*, however, are not conditions of the moral law" (140). He then observes that what he calls "the enigma of the critical philosophy" is here properly explained: that, while we deny objective status to the supersensible use of the categories of the understanding, we "*grant* them this *reality* with respect to the objects of pure practical reason" (141). At this point in his discussion Kant introduces the concept of desire in order to distinguish it from the *feeling of pleasure*" (143). In simple terms, desire, as we shall continue to see, is to be understood as identical with will (as practical reason). He concludes the Introduction "on the idea of a critique of practical reason" with the statement that "the law of causality from freedom, that is, some pure practical rational principle, constitutes the unavoidable beginning and determines the objects to which alone it can be referred" (148–49). For here "we have to do with a will and have to consider reason, not in its relation to objects but in relation to this will and its causality" (149).

In initiating his discussion of what he calls "the Principles of Pure Practical Reason," Kant observes that "practical principles," when understood as determining the will, are at one and the same time subjective maxims and objective, i.e., universal and necessary, practical *laws* that hold "for the will of every rational being" (153). We are here in the familiar territory where practical laws are imperatives that are at once universal and necessary. "Thus freedom and unconditional practical law," Kant writes, "reciprocally imply each other" (162). Whence we have the formulation for which Kant is famous: "So act that the maxim of your will [i.e., what you desire] could always hold at the same time as a principle in giving a universal law" that is true for all people and thus is what all individuals desire. But it is then particularly interesting to note that Kant declares that consciousness "of this fundamental law may be called a fact of reason because one cannot reason it out from antecedent data of reason . . . and because it instead forces itself upon us of itself as a synthetic a priori proposition" (164). But he is careful to add that the fact that we are originally conscious of the moral law "is not an empirical fact but the sole fact of pure reason which, by it, announces itself as originally lawgiving" (164–65). He adds yet further that we cannot deny this fact of reason since it is evident that "the judgment that people pass on the lawfulness of their action" always involves their holding "the maxim of the will in an action up to the pure will." Indeed, the principle of morality is "not limited to human beings only but also applies to all finite beings that have reason and will [angels?] and even includes the infinite being as the supreme intelligence" (165). But since our human will is not holy as God's will is holy, the moral law is for us an obligatory imperative, a duty. Still, "the concept of *holiness* . . . is nevertheless a practical *idea*, which must necessarily serve as a *model* to which all finite rational beings can only approximate without end and which the pure moral law, itself called holy because of this, constantly and rightly holds before their eyes" (166).

In next proceeding to distinguish between moral autonomy and moral heteronomy Kant articulates the difference between the autonomous principle of morality and "the [heteronymous] principle of *one's own* happiness [when it is] made the determining the ground of the will" (168). He observes that the fundamental difference between "the maxim of self-love," which cannot be universalized without falling into self-contradiction, and the moral law, which commands what is true for all, is plain to all. "To satisfy the categorical imperative of morality is within everyone's power at all times; to satisfy the empirically conditioned precept of happiness is but seldom possible.... A command that everyone should seek to make himself happy would be foolish, for one never commands of someone what he unavoidably wants already" (169–70). It is important to take note of the fact that Kant includes among the heteronymous grounds of the will, as merely subjective and empirical, the will of God (as found among "theological moralists") (172).

Having established the ground of the moral law in the "fact," transcendental and so practical, and not empirical and so theoretical, of the autonomous, free, universal, and necessary actions of human beings, as recognized by everyone, Kant, in the remaining sections of *The Critique of Practical Reason*, proceeds to elaborate his basic principles, often with rich insights. It is important, I think, to savor this richness. Thus, he writes that

> we are conscious through reason of a law to which all our maxims are subject, as if a natural order must at the same tine arise from our will. This law must therefore be the idea of a nature not given empirically and yet possible through freedom, hence a supersensible nature to which we give objective reality, at least in a practical respect, since we regard it as an object of our will as pure rational beings. Hence the difference between the laws of nature to which *the will is subject* and of a *nature which* is subject *to a will*. (175)

Kant proceeds to point out, as is already evident to us, that the critique of reason involves two altogether different problems: "how, *on the one side*, pure reason can *know* objects a priori and how, *on the other side*, it can be an immediate determining ground of the will, that is, of the causality of a rational being with respect to the reality of objects (merely through the thought of the universal validity of its own maxims as law)"

(175–76). Thus, we do not ask "how objects of the faculty of desire are possible... but only how reason can determine maxims of the will" (176). For we recognize that pure, practical "laws are possible only in relation to the freedom of the will; but on the presupposition of freedom they are necessary or, conversely, freedom is necessary because those laws are necessary as practical postulates. How this consciousness of moral laws or, what is the same thing, this consciousness of freedom is possible cannot be further explained." We see, consequently, that "the moral law is given . . . as a fact of pure reason of which we are a priori conscious and which is apodictically certain" (177). Thus, we have what Kant calls the "paradoxical" situation that, while the moral principle itself cannot be transcendentally deduced, since it is the actuality that freely, universally, and necessarily underlies all possibility, it is the principle on which the transcendental deduction of the categories of possible experience rests. It is evident, then, that "the moral law thus determines that which speculative philosophy had to leave undetermined, namely the law for a causality the concept of which was only negative in the latter, and thus for the first time provides objective reality to this concept" (178).

Having explained yet again that we can deduce and hence justify our knowledge of the objects of possible experience solely on the basis of the freely self-determining will of the subject whose practical reason constitutes the fact of necessary existence, Kant proceeds to discuss good and evil as the "only objects of a practical reason" (186). The issue, consequently, to be addressed is whether the objects of good and evil determine the will or whether the will determines the objects of good and evil. Either/or. Thus, Kant writes "that either desire is the determining ground of the concept of the object as a good, or the concept of the good is the determining ground of desire (of the will)" (188). In the first case, what desire wills—in doing its duty—determines what the good is. In the second case, our feelings and inclinations—happiness—determines the good for us. Kant acknowledges that, because we human beings are creatures of need, "our well-being and woe count for a *very great deal* in the appraisal of our practical reason, and, as far as our nature as sensible beings is concerned, *all* that counts is our happiness . . . ; but happiness is not *the only thing* that counts" (189). For we are, first and foremost, creatures whose life is grounded in the moral law. This is, consequently, "the place," Kant tells us,

> to explain the paradox of method in a *Critique of Practical Reason*, namely, that the concept of good and evil must not be determined before the moral law ... but only ... after it and by means of it.... [I]t is ... the moral law that first determines and make possible the concept of the good, insofar as it deserves this name absolutely. This remark ... explains at once the occasioning ground of all the errors of philosophers with respect to the supreme principle of morals. For they sought an object of the will in order to make it into the matter and ground of a law ..., whereas they should first have searched for a law that determined the will, a priori and immediately, and only then determined the object conformable to the will. (190–91)

Then, Kant repeats what he has already shown us. Whether these philosophers "placed this object of pleasure, which was to yield the supreme concept of good, in happiness, in perfection, in moral feeing, or in the will of God, their principle was in every case heteronomy" (191–92). In making our feeling the determining ground of good and evil, they reduced the moral law to empirical (and so merely contingent) conditions. For it is only the law that, in prescribing "to reason nothing more than the form of its universal lawgiving as the supreme condition of maxims, can be a priori a determining ground of practical reason" (192).

Kant observes yet again that "how a law can be of itself, and immediately, a determining ground of the will (though this is what is essential in all morality), is for human reason an insoluble problem and identical with that of how a free will is possible" (198). What counts, consequently, is not to supply an incentive for the moral law but to grasp how the moral law must be viewed as its own incentive. We do not will the good because it pleases us or makes us happy. For it is, indeed, the moral law that strikes down our self-love and self-conceit in building up in us our "respect for the moral law.... Hence the moral law unavoidably humiliates every human being when he compares with it the sensible propensity of his nature. If something represented *as a determining ground of our will* humiliates us in our self-consciousness, it awakens *respect* for itself insofar as it is positive and a determining ground" (199–200). But Kant is then careful to point out that "respect for the law is not the incentive to morality," but rather it is morality, "by rejecting all the claims of self-love in opposition with its own," that is its own incentive (201). It is evident, then, that respect "is directed only to persons never to things." We may love our pets and fear beasts of prey, but we do not give them our respect.

Extraordinary scenes of nature and extraordinary feats of human beings may generate in us feelings of admiration and even amazement, but not respect. So Kant writes:

> Fontenelle [died 1757] says: "*I bow before an eminent man but my spirit does not bow.*" I can add: before a humble, common man in whom I perceive uprightness of character in a higher degree than I am aware of in myself *my spirit bows*, whether I want it or whether I do not [want it] and hold my head ever so high that he may not overlook my superior position.... *Respect* is a *tribute* that we cannot refuse to pay to merit, whether we want to or not; we may indeed withhold it outwardly, but we still cannot help feeling it inwardly.... Respect for the moral law is therefore the sole and also the undoubted moral incentive, and this feeling is also directed to no object except on this basis. (202–3)

Kant adds further that, while respect for the moral law inevitably humbles us in lowering our "pretensions to moral self-esteem," it also at the same time represents "an elevation of the moral—that is, practical—esteem for the law itself on the intellectual side" (203–4). The idea of a moral incentive involves, then, the idea of "an *interest*, which can never be attributed to any being unless it has reason and which signifies an *incentive* of the will insofar as it is *represented by reason*." Since the moral law must be the incentive for a morally good will, "the *moral interest* is a pure sense-free interest of practical reason alone." It is, then, what in truth interests us that constitutes our maxims (opinions, judgments, feelings, ideas . . .). Our maxims, consequently, are genuinely moral and so necessary and universal insofar as they rest "solely on the interest one takes in compliance with the law" (204).

I take the opportunity here of raising the following question: When we say that something interests us (that we find it interesting), is this because it merely arouses our feelings (of self-interest as self-love) or because it truly engages us in thinking about the moral consequences involved? Thus, Kant comments yet again on the singular fact that, and I paraphrase him, all human beings take an interest in the moral law, i.e., that there is one thing that cannot be thought (or willed) by them without necessarily existing, and that is the moral law. To think (to act) is to constitute the moral law as truly interesting for all persons, including oneself. "There is," Kant writes, something so singular in the boundless esteem for the pure moral law stripped of all advantage—as practical reason, whose voice makes even the boldest evildoer tremble and forces him to hide from its sight, presents it to us for obedience—that one cannot wonder at finding this influence of a mere intellectual idea on feeling quite impenetrable for speculative reason and at having to be satisfied that one can yet see a priori this much: that such a feeling is inseparably connected with the representation of the moral law in every finite rational being. (204)

What is singularly interesting, consequently, about the moral law is that, while it cannot be known by theoretical reason (the understanding), it can and must be practiced by all human beings as that which constitutes the fundamental priority of their lives. We are once again in the presence of the ontological argument, as I paraphrased it earlier in this paragraph.

Kant proceeds, then, to discuss respect for the law at some length. It involves both the "consciousness of a *free* submission of the will to the law, yet as combined with an unavoidable constraint put on all inclinations [of self-interest] though only by one's own reason" (204–5). An action that is done in accordance with the law, in excluding "every determining ground of inclination, is called duty" as necessitating our "determination to action." While our necessary submission to the law may induce displeasure in us, still, "since this constraint is exercised only by the lawgiving of our *own* reason, it also contains something *elevating*," our feeling of self-approbation (205).[100] When we are determined to act solely by the law, without self-interest, we find that we become "conscious of an altogether different interest, subjectively produced by the law, which is purely practical and *free*" (205). It is the self-approbation, or, in other words, the self-respect that is consciously the product of our moral interest in the law, not our self interest, that leads to the distinction that Kant makes "between consciousness of having acted *in conformity with duty* and *from duty*." Whereas to act "in conformity with duty" is to conform legally to what others say and do, "moral worth . . . must be placed solely in this: that the action takes place from duty, that is, for the sake of the law alone" (205). Kant then waxes eloquent on the sublimity of duty. Duty, he writes, and what we owe to duty, is the sole name

> that we must give to our relation to the moral law. We are indeed lawgiving members of a kingdom of morals possible through freedom and represented to us by practical reason for our respect; but we are at the same time subjects in it, not

its sovereign, and to fail to recognize our inferior position as creatures and to deny from self-conceit the authority of the holy law is already to defect from its spirit, even though the letter of the law is fulfilled. (206)

Having thus shown that to live according to the spirit of the law is to act from duty while to live in accordance with the letter of the law is to act in conformity with duty, Kant hails "*Duty!* Sublime and mighty name that embraces nothing charming or insinuating but requires submission, and yet does not seek to move the will by threatening anything that would arouse natural aversion or terror in the mind." What "origin is there worthy of you," he asks, "and where is to be found the root of your noble descent which proudly rejects all kinship with the inclinations, descent from which is the indispensable condition of that worth which human beings alone can give themselves?" (209). He answers: "It can be nothing less than what elevates a human being above himself (as a part of the sensible world [of time and space]), what connects him with an order of things" in which the practice of reason constitutes the kingdom of moral ends. It is thus "personality," which is at one and the same time our "freedom and independence from the mechanism of the whole of nature" and our capacity as human beings to be subject to "pure, practical laws," as given by our own reason, that makes it possible to view our "highest vocation only with reverence and its laws with the highest respect." Kant then goes on to tell us that connected with this origin of the moral law are "many expressions that indicate the worth of objects according to moral ideas." We call the moral law "*holy* (inviolable")" even though a "human being is indeed unholy enough but the *humanity* in his person must be holy to him." While there is nothing in the whole of creation that cannot serve merely as a means, "a human being alone, and with him every rational creature [God, angels?], is an *end in itself*; by virtue of the autonomy of his freedom he is the subject of the *moral law*, which is holy." Because human beings are persons and not merely things, they are "to be used never merely as a means but as at the same time an end. We rightly attribute this condition even to the divine will with respect to the rational beings in the world as its creatures, inasmuch as it rests on their *personality*, by which alone they are ends in themselves" (210).

That the "idea of personality" reveals "the sublimity of our nature (in its vocation)," while at the same time "striking down [our] self-conceit," is naturally evident, Kant continues to emphasize, "even to the most common human nature and is easily observed" (210). When we behold, he continues, "an upright man [who] is in the greatest distress, which he could have avoided if he could only have disregarded duty," do we not find that this man is "sustained by the consciousness that he has maintained humanity in its proper dignity in his own person and honored it, that he has no cause to shame himself in his own eyes and to dread the inward view of self-examination?" (210–11). While his consolation is not happiness, still, he is upbuilt in his sense of self-worth and dignity. "This is how the genuine moral incentive of pure practical reason is constituted," Kant writes. "It is nothing other than the pure moral law itself insofar as it lets us discover the sublimity of our own supersensible existence and subjectively effects respect in human beings for their higher vocation. . . . The majesty of duty has nothing to do with the enjoyment of life; it has its own law and also its own court" (211).

While it is evident that Kant is a demanding moralist—Do your duty and bear (suffer) the consequences!—still, in no sense does he view the moral law of practical reason as dualistically opposed to human happiness, enjoyment, or pleasure. Indeed, Kant will proceed to point out that the critical distinction between the principles of morality and happiness involves, not an opposition between them but simply the subordination of the second to the first. "It can even in certain respect," he writes, be a duty to attend to one's happiness, "partly because happiness (in which belong skill, health, wealth) contains means for the fulfillment of one's duty, and partly because lack of it (e.g., poverty) contains temptations to transgress one's duty. However, it can never be a direct duty to promote one's happiness, still less can it be a principle of all duty" (214–15). What Kant thus opposes is eudaimonism whose philosophical proponents claim that the incentives of the moral law are pleasure and pain. Indeed, we shall see that, with his two postulates of the immortality of the soul, which involves infinite progress, and of God as the principle of the highest good, Kant will make human happiness, while not providing the incentives for our moral practice, the necessary creation of the moral law. Moral practice leads to true happiness. Happiness itself, however, does not lead to moral practice. Just as Kant in *The Critique of Pure Reason* limits knowledge to objects of possible appearance by showing that all claims to know the thing in itself are purely dialectical and thus illusory, so in *The Critique of Practical Reason* he shows that, if we base the incentives of the moral law on sensible objects (those involving pleasure and pain), we shall fall, with Hume, into a contradictory skepticism that is but the mirror opposite of contradictory dogmatism.

Before, however, taking up the postulates of the immortality of the soul and of God, it is important, first, to ponder the extraordinary implications of the claims that Kant makes on behalf of duty. I want to emphasize three points. First, Kant observes that, while human beings are unholy enough, their humanity—their personality, their very personhood, we may say—is holy. The moral law, in its holiness, is our majestic, noble, sublime sovereign with its own court. Indeed, God himself is subject to the sovereign moral law. Notwithstanding the omnipotence and the omniscience of God, he, too, is under the obligation of treating all rational beings as ends in themselves and not as means, as subjects and not as natural objects (or things). God, too, is subject to the sovereign law of morality. Additionally, human beings are, like God, supersensible (i.e., supernatural). But the supersensible, i.e., the transcendental, we remember, constitutes the realm of human practice and so the kingdom of ends (of God) on earth. We see, then, that Kant, in showing how metaphysics (as involving the postulates of freedom, the soul, and God) is possible, demonstrates that it is actual in and through the moral practice of rational human beings. The supersensible, it is evident, is the kingdom of God on earth. The holy will of every human being, and so the "common man," is the earthly sovereign before whom we all bow in dutiful humility. The Lord our God is subject to the mighty sovereignty of the moral law. And the Lord our King (of Prussia), too?

The second point regarding the implications that arise from the concept of duty and that I want to emphasize here is closely related to the first. Kant is emphatic that the concept of duty, as universally subjecting our will to the obligations of the moral law, is evident to all persons, to the common man no less than to those whose elevated rank reflects the particularity of their (natural) birth, not the universality of their (moral) being. Kant does not, however, directly (politically, in politeness!) pursue the implications of this second point any more than of the first. Our third and final point concerns the origin of the moral law. We saw Kant pose the question of what origin there could possibly be that would be worthy of duty and where could there possibly be found the root of its noble descent that alone provides "the indispensable condition of that worth which human beings alone can give themselves." While Kant, unlike his contemporaries such as Herder or his nineteenth century successors, like Hegel and Marx and their followers, does not directly take up the question of the historical origin of the concept of the moral law and so of the concept of reason as practice, still, he does make it evident, as we have already seen and as we shall soon again see, that it is found in the Bible and not in ancient Greek philosophy. At the same time, however, he does continue to remind us that, unless we adopt the twofold standpoint of natural law and of moral law, we shall remain inescapably lost in the antinomy of pure reason. Kant thus appears to leave hanging the question of the origin, at once historical and ontological, of his twofold standpoint. Or does he?

Since we are not able to provide a transcendental "deduction of the supreme principle of pure practical reason—that is, the explanation of the possibility of such a cognition a priori," we are, Kant writes, "now forced to assume it and are thereby justified in doing so by the moral law, which postulates it." He reminds us that "there are many" (like Hume) who, in claiming to explain freedom on the basis of empirical principles, hold that it is a natural, "psychological property" and not a "*transcendental* predicate of the causality of a being that belongs to the sensible world" (215). Thus, it is, Kant continues, that these philosophers

> deprive us of the grand disclosure [*Eröffnung*] brought to us through practical reason by means of the moral law, the disclosure, namely, of an intelligible [transcendental] world through realization of the otherwise transcendent concept of freedom, and with this deprive us of the moral law itself, which admits absolutely no empirically determining ground. (215)

Kant then proceeds to expose the disastrous results that follow when freedom is viewed, not as beginning from itself alone and thus as self-determining, but, instead, as determined by the inclinations of pain and pleasure.

Before, however, we review Kant's brilliant critique of the dialectical illusion of the empiricists, I want, first, to consider what we are to understand by the "grand disclosure" of the moral law of which these empirical philosophers deprive us. Once again, we have seen Kant resolutely insist that we cannot provide a transcendental deduction of practical reason—since, indeed, the transcendental deduction of the categories of the objects of possible appearance itself rests on (i.e., presupposes) the concept of transcendental reason (self-consciousness) as practical. But how, then, do we begin? What is the origin, the root, of the moral law? What does it mean to say that we are "forced to assume it," as we saw Kant write above? Is freedom itself to be understood as the force that compels us to be free? I am equally resolute in wanting to be clear that, while Kant truly understands the importance of grounding nature in freedom—the object in the subject, knowledge of objects of possible experience in the thing in itself, which cannot be known as a natural object—he continues in his failure to see that his twofold standpoint is grounded in the concept of necessary existence as demonstrated by the ontological argument. Kant commits no error as such here. He knows that he must begin with freedom as the necessary (absolute, unconditional) condition of the contingent conditions of nature. Indeed, it is thanks to the "grand disclosure brought to us through practical reason by means of the moral law" that we know that we belong to an intelligible (supersensible, transcendental) world: I think, *ergo* I am. It is evident, surely, to us, that this "grand discourse" is revelation. Indeed, we shall see that Kant directly associates the moral law of freedom with the biblical command to love God above all and your neighbor as yourself. We shall also see that Kant directly associates the biblical idea of divine creation with the noumenal world (of practical reason) and not with the phenomenal world (of nature), while at the same time drawing an absolute distinction between the moral law, as found in biblical theology, and the concepts of morality, as found in Greek philosophy. It is the rare philosopher or theologian, indeed, who recognizes that biblical revelation incarnates the ontological argument—the necessity of thinking (willing) existence—that to think (to be conscious) is to disclose the existence of the moral law.

Still, it is hardly surprising that, as we shall now see, Kant directly connects the moral law with the Bible. For, as we found in the previous chapter, the major aim that he has in his two major works on religion, together with his essay on the "Conjectural Beginning of Human History," is to show that practical reason constitutes the very core of biblical religion. Indeed, Kant states, to recall what he wrote earlier in *The Critique of Practical Reason*, that we are "lawgiving members of a kingdom of morals possible through freedom" who are "subjects in it, not its sovereign." If, however, we "fail to recognize our inferior position as creatures" and thus "deny from self-conceit the authority of the holy law," we consequently "defect from it in spirit, even though the letter of the law is fulfilled" (206). Kant then proceeds to observe that this is consistent with "such a commandment as *Love God above all, and your neighbor as yourself*" (see Matt 22:37–40). If, however, he observes, we make the "principle of one's own happiness . . . the supreme principle of morality," then we would have the following commandment: "*Love yourself above all but God and your neighbor for your own sake.*" Because love of God and neighbor cannot truly be based on inclinations or dispositions (self-love), only "*practical love*" can be viewed as the "kernel of all laws." To obey the command to love God and neighbor means to do so "gladly." This is why, Kant observes, that the "law of all laws, therefore, like all the moral precepts of the Gospel, presents the moral disposition in its complete perfection, in such a way that as an ideal of holiness it is not attainable by any creature but is yet the archetype which we should strive to approach and resemble in an uninterrupted but endless progress." In other words, if a human being "could ever reach the stage of thoroughly *liking* to fulfill all moral laws," he would be perfectly holy (like God himself) and so be beyond all possible deviation from them in following his inclinations. In order, however, for human beings to overcome their self-love there is required "some sacrifice and ... self-constraint, that is, inner [moral] necessitation to [do] what one does not altogether like to do" (207). It is thus always necessary for a human being "to base the disposition of his maxims on moral necessitation, not on ready fidelity but on respect, which *demands* compliance with the law even though this is done reluctantly" (207–8). Indeed, Kant points out that it is only because the moral law causes conflict in us that, in overcoming it, we can be said to be virtuous (moral). Or, in terms of traditional Christian theology: without sin there is no salvation. *O felix culpa*! O happy sin! Paradise lost is paradise regained. The fall of Adam and Eve into the knowledge of good and evil is the conjectural beginning of human history that is repeated in the moral story of every human being.

Kant, however, makes clear to us that his aim in elucidating the concepts fundamental to "the evangelical command" is not primarily "to prevent *religious enthusiasm* in regard to love of God" but rather "to determine accurately the moral disposition ... in regard to our duties toward human beings" and so "to check ... a *merely moral* enthusiasm which infects many people" (208). Keeping in mind that "enthusiasm" (Kant's term in German is *Schwärmerei*) means "in God" (or "God within": *entheos*), Kant views "enthusiasm" as overstepping the bounds of reason and so "moral enthusiasm" as overstepping "the bounds that practical, pure reason sets to humanity ... [in] forbidding us to place the subjective, determining ground of dutiful actions—that is, their moral motive—anywhere else than ... in respect for this law and so [in] commanding us to make the thought of duty, which strikes down all *arrogance* as well as vain *self-love*, the supreme *life-principle* of all morality in human beings." Kant then concludes his reflections on "the moral teachings of the Gospel" by pointing out that

> by the purity of its moral principles but at the same time by the suitability of this principle to the limitations of finite beings, it first subjected all good conduct of man to the discipline of a duty laid before his eyes, which does not allow them to rove among fancied moral perfections [as filled with moral enthusiasm] and sets limits of humility (i.e., self-knowledge) to self-conceit as well as to self-love, both of which are ready to mistake their boundaries. (209)

Having now shown that the "grand disclosure" of the moral law in and through practical reason is consistent with the biblical imperative to love God and neighbor, Kant next undertakes to explain what it means for us human beings to have disclosed to us an intelligible world of freedom. He is concerned, as always, to distinguish carefully between the two concepts of necessity, natural necessity and freedom, and so between sensible objects as determined by natural law and intelligible subjects as self-determining persons. Since the account that Kant gives of this fundamental distinction in *Practical Reason* is not fundamentally different from that found in the third antinomy of *Pure Reason* and that I discussed earlier, I shall highlight only its key passages. What is especially important to take note of here is that the intelligible and the sensible worlds involve completely different notions of time. But, as we shall see, Kant has no ready term for his idea of our human existence as intelligibly temporal (timely!), as distinct from the time of our sensible existence.

Kant begins his account of freedom with the invocation of his critically important distinction between "causality as *natural necessity*" and "causality as *freedom*." Whereas the first "concerns only the existence of things insofar as it is *determinable in time* and hence as appearances," the second refers to "their causality as things in themselves" (215). He reminds us that, if we take "the determinations of the existence of things in time for determinations of things in themselves (which is the most usual way of representing them)," then we shall find ourselves in the grips of an insoluble antinomy. For we must keep in mind

> that every event, and consequently every action that takes place at a point of time is necessary under the condition of what was in the preceding time. Now, since time past is no longer within my control, every action that I perform must be necessary by determining grounds *that are not within my control*, that is, I am

> never free at the point of time in which I act.... Consequently, if one still wants to save it [freedom], no other path remains than to ascribe the existence of a thing so far as it is determinable in time, and so too its causality in accordance with the law of *natural necessity, only to appearance, and to ascribe freedom to the same being as a thing in itself.* (216)

Kant points out, as he also did in *Pure Reason*, that, if I commit an evil deed "in accordance with the natural law of causality," then it is impossible that it could have been left undone or that I could ever repent for having done it and so take responsibility for it (216). We would be a mere *automaton materiale*. But if I view myself, not only as an object whose actions follow from natural necessity but also as a subject who is "conscious of himself as a thing in itself," then I view my "existence *insofar as it does not stand under conditions of time* and ... [consequently] as determinable only through laws" that I give to myself "by reason." When, then, in the existence of an individual—and here it is important once again to cite Kant's dense presentation verbatim—

> nothing is, for him, antecedent to the determination of his will, ... [then,] every action ... is to be regarded [by him] in the consciousness of his intelligible existence as nothing but the consequence and never as the determining ground of his causality as a *noumenon*. So considered, a rational being can now rightly say of every unlawful action he performed that he could have omitted it even though as appearance it is sufficiently determined in the past and, so far, is inevitably necessary; for this action, with all the past which determines it, belongs to a single phenomenon of his character, which he gives to himself and in accordance with which he imputes to himself, as a cause independent of all sensibility, the causality of those appearances. (218)

In the above passage Kant distinguishes between two concepts of the present. In one case the present is but the consequence of past events in a never-ending chain of natural causation. In the other case the present is the consequence of my action the unity of which I constitute in my consciousness as consequential (momentous, far-reaching . . .), as having consequences. In the first case, I am, as an object of possible experience, part of a finite whole that remains indefinitely partial unto the end of time. In the second case, I am, as a thing in itself, an infinite whole whose existence is the consequence of my free will. The past is consequential solely because I am wholly responsible for it as the creation of my freedom. Yes, it is true, that I cannot change the past—so long as I am honest: the facts are the facts. But as an individual who freely determines himself I am responsible for the future consequences of the facts. My future is not the natural consequence of the past. Rather, the past is the intelligible consequence of my future, of what I will to do now.

It is evident that I here go beyond Kant in drawing out the implications of the critical difference that he makes between the empirical time of nature and the noumenal time of freedom. My point is to indicate that, while he leaves nameless the time that is the product of my freedom, we surely recognize it to be history as the realization of the future consequences of past events. In Hegelian terms, our task is to render what actually happened in the past, what it is that I actually did, rationally consequential in the future. The past is the future rendered eternal—*in saecula saeculorum*—in and as my present. Kant thus clearly sees that, if we are to possess a concept of freedom, when properly distinguished from natural necessity, as necessarily expressing self-determination, then it will constitute a unity, a wholeness that, in demanding a concept of temporal existence as noumenal (intelligible), is essentially different from sensible existence.

If, however, we fail to adhere to the "ideality of natural time and space" and thus to the empirical (contingent) reality of things appearing in time and space, disastrous consequences follow. For then, Kant observes, we view space and time as "essential determinations of the original being itself," with the result that "the things dependent upon it are not [viewed as] substances but merely [as] accidents inhering in it" (221).[101] What here is at issue is the very concept of creation, of which Kant now proceeds to provide a truly penetrating analysis. He writes that, if

> existence *in time* is only a sensible way of representing things which belong to thinking beings in the world and consequently does not apply to them as things in themselves, then the creation of these beings is a creation of things in themselves, since the concept of a creation does not belong to the sensible way of representing existence or causality but can only be referred to noumena. Consequently, if I say of beings in the sensible world that they are created, I so far regard them as noumena. (221–22)

It follows, then, that it is contradictory to consider God as the creator of appearances or, as creator, "the cause of actions in the sensible world" of appearances, "even though he is the cause of the existence of the acting beings (as noumena)" (222). What this clearly means, Kant continues, is that we can "affirm freedom without compromising the natural mechanism of actions as appearances," since it is appearances, not things in themselves, that exist in time. It follows, then, that we have no problem in holding that "acting beings are creatures, since creation has to do with their intelligible, but not their sensible existence." If, however, "the beings in the world existed as things in themselves *in time*," then "the creator of substance would also [have] to be the author of the entire mechanism in this substance" (222).

It is, I presume, by no means evident how Kant, in the above passage on creation, intends us to understand God as "the cause of the existence of the acting beings (as noumena)." Before, however, undertaking to address that question, I want, first, to underscore the import of his radical conception of creation. God is not the creator of phenomenal nature. God did not create the world of sensible objects (as studied by the natural sciences). God is the creator of noumenal existence. God did create the world of human subjects as things in themselves. If we do not distinguish between things as knowable objects of possible appearance and things in themselves as actual subjects who determine their existence in and through practical reason, then we lose both God and the human being. They become mere idols of illusion whose reflections are no less skeptical (one is all) than dogmatic (all is one). It is important, however, to recall here that Kant bases the entire structure of reason as at once theoretical and practical, and so as involving both objects as known to be determined and subjects as self-determinately willing, on the priority of self-conscious existence. In other words, while God did not create the world of nature (for natural data are what they are empirically), still our knowledge of the natural world depends, we may say, on our creation in the image of God. If human beings were not created—by God—they would possess no systematic and comprehensive science of nature. The creation of human beings by God as things in themselves is the presupposition underlying knowledge of the natural world. It is the very concept of creation, the idea that human beings are created from nothing, from nothing natural, that discloses (reveals) them to exist in themselves, not as objects of possible appearance but as self-creating, free subjects who determine themselves to be members of the kingdom of God.

In concluding his discussion of freedom, without further mention of the concept of creation, Kant recurs one last time to his demonstration in the Transcendental Dialectic of *Pure Reason* that "the two seemingly opposed ways of finding the unconditioned for the conditioned" can be reconciled as not contradicting each other and so with each held to be true. The same action can be viewed both as "sensibly conditioned—that is, mechanically necessary"—and "as belonging to the causality of an acting being [in] so far as it belongs to the intelligible world . . . and so thought to be as free. Then, the only point at issue was whether this *can* [can] be changed into *is*." *Is* there, consequently, "an actual case" in which such an action is shown to be "practically necessary"? (223). We know, Kant continues, that it is not given in sensible experience

> since causality through freedom must always be sought outside the sensible world in the intelligible world. But other things, things outside the sensible world, are not given to perception and observation. Hence nothing remained but that there might be found an incontestable and indeed an objective principle of causality that excludes all sensible conditions from its determination, that is, a principle in which reason does not call upon something *else* as the determining ground with respect to its causality but already itself contains this determining ground by that principle, and in which it is therefore as *pure reason* itself practical.

But Kant immediately adds that "this principle does not need to be searched for or devised; it has long been present in the reason of all human beings and incorporated in their being and is the principle of *morality*" (224). The principle of freedom, as founded on the moral law, cannot and need not, therefore, be transcendentally deduced (justified). It *is* (although it cannot be empirically perceived or observed). It exists and has long existed (but not for ever?) in the rational practice of all human beings.

We might ask how and why it was that Kant was able to "see" in the practice of all human beings—at least, as for long present—what philosophers like Hume and Leibniz and so many others, both dogmatists (theologians) and skeptics (philosophers), failed to see. More relevant for our present purposes, however, is to ask how we are to understand (conceptualize) his argument that the moral law, together with practical reason as constituted in and through freedom, *is* present before us, although only in our mind's eye as the actual thing in itself and not as an object of possible (visual) appearance. The short answer to this question is that his argument is at once historical and ontological—precisely because the concept of history presupposes the argument demonstrating the necessity of existence as freedom and the ontological argument presupposes existence as history precisely as Kant shows us in his reflections on the conjectural beginning of human history as originating with the first man and woman—in history (if not in nature). Indeed, Kant makes it clear to us, although he does not conceptualize his insight, that we begin with our existence as that which we think (will): I think, *ergo* I exist. I do not know "why" I exist. All I know is that, in order for me to question, to doubt, to provide a critique of my existence, I thereby presuppose and so prove and thus constitute my existence. We have also seen that Kant, in addition to showing in his major works on religion that practical reason constitutes the very core of biblical religion, directly aligns the principle of the moral law, as grounded in freedom, with the story of Adam and Eve, with the biblical principle of creation, and with the Gospel's command to love God and neighbor. Still, as I continue to point out, he does not directly address the question of the ontological origin of the moral law as brought into historical existence by and through the free practice of self-determining reason.

At the same time, however, Kant does undertake to show, in the "Dialectic" of *The Critique of Practical Reason*, that the moral law, and so the very concept of reason as fundamentally practice, thought, will, and desire is not to be found in the philosophy of the ancient Greeks. He frames the issue in terms of how we conceive of what he calls the highest good. He begins by reminding us that, because "reason always has its dialectic," it falls into "an avoidable illusion" since it inevitably attempts to apply the "rational idea of the totality of conditions (and so of the unconditioned) to appearances as if they were things in themselves." Dialectical illusion would, however, go unnoticed by us, Kant tells us, if it were not unavoidably "revealed by a *conflict* of reason within itself," whereby "reason is forced to investigate this illusion—whence it arises and how it can be removed—and this can be done only through a complete critical examination" of the faculty of reason itself. Indeed, he continues,

> the antinomy of pure reason, which becomes evident in its dialectic, is in fact the most beneficial error into which human reason could ever have fallen, inasmuch as it finally drives us to search for the key to escape from this labyrinth; and when this key is found, it further discovers what we did not seek and yet need, namely a view into a higher, immutable order of things in which we already are and in which we can henceforth be

directed, by determinate concepts, to carry on our existence in accordance with the highest vocation of reason. (226)

Thus it is, Kant observes, that we seek "the unconditioned totality of the object of pure practical reason under the name of the *highest good*" (226–27). Dialectical illusion emerges, consequently, when we view the highest good as the "*determining ground*" of practical reason, whereas "the moral law alone must be viewed as the ground for making the highest good and its realization or promotion the object" of our will (228).

Again, Kant presents us with two complex questions. He tells us that error (dialectical illusion), the contradictory conflict of reason with itself, is fruitful, not only because it drives us to find a way out of it but also because it reveals to us "a higher, immutable order of things in which we already are." Whence our first question: How do we discern our error, i.e., how do we discover that our reason is in conflict with itself in holding contradictory ideas? How, in other words, do we know *what* our error is? We remember that, while Hume acknowledged *that* he was in total contradiction with himself, he nevertheless altogether failed to recognize *what* his error was. His error did not lead him to find a solution for it. We shall also find that, when Kant discusses the concept of the good that was held by Greek philosophers, he shows that it was completely erroneous. But the Greeks did not, indeed, could not recognize that they contradicted themselves, since for them error was, to recall Socrates, ignorance of the truth. In holding that we can and in that sense must recognize our errors (sin), Kant yet again reveals (indirectly) to us his adherence to biblical doctrine, in this case, that we are like God in knowing good and evil. I cannot *not* know what my sin is (although I may, indeed, deny, repress, hide from . . . it). It is also important here to take into account the fundamental source of the dialectical illusion or error that emerges when we confuse or conflate our two concepts of necessity, freedom and nature, or, in the case at hand, when we make the highest good (as happiness) the determining ground of practical reason (the moral law). Philosophers, of whom Hume is so apt an example, continued to ground logic and so thinking (and existence) on the law of contradiction.[102] But we remember that Kant founds his concept of thinking (and existence) on transcendental logic, not on the "general logic" of contradiction as inherited from Aristotle. (Descartes and Spinoza were rare exceptions to the conventional norms of the philosophical tradition in breaking with the domination of Aristotelian logic.) The "I think" embodies the thing in itself as practical reason. I am who I am in founding my life on willing the good. The good is *what* I will. I am the foundation of good (the good is not the foundation of my will, of my existence.) Thus we see, yet again, that Kant, in making *what* I think the good of my existence, and so in rejecting the law of contradiction as the basis of logic, aligns himself, as always, with the ontological argument and, consequently, with the *logos* of the Bible.

The second question involves our understanding of how it is that "a higher, immutable order of things in which we already are" is disclosed to us and what it is. Since this higher, eternal order of things is, patently, the moral law, what Kant proceeds to show us is that the moral law leads to, but is not grounded in, God as the highest good, that virtue, in other words, leads to, but is not grounded in, happiness and that, consequently, the highest good involves both the immortality of the soul as infinite progress (i.e., historical development and advance) and God (i.e., the ontology of "I am").

In telling us that virtue and happiness together constitute possession of the highest good in a person, Kant goes to some considerable length in making it clear that respect, "and not the gratification or enjoyment of happiness, is thus something for which there can be no feeling *antecedent* to reason and underlying it (for this would always be aesthetic and pathological): respect as consciousness of direct necessitation of the will by the law is hardly an analogue of the feeling of pleasure," which, although it is like "desire," comes from merely empirical sources (234). Indeed, we can and do possess self-contentment—*Selbstfriedenheit*—in being conscious of freely adhering to the moral law. Thus, we can think that it is "natural and necessary" for us to connect "the consciousness of morality and the expectation of a happiness proportionate to it, . . . though certainly not, on this account, known and understood" since the "principles of the pursuit of happiness cannot possibly produce morality" (235). It is evident, consequently, that, insofar as morality is understood to constitute the first condition of the highest good, happiness can to be understood to be its second element. "Only with this subordination is the *highest good* the whole object of pure practical reason, which must necessarily represent it as possible since it commands us to contribute everything possible to its production" (236). It is thus a question of what "interests" us, Kant explains further. Since, however, reason is the power that determines its own interests, it "determines the interests of all the [other] powers of the mind but itself determines its own" (236).

We arrive, then, at the two postulates of practical reason, the immortality of the soul and the existence of God, which rest on, and do not constitute, the moral law with its ground in freedom (as the first postulate of practical reason). "For a rational but finite being," Kant explains to us, "only endless [or infinite: *unendlichen*] progress from lower to higher stages of moral perfection is possible." Insofar as the individual has always progressed, in his life, from the morally worse to the morally better, he may, then, "hope for a further uninterrupted continuance of this progress, however long his existence may last, even beyond this life" while yet neither now nor ever hoping that he will "be fully adequate to God's will . . . ; he can hope to be so only in the endlessness [infinity] of his duration (which God alone can survey)." Kant adds that, because beatitude, like holiness, designates a state free of all contingency, it "is an idea that can be contained only in an endless [infinite] progress . . . and hence is never fully attained by a creature" (239). Thus it is that the immortality of the soul, as postulated by pure reason, represents the possibility of our infinite progress from the good of our moral being to the ever greater good of containing within rational practice the happiness of enjoying our mortally contingent life.

It is important to keep in mind that, while Kant typically calls human beings "finite," he also has made it clear, as we have seen, that human beings, in living by the categorical demands of the moral law, are supersensible (supernatural)—as made in the image of God in knowing good and evil. Human beings, as things in themselves, are not finite as the objects of possible appearance are finite. It is thus no less important to remember that infinite progress involves, not progress to the good but progress from the absolute good of the moral law to ever fuller, more ample practice of the good. But is not our concept of God also that than which we can think nothing greater, as we progress towards ever more profound comprehension of God as the supreme good of our lives?

So we have arrived at the existence of God as a postulate of practical reason. Because morality is, for Kant, "the first and principal part of the highest good," which "can be fully accomplished only in an eternity," it follows, he argues, that the possibility of making happiness fully compatible with morality presupposes the existence of God. He defines happiness as "the state of a rational being in the world in the whole of whose existence *everything goes according to his wish and will*, and [that] rests, therefore, on the harmony of nature with his whole end as well as with the essential determining ground of his will." However, because the self-determining laws of practical reason are independent of nature, all we can say, therefore, Kant continues, is that the attainment of the highest good ought to be possible. "Accordingly, the existence of a cause of all nature, distinct from nature, which contains the ground of this connection, namely of the exact correspondence of happiness with morality, is also *postulated*" (240). Since it is our duty to promote the highest good, we find that its possibility can be made actual "only under the condition of the existence of God ... ; that is, it is morally necessary to assume [postulate] the existence of God" (241). But Kant immediately adds that "this moral necessity" is a subjective need, not an objective law of duty. Thus, "it can be called *belief* [*Glaube*: faith] and, indeed, a pure *rational belief*, since pure reason alone ... is the source from which it springs" (241).

Kant proceeds then to point out that it is "this *deduction*" (justification) of the postulate of the existence of God as the highest good for human beings that explains "why the *Greek* schools could never solve their problem of the practical possibility of the highest good" (241). In making human sufficiency adequate to attaining it, they excluded the necessity of the existence of God.[103] On the one hand, the Epicureans falsely held that (sensuous) happiness leads to (rational) virtue, while, on the other hand, the Stoics, while properly viewing virtue as the condition of the highest good, falsely believed that it was fully attainable in this life—by the wise man or sage, if not by all human beings. In turning the sage into a god as one who was absolutely free from the ills of life and thus also from evil, the Stoics actually "left out the second element of the highest good, namely one's own happiness." In other words, while the Epicureans sacrificed virtue to happiness, the Stoics sacrificed happiness to virtue. Still, Kant observes, it "is commonly held that the Christian precept of morals has no advantage with respect to its purity over the moral concepts of the Stoics; but," he insists, "the difference between them is nonetheless very obvious." In elevating the sage "above the animal nature of the human being" and thus in making him "sufficient to himself," the Stoics put the wise man beyond "any temptation to transgress the moral law." The Stoic wise man was the perfect god in himself. Kant adds that the Stoics could not have done this "if they had represented this law in all its purity and strictness, as the precept of the Gospel does." Indeed, "the moral ideas, as archetypes of practical perfection, serve as the indispensable rule of moral conduct and also as the *standard of comparison.*" Kant proceeds, then, to provide his readers with a simple table in which he contrasts

"*Christian morals* on their philosophic side . . . with the ideas [i.e., the principles] of the Greek schools":

> Christians: holiness;
> Cynics: natural simplicity;
> Epicureans: prudence; and
> Stoics: wisdom. (242)

What consequently distinguished these three Greek schools of philosophy from each other, in respect of making their ideas real, Kant continues, was that, while "the Cynics found *common human understanding* [*Menschenverstand*] sufficient," both the Epicureans and the Stoics made "the path of *science* [*Wissenschaft*] sufficient" (242). Thus, all three schools "found the mere *use of natural powers* sufficient for" attaining the highest good (243). When Kant then observes that "Aristotle and Plato differed only with respect to the *origin* of our moral concepts," I understand him to mean that they, too, grounded morality in our merely "natural powers." In contrast to all these schools of Greek philosophy, he continues,

> Christian morals, because it frames its precept so purely and inflexibly (as must be done), deprives the human being of confidence that he can be fully adequate to it, at least in this life, but again sets it up by enabling us to hope that if we act as well as is within our *power*, then what is not within our power will come to our aid from another source, whether or not we know in what way. (243)

Two things thus become readily evident. First, we are all sinners—*O felix culpa!*—since, according to Kant, the moral law represents the "philosophic" import of the Gospel. Second, practical reason postulates the existence of the immortality of the soul and of the existence of God as the very incarnation of hope, faith, and, indeed, love.

But then Kant proceeds to point out that, while the moral law, in leading to our ideas of the immortality of the soul and of God, is consistent with the Gospel, it is not itself to be considered religion. Indeed, he writes that the moral law leads "through the concept of the highest good, as the object and final end of pure practical reason, *to religion, that is, to the recognition of all duties as divine commands*" (243-44). But he is careful to add that we must not confuse *duties* as divine commands with *sanctions* as imposed on us by the will of another. In other words, we must regard what are the

> essential *laws* of every free will in itself . . . as commands of the supreme being because only from a will that is morally perfect (holy and beneficent) and at the same time all-powerful, and so through harmony with this will, can we hope to attain the highest good, which the moral law makes it our duty to take as the object of our endeavors. . . . The moral law commands me to make the highest possible good in a world the final object of all my conduct. But I cannot hope to produce this except by the harmony of my will with that of a holy and beneficent author of the world.

It is evident, consequently, that "morals is not properly the doctrine of how we are to *make* ourselves happy but of how we are to become *worthy* of happiness. Only if religion is added to it does there also enter the hope of some day participating in happiness to the degree that we have been intent upon not being unworthy of it" (244). Since "all worthiness depends upon moral conduct, . . . *morals* in itself must never be treated as a *doctrine of happiness*, that is, as instruction in how to become happy" (244). It follows, then, that "it is only with religion that the *hope* of happiness first arises" (245).

If, however, we ask what was "*God's final end* in creating the world," the answer lies, not in the happiness of human beings but in "*the highest good* . . . [as] the condition of being worthy of happiness." When people, consequently, "put the end of creation in the glory of God," they bear witness to the fact that "nothing glorifies God more than what is most estimable in the world, [which is] respect for his command, [that is,] observance of the holy duty that his law lays upon us" as crowned "with corresponding happiness" (245). But thus it "follows of itself," Kant proceeds next to observe, "that, in the order of ends, the human being . . . is an *end in itself* . . . [who] can never be used merely as a means by anyone (not even by God) without being at the same time himself an end, and that humanity in our person must, accordingly, be *holy* to ourselves; for he [i.e., the human being] is the *subject of the moral law* and so of that which is holy in itself, on account of which and in agreement with which alone can anything be called holy" (245–46). Because the "moral law is based on the autonomy" of the subject's will, this will, "as a free will" that accords with the universal laws of morality, "must necessarily be able at the same time *to agree* to that to which it is to *subject* itself" (246).[104]

In the last sentence cited above Kant reiterates two radically significant claims that we have seen him make previously but that he emphasizes now in the context of discussing the existence of God as a postulate of practical reason. First, because the end of the creation of the—noumenal!—world by God constitutes the revelation that human beings are the true end of the divine will of creation, God Himself is obligated to respect them as holy ends in themselves. Second, since human beings are, as ends in themselves, autonomous agents whose free will constitutes the moral law in its universality, they are subject solely to that to which they agree to be subject. In other words, they enter into the covenant with God as free and equal partners. The implications incarnated in the idea that human beings are created in the image of God in knowing good and evil are radical, indeed—*in deed*!

Kant has now concluded his account of the three postulates of practical reason—freedom, the immortality of the soul, and God. In the four remaining sections of *Practical Reason* on the postulates he continues to demonstrate the critical importance of addressing his original question: How is metaphysics possible?[105] Metaphysics is possible because its key ideas are postulated by practical reason as actually necessary to the fulfillment of the moral law in its universality. As always, I shall highlight only those passages in these four sections where Kant, in providing us with additionally illuminating comments on the postulates of practical reason, advances our understanding of their significance.

Because the postulates "proceed from the principle of morality, which is not a postulate but a law by which reason determines the will," they "are not," Kant observes, "theoretical dogmas but *presuppositions* having a necessarily practical reference" (246). The postulate of the immortality of the soul "flows from the practically necessarily condition" of having sufficient time in which the moral law can be completely fulfilled. The postulate of freedom presupposes our necessary "independence from the sensible world" and thus "our capacity" to determine our will "by the law of an intelligible world, that is, the law of freedom." The postulate of God provides the necessary condition "for such an intelligible world to be the highest good through the presupposition of the highest independent good, that is, of the existence of God" (246). Kant reiterates, yet again, that "we thereby know neither the nature of our souls, nor the intelligible world [of freedom], nor the supreme being as to what they are in themselves." How, then, the soul, freedom, and God are possible theoretically "no human understanding will ever fathom although no sophistry will ever convince even the most common human being that they are not true concepts" (247).

Kant next observes that, because our "knowledge of God" is purely practical, we "can confidently challenge all supposed *natural theologians*" since it is evident that "*the concept of God*" belongs, not to physics but to morals. (250–51) Indeed, we are not able to proceed metaphysically "*by sure inferences* from knowledge of this world to the concept of God and to the proof of his existence" (250). Kant thus recalls here his refutation of the teleological and the cosmological arguments for the existence of God in the Transcendental Dialectic of *The Critique of Pure Reason*. He observes yet further that it is also "absolutely impossible to know the existence [*die Existenz*] of this being from mere concepts because every existential proposition [*ein jeder Existentialsatz*]—that is, every proposition that says, of a being of which I frame a concept, that it exists [*dass es existiere*]—is a synthetic proposition [based on sensible experience], that is, one by which I go beyond that concept and say more about it than was thought in the concept" (251). In other words, I presuppose in this case the existence of an object of sensibility separate from the understanding. Kant thus rejects the ontological argument (without so naming it here), consistent with his refutation of it in the Transcendental Dialectic. It follows, then, he continues, that

> there remains for reason only one single procedure by which to arrive at this knowledge, namely, as pure reason to start from the supreme principle of its pure practical use (inasmuch as this is always directed simply to the *existence* [*die Existenz*] of something as a result of reason) and [to] determine its object. And, then, in its unavoidable problem, namely that of the necessary direction of the will to the highest good, there is shown not only the necessity of assuming such an original being in relation to the possibility of this good in the world but [also]—what is most remarkable—something that was quite lacking in the progress of reason on the path of nature, *a precisely determined concept of this original being*. (251–52)

While "we can well infer" from the "order, purposiveness, and magnitude" of the natural world, Kant observes, an author of it who is "*wise, beneficent, powerful*, and so forth," it is evident that the conception of God as omniscient, all-beneficent, and omnipotent, etc., depends solely on reason as practical (252).

It is of the upmost importance to see that in the above paragraph Kant presents us with two entirely different concepts of existence: *die Existenz*. In the first case, "existence" is understood to be synthetic and so to refer to the empirical existence of objects of possible experience. In the second case, however, "existence" is said by Kant (within parentheses!) to be the product of practical reason. It is evident, consequently, that that being whose existence practical reason necessarily determines as an actual thing existing in itself is at once synthetic and *a priori*. It is no less evident that Kant, in declaring that the necessary existence of God, as the highest good for human beings, results from practical reason (and not from theoretical understanding in its knowledge of objects of possible appearance), simply invokes here the ontological argument—that there is one thing that cannot be thought (or willed by practical reason) without existing necessarily, and that is God. When Kant then proceeds to address what he calls "the [absolute] need" of practical reason to postulate the existence of God, he writes that we have before us "a problematic but yet unavoidable concept of reason, namely that of an absolutely necessary being" (254). The *"need of reason,"* he writes, arises

> from an *objective* determining ground of the will, namely the moral law, which necessarily binds every rational being and therefore justifies him a priori in presupposing in nature the condition befitting it and makes the latter inseparable from the complete practical use of reason. It is a duty to realize [i.e., to make real the existence of] the highest good to the utmost of our capacity; therefore, it must be possible; hence it is also unavoidable for every rational being in the world to assume [i.e., to think, to will] what is necessary for its objective possibility. The assumption is as necessary as the moral law, in relation to which alone it is valid.

Kant goes on to observe that, because "the pure moral law inflexibly binds everyone as a command (not as a rule of prudence), the upright man may well say:

> I *will* that there be a God, that my existence [*mein Dasein*] in this world be also an existence in a pure world of the understanding [*in einer reinen Verstandeswelt*] beyond natural connections, and finally that my duration be endless; I stand by this, without paying attention to rationalizations, however little I may be able to answer them or to oppose them with others more plausible, and I will not let this belief be taken from me; for this is the only case in which my interest, because I *may* not give up anything of it, unavoidably determines my judgment. (255)[106]

Kant has now completed his account of the postulates of practical reason and thus his critical accounting for the absolute necessity of conceiving of reason as determinately, because freely, obligated to bring into existence the kingdom of God as universally and necessarily grounded in the practice of the moral law.[107] In showing that synthetic *a priori* judgments are possible solely because they are made metaphysically actual by practical reason, Kant revolutionizes philosophy—consistent, we may say, with the American and the French revolutions that occurred in the very same period of the later eighteenth century when Kant wrote his great works. Because the entire history of philosophy, and also of religion, and thus the ever complex and fraught relationship between philosophy and religion, between human being and divine being, is at play here, there is no summary of the magnitude of Kant's philosophical achievement that will ever suffice. Still, it is my duty, and desire, to provide a summary. It is necessary, although not sufficient.

CONCLUSION

In thinking through the complex of ideas that for Kant constitutes the very core of his philosophy, I shall concentrate on the twofold distinction that he makes critically fundamental in distinguishing between (while preserving the relative importance of both) nature and freedom, knowledge and practice, natural law and moral law, things of possible appearance and things in themselves, theory and practice, the sensible and the transcendental, the hypothetical and the categorical, object and subject, phenomenal and noumenal, letter and spirit, possibility and actuality The list goes on. But what is especially important here is how Kant justifies ("deduces") this twofold distinction. We may say that he takes two distinct (yet closely related) approaches in advancing his argument in support of the absolute necessity (as our duty) of distinguishing between causal determination (natural law) and self-determining causation (freedom). First, he truly contends: either/or. Either both nature and freedom. Or neither nature nor freedom. Either we show that we can possess, do possess, and must possess true, universal, and necessary concepts of both natural causation and human freedom. Or we remain lost in the dialectical illusions, whether skeptical or dogmatic, of failing to see that we cannot possess the truth of the natural world without at the same time possessing the truth of the human world as two entirely different, yet *not* contradictory, realms of truth.

But thus it is that the two-fold distinction between natural law and moral law depends on yet another fundamental difference, that between what Kant calls general logic, which is based on the law of contradiction, and transcendental logic, which is based on the necessary relationship between thinking and existence: I think, *ergo* I exist. There *is* one thing whose existence can*not* be denied without contradiction, and that is the existence of the one who cannot deny, doubt, question, or critique his or her necessary existence without at the very same time affirming it. We arrive, then, at the second approach that Kant takes in justifying, in affirming, the reality of both natural law (science) and human law (morality). Look about the world, he tells us. We see that common folk have for long been living the truth of the moral law in their everyday practice—at least since the time when the categorical command to love God and neighbor was revealed to them in and through, and so as, the Gospel of the moral law. It is no less the case that, when we look at the demonstrably true and so necessarily universal findings of science that natural philosophers in the past two centuries like Copernicus, Galileo, and Newton have established for us, it is evident that the hypothetically (theoretically) certain results of science depend on the transcendental deduction of the categories of experience as founded on (i.e., as presupposing) the existence of the mind as the thing in itself, which cannot be known as an object but can only be willed into existence in and through the practice of the moral law. Theoretical understanding depends on practical reason. We know that the science of nature exists as a hypothetically true body of universally necessary laws. But, in order to know this body of natural law we are required to acknowledge that we do not know, as an object, that on which our knowledge of objects rests, the human subject. But how, then, do we justify our beginning as free, self-determining human subjects if we do not and cannot know our original beginning as a thing in itself? Well, Kant responds (as we already know): look around the world and you will see that this is how people act and live—except for philosophers who have skeptically denied the truths of metaphysics as natural and for theologians who have dogmatically asserted the truths of metaphysics as supernatural.

It is, then, quite extraordinary to see that Kant, in saving the truths of metaphysics from both the skeptics and the dogmatists, calls upon on the authority of the common folk to support his claim that they are founded on practical reason, not on theoretical reason. We necessarily postulate the truths of freedom (as presupposed by the moral law), of the immortality of the soul (as infinite progress towards the highest good), and of the existence of God (as the ideal good in which morality and happiness, mind and body, are united) as the ends that we are morally duty-bound to realize and so to make actual in our practice as human beings.

Not only, however, do the common folk know by practicing what the schooled philosophers and theologians practice, presumably, yet fail to acknowledge consciously. But also two additional points follow that are truly radical in their implications, implications that are at once ontological and historical. First, it is by no means evident how the human being, whom Kant shows to be, as a thing in itself, supersensuous (supernatural) and so subjectively infinite, is to be differentiated from God. Yes, it is true that human beings are not objectively infinite: they are not objects that can be known as infinite. (Yet God, also, cannot be known as an object.) Presumably, then, this is why Kant typically calls human beings finite (as distinct from God who is infinite). Human beings are mortal: they die. At the same time, however, we have seen Kant make absolutely clear that human beings, as ends in themselves, are holy as God as holy. They are holy in their personality, in their humanity. Indeed, the moral law, which obligates human beings to make God their ideal of the highest good in their everyday practice, is the ground of the God of religion. Morality leads to God, not God to morality. Yes, it is true, as Kant constantly reminds us, that human beings are endlessly unholy in their failure to adhere to the moral law. Still, human beings are made in the image of God. But this means that God is the true image, the archetype of humanity, the very image of the person that each human being must will to be, even as he or she fails to live up to this standard of moral purity.

But this brings me to the second point that follows from the "fact" that all (but dialectically confused philosophers and theologians) recognize and so accept as true, which is that the moral law is universally and necessarily valid precisely because it practiced by all people. This "fact" is ontological, not empirical; practical, not theoretical; transcendental, not natural. (It is also "historical" and not merely a contingent happening or occurrence. My birth happens. What I make of this occurrence is my history. But I shall for the present defer further discussion of history.) The fact of my existence indicates not only *that* I exist but also *what* my existence is—a self-conscious subject who absolutely distinguishes the actual self of existence from an object of possible (sensuous) existence. It is, surely, evident, yet again, that we are in the presence of the ontological argument necessarily proving the existence of—the thing itself as at once divine and human, both infinite and supersensuous (supernatural). We see, then, that there are two distinctly different concepts of existence—empirical (natural) and rational (moral). We can transcendentally deduce the categories of possible (empirical or factual) existence solely because we exist as the very fact of creative life itself, i.e., as persons who exist as ends in themselves and so as created from nothing, from nothing that can be known as an object of possible appearance.

It is evident, consequently, that the ontological argument is nothing more or less than the moral law whose necessary and universal validity all human beings are obligated to prove (to justify) in accepting as their duty the task of constituting their lives, the historical fact of their existence, in and through the kingdom of ends. We also remember that Kant is unequivocal in showing how important it is to acknowledge that, because divine power is freely embodied in love, God, too, is duty-bound to treat human being as things in themselves and not merely as means. The moral law is the sovereign to which both God and human beings are subject. Furthermore, Kant no less insists that human beings are subject only to those laws that they agree to accept as sovereign, i.e. that they are subject solely to those laws that they freely impose on themselves. We remember that Kant tells us in the *Groundwork of the Metaphysics of Morals* that we accept as true the revelation of the moral law in the Gospel as the obligation to love our neighbor as ourselves, not because it is given to us in and by the divine Word of the Lord God as incarnate in Jesus as the Christ but because we acknowledge, in the depths of our hearts and souls, that it is this very word that constitutes the foundation of human existence. To *prove*—to justify—the fact of human existence is to prove, and thereby justify, the existence of God as that than which we can think—will and desire—no higher good as the existence of human beings.

In preparing, now, to bring Wordsworth and Kant, poetry and philosophy, together in the Conclusion of my book, let us return to the "Conclusion" of *The Critique of Practical Reason* with which I initiated the present chapter. Two things, Kant tells us, fill our minds with ever new and expanding "admiration [*Bewunderung*] and awe [*Ehrfurcht*] the more often and the more steadily we reflect on them": the starry heavens above us and the moral law within us. I do not have to search for these realities in the obscure regions of transcendent metaphysics. For, in seeing them before me, I directly connect them "with the consciousness of my existence [*mit dem Bewusstsein meiner Existenz*]." The first is the finite realm of visible nature whose unending wonders reveal to me my utter insignificance as a mere speck of matter. The second is the truly infinite world of the invisible self of my personality whose universal necessity "infinitely raises my worth as an *intelligence*" through which the moral law is revealed to me as "the purposive determination of my existence [*meines Daseins*]," which, in not being restricted by space and time, reaches "into the infinite." Kant here provides us, surely, with an apt summary of the poetry of Wordsworth and, above all, of *The Prelude*. The poet, in relating the story of his life, in which the child is revealed, as the father of man, to be the true philosopher, shows us that, the more often and steadily we reflect on, not just the wonders of nature but, above all, the wonders of the human mind in its capacity to intensify its consciousness of the moral dignity of human kind through the contemplation of nature, the deeper is our appreciation of nature as that through and in which the mind intensifies its self-consciousness as a thing infinite in itself and not as a finite object of nature, to recur to Kant's seemingly non-poetic formulation. But what we thus see, as I am sure the reader now fully appreciates, is that both Kant and Wordsworth, in their distinctively philosophic and poetic manners, verify the insight of Kierkegaard, with which I initiated my study. All language of the spirit, i.e., of the thing in itself, including the language of the Bible, not to mention the language of philosophers who truly see that spirit incarnates practical reason as the truth of the moral law that is necessarily and universally known to all human beings, is transferred language. We are transferred, by the critique of practical reason, from the world of nature to the realm of metaphor in which we justify—deduce transcendentally—the world of nature as truly the creation of the human mind. We begin in nature, as both Kant and Wordsworth show us, only to discover (to have disclosed to us) that our beginning is truly in and through the metaphorical practice of critical reason. We are creative beings whose existence we constitute through those practices that, in revealing to us our dignity as human persons, constitute our moral worth. Those practices embrace at one and the same time poetry, together with all the arts, and philosophy, together with all the others interests in and through which we human beings reveal the depth of our commitment to establishing the kingdom of God on earth.

I cannot and do not claim to be a poet. But I trust that my philosophic endeavors show that, in pondering in depth both the poetry of Wordsworth and the philosophy of Kant, we properly affirm and reaffirm that all truly human practice—individual, social, artistic, philosophic . . . —is no less transcendental and godly in bearing witness to the dignity of all human beings. To think, poetically and philosophically, is to demonstrate *in saecula saeculorum: ergo*, I am. I can only hope, then, that we—both my reader and I—are ready now to leave behind the seemingly secure island of natural appearances and to embark, in concluding my book, upon the apparently stormy but, in reality, transfigured sea in which we meet with the poetry of true philosophy and the philosophy of true poetry. To think metaphorically is the critique of poetry. To think critically is the metaphor of philosophy.

CHAPTER 6

Conclusion

The Metaphoric Critique of Poetic and Philosophic Practice

I HAVE UNDERTAKEN TO show in the preceding chapters, in my engagement with the poetry of Wordsworth and the philosophy of Kant, the profound truth, at once historical and ontological, of Kierkegaard's inspired insight that all human speech about the spirit, including the divine speech of the Bible, is transferred speech. We are transferred and so metaphorically borne from the sensate to the spiritual, from the world of nature to the world of spirit. Wordsworth attests to the truth of this insight by showing in his poetry and, above all, in and through the grandeur of his singular achievement, *The Prelude*, that, in beholding the glories of nature, we bear witness to the creative powers of the mind. Nature, in truth, is but a metaphor of spirit. Kant, for his part, demonstrates that *that* by which we know natural objects we cannot know as a sensible object of nature but can only will—practice—as a transcendental (supersensuous) subject. Our very knowledge of nature presupposes our critical transfer to the practice of the never ending and ever yet to be completed critique of practical reason. The critical practice of philosophy at once constitutes and is constituted by the metaphoric practice of poetry. The poetic critique of metaphor at once constitutes and is constituted by the philosophic metaphor of critique

Both poetry and philosophy confirm the moral truth of the Bible that, while we live in the world, we do not live by the world. Our material being—our body, our flesh—is the given that it is our duty to transform into the gift of spirit that is the practice of at once metaphor and critique. But nature is our gift only insofar as we receive it actively by creating and recreating our lives as the kingdom of God on earth. The earth is not holy and holiness is not earthly except insofar as we constantly (eternally) and unendingly (infinitely) endeavor to establish the kingdom of ends in and through the critical practice of metaphor and the metaphoric practice of critique. All substantial poetry and all substantial philosophy verify by confirming the truth, at once individual and universal, both personal and social: I think, *ergo* I exist. Thinking—self-consciousness—presupposes a thinker (who exists). A thinker (one who exists) presupposes one who says I think (I will, I desire), *ergo* I exist. To think, to be self-conscious, is to think oneself existing. To exist, to utter "I am who I am," is to acknowledge that my existence involves and expresses consciousness of the self. Insofar, then, as poetry and philosophy affirm the truth that all speech about the spirit, like the divine speech of the Bible, involves and expresses the metaphoric transfer from the objects of nature to self-determining subjects who practice rational critique, they speak the same veritable language.

We need always to keep in mind that, in light of the good news that the Word of the Spirit of God is in the world, there is much speech that, insofar as it does not reveal human beings to be made in the image of God as bearing critical knowledge of good and evil, is not substantially true. In other words, it lives in and through idols. Much philosophy is not truly philosophic, notwithstanding its logical form, and much poetry is not truly poetic whatever its verse form. This has not been the place, as I indicated at the beginning of my study, for me to provide a history of either poetry or philosophy, although, as we have seen, it is critically important to take into account, to justify, at once historically and ontologically, our poetic and philosophic origins in and through the biblical stories of creation and covenant. All truly substantial creation is the creation from nothing, from nothing prior to or other than the covenantal relations that Kant calls the kingdom of ends and Wordsworth the dignity of the common man. Creation substantiates the life of the covenant. The covenant substantiates the life of creation. Creative life is covenantal in embodying what Wordsworth shows us to be the critical practice of metaphor. Covenantal life is creative in embodying the practice that Kant calls the critique of reason.

All substantially creative poetry and philosophy covenantally embrace their readers in holding both the content of their own writing (as communicative action) and the content of their readers' lives up to the same absolute standards of metaphoric critique. All true speech demands of their listeners (their readers) that they substantiate it by showing that, in being truly interesting to them, the interest that they take in their own lives and in the lives of others is deepened and enriched. Others words, then, for merely idle or idolatrous speech are entertainment, distraction, the filling in of the time and space of our lives such that the time is spent without revealing to us the promise of the space that is to be opened up to us in our future lives. True poetry and philosophy are at once gracious and spacious.

Wordsworth makes it plain in his prefatory writings on poetry (as found in the *Lyrical Ballads*, in its first edition of 1798 jointly prepared by him and Coleridge, and then in his own poems that he wrote up to 1815, the end of his truly creative period of poetic creation), that there is no essential difference between poetry (written in meter) and prose. For what truly distinguishes creatively interesting writing from writing that does not truly create interest in us is not its form or manner but rather the matter of its content. What does it say to us? What, in response, do we say to it in return? It is evident that neither Wordsworth nor Kant explicitly addresses these questions. Wordsworth does not discuss philosophic prose, and Kant shows little interest in poetry (although it perhaps should be noted that there was hardly anything of significance written in German verse until poets like Goethe and Schiller emerged in the late eighteenth century). Why, then, do we have both poetry and prose (together with literary writing in both verse and prose)? Why does *prosaic* mean banal, mundane, pedestrian, commonplace . . . ? Why does *poetic* tend to imply the form of graceful, flowery, sensitive expression without consideration of its content? To these questions there are no simple answers.[108] If we were to respond in the non-poetic but exactingly prosaic manner of Kant, we could respond that our proper question is not "why" but "how." How is poetry and how is philosophy possible? In other words, all we can do, which is what I hope that I have done in my book, is to reveal the possibilities of poetry and philosophy through an intensive and, I trust, interesting, indeed, bracing engagement with the actual poetry of a great poet and the actual prose of a great philosopher. What they say is what counts. We do not dismiss the form or manner of their presentation as without interest, but it is interesting primarily in terms of the content of their writing.[109]

CONCLUSION 249

I want, then, to summarize the content of our poet and of our philosopher—such as it is displayed in their great works. It is evident to the reader, surely, that one way in which we can distinguish between the content of poetry and the content of philosophy is that the first (in belonging to the fine arts) is fictive and the second real. In other words, poetry embodies in metaphor the fictive story of our human lives while philosophy embodies in critique the principles of our lives. There is a sense, then, that poetry (like all artful fiction) demonstrates the truth of philosophical principles by showing how they play out in the (fictively) actual lives of individuals and that philosophy demonstrates the truth of fictional story by articulating the principles on the basis of which human beings construct their lives. I do not disagree with or dispute the importance of taking due note of the difference between poetic fiction and philosophic principle. Still, *The Prelude* of Wordsworth is neither fundamentally fictive narrative nor strictly autobiographical story. Rather, what Wordsworth undertakes to show in his poem is that it is the growth of the mind of the poet that truly reveals poetic practice to be the metaphorical critique of nature.

The paradox of my undertaking to bring together within a common framework the content of poetry and the content of philosophy—or is it a limitation of my approach?—is that I write as a philosopher who is interested above all in the articulation, no less artistic than philosophic, of the principles that undergird the lives of us human beings. But what interests me above all, as I have stressed in the above chapters, is Kant's demonstration that reason is fundamentally critical practice, the practice of critique. Reason is action, will, desire, thinking—the practice of making human lives creatively covenantal and covenantally creative. Our human practice is at once personal and social, both individual and universal. Practice is thus centered on the moral law whose categorical imperative makes it our duty to look upon all human beings as things in themselves, as persons and so not merely as objects of possible appearance. But what interests me equally, then, is that philosophy is no less fictive than poetry. For philosophy begins, not with the scientific knowledge of natural fact but with what Kant calls, never systematically, a presupposition, an assumption, a conjecture regarding our beginning, i.e., our origins, at once historical and ontological. He is systematic, however, in making it clear to us that the answer to the question—How do we explain the fact that the universal and necessary knowledge of the natural world is possible (as, however, always hypothetical and theoretical)—is to answer the question: How is metaphysics possible? As we have seen, Kant shows us that, in order to answer the question how the science of nature is possible, we must first answer (i.e., have already answered) our second question regarding how metaphysics is possible. The conundrum, always, is that the knowledge of nature, as constituted by the objects of possible appearance, presupposes, in resting on, the subject that cannot be known as an existing object but can only be and must be thought as necessarily and freely existing in and through the critical practice of reason: I think, *ergo* I exist.

But what, then, is extraordinary is that Kant, in demonstrating that the possibility of actually possessing knowledge of nature rests on the possibility that metaphysics is actual, shows that metaphysics is rooted in the free, moral and so transcendental and thus supersensuous (supernatural) practice of human beings. While human beings are creatures of nature, they know themselves to be objects of possible appearance that are universally and necessarily subject to the laws of nature solely because they do not, cannot, and will never know what they are in themselves as actually rational, willing human beings. Indeed, we remember that Kant shows us that logical possibility is not a field larger than what we may call the actuality of human existence. For, while not everything logically possible is actual, everything actual, as "absolute possibility," is possible. The actual is infinite in its possibilities, practically and so transcendentally, not hypothetically (as an object of nature) or logically (as a topic of analytic judgment consistent with the law of contradiction). Synthetic, *a priori* judgments are possible precisely because human beings freely and so self-consciously will to ascribe priority to their existence: I think, *ergo* I am. This *ergo* represents, therefore (*sic!*), neither analytic deduction nor synthetic induction—from the contradictory opposition of which Hume, as we saw, knew no escape. Rather, the "therefore" here represents the self-determination on the part of human beings to bind together the necessity of their existence and the existence of their necessity. The one thing that human beings cannot think (will, desire) and so practice without making it their absolute priority is the necessity of their existence, that they exist necessarily. All human practice—will, effort, labor, desire, interest, concern, purpose, intent—emerges out of, in beginning with, the necessity of constituting existence in and through the synthesis of priorities. As Kant shows us in, above all, *The Critique of Practical Reason*, together with the *Groundwork of the Metaphysics of Morals*, plus his writings on religion and shorter essays such as "Conjectural Beginning of Human History," the moral law is the necessary ground of our existence. The transcendental deduction (justification) of the categories of the objects of possible appearance is only possible because we human beings actually exist as subjects who are duty bound to treat every person as a thing in itself and not merely as an object of possible (sensible or empirical) appearance. We begin in nature only to have it revealed to us (as self-conscious persons) that, having been created in the image of God with knowledge of good and evil, our existence is freely and so necessarily self-determinable. But it is always important to bear in mind that the content of the moral law as knowledge of good and evil is not predetermined for us. We may read in the Bible about the duty of loving God and human beings. We may read in Kant that there is only one thing that is good in itself, whether within or even without the world, and that is the will (of all rational beings). But since the good of the will includes its freedom to do evil, every human being and so all human beings must begin anew in submitting their lives to the trial of existence in learning what it means to be responsible in their lives for good as for evil.

It is no less extraordinary that Wordsworth in the *Prelude* celebrates what is surely his crowning, poetic achievement in telling us that, having completed his poem, he now feels ready to don the prophetic mantle of the poet. He arrives at the end of his magisterial poem only to find that he is at the prelude to his life as a poet whose significant achievement now lies before him. Wordsworth depicts the growth of the poet's mind in and through the very poem that at one and the same time embodies the double movement of then, in the past, and of now, as the product of this past, and also of now, in the present, and of then, as the product of the present. The poet finds that in the present now he is the product of his past then. The double movement of time—of *then and now* and of *now and then*—captures, by making historical, the growth of the poet's mind.

I repeat: All human practice—will, effort, labor, desire, interest, concern, purpose, intent—emerges out of, in beginning with, the priority of making our human existence necessary by constituting the synthesis of priorities as the necessary basis of our life. We begin at the end only to find that our end is in our beginning. But it is no less true that we begin in the beginning only to have it revealed to us that our beginning is in the end as we recount the story of the growth of the poet's mind as the past made present and as the present made past. The poet did not know and could not have known in the beginning that it was his destiny to become the poet that he will become and that he has become today. Still, he makes clear to us that he could not have become and would not have become the poet that he is without beginning as the poet he was to become. Wordsworth thus shows us that his earliest encounters with nature unconsciously lead him to the conscious awareness that the imagination is at once both the product of nature and the very creation of nature as the act of the mind that constitutes its historical growth. The imagination passively allows the extraordinary elements of nature to enter into the mind of the child while at the same time empowering the growing and maturing poet to meditate on the active powers of creating poetry in and through which he celebrates the sublime originality and, indeed, divinity of the human mind. In concluding *The Prelude* Wordsworth recalls to his dear friend and fellow-poet, Coleridge, as we have seen, that they will "be Blessed with true happiness if," as "Prophets of Nature," they may inspire others in sanctifying them "By reason and truth." For

> what we have loved
> Others will love; and we may teach them how;
> Instruct them how the mind of man becomes
> A thousand times more beautiful than the earth
> On which he dwells, above this Frame of things
> (Which, 'mid all revolutions in the hopes
> And fears of men, doth still remain unchanged)
> In beauty exalted, as it is itself,
> Of substance and of fabric more divine.

Overall, then, I chose Wordsworth to represent the truth of poetry and Kant to represent the truth of philosophy because, both singly and together, they so amply embody and demonstrate the profundity of Kierkegaard's dictum that all human speech, including the speech of the Bible, is critically metaphoric in transferring human beings from the world of nature to the world of spirit. What I want, then, to emphasize in my final, concluding remarks, is that this transfer is at once ontological and historical. In the traditional terms of formal philosophy this transfer, this conversion to the world of spirit, involves both the moral law as the kingdom of ends and the ontological argument demonstrating the necessary relationship between thought and existence. It is especially important, consequently, to discern the temporal dimension, i.e., the role that time plays in our realization of the moral law on earth. We begin as moral creatures only to discover our sinfulness, our inadequacy in meeting the universal demands of covenantal love. Thus, Kant shows us that metaphysics is possible in our human lives solely as the practice of freedom and so, too, as containing the hope of realizing the moral law in and through the infinite progress that lies ahead of us and so of uniting the moral law with our happiness as human beings in and through God as the highest good. Kant thus distinguishes, in absolute terms, between sensible space and time, which are finite, and the infinite (qualitative) dimensions, both spatial and temporal, of the moral law that lies within us. Still, it is true, as I have emphasized, that Kant does not yet name or thus explicate as *historical* the moral, practical dimension of time (and space) that is implied by his postulates of the immortality of the soul and of God. It is perhaps ironic that it is Wordsworth who, in a truly philosophic sense, profoundly embodies the temporal dimension of moral existence in his depiction in *The Prelude* of the growth of a poet's mind. Still, both philosopher and poet make use of the idea of progress, then common in their day, but understood by them to designate the moral (sanctifying) development of the individual (and not primarily social or even technological change).

The point that I especially want to emphasize is what it actually is that Wordsworth and Kant reveal to us in and through their demonstrations, at once poetic and philosophic, that the human speech of true poetry and of true philosophy, like the divine speech of the Bible, transfers us metaphorically to the realm of the mind by the critique of reason as practice. The realm of the mind that we occupy as both poets and philosophers is, Wordsworth and Kant show us, the realm of the moral law as occupied by all human beings whose common speech, Kant reminds us, has long been universally used by human beings. All the touching stories that Wordsworth relates in *The Prelude* involve those reflecting compassionate love for and moral interest in others. But it turns out that it is precisely the moral law that lies at the basis of, and so authorizes, the necessary relationship of thought (will, desire) and existence that we call, since Kant, the ontological argument proving the necessary existence of God. The necessary relatedness of thought and existence is precisely the *a priori* synthetic proposition that is shown to exist in response to the question: How is metaphysics possible? Metaphysics is possible because it is actually shown by us to enable the very possibility of posing the question of how it is possible. Everything that is metaphysically (and not merely logically) possible is actual—practically, necessarily, existentially. To think is to think—something existing (both the "I" that thinks and what the "I" thinks). To exist is to be conscious not simply that I exist but that "I" am something that thinks something. It is little wonder, then, that Spinoza, as I indicated earlier, initiates his *Ethics* with the ontological argument demonstrating the necessary existence of God and that Kant, in showing that reason constitutes the free practice of morality, demonstrates, without explicit acknowledgement, that the moral law embodies the ontological argument: I think, *ergo* I will to exist freely in and through the kingdom of ends of human dignity and equality.

Not only, then, does the moral law embody the ontological argument by demonstrating the necessary relationship between thought and existence—there is one fact whose non-existence is contradictory, i.e. there is one fact that I cannot think, or will, without demonstrating its necessary existence. But also the ontological necessity of the relationship between thought (I will) and existence (I exist) is an historical necessity. As Kant unceasingly reminds us and as Wordsworth continuously shows us, our existence is necessarily progress or growth in and through time (and, we should also add, place)—as historical, not natural. While human beings as creatures of nature participate in the temporal and circular dimensions of time (and space)—they live linearly from birth to death in repeating the circularity of the generations—they are also moral, free, transcendental, noumenal, creative beings whose lives, at once poetic and philosophic, repeat the story of their original forebears, Adam and Eve. Created in the image of God with knowledge of good and evil and consequently from nothing that is not metaphorical, they bear the eternal responsibility of constituting the transfer from nature to spirit in and through the historical existence of the moral kingdom of God. We could pose, in Kantian terms, the question that is metaphysical at once historically and ontologically: How is existence possible? The question is *not*: Is existence possible? It is *not*: *Why* is existence is possible? *Nor* is it why something exists and not nothing. The question is: How is existence possible? The answer, consequently, is that existence is possible only as necessarily and historically actual. We may recall the ancient saying: *vita brevis, ars longa*. Life is short, art (poetry, philosophy . . .) is long. We could equally say: *vita brevis, historia longa*. Life, the existence of each individual, human being, is brief. But *historia*, the life of the community of human beings, is long. We begin, each of us, to recall Descartes, with a whole and a complete mind (not with a partial mind or only with a part of our mind). We begin wholly with the moral law, which is complete in the beginning: do unto others what you want others to do unto you. There is nothing more (i.e., other) to think or to do (to be). Yet, the paradox is that

CONCLUSION

everything remains, for each of us, to think, to be, to do, to carry out, to make actual, to realize, to bear out in the historical practice of our lives.

God begins complete and whole. Still, the existence of God is historical. For the very idea of creation, as Kant makes clear to us, is noumenal, not phenomenal. Creation involves persons, not things; freedom, not nature; the moral law, not natural law. God, like the moral law, like every human being, is complete and whole in the beginning. God is not just partly God. But there's the rub. Our concept of God as that than which we cannot think anything greater is ever yet to be developed historically and ontologically in and through the covenantal existence of the kingdom of ends on earth.

In sum, all human speech about the spirit, like the divine speech of the Bible, is a work of love—insofar as it is true speech. In undertaking to inspire others by sanctifying them through the truthful practice of reason, it teaches them to love what we have loved. The poetry of Wordsworth, as found, above all, in *The Prelude*, and the philosophy of Kant, as found, above all, in *The Critique of Practical Reason*, show us that all truly human speech about the spirit must be rationally grounded in the moral law, as found in the Bible, and must bear practical witness, historically and ontologically, to the necessary existence of human beings as divine.

Notes

Chapter 1

1. The translator indicates in square brackets that the Danish for "metaphorical" is "*overført,* carried over." I modify the order of the phrases in this opening sentence of Part II of *Works of Love*. For the texts cited in my study see the Bibliography.

2. When, within a given paragraph of my study, quotations are taken from the same page of the text that is cited, the page number is given at the end of the last passage quoted.

3. It is important to keep in mind that "German" refers properly to the language in which a text is written, not the country from which the writer comes, since Germany did not exist as a (modern) country or nation state before 1870.

4. I want to point out here, briefly and thus without extended commentary, that I do not include *The Critique of the Power of Judgment*, with its two parts, "The Critique of the Aesthetic Power of Judgment" and "The Critique of the Teleological Power of Judgment," among the works of Kant that I discuss in my present book. As I have explained in earlier studies of Kant, the second part of *The Critique of the Power of Judgment*, while providing a significant overview of his philosophy, adds nothing fundamentally new to it. In the first part on aesthetic judgment, however, Kant continues to view the "aesthetic" in the Enlightenment tradition of A. G. Baumgarten (d. 1757). Thus, he altogether fails to see that art belongs to rational practice and not to the realm of sensible nature. In his work, consequently, Kant associates the imagination with sensibility and understanding, not with the moral practice of reason. It is thus Wordsworth, not Kant, who, together with Coleridge and other romantic poets, is truly Kantian in associating the imagination with the morally creative power of practical reason, as we shall see.

5. In his introduction to Kant's work the translator comments on the challenge that he faced in choosing to translate its title—*blosse Vernunft*—as "mere reason," meaning pure, unmixed, naked, sole reason. "Certainly, it was Kant's intention to examine religion in the light of unaided reason," he writes: "to establish its 'mere' rights as contrasted with those it had acquired historically. 'Mere reason' thus seems to me to convey at least the basic metaphors elicited by *blosse Vernunft*" (53).

6. The editor discusses on pp. 41ff what he calls "Kant's famous confrontation with censorship" (42).

7. See *Concluding Unscientific Postscript to Philosophical Fragments*.

Chapter 2

8. Boldface is added. See n. 9.

9. See the Bibliography for the editions of Wordsworth, Coleridge, and Shelley that I use.

10. It is also curious to note that Wordsworth was named the Poet Laureate of England in 1843 (following the death of the Poet Laureate Robert Southey), although what we now view as his greatest poem (not to mention as the greatest poem of the nineteenth century and what Coleridge called the greatest philosophic poem since Milton's *Paradise Lost*) had not been published and was unknown to the public.

11. Gill points out in his "Note on the Text" (in his edition of Wordsworth's poetry) that Wordsworth between 1793 and 1850 published "fifteen new volumes of verse (excluding from consideration reprint editions, selections and pamphlets), and from 1815 [on] nine collected editions (again excluding reprints, American and other unauthorized editions). Each new collection contained fresh verse . . . and presented Wordsworth's latest revisions of the old." But he adds that, while The Collected Edition of 1849–50 must "be regarded as the poet's final authorized text," still, in consideration of "the development of Wordsworth's art, . . . this last edition is most unsatisfactory." While the 1849–50 edition can be considered canonical, biographically, "it does not present all of the poetry, nor the poems as they appeared to Wordsworth's first readers." It is also the case that in the later editions of the poems Wordsworth arranged them, not chronologically, but in ever-shifting categories. Thus, Gill concludes: "In the belief that a chronological presentation can best reveal the growth of the poet's mind (the subject, after all, of his greatest poem, *The Prelude*) and the unfolding of his imagination, this volume is ordered according to date of composition. It follows . . . that one *must* print a text which comes as close as possible to the state of a poem when it was first completed. To place a poem under 1795 in a text encrusted with the revisions of perhaps forty years . . . is, to say the least, confusing" (Gill, xxx-xxxi).

12. I omit lines 145–50 as at once neither clear nor significant.

13. Gill points out that Wordsworth wrote in a note that, since the fiction of "a pre-existent state has entered into the popular creeds of many nations, and . . . is known as an ingredient in Platonic philosophy . . . , I took hold of the notion of pre-existence as having sufficient foundation in humanity for authorizing me to make for my purpose the best use of it I could as a Poet" (Gill, 714). In his *Biographia Literaria* Coleridge points out that, since the "Immortality Ode" was intended only for readers who were "accustomed to watch the flux and reflux of their inmost nature . . . and to feel a deep interest in modes of inmost being" for which they know only the "symbols of time and space" are applicable, such readers "will be as little disposed to charge Mr. Wordsworth with believing the platonic pre-existence . . . as I am to believe that Plato himself ever meant or taught it" (Ch. 22, 147). While neither Wordsworth nor Coleridge raises the question whether or how the notion of the immortality (or pre-existence) of the soul is compatible with the biblical concepts of creation and eternity, etc., it is noteworthy that Wordsworth writes that he poetically makes use of it for his own purpose as commonly known. He does not say, however, either what that use was or what was commonly understood by the immortality of the soul. Coleridge, on the other hand, while he denies that Wordsworth is to be understood as believing in

the Platonic pre-existence (immortality) of the soul (as if it were incompatible with Christian doctrine), also denies, erroneously, that Plato held this belief.

14. Baker, 200–2.

15. Let me add here that I follow the standard scholarship on Wordsworth in not considering in my study the two existing fragments of *The Recluse* (except for that part of *Home at Grasmere* that serves as the Prospectus to *The Excursion*). Neither of the editions of Wordsworth that I use in my study includes *The Excursion*.

16. This is the spelling of the title of the poem as published in 1834. In the first (1798) edition of the *Lyrical Ballads* the title appeared as "The Rime of the Ancyent Marinere."

17. I want to outline here my citation protocol. When two or more quotations, which follow upon one another within the same paragraph, come from the same page of the text that is cited, the reference is provided at the end of the last quotation given. When I cite the prose (but not the poetic) works of Wordsworth and also the prose works of Coleridge and Shelley, I shall, for the purpose of ensuring proper clarity, occasionally modify the capitalization and the punctuation (and also the syntax) that are found in the original texts. Italics and capital letters are in the original unless otherwise indicated. Bold face is added. Emphasis is in the original unless otherwise indicated.

18. Wordsworth also refers to Sir Joshua Reynolds as his authority in a similar passage that is found near the end of the Preface to the *Lyrical Ballads* (1800) (Baker, 30).

19. Wordsworth repeats on the following page: "It may be safely affirmed that there neither is, nor can be, any *essential* difference between the language of prose and metrical composition." They embody the same human affections, the same human tears, the same vital juices, and "the same human blood circulates through the veins of them both" (Baker, 11).

20. Wordsworth concludes the Appendix to the Preface of the *Lyrical Ballads* (1802) with the observation "that in works of *imagination and sentiment*, for only of those have I been treating, in proportion as ideas and feelings are valuable, whether the composition be in prose or in verse, they require and exact one and the same language. Metre is but adventitious [accidental, extrinsic] to composition, and the phraseology for which that passport is necessary, even where it may be graceful at all, will be little valued by the judicious" (Baker, 38).

21. I have omitted from this passage, for the sake of economy, Wordsworth's concern to distinguish the poet from "the man of science." But the following passage captures the essence of the distinction that he makes: "The knowledge both of the poet and the man of science is pleasure; but the knowledge of the one [the poet] cleaves to us as a necessary part of our existence, our natural and unalienable inheritance; the other [the scientist] is a personal and individual acquisition, slow to come to us, and by no means habitual and [involving] direct sympathy connecting us with our fellow-beings" (Baker, 18).

22. See Prickett (*Words and* The Word) and Drury for information on Robert Lowth whose *Lectures on the Sacred Poetry of the Hebrews* (1753; trans. from Latin into English, 1787) revolutionized the modern understanding of Hebrew prosody.

23. Emphasis added.

24. One of the problematic elements involved in how Wordsworth conceives of the relationship between poetry and prose is what he means by "prose." Today, we would doubtlessly be primarily interested in considering the relationship between poetry and prose fiction as found in novels and short stories and also in plays. The only time that Wordsworth makes reference to the great English fiction of the eighteenth century (which saw the birth of the modern novel) is when he appeals "to the reader's own experience of the reluctance with which he comes to the reperusal of the distressful parts of *Clarrisa Harlowe* [the novel, *Clarrisa: Or, The History of a Young Lady*, by Samuel Richardson, 1748] or *The Gamester* [a play by Edward Moore, 1753]." In contrast, "Shakespeare's writings, in the most pathetic scenes, never act upon us as pathetic beyond the bounds of pleasure . . . which . . . is to be ascribed to small but continual and regular impulses of pleasurable surprise from the metrical arrangement" (Baker, 24). Wordsworth, like countless other readers of Shakespeare, fails not only to point out that his plays, including his tragedies, contain both verse and prose passages but also to account for the significance of the formal difference between them.

25. Emphasis added.

26. In a passage of considerable ambiguity and also, perhaps, of considerable uncertainty about how to proceed, Wordsworth indicates that nothing would have contributed further to the end that he had in mind than to have shown both the kind of pleasure "metrical composition" produces and how it produces a pleasure different from that which he has endeavored to recommend. If the reader says that a composition has pleased him, "what," Wordsworth asks, "can I do more for him?" For "all men feel an habitual gratitude and something of an honorable bigotry for the objects which have long continued to please them; we not only wish to be pleased but to be pleased in that particular way in which we have been accustomed to be pleased." What he is not willing to do, Wordsworth writes, is to maintain "that, in order entirely to enjoy the Poetry which I am recommending, it would be necessary to give up much of what is ordinarily enjoyed." Still, he adds that, if the limits of his Preface had permitted it, "I might have removed many obstacles and assisted my Reader in perceiving that the powers of language are not so limited as he may suppose; and that it is possible that poetry may give other enjoyments of a purer, more lasting, and more exquisite nature" (614). It is evident, surely, that the pleasure that, according to Wordsworth, is to be received from poetry is no ordinary or habitual pleasure (immediate gratification). For us, the true test of the pleasure of poetry will be *The Prelude*.

27. It is fitting, I believe, to recall that the verb "tantalize" (together with its gerundive adjective, "tantalizing") is a metaphoric expression recalling Tantalus, the figure in ancient Greek mythology who was condemned for all eternity to reach for food and drink that were always just beyond his reach.

28. Wordsworth concludes his sentence in writing that he cannot forebear adding the works of Spencer to those of Milton.

29. It is useful to recall that "enthusiasm," with its roots in Greek—*en* ("in") and *theós* ("god")—is itself a metaphoric expression.

30. Although Spencer, unlike Milton, did not directly engage the biblical story of fall and redemption in his great epic, the *Fairie Queene*, Wordsworth observes that, thanks to "his allegorical spirit," he was able, "by a superior effort of genius, to give universality and permanence of abstractions to his humans beings by means of attributes

and emblems that belong to the highest moral truths and purest sensations—of which his character of Una is a glorious example" (634–35).

31. *Biographia Literaria* (10, 222, lines 65–75). The standard, scholarly edition of the *Biographia Literaria* (ed. by Engell and Bate) is divided into two volumes, with the chapters numbered consecutively from Chapter 1 to Chapter 24 but with the pagination of each volume provided separately. Consequently, I shall identify the passages that I cite by chapter and page number. (Both Chapter 1 and Chapter 14 begin on p. 5.)

32. A significant portion of the *Biographia Literaria* is taken up by the notes of the editors in which they provide the sources for the texts that Coleridge cites (falsely) as his own or for writings of his own as found in previously published books or journals or in personal letters.

33. Coleridge does write that in "Schelling's *Natur-Philosophie* and the *System des Transcendentalen Idealismus* I first found a genial coincidence with much that I had toiled out for myself and a powerful assistance in what I had yet to do" (9, 160). He adds that with the "exception of one or two fundamental ideas, . . . to Schelling we owe the completion and the most important victories of this revolution in philosophy" (9, 163). Still, Coleridge provides no sustained philosophical argument in support of these claims. Additionally, he addresses the issue of his plagiarism in Chapter 9 (161 and 164). I also want to point out that Coleridge remains silent on Hegel. While it is true that Hegel produced the bulk of his mature works, both books and lecture series, in the years following the publication of the *Biographia Literaria* (1817), he initiated his ground-breaking career in philosophy with the publication of *The Phenomenology of Spirit* in 1807. Hegel became famous throughout Europe for his lectures on philosophy and religion that he gave as the chair in philosophy at the University of Berlin (in the Kingdom of Prussia) from 1818 to his death in 1831.

34. The structural incoherence of the *Biographia Literaria* is reflected in the work's chapters, taken both individually and as a collective whole, together with their titles. Chapter 12 is entitled "A Chapter of requests and premonitions concerning the perusal or omission of the chapter that follows." It thus gives no indication that it is here in this chapter that Coleridge outlines the fundamental principles of his philosophy, although it does serve as a warning that he views it as incomplete.

35. Coleridge then cites Juvenal (in Latin)—"It descended from heaven"—(and in Greek) *know thyself*? But he does not tell us that the words "Know thyself" were inscribed over the Temple of Apollo at Delphi, from which Socrates (as he tells us in Plato's *Apology*) received the oracle informing him that he was the wisest man in Greece—because he knew that he was ignorant of the truth.

36. Judge William continues: "The self the individual knows is simultaneously the actual self and the ideal self, which the individual has outside himself as the image in whose likeness he is to form himself, and which on the other hand he has within himself, since it is he himself. . . . That is why the ethical life has this duplexity, in which the individual has himself outside himself within himself. Meanwhile the exemplary self is an imperfect self, for it is only a prophecy, and thus not the actual self. . . . What [t]he [individual] wants to actualize is certainly himself, but it is his ideal self, which he cannot acquire anywhere but within himself. If he does not hold firmly to the truth that the individual has the ideal self within himself, all of his aspiring and striving becomes abstract" (259). In citing this passage on the ethical from Kierkegaard's Judge William,

I want to emphasize two points that are frequently misrepresented or even distorted by Kierkegaard scholars. First, while Judge Williams is a pseudonymous figure within a work whose editor is Victor Eremita (and whose name is given on the title page of *Either/Or*, Part II), the views that he puts forth are fully compatible with Kierkegaard's own (as found, for example, in *Works of Love*). Second, the conception of the ethical individual that Judge William articulates here is completely different from the conception of "the ethical" that we find in *Fear and Trembling*. In that work the ethical is represented by the tragic hero of ancient Greek drama, together with Socrates, who is called an intellectual tragic hero (with the tragic hero being absolutely distinguished from the knight of faith who, in the figure of Abraham, represents the "religious.") The "ethical" of Judge Williams is fully consistent with the "religious" of *Fear and Trembling* and with the command to live by the golden rule (in *Works of Love*).

37. I omit here the critique of Descartes' *Cogito, ergo sum* that Coleridge includes in a note to Thesis VI. (In my judgment his critique is, at best, altogether misleading.)

38. I have here reconfigured the sentence structure and corrected Coleridge's grammar.

39. Additionally, Coleridge states in the third and last paragraph on the imagination, which contains but one sentence, that whatever more than what he thinks it fit to write about the imagination in the present work "will be found in the critical essay on the uses of the Supernatural in poetry and the principles that regulate its introduction, which the reader will find prefixed to the poem of 'The Ancient Mariner.'" The editors observe in a note: "This essay, if written, has not survived" (13, 306).

40. As always, the editors of the *Biographia Literaria* provide copious notes here.

41. I omit the (irregular) capitalization that Coleridge uses in this sentence.

42. I transpose Wordsworth's statement as cited by Coleridge.

43. *Poetics*, 9.1–4.

44. In praising Lessing Coleridge writes that it was he "who first proved to all thinking men, even to Shakespeare's own countrymen, the true nature of . . . [the] apparent irregularities" that are found in his plays, since these "were deviations only from the *Accidents* of Greek Tragedy . . . [that] hung [like] a heavy weight on the wings of the Greek Poets" (23, 210). What Coleridge writes here, the editors point out, "is so completely at variance with the facts (the defence and understanding of Shakespeare's 'apparent irregularities' are common in eighteenth-century English criticism . . .) that one can only assume that Coleridge at this moment is nodding or partly thinking of something else when dictating" his manuscript (23, 209).

45. In discussing the defects that he finds in Wordsworth's poetry Coleridge supports his claims with numerous citations of lines and passages from individual poems.

46. Earlier in the *Biographia Literaria* Coleridge writes that Spinoza's *Ethics* "may, or may not, be an instance" of "irreligious PANTHEISM. . . . But at no time could I believe, that *in itself* and *essentially* it is incompatible with religion, natural or revealed: and now I am most thoroughly persuaded of the contrary" (9, 152–53). Coleridge typically does not provide textual evidence from the *Ethics* in support of his claims. He also does not explain what he understands to be the difference between natural religion (Platonism?) and revealed religion (Christianity).

47. See Rousseau's *Second Discourse on Inequality* (234). In the *Social Contract* Rousseau writes: "To renounce one's liberty is to renounce one's quality as a man, the rights and also the duties of humanity.... Such a renunciation is incompatible with man's nature, for to take away all freedom from his will is to take away all morality from his actions" (12–13). Again, the paradox here is that, if I were to renounce my freedom, I would not even know that I had given up my freedom, that I was unfree.

48. Shelley notes here that "the limits of this essay... forbid citation" (977/col. 1).

49. In his essay Peacock "maintained that in savage and barbarous ages poetry had been appropriate, but that in modern times it had become an anachronism." Thus, he wrote that "A poet in our times is"
- a semi-barbarian in a civilized community,
- a morbid dreamer,
- a driveler and mountebank,
- [and not] a useful or rational man [such as a mathematician, politician, or chemist] (*Anthology of Romanticism*, editor's note, 1212).

50. I have changed the word order of Shelley's sentence.

51. There are numerous, odd omissions in *A Defense of Poetry*. Shelley does not point out, for example, that in the final book of the *Republic* Plato famously expels the poets, Homer, above all, from the perfect republic of words. He also does not mention Aristotle's *Poetics*. Additionally, he gives no indication that he even knows of Gianbattista Vico's *New Science*, the definitive edition of which was published in 1744 (the year of the author's death). In his work Vico systematically distinguishes the "inhuman" (non-humane) gentes or pagans (as found in Homer and the ancient Greeks, above all) from the humane Hebrews of the Bible and their Christian successors. It is also important to note that, while we know that Shelley does not discuss in detail (in what is, he tells us, only the first part of his *Defense of Poetry*) the present poetic and philosophical age, still, he does make urgent (if relatively indirect) reference to it in his criticism both of utilitarianism and of what he refers to as the overwhelming piling up of scientific facts. More importantly, he points out that it was the chivalric and Christian poets who, in their songs in praise of love, provided the very principle for rejecting the basis on which the *polis* of the ancients was constituted: slavery and the subordination of women (in confusing diversity with inequality). In this context it is odd that Shelley makes no reference to the American and French revolutions as based on the principles of equality, freedom, and fraternity (love) and never mentions democracy. He also evinces no awareness that Spinoza, in his *Theologico-Political Treatise*, demonstrates that democracy, as the sole commonwealth truly based on the freedom of all, has its origins, both historical and ontological, in the biblical covenant whose fundamental law is love (respect for the other) and thus, by evident implication, not in the "democracy" of the ancient, Greek *polis* as based on the rule of many over (most) others.

Chapter 3

52. When quoting from *The Prelude* I provide the reference for citations (book and line numbers) at the end of the last passage cited from a single book within a single paragraph.

53. I want here to point out, without further comment, that Wordsworth misleadingly exemplifies the conversation on "rational liberty" that took place between him and the Patriot officer in France with "the philosophic war" against tyranny as "Led by Philosophers" in antiquity (9.423–24).

54. Laudanum, a tincture of opium, was, in the time of Wordsworth and Coleridge, widely taken by many, frequently with brandy, not only for medicinal but also for leisure purposes.

55. Wordsworth continues in this passage to laud the ancients, consistent with his appeal to ancient philosophers that we noted in Book 9 (see note 2):

> a Land
> Glorious indeed, substantially renowned
> Of Simple vertue once, and manly praise,
> Now without one memorial hope, not even
> A hope to be deferred. (10.959–64)

He persists in his praise of ancient Sicily, land of shepherds, poets, and philosophers, to the end of Book 10.

56. A few lines further along in *The Prelude* Wordsworth associates false education with those for whom "strong affections, love / Known by whatever name," is not a gift of what they call "vulgar Nature" but the product of "Retirement, leisure, language purified / By manners thoughtful and elaborate." (12.185–90). Still a bit further on he observes that human beings, with their books, mislead each other in "looking for their fame" in "judgments of the wealthy Few" and "debase / The Many for the pleasure of those few." In judging the differences among men according to "the outside marks by which / Society has parted man from man," they neglect "the universal heart" (12.207–19).

57. I have altered the order of Wordsworth's phrases.

58. Emphasis added. Wordsworth modifies the sharp contrast between "thy" merely human love and "this" divine love in the 1850 version of this passage. There he writes that the "delight" in "The one who is thy choice of all the world" is "pitiable"

> Unless this love by a still higher love
> Be hallowed, love that breathes not without awe;
> Love that adores, but on the knees of prayer,
> By heaven inspired; that frees from chains the soul,
> Lifted, in union with the purest, best,
> Of earth-born passions, on the wings of praise
> Bearing a tribute to the Almighty's Throne.
> (14.178–87)

59. The following epigram is found on the title page of Nietzsche's *Ecce Homo*: "How One Becomes What One Is." Nietzsche comments on this epigram in the section of *Ecce Homo* entitled "Why I am so Clever," no. 9.

60. I want to point out here that Wordsworth, in viewing the mind as infinitely more beautiful than the earth, i.e., in making beauty an attribute of spirit and not of sensate nature, conveys a conception of "man" (humankind) fundamentally different

from that found in Keats' "Ode on a Grecian Urn." After contemplating the figures frozen in time on an antique vase, Keats famously ends his poem:

> Beauty is truth, truth beauty, that is all
> Ye know on earth, and all ye need to know.
> (Bernhaum, lines 49–50)

The scene that Keats depicts in his poem is one in which, just as the promise of spring goes eternally unfulfilled, so the possibilities of our life are never actualized or made real and our life's goals are never attained or realized. Keats addresses the "Fair youth" who is portrayed on the urn as follows:

> Bold Lover, never, never can't thou kiss,
> Though winning [i.e., getting] near the goal—yet, do not grieve;
> She cannot fade, though thou hast not thy bliss.
> For ever will thou love, and she be fair! (lines 17–20)

In the world depicted on the antique urn there is no birth or death, no sin or redemption, no growth of the human spirit in and through its historically self-conscious development. Indeed, what Keats give us in his poem is a perfect image of the Greek world as reflected in the myth of Tantalus, for whom the fruits of life are forever just out of reach. Keats' poem is also consistent with the teaching of Socrates who demonstrates in Plato's dialogues that to love, to desire, to seek the good is fatally to prove that you eternally lack the good or, in other words, that you are ignorant of that which you love, desire, or seek. It follows, then, that to know the good, to attain your end or goal, is to be identical with it as that which is eternally unchanging. When you love, the good (the end of your life) is but a tantalizing appearance forever unattained and unattainable. When you attain your good (in being identical with it), then love is forever absent. The world that Keats depicts in his "Ode on a Grecian Urn" is, consequently, one in which beauty and truth are never realized on earth as the happiness of actual human love. It is evident that, in light of the values that we find expressed in *The Prelude*, the beauty that is depicted in Keats' poem is devoid of truth and the truth that is articulated in it is devoid of beauty. For neither is founded on love. We remember Wordsworth's declaration:

> From love . . . all grandeur comes,
> All truth and beauty, from pervading love.
> That gone, we are as dust. (*The Prelude*, 10.725–27)

One wonders, then, what Keats saw in a painting or sculpture of the crucified Christ or, indeed, in Milton's portrayal in *Paradise Lost* of paradise lost as paradise regained!

61. We do have the strange anomaly that Wordsworth added to the 1836–37 edition of his poem "Ode to Duty" (first published in 1807) a one-sentence quotation from Seneca, the Roman Stoic philosopher, as an aphorism—in Latin without attribution. (See Gill for the earlier and Baker for the later versions of the poem.) Seneca writes: "I am no longer good through deliberation (*consilio*). But, having been conducted there by habit (*more*), I am not only able to act rightly (*recte facere*) but I am unable not to act rightly." The idea that duty (morality) becomes in our life unthinking habit (custom) is totally foreign to the biblical idea of moral duty as willed. The very idea of willing the good (the concept of will) is unknown to Seneca, as to the all of the ancients. Wordsworth concludes the "Ode to Duty" with an address to the "awful Power" of Duty:

> I myself commend
> Unto thy guidance from this hour;
> Oh! Let my weakness have an end!
> Give unto me, made lowly wise,
> The spirit of self-sacrifice;
> The confidence of reason give;
> And in the light of truth thy Bondsman let me live! (Gill, 57–64)

Again, the "confidence of reason" is not habit but self-conscious realization on the part of individuals that willing the good—in loving the neighbor as themselves—is but the prelude to a yet fuller life of sinning and loving.

I also want to note that in Book 2 of *The Prelude*, when Wordsworth (in the context of having returned to the natural solace of Grasmere in 1799) refers to "these times of fear, . . . / of hopes o'erthrown, . . . / indifference and apathy, / And wicked exultation," he then continues:

> if in this time
> Of dereliction and dismay, I yet
> Despair not of our nature; but retain
> A more than Roman confidence, a faith
> That fails not, in all sorrow my support,
> The blessing of my life, the gift is yours,
> Yet mountains! thine, O Nature! Thou hast fed
> My lofty speculations; and in thee
> For this uneasy heart of ours I find
> A never-failing principle of joy,
> And purest passion. (2.448–66)

The confidence "more than Roman" that Wordsworth invokes here results, not from habit but from self-determining deliberation to find the blessing of his life in the gift of self-acknowledgment that the infinitely mighty (and tender!) mind of man, of Nature, and of God is encountered in the earthly scenes of daily life. I hardly need add that Wordsworth's concept of Nature is totally different from the ancients' concept of nature as the unchanging, finite, and divine cosmos.

Chapter 4

62. Kant's "critical writings" begin with the publication of *The Critique of Pure Reason* in 1781.

63. Descartes writes in his *Second Meditation*: "But what then am I? A thing that thinks. What is that? A thing that doubts, understands, affirms, denies, is willing, is unwilling, and also imagines and has sensory perceptions" (19).

64. Aristotle formally distinguishes between timocracy as the good rule and democracy as the bad rule of the many.

65. I have modified Kant's syntax by substituting "human beings" for "man."

66. Francesco Cavalli's *Elena* (*Helen of Troy*), 1659.

67. Croce, *History as the Story of Liberty*.

68. I distinguish "anti-Judaism" from the anti-Semitism that was formulated in the nineteenth century in explicitly racist terms.

69. Spinoza makes acute comments on the story of Adam in both his *Theologico-Political Treatise* and his *Political Treatise*. In the latter work he points out that Adam was not "free" to fall into knowledge of good and evil, since freedom presupposes knowledge of good and evil (and vice-versa) (271). But Spinoza does not then acknowledge the "analogy" between the Garden of natural Paradise and the state of nature. The contract theorists (Hobbes, Spinoza, Rousseau) always found themselves beset with the problem of explaining the passage, the transition, from the state of nature (red in tooth and claw, to recall Tennyson in his poem *In Memoriam*) to the civil state of peaceful relationships, from nature to freedom. There is "nothing" in the state of nature (and so nothing in either the Garden of Paradise or the pagan world of the Greeks) that can account for history as the story of reason made the practice of freedom. Kant is the first thinker ever to realize, explicitly, that our beginning in the state of nature is a "conjecture" that we can and, indeed, must make—yet only subsequent to our "fall" into the knowledge of good and evil. We begin in nature, but we can account for that beginning only from the perspective of our beginning as rational, historical, free agents. The relationship between nature and freedom is transcendental, that is, conjectural. But even Kant does not directly connect the story of Adam and Eve with the account of creation with which the Bible begins. Our human beginning is from itself alone. We are created from nothing, from nothing natural, from nothing that is not in the beginning truly covenantal and so founded on the categorical imperative of duty: love your neighbor as yourself.

Christian theologians, from the time of the Church Fathers through the Middle Ages, continually commented on "the fall of man," as did the Jewish rabbis in their biblical commentaries. Still, it was only St. Augustine, within the Christian tradition, who fundamentally grasped the idea of "happy sin" (*felix culpa!*)—that human beings can will the good only in confronting themselves as sinners whose evil they must work to overcome. We also have the extraordinary recognition on the part of Milton in *Paradise Lost* that, consistent with Kant, the fall from the (natural) paradise (without) into the knowledge of good and evil is the "happier far" gain of (covenantal) paradise within. Hegel, too, following Kant, includes within several of his major works penetrating commentaries on the story of Adam and Eve as providing the history of human reason.

70. It is also relevant here to recall that angels, as immortal (supernatural), were traditionally viewed as male and so without sexual inclinations. Milton in *Paradise Lost* pens a delightful riff on this story when the archangel Michael, in response to Adam's question about his attraction to sensuous delights such as food (apples!) and sex, blushes.

71. In Parts 2 and 3 of *The Conflict of the Faculties* Kant examines the relationship of the Faculty of Philosophy to the Faculties of Law and of Medicine.

72. The full text reads: "unless he speaks to us through our own understanding and reason." I omitted "understanding" for the sake of simplicity. When Kant uses "understanding" (*Verstehen*) in its formal sense, he carefully distinguishes it from "reason" (*Vernunft*), as we shall see in the *Critique of Pure Reason*.

73. Benjamin Jowett, "On the Interpretation of Scripture" (1860).

74. Kant attached to his essay on *The Conflict* of the philosophy faculty with the theology faculty an Appendix entitled "On a Pure Mysticism in Religion." He explains in a note that the Appendix is a letter that a student enclosed with his dissertation entitled (in Latin) "On the Similarity between Pure Mysticism and the Kantian Doctrine of Religion" (1797) and addressed to Kant, his "venerable father" (a term of address that the student uses in the letter). In his letter the author of the dissertation writes: "Ancient philosophers were quite mistaken in the role they assigned the human being in the world, since they considered him a machine within it, entirely dependent on the world or on external things and circumstances, and so made him an all but passive part of the world — Now the critique of reason has appeared and assigned the human being a thoroughly *active* existence in the world" (288). He mentions later in his letter that, while studying Kant's philosophy, he became acquainted with a group of "separatists," who, while they view themselves as Christians, "take as their code not the Bible, but only the precepts of an inward Christianity dwelling in us from eternity." He adds that he found in "their teachings and principles . . . the essentials of your entire moral and religious doctrine, though with this difference: that they consider the inner law, as they call it, an inward revelation and so regard God as definitely its author." Our letter writer adds further that, while they regard the Bible as divine in origin, "one finds that they infer the divine origin of the Bible from the consistency of the doctrine it contains with their inner law." Thus, they hold: "The Bible is validated in my heart, as you will find it in yours if you obey the precepts of your inner law or the teachings of the Bible." Consequently, they do not view the Bible "as their code of laws but only as a historical confirmation in which they recognize what is originally grounded in themselves. In a word, if these people were philosophers, they would be (pardon the term) true Kantians." Indeed, most of them are "merchants, artisans, and peasants" with few among them "in higher stations" or educated (292).

75. The work as translated in the Cambridge edition of Kant is the revised edition of 1794. Di Giovanni (one of the two translators of the work) notes in the "Translator's Introduction" that, once *Religion* was published in 1793, it "quickly went through a succession of reprints and new editions," notwithstanding "censorship obstacles," with Kant adding in the second edition of his work (1794) "a new preface and many important new notes." The translator also points out that "it was not long before the book began to be publicized in Great Britain as well." Before 1800 both "a brief exposition of its content" and a selection from the work were published, although it was not until 1838 that the "first complete and direct translation of Kant's book" was published (in Scotland). He adds that Kant's language, "because of the diffuseness of its syntax, even by German standards," is a challenge for the translator. Still, he writes: "I suggest that the best way of reading Kant is to 'hear' him speak. The force of his rhetoric is that of the spoken word. Kant is the teacher forever pursuing an elusive thought before his audience of students . . . and not letting up until the full thought . . . has finally been expressed. As in spoken language, so too in Kant's writing—what counts at the end is not syntactical elegance but rhetorical strength" (50–52).

76. Here Kant directly refers to passages in John (3:5) and Genesis (1:2) indicating that the transformation of human beings, whereby they become worthy of heaven and of the creative transformation of the dark, formless earth on the part of God, involves spirit.

77. I have slightly modified Kant's syntax.

78. In a subsequent passage Kant calls "Scripture" the "norm" of "ecclesiastical faith" and the *"religion of reason"* the "expositor" of Scripture (145).

79. Kant also points out that the Parsee "followers of the religion of Zoroaster . . . have until now retained their faith in spite of their dispersion, because their *'dustoors'* [high priests] possessed the Zendavesta [the sacred book of Zoroastrianism which, while having a creator God, maintains a dualistic conception of good and evil]" (163).

80. Kant adds, however, that, while Jews find in their preservation, notwithstanding their dispersion, "the proof of a special beneficent providence which is saving . . . [them] for a future kingdom on earth," Christians see in the preservation of the Jews "nothing but the admonishing ruins of a devastated state which stands in the way of the Kingdom of Heaven to come but which a particular providence still sustains, partly to preserve in memory the old prophecy of a messiah issuing from this people, and partly to make of it an example of punitive justice, because, in its stiffneckedness, that people wanted to make a political and not a moral concept of this messiah" (164).

81. It may be remembered that in Kierkegaard's *Fear and Trembling* Socrates is likened to the tragic heroes of ancient Greek drama in being called there an intellectual tragic hero.

82. Kant observes in a note that a "hereditary kingdom [e.g., Prussia] is not a state which can be inherited by another state, but the right to govern it can be inherited by another" individual. While the "state thereby acquires a ruler," the ruler "does not acquire the state" (86).

83. Kant here cites Virgil's *Aeneid: tu ne cede malis, sed contra audentior ito*.

84. Kant actually writes, in Beck's translation: "Moral evil has the indiscerptible property of being opposed to."

85. *Candide, ou l'Optimisme* (1759).

86. *Essais de Théodicée sur la Bonté de Dieu, la Liberté de l'Homme et l'Origine du Mal* (1710). It was in this work that Leibniz coined the term "theodicy."

87. In Ellington's translation: "I immediately become aware that I can indeed will the lie but cannot at all will a universal law to lie. For by such a law there would be really no promises at all. . . . Therefore, my maxim would necessarily destroy itself just as soon as it was made a universal law" (15).

88. I want to note here two passages in which Kant states that the universal religion of reason is found in all peoples.

(1) In the first passage he states that the three-fold (Trinitarian) nature of God—as (i) *"holy* lawgiver (creator)," (ii) "preserver of the human race" and so its *benevolent* ruler and moral guardian," and (iii) *"just* judge"—accords with the "need of practical reason" in showing that "the universal true religious faith is faith in God. . . . This faith really contains no [hidden] mystery, since it expresses solely God's moral bearing toward the human race. It is also by nature available to all human reason and is therefore to be met with in the religion of most civilized peoples." Kant adds that it "is hard to give a reason why so many ancient peoples hit upon this [Trinitarian] idea, unless it is that the idea lies in human reason universally." He mentions the religions of, in particular, Zoroaster, the Hindus, the Egyptians, the Goths, and "even the Jews" (165–66).

(2) In the second passage on "the pure faith of religion" (which is itself based on the moral law of practical reason) as the "supreme interpreter" of "ecclesiastical faith," Kant writes that it has always been true of "all types of faith," both ancient and new, oral as well as written, "that rational and thoughtful teachers of the people have kept on interpreting them until, gradually, they brought them, as regards their essential content, in agreement with the universal principles of moral faith. The moral philosophers among the Greeks and, later, among the Romans, did exactly the same with their legends concerning the gods. They knew in the end how to interpret even the coarsest polytheism as just a symbolic representation of the properties of the one divine being; and how to invest all sorts of depraved actions, and even the wild yet beautiful fancies of their poets, with a mystical meaning that brought popular faith ... close to a moral doctrine intelligible to all human beings and also beneficial" (142–43).

I cite these two passages as further evidence that Kant does not yet have a fully consistent concept of the relationship between history and ontology. There are two things, in particular, that he does not fully comprehend: first, that religion, as the written Word of the God of the Bible, is, at one and the same time, revealed, rational, and historical; and, second, that philosophy is grounded in the biblical concepts of creation and covenant. While Kant, at times, indulges in making loose analogies between non-biblical religions and the religion of the Bible, still, he does possess, as we have seen, rich and original insight into the Bible as providing us with the true story of the beginning and thus with the universal history of human reason.

Chapter 5

89. Heidegger opens the initial chapter, entitled "The Fundamental Question of Metaphysics," to his *An Introduction to Metaphysics* (1935, revised 1953) as follows: "Why are there essents [existing things] rather than nothing? That is the question" (1). It is evident that this is not Hamlet's question: to be or not to be.

90. Kant adds that whoever "undertakes to judge or, still more, to construct a system of metaphysics must satisfy the demands here made, either by adopting my solution or by thoroughly refuting it and substituting another. To evade it is impossible" (11).

91. The verb Kant uses for "negate" ("overcome") is *aufheben*, made famous by Hegel as the negation whereby we overcome (appropriate) that which we negate.

92. Kant adds later in the preface to the first edition of *Pure Reason*: "Nothing here can escape us, because what reason brings forth entirely out of itself cannot be hidden, but is brought to light by reason itself as soon as reason's common principle has been discovered." We see, then, that "this unconditioned completeness [of reason is] not only feasible but also necessary" (104).

93. I translate Kant's terms *erkennen* as "to know" and *Erkenntnis* as "knowledge" (instead of as "to cognize" and "cognition" as used by the Cambridge editors).

94. What Kant states here about mathematics is misleading since he will, indeed, proceed to demonstrate that mathematical propositions are also synthetic *a priori* and not merely analytic (or *a priori*).

95. Kant observes later that "freedom in the practical furnishes an actual law of

causality, which is not empirical, and therefore is the actually which, concerning its quality, not only proves the actually of something extrasensible but also determines it" (553).

96. Kant adds a page later that the "duty to choose would here tip the indecisiveness of speculation out of balance through a practical addition" (562). He also notes later that "moral theology . . . is a conviction of the existence of a highest being which grounds itself on moral laws" (584).

97. In his critique of the academic philosophers of antiquity (the skeptics who followed in the tradition of Plato's Academy) Montaigne asks: "But how can they let themselves be inclined toward the likeness [the appearance] of truth if they know not the truth? How do they know the semblance of that whose essence they do not know?" He answers: "Either we judge absolutely, or we absolutely cannot" ("Apology for Raymond Sebond," 422).

98. It is important to remember that in the *Ethics* Spinoza summarizes what he calls the dictates of reason (*rationis dictatima*) as not doing unto others what you do not want others to do unto you (Part IV, Proposition 18, *Scholium*).

99. It is striking that in *Les Misérables* (1862) Hugo declares the following: "This book is a drama whose main character is the infinite. Man is the second character" (460).

100. I have slightly reworded the phrase cited in this sentence.

101. The context of Kant's discussion here is "Spinozism," which I do not directly take up.

102. Together with its sister laws of identity and the excluded middle.

103. Kant actually writes: "it was because they made the rule of the use which the human will makes of its freedom the sole and sufficient ground of this possibility" that they did without the existence of God (241). His language here is misleading. The concepts of the human will and of freedom were unknown to the ancient Greek philosophers, as Kant himself shows (although only indirectly).

104. I have reworded Kant's convoluted sentence in order to render it properly lucid.

105. I think it is useful to provide here the titles of these four sections:
    VI. "On the Postulates of Pure Practical Reason in General"
    VII. "How is it Possible to Think of an Extension of Pure Reason for Practical Purposes without thereby also Extending its Knowledge as Speculative?"
    VIII. "On Assent From a Need of Pure Reason" (i.e., On the Need on the part of Pure Reason to Assent to the Existence of the Soul and of God)
    IX. "On the Wise Adaptation of the Human Being's Cognitive Faculties to his Practical Vocation"

106. Earlier in this same paragraph Kant calls again upon his common nostrum: "I must suppose" the possibility and hence also "the conditions for this, namely, God, freedom, and immortality, because I cannot" either prove or refute them "by my speculative reason" (254).

107. I do not discuss here Part II of *The Critique of Practical Reason*, entitled "Doctrine of the Method [*Methodenlehre*] of Pure Practical Reason," just as, when analyzing *The Critique of Pure Reason*, I omitted consideration of Part II of the work, entitled "Transcendental Doctrine of Method." While Kant in the "methodology" sections of each of his two major works continues to amplify our insight into how synthetic *a priori* judgments are possible, he adds nothing critically new to his concept of reason as first and last practical.

Chapter 6

108. We have the curious phrase "to wax poetic" (which I myself have used in this study!) and the intriguing idea of "poetic justice" (somebody deserved what he got).

109. Still, I observe, with no little anxiety, that, as I indicated at the beginning of my study, I felt it incumbent on me to center my discussion on poetry that was written in English and not in a language other than English because of the importance of attending carefully to poetic diction, including meter (and rhyme, when present). Is this an instance of poetic justice? On the other hand, I acknowledge that I make use of English translations of the Hebrew and Christian Bibles (for, while I do possess basic knowledge of Greek, I do not know Hebrew).

Bibliography

Abrams, M. H. *Natural Supernaturalism: Tradition and Revolution in Romantic Literature*. New York: Norton, 1971.
Agamben, Giorgio. *Saint Paul: The Foundation of Universalism*. Translated by Ray Brassier. Stanford: Stanford University Press, 2003.
———. *The Time that Remains: A Commentary on the Letter to the Romans*. Translated by Patricia Daley. Stanford: Stanford University Press, 2005.
Alter, Robert, trans. *The Five Books of Moses*. New York: Norton, 2004.
Aristotle. *The Complete Works*. Edited by Jonathan Barnes. 2 vols. Princeton: Princeton University Press, 1984.
Auerbach, Erich. *Mimesis: The Representation of Reality in Western Literature*. Translated by Willard R. Trask. Princeton: Princeton University Press, 1968.
Augustine, Saint. *The City of God*. Translated by Marcus Dods. New York: The Modern Library, 1950.
Badiou, Alain. *The True Life*. Translated by Susan Spitzer. Cambridge: Polity, 2017.
Balfour, Ian. *The Rhetoric of Romantic Prophecy*. Stanford: Stanford University Press, 2002.
Barfield, Owen. *Poetic Diction: A Study in Meaning*. 3rd ed. Middletown: Wesleyan University Press, 1973.
———. *Saving the Appearances: A Study in Idolatry*. New York: Harcourt, Brace & World, n.d.
———. *What Coleridge Thought*. Middletown: Wesleyan University Press, 1971.
Barth, J. Robert. *Romanticism and Transcendence: Wordsworth, Coleridge, and the Religious Imagination*. Columbia: University of Missouri Press, 2003.
Bate, Jonathan. *Radical Wordsworth: The Poet Who Changed the World*. New Haven: Yale University Press, 2020.
Batnitzky, Leora. *How Judaism Became a Religion: An Introduction to Modern Thought*. Princeton: Princeton University Press, 2011.
Berkeley, Richard. *Coleridge and the Crisis of Reason*. Houndmills: Palgrave Macmillan, 2007.
Biale, David. *Not in the Heavens: The Tradition of Jewish Secular Thought*. Princeton: Princeton University Press, 2011.
Bloch, Ernst. *The Principle of Hope*. Translated by Neville Plaice et al. Oxford: Blackwell, 1986.
Bowie, Andrew. *Aesthetics and Subjectivity: From Kant to Nietzsche*. 2nd ed. Manchester: Manchester University Press, 2003.

———. *Introduction to German Philosophy: From Kant to Habermas*. Cambridge: Polity, 2003.
Bowker, John. *The Religious Imagination and the Sense of God*. Oxford: Oxford University Press, 1978.
Breton, Stanislas. *A Radical Philosophy of Saint Paul*. Translated by Joseph N. Ballan. New York: Columbia University Press, 2011.
Buber, Martin. *I and Thou*. Translated by Walter Kaufmann. New York: Scribner's, 1970.
———. *On the Bible*. Edited by Nathan N. Glatzer. New York: Schocken, 1968.
Cahill, Thomas. *The Gifts of the Jews*. New York: Anchor, 1998.
Cahn, Steven M. *God, Reason, and Religion*. Belmont: Wadsworth, 2006.
Caputo, John D., and Gianni Vattimo. *After the Death of God*. Edited by Jeffrey W. Robbins with an Afterword by Gabriel Vahanian. New York: Columbia University Press, 2009.
Caputo, John D., and Michael J. Scanlon, eds. *God, The Gift, and Postmodernism*. Bloomington: Indiana University Press, 1999.
———. *The Prayers and Tears of Jacques Derrida*. Indianapolis: Indiana University Press, 1997.
Carr, E. H. *What is History?* Harmondsworth: Penguin, 1974.
Class, Monika. *Coleridge and Kantian Ideas in England, 1796–1817: Coleridge's Responses to German Philosophy*. London: Bloomsbury, 2012.
Coleridge, Samuel Taylor. *Biographia Literaria or Biographical Sketches of My Literary Life and Opinions*. 2 vols. Edited by James Engell and W. Jackson Bate. Bollingen Series LXXV. Vol. 7 of *The Collected Works of Samuel Taylor Coleridge*. Princeton: Princeton University Press, 1983; paperback ed., 1 vol., 1984.
———. *The Complete Poems*. Edited by William Keach. London: Penguin, 2004.
Collingwood, R. G. *The Principles of Art*. Oxford: Oxford University Press, 1938.
Croce, Benedetto. *History as the Story of Liberty*. Translated by Sylvia Sprigge. New York: Norton, 1941.
Davidson, Donald. *Subjective, Intersubjective, Objective*. Oxford: Oxford University Press, 2001.
Delpech-Ramsey, Joshua. "An Interview with Slavoj Zizek 'On Divine Self-Limitation and Revolutionary Love.'" *Journal of Philosophy and Scripture* 1 (2004) 32–38.
Derrida, Jacques. *Acts of Religion*. Edited by Gil Anidjar. New York: Routledge, 2002.
———. *Deconstruction and the Possibility of Justice*. Edited by Drucilla Cornell et al. New York: Routledge, 1992.
———. *Gift of Death*. Translated by David Wells. Chicago: University of Chicago Press, 1992.
———. *Of Grammatology*. Corrected ed. Translated by Gayatri Chakravorty Spivak. Baltimore: Johns Hopkins University Press, 1998.
———. *Writing and Difference*. Translated by Alan Bass. London: Routledge, 2001.
Derrida, Jacques, and Gianni Vattimo, eds. *Religion*. Stanford: Stanford University Press, 1998.
Descartes, René. *The Philosophical Writings*. 2 vols. Translated by John Cottingham et al. Cambridge: Cambridge University Press, 1998.
Devisch, Ignaas. *Jean-Luc Nancy and the Question of Community*. London: Bloomsbury, 2013.
Drury, John, ed. *Critics of the Bible: 1724–1873*. Cambridge: Cambridge University Press, 1989.

Eliade, Mircea. *The Sacred and the Profane: The Nature of Religion*. Translated by Willard R. Trask. New York: Harvest, 1959.
Engell, James. *The Creative Imagination: Enlightenment to Romanticism*. Cambridge: Harvard University Press, 1981.
Estlund, David M. *Democratic Authority: A Philosophical Framework*. Princeton: Princeton University Press, 2008.
Fackenheim Emil. *Encounters Between Judaism and Modern Philosophy*. New York: Schocken, 1980.
Ferry, Luc. *Man Made God: The Meaning of Life*. Translated by David Pellauer. Chicago: University of Chicago Press, 2002.
———. *On Love: A Philosophy for the Twenty-First Century*. Translated by Andrew Brown. Cambridge: Polity, 2013.
Flew, Anthony. *God and Philosophy*. Amherst: Prometheus, 2005.
Foss, Martin. *The Idea of Perfection in the Western World*. Lincoln: University of Nebraska Press, 1946.
———. *Symbol and Metaphor in Human Experience*. Lincoln: University of Nebraska Press, 1949.
Fredriksen, Paula. *Sin: The Early History of an Idea*. Princeton: Princeton University Press, 2012.
Gauchet, Marcel. *The Disenchantment of the World: A Political History of Religion*. Translated by Oscar Burge. Princeton: Princeton University Press, 1997.
Gill, Stephen. *William Wordsworth: A Life*. Oxford: Oxford University Press, 1989.
———. *William Wordsworth: The Prelude*. Cambridge: Cambridge University Press, 1991.
Girard, René. *Job: The Victim of His People*. Translated by Yvonne Freccero. Stanford: Stanford University Press, 1987.
———. *Things Hidden Since the Foundation of the World*. Stanford: Stanford University Press, 1987.
Glouberman, Mark. *The Raven, the Dove, and the Owl of Minerva: The Creation of Humankind in Athens and Jerusalem*. Toronto: University of Toronto Press, 2012.
Gray, John. "Faith in Reason; Secular Fantasies of a Godless Age." *Harper's Magazine*, January 2008.
Green, Ronald M. *Kierkegaard and Kant: The Hidden Debt*. Albany: State University of New York Press, 1992.
Guyer, Paul. *Knowledge, Reason, and Taste: Kant's Response to Hume*. Princeton: Princeton University Press, 2008.
Habermas, Jürgen. *The Philosophical Discourse of Modernity*. Translated by Frederick Lawrence. Cambridge: MIT Press, 1990.
———. *The Theory of Communicative Action*. Translated by Thomas McCarthy. Boston: Beacon, 1984.
Harrison, Peter. *The Territories of Science and Religion*. Chicago: University of Chicago Press, 2015.
Hartman, Geoffrey H. *The Unremarkable Wordsworth*. Minneapolis: University of Minnesota Press, 1987.
———. *Wordsworth's Poetry 1787–1814*. New Haven: Yale University Press, 1964.
Hazony, Yoram. *The Philosophy of Hebrew Scripture*. Cambridge: Cambridge University Press, 2012.

Hegel, G. W. F. *Aesthetics: Lectures on Fine Art*. 2 vols. Translated by T. M. Knox. Oxford: Oxford University Press, 1975.

———. *The Encyclopaedia Logic, with the Zusätze*. Translated by T. F. Geraets et al. Indianapolis: Hackett, 1991.

———. *Lectures on the Philosophy of Religion*. 3 vols. Edited by Peter C. Hodgson. Berkeley: University of California Press, 1984.

———. *Phenomenology of Spirit*. Translated by A. V. Miller. Oxford: Oxford University Press, 1977.

———. *The Philosophy of History*. Translated by J. Sibree. New York: Dover, 1956.

———. *Philosophy of Mind*. Part III of *The Encyclopaedia of the Philosophical Sciences*. Translated by William Wallace. Oxford: Oxford University Press, 1971.

Heidegger, Martin. *An Introduction to Metaphysics*. Translated by Gregory Fried and Richard Polt. New Haven: Yale University Press, 2000.

———. *Kant and the Problem of Metaphysics*. Translated by James S. Churchill. Bloomington: Indiana University Press, 1972.

———. *What Is Called Thinking?* Translated by Fred D. Wieck and J. Glenn Gray. New York: Harper & Row, 1968.

———. *What Is Philosophy?* Translated by Jean T. Wilde and William Kluback. New Haven: College and University Press, 1955.

Heschel, Abraham Joshua. *God in Search of Man: A Philosophy of Judaism*. New York: Ferrar, Straus, and Giroux, 1983.

Hoult, Jason. "The Art of Ethics and the Ethics of Art: Between Kant and Wallace Stevens." PhD diss., York University, 2018.

Hugo, Victor. *Les Misérables*. Translated by Christine Donougher. New York: Penguin, 2013.

Israel, Jonathan I. *Radical Enlightenment: Philosophy and the Making of Modernity 1650–1750*. Oxford: Oxford University Press, 2001.

Jaspers, Karl, and Rudolf Bultmann. *Myth and Christianity: An Inquiry into the Possibility of Religion without Myth*. New York: Noonday, 1968.

Jung, C. G. *Modern Man in Search of a Soul*. Translated by W. S. Dell and Cary F. Baynes. San Diego: Harvest/HBJ, 1933.

Kahn, Paul W. *Out of Eden: Adam and Eve and the Problem of Evil*. Princeton: Princeton University Press, 2007.

Kant, Immanuel. *The Conflict of the Faculties*. In *Religion and Rational Theology*. Edited and translated by Allen W. Wood and George di Giovanni. Cambridge: Cambridge University Press, 1996.

———. "Conjectural Beginning of Human History." In *On History*, edited by L. W. Beck. Indianapolis: Library of Liberal Arts, 1963.

———. *Critique of the Power of Judgment*. Edited by Paul Guyer. Cambridge: Cambridge University Press, 2000.

———. *Critique of Pure Reason*. Edited and translated by Paul Guyer and Allen W. Wood. Cambridge: Cambridge University Press, 1998.

———. *Grounding for the Metaphysics of Morals*. 3rd ed. Translated by James W. Ellington. Indianapolis: Hackett, 1993.

———. *Grundlegung zur Metaphysik der Sitten*. Edited by Karl Vorländer. Hamburg: Meiner, 1965.

———. *Kritik der Praktischen Vernunft*. Edited by Karl Vorländer. Hamburg: Meiner, 1967.

———. *Kritik der Reinen Vernunft*. Edited by Raymund Schmidt. Hamburg: Meiner, 1956.
———. *Kritik der Urteilskraft*. Edited by Karl Vorländer. Hamburg: Meiner, 1968.
———. *Practical Philosophy* [includes *Groundwork of the Metaphysics of Morals* & *The Critique of Practical Reason*]. Edited and translated by Mary J. Gregor. Cambridge: Cambridge University Press, 1996.
———. *Die Religion innerhalb der Grenzen der blossen Vernunft*. Edited by Karl Vorländer. Hamburg: Meiner, 1966.
———. *Der Streit der Facultäten Anthropologie in Pragmatischer Hinsicht*. Vol. 7 of *Kant's Werke*. London: Forgotten, 2017.
Keats, John. "'Ode on a Grecian Urn' and other poems." In *Anthology of Romanticism*, edited by Ernest Bernbaum. New York: Ronald, 1948.
Kierkegaard, Søren. *Concluding Unscientific Postscript to Philosophical Fragments*. 2 vols. Translated by Howard V. Hong and Edna H. Hong. Princeton: Princeton University Press, 1992.
———. *Either/Or*. Parts I and II. Translated by Howard V. Hong and Edna H. Hong. Princeton: Princeton University Press, 1987.
———. *Fear and Trembling*. Translated by Howard V Hong and Edna H. Hong. Princeton: Princeton University Press, 1983.
———. *Philosophical Fragments*. Translated by Howard V. Hong and Edna H. Hong. Princeton: Princeton University Press, 1985.
———. *Practice in Christianity*. Translated by Howard V. Hong and Edna H. Hong. Princeton: Princeton University Press, 1991.
———. *The Purity of Heart Is To Will One Thing*. Translated by Douglas V. Steere. New York: Harper & Row, 1956.
———. *The Sickness unto Death*. Translated by Howard V. Hong and Edna H. Hong. Princeton: Princeton University Press, 1980.
———. *Works of Love*. Translated by Howard V. Hong and Edna H. Hong. Princeton: Princeton University Press, 1995.
Kind, Amy, ed. *The Routledge Handbook of Philosophy of Imagination*. London: Routledge, 2016.
Kirby, Torrance, et al., eds. *Philosophy and the Abrahamic Religions: Scriptural Hermeneutics and Epistemology*. Newcastle upon Tyne: Cambridge Scholars, 2013.
Kolakowski, Leszek. *Modernity on Endless Trial*. Chicago: University of Chicago Press, 1990.
———. *My Correct Views on Everything*. Edited by Zbigniew Janowski. South Bend: St. Augustine's, 2005.
———. *The Two Eyes of Spinoza and Other Essays on Philosophers*. Edited by Zbigniew Janowski. South Bend: St. Augustine's, 2004.
———. *Why Is There Something Rather Than Nothing? 23 Questions from Great Philosophers*. Translated by Agnieszka Kołakowska. London: Lane, 2007.
Leeuwen, Arend Theodoor van. *Christianity in World History: The Meeting of the Faiths of East and West*. Translated by H. H. Hoskins. London: Edinburgh House Press, 1966.
Levinas, Emmanuel. *Outside the Subject*. Translated by Michael B. Smith. London: Continuum, 2008.
Lilla, Mark. *The Stillborn God: Religion, Politics, and the Modern West*. New York: Knopf, 2007.

Machiavelli, Niccolò. *Opere*. Edited by Mario Bonfantini. Milano: Ricciardi, 1954.
Macmurray, John. *The Self as Agent*. London: Faber and Faber, 1969.
———. *Persons in Relation*. New York: Random House, 1998.
Mason, Emma. *The Cambridge Introduction to Wordsworth*. Cambridge: Cambridge University Press, 2010.
Milton, John. *Paradise Lost*. Edited by Alastair Fowler. London: Longman, 1971.
Montaigne, Michel de. *The Complete Essays*. Translated by Donald M. Frame. Stanford: Stanford University Press, 1965.
Nancy, Jean-Luc. *Being Singular Plural*. Translated by Robert D. Richardson and Anne E. O'Byrne. Stanford: Stanford University Press, 2000.
———. *Dis-Enclosure: The Deconstruction of Christianity*. Translated by Bettina Bergo et al. New York: Fordham University Press, 2008.
Neiman, Susan. *Moral Clarity: A Guide for Grown-Up Idealists*. Revised ed. Princeton: Princeton University Press, 2009.
Nietzsche, Friedrich. *The Gay Science*. Translated by Walter Kaufmann. New York: Vintage, 1974.
———. *On the Genealogy of Morals* and *Ecce Homo*. Translated by Walter Kaufmann. New York: Vintage, 1969.
O'Neill, Michael, ed. *The Cambridge History of English Poetry*. Cambridge: Cambridge University Press, 2010.
Pascal, Blaise. *Pensées sur la Religion et sur Quelques Autres Sujets*. 3rd ed. Edited by Louis Lafuma. Paris: Delmas, 1960.
———. *Selections from the Thoughts*. Edited and translated by Arthur H. Beattie. New York: Appleton-Century-Crofts, 1965.
Plato. *Republic*. Translated by G. M. A. Grube, revised by C. D. C. Reeve. Indianapolis: Hackett, 1992.
———. *Five Dialogues* [*Euthyphro, Apology, Crito, Meno, Phaedo*]. Translated by G. M. A. Grube. Indianapolis: Hackett, 1985.
———. *Symposium*. Translated by Benjamin Jowett. New York: Library of Liberal Arts, 1956.
———. *Gorgias*. Translated by Donald J. Zehl. Indianapolis: Hackett, 1987.
Polka, Brayton. "Covenantal Sinning as the Truth of History and Morality." *The European Legacy* 19.6 (2014) 774–81.
———. "Democracy as the Liberating Story of Historical Critique." *The European Legacy*, forthcoming.
———. *The Dialectic of Biblical Critique: Interpretation and Existence*. London: Macmillan, 1986.
———. "Enlightenment Heroes and the Ideal of Moral Clarity." *The European Legacy* 16.1 (2011) 91–96.
———. "The Fall of Adam and Eve: Cultural Transformative Story as the Critique of Culture." *The European Legacy* 17.7 (2012) 934–39.
———. "Freud, the Bible, and Hermeneutics." *The European Legacy* 6.3 (2001) 319–32.
———. "Hebrew Scripture and the Wisdom of Philosophical Reason, or What has Athens to do with Jerusalem?" *The European Legacy* 20.3–4 (2015) 273–83.
———. "Hobbes and the Sovereignty of the Golden Rule." *The European Legacy* 18.4 (2013) 628–34.

———. "Interpretation and the Bible: The Dialectic of Concept and Content in Interpretative Practice." In *Hermeneutics, the Bible and Literary Criticism*, edited by A. Loades and M. McLain, 27–45. London: Macmillan, 1992.

———. "Is Covenantal Theology a Hermeneutics of Allegory? A Radical Reading of Saint Paul." *The European Legacy* 18.4 (2013) 483–86.

———. "Kierkegaard and Theology." *The European Legacy* 18.3 (2013) 358–66.

———. "Levinas between the Bible and Philosophy." *The European Legacy* 15.5 (2010) 637–42.

———. "The Metaphysics of Thinking Necessary Existence: Kant and the Ontological Argument." *The European Legacy* 17.5 (2012) 583–91.

———. "Of Scripture, Paradox, and Interpretation." In *Literary Criticism and Biblical Hermeneutics*, edited by T. Fabiny, 127–40. Szeged: Attila Jozsef University, 1992.

———. "On Reading Spinoza: Has Philosophy Replaced the Bible?" *The European Legacy* 18.6 (2013).

———. "On Sin as Human History Comprehended." *The European Legacy* 20.2 (2015).

———. "On Thinking *The Modern Revolution* in Light of the Bible." *The European Legacy* 15.2 (2010) 221–32.

———. "On Thinking the Secular and the Religious." In *The Holy and the Worldly (Studies in Cultural Meaning)*, edited by D. Paycha and B. Zelechow. Cergy-Pontoise: Les cahiers du CICC, 2001.

———. "The Ontological Argument for Existence." In *Difference in Philosophy of Religion*, edited by Philip Goodchild, 15–32. London: Ashgate, 2001.

———. "Philosophy without God? God without Philosophy? Critical Reflections on Flew's *God & Philosophy*." *The European Legacy* 11.1 (2006) 35–46.

———. "Reason within the Limits of Purely Subjective Faith." *The European Legacy*, forthcoming.

———. "The Self in Shakespeare and Modernity." *The European Legacy* 18.5 (2013) 917–28.

———. "Self-Referentiality and Philosophy." *The European Legacy* 19.7 (2014) 906–9.

———. *Shakespeare and Interpretation, or What You Will*. Newark: University of Delaware Press, 2011.

———. "The Single Individual in Kierkegaard: Religious or Secular?" Part 1, *The European Legacy* 19.2 (2014) 309–22; Part 2, *The European Legacy* 19.3 (2014) 442–55.

———. "Spinoza and Biblical Interpretation: The Paradox of Modernity." *The European Legacy* 1.5 (1996) 1673–82.

———. "Spinoza and the Separation Between Philosophy and Theology." *Journal of Religious Studies* 16.1–2 (1990) 91–119.

———. *Spinoza, the Bible, and Modernity*—Vol. I: *Hermeneutics and Ontology*; Vol. II: *Politics and Ethics*. Lanham: Lexington, 2007. Paperback, 2009.

———. "Spinoza's Concept of Biblical Interpretation." *The Journal of Jewish Thought and Philosophy* 2 (1992) 19–44.

———. "Spinoza vs. Maimonides: On the Relation of the Secular and the Religious." *The European Legacy* 17.4 (2012) 529–36.

———. "Theology and the Deconstruction of Derrida." *The European Legacy* 18.2 (2013) 209–215.

———. "Thinking—Between Kant and Kierkegaard—Modernity and the Bible." In *Studies in Cultural Meaning*, vol. I, edited by D. Paycha and B. Zelechow. Cergy-Pontoise: Les Cahiers du CICC, 1999.

———. *Truth and Interpretation: An Essay in Thinking*. New York: St. Martin's, 1990.

———. "Truth and Metaphor: Interpretation as Philosophical and Literary Practice." *Diogenes* 143 (1988) 111–28.

———. "What Does the Bible Have To Do with Philosophy?" *The European Legacy*, forthcoming.

———. "What Ought We To Do? Democracy as the Liberating Story of Historical Critique." *The European Legacy* 16.5 (2011) 649–52.

———. "What Is Democracy? Reflections on Sen's Idea of Justice." *The European Legacy* 15.6 (2010) 769–77.

———. "Who is the Single Individual? On the Religious and the Secular in Kierkegaard." *Philosophy and Theology* 17.1–2 (2005) 157–75.

Prickett, Stephen. *Words and The Word: Language, Poetics, and Biblical Interpretation*. Cambridge: Cambridge University Press, 1986.

———. *Wordsworth and Coleridge: The Lyrical Ballads*. London: Arnold, 1975.

Rawls, John. *Lectures on the History of Moral Philosophy*. Cambridge: Harvard University Press, 2000.

Ricoeur, Paul. *The Conflict of Interpretations: Essays in Hermeneutics*. Edited by Don Ihde. Evanston: Northwestern University Press, 1974.

Roberts, Jonathan. *Blake. Wordsworth. Religion*. Coventry: University of Warwick Press, 2010.

Rorty, Richard, and Gianni Vattimo. *The Future of Religion*. Edited by Santiago Zabala. New York: Columbia University Press, 2005.

Rougement, Denis de. *Love in the Western World*. Revised and augmented ed. Translated by Montgomery Belgion. New York: Pantheon, 1956.

Rousseau, Jean-Jacques. *Du Contrat Social* [including both *Discourses*]. Paris: Garnier Frères, 1962.

———. *The Social Contract* (together with the *Discourse on the Origin of Inequality*). Edited by Lester G. Crocker. New York: Washington Square, 1967.

Segal, Alan F. *Sinning in the Hebrew Bible: How the Worst Stories Speak for its Truth*. New York: Columbia University Press, 2012.

Sen, Amartya. *The Idea of Justice*. Cambridge: Harvard University Press, 2009.

Shakespeare, Steven. *Derrida and Theology*. London: T&T Clark, 2009.

Shelley, Percy Bysshe. *A Defense of Poetry*. In *Anthology of Romanticism*, edited by Ernest Bernbaum. New York: Ronald, 1948.

Spinoza, Benedict de. *Ethics*. In *The Collected Works of Spinoza*, edited and translated by Edwin Curley, vol. 1. Princeton: Princeton University Press, 1985.

———. *The Letters*. Translated by Samuel Shirley. Indianapolis: Hackett, 1995.

———. *Opera*. 4 vols. Edited by Carl Gebhardt. Heidelberg: Carl Winters Universitaetsbuchhandlung, 1925.

———. *The Political Works* [*Tractatus Theologico-Politicus*, in part; *Tractatus Politicus*]. Edited and translated by A. G. Wernham. Oxford: Oxford University Press, 1958.

———. *Theological-Political Treatise*. Translated by Samuel Shirley. Indianapolis: Hackett, 1998. [Note that the second edition of 2001 is not a revised translation. Nor are all the errors found in the first edition corrected.]

Steinberg, Leo. *The Sexuality of Christ in Renaissance Art and in Modern Oblivion*. 2nd revised ed. Chicago: University of Chicago Press, 1996.
Stendahl, Krister, ed. *Immortality and Resurrection: Death in the Western World: Two Conflicting Currents of Thought*. New York: Macmillan, 1968.
Strauss, Leo. *Jewish Philosophy and the Crisis of Modernity: Essays in Modern Jewish Thought*. Edited by Kenneth Hart Green. Albany: State University of New York Press, 1997.
Taylor, Charles. *A Secular Age*. Cambridge: Harvard University Press, 2007.
———. *Sources of the Self: The Making of Modern Identity*. Cambridge: Harvard University Press, 1989.
Thomas-Fogiel, Isabelle. *The Death of Philosophy: Reference and Self-Reference in Contemporary Thought*. Translated by Richard A. Lynch. New York: Columbia University Press, 2011.
Tillich, Paul. *Biblical Religion and the Search for Ultimate Reality*. Chicago: University of Chicago Press, 1968.
Todorov, Tzvetan. *Imperfect Garden: The Legacy of Humanism*. Translated by Carol Cosman. Princeton: Princeton University Press, 2002.
Ulmer, William A. *The Christian Wordsworth 1798–1805*. Albany: State University of New York Press, 2001.
Vattimo, Gianni. *After Christianity*. Translated by Luca D'Isanto. New York: Columbia University Press, 2002.
———. *Art's Claim to Truth*. Edited by Santiago Zabala. Translated by Luca D'Isanto. New York: Columbia University Press, 2008.
Vico, Giambattista. *The New Science*. Revised translation of the third edition (1744). Translated by T. G. Bergin and M. H. Fisch. Ithaca: Cornell University Press, 1968.
Vries, Hent de. *Philosophy and the Turn to Religion*. Baltimore: Johns Hopkins University Press, 1999.
———. *Religion within the Limits of Reason Alone and Violence: Philosophical Perspectives from Kant to Derrida*. Baltimore: Johns Hopkins University Press, 2002.
Walsh, David. *The Modern Philosophical Revolution: The Luminosity of Existence*. New York: Cambridge University Press, 2008.
Williams, Bernard. *In the Beginning Was the Deed: Realism and Moralism in Political Argument*. Princeton: Princeton University Press, 2005.
Wordsworth, William. *The Excursion*. Middletown: Portable Poetry, 2017.
———. *The Major Works* [including the 13-book *Prelude*]. Edited by Stephen Gill. Oxford: Oxford University Press, 2008.
———. *The Prelude* [in 14 books] *with a Selection from the Shorter Poems, the Sonnets, The Recluse, and The Excursion and Three Essays on The Art of Poetry*. Edited by Carlos Baker. New York: Holt, Rinehart and Winston, 1954.
Worthen, John. *The Cambridge Introduction to Samuel Taylor Coleridge*. Cambridge: Cambridge University Press, 2010.
Zabala, Santiago. *The Remains of Being: Hermeneutic Ontology after Metaphysics*. New York: Columbia University Press, 2009.
Zimmermann, Jens. *Humanism and Religion: A Call for the Renewal of Western Culture*. Oxford: Oxford University Press, 2012.
Žižek, Slavoj. *On Belief*. London: Routledge, 2001.

Žižek, Slavoj, and John Millbank. *The Monstrosity of Christ: Paradox or Dialectic?* Cambridge: MIT Press, 2009.

Žižek, Slavoj, et al., eds. *Hegel and the Infinite: Religion, Politics, and Dialectic.* New York: Columbia University Press, 2011.

About the Author

Brayton Polka is Professor of Humanities Emeritus and Senior Scholar at York University (in Toronto, Canada). He is the author of numerous books and articles in philosophy, religion, literature, music, psychology and thus, more generally, the history of ideas, including his latest book, *Paradox and Contradiction in the Biblical Traditions: The Two Ways of the World*. His principal interest is hermeneutical. He argues that the principle of interpretation that we bring to the oeuvres we engage is precisely the principle by and through which they interpret us who engage them. As you measure, so are you measured. As you judge, so are you judged. The interpretative imperative—read others as you want others to read you—is a reworking of the golden rule of the Bible: do unto others as you want others to do unto others. Because this imperative is at once divine and human, Professor Polka makes the exploration of the relationship of the religious and the secular in the western intellectual tradition central to his work.

Index

Adam and Eve: *felix culpa* paradox, 40; Kant on, 124; in *The Prelude,* 97, 114; in *Religion within the Bounds of Mere Reason,* 146; Wordsworth on, 40
Aeschylus, 71
ages of ages. See *saecula saeculorum*
allegory, in religion, 71
analytic reason. *See* deductive reason
analytical knowledge, in *Critique of Pure Reason,* 184
ancient Greece: metaphor in, 3–4; metaphysics in, 13; modern poetry influenced by, 69
Anselm (Saint), 7, 114, 158, 209, 211
anti-Judaism: Christianity and, 12; of Kant, 12, 126, 155–56, 269n80
antimony, 197; law and, 199
"Antimony of Pure Reason, The" (Kant), 199–204
Aristotle, 3, 126, 131; Coleridge influenced by, 63; on general logic of contradiction, 231–32; on God, 81, 97, 123; golden mean, 60–61; metaphysics and, 189; on moral concepts, origins of, 235; on poetry, 60; *polis,* 120–21; on slaves, 120; on timocracy, 266n64
atheism, 183

Augustine (Saint), 267n69
autonomy. *See* moral autonomy

Bacon, Francis, 181–82
baptism, symbolism of, 143
Baumgarten, A. G., 257n4
being and knowledge, principle of, 56
Bible, The: in *The Conflict of the Faculties,* as vehicle of religion, 135–36, 138; Latin Vulgate and, 3; metaphor in, 2; moral truth of, 246–47; as poetic, 6; "religion of reason" in, 126; as theodicy, 166. *See also* Holy Scripture; New Testament; Old Testament
Biographia Literaria (Coleridge), 11, 258n13, 261n31–34, 262n46; Christianity in, 65–67; critique of poetry in, 20, 28–29; diversity of content in, 50; imagination in, 36; "Immortality Ode" and, 18; philosophical principles in, 50; poetry compared to prose in, 62; structure of, 50
body, mind and, distinction between, 131–32
Buber, Martin, 113

Candide (Voltaire), 163
causality, as freedom, 225
censorship, 257n6

285

Charles I (King), 45
Charles II (King), 45
childhood: in "Immortality Ode," 23; in *The Prelude*, 89
Christianity/Christendom: anti-Judaism embedded in, 12; baptism in, symbolism of, 143; in *Biographia Literaria*, 65–67; *Ethics* and, 66–67; holy mysteries of, 158; Kierkegaard on, 68; moral law and, 123; Neoplatonic dualism and, 73; paganism and, 68, 131; philosophy and, incompatibility with, 65–66; in *Religion within the Bounds of Mere Reason*, 146, 153; as religious reform, 146. *See also* The Bible; Holy Scripture
civil state, 161
Clarissa Harlowe (Richardson), 260n24
Coleridge, Samuel Taylor, 5; Aristotle as influence on, 63; Christian faith of, 67; on fancy, 57; friendship with Wordsworth, 101–2; on imagination, 57, 262n39; on Kant, 11, 53; "Know Thyself," 68–69; *logosophia* for, 53–56; *Lyrical Ballads*, 8, 27–31; Plato as influence on, 63; poems defined by, 58–59; on poetic imagination, 64–65; in *The Prelude*, 91; principle of being and knowledge, 56; principle of self-consciousness, 56; on principles of criticism, 62; as "Prophet of Nature," 9, 111; "The Rime of the Ancient Mariner," 262n39; on rustic life, 59–60; on self-knowledge, 52–53; Shakespeare as influence on, 61; slander of, 66; "To William Wordsworth," 18–19, 26–27, 47–52, 102, 112; on Wordsworth, 47–69. *See also Biographia Literaria*; *Lyrical Ballads*
concepts of understanding, in *Critique of Pure Reason*, 191–92
Conflict of the Faculties, The (Kant), 14, 118, 268n74; The Bible in, as vehicle of religion, 135–36, 138; "The Conflict of the Philosophy Faculty with the Theology Faculty," 133–34; moral law in, 136; reason in, 135, 137; religion in, 133–40; supersensible human being in, ascendancy of, 138–39
"Conflict of the Philosophy Faculty with the Theology Faculty, The" (Kant), 133–34
"Conjectural Beginning of Human History" (Kant), 118, 124, 126, 128–33, 223, 251; original sin in, 130–32, 143
consciousness of the Self, 192
Copernicus, Nicolaus, 181–82, 241
1 Corinthians, 8:1, 9
cosmology, 185; in *Critique of Pure Reason*, 203; in metaphysics, 195
covenant, creation and, 171, 247
covenantal law, 171–73
creation: covenant and, 171, 247; in *The Prelude*, 107; revelation and, 171; theodicy and, 170–71
critical philosophy, Kant as father of, 50
criticism, principles of, Coleridge on, 62
Critique of Practical Reason (Kant), 10–11, 15, 51, 174, 209–40, 250–51, 272n107; as account of moral life, 82; desire in, 213; dialectical illusion in, 230–31, 240; dogmatism in, 229; duty in, 218–19; eudaimonism in, 220; evil in, 215; existence concepts

in, 238–39; freedom in, 69, 213, 225, 228–29; God in, 69, 228, 233–34, 238; good in, 215, 231; holiness as concept in, 213–14; immortality in, 69; law in, 213; metaphysics in, 210–12, 237; moral autonomy in, 214; moral heteronomy in, 214; moral law in, 212, 215–19, 222–25, 229, 235–37, 239–40; moral necessity in, 225, 234; morality in, 213, 221, 229, 235; natural law in, 240–41; natural necessity in, 225–27; natural objects in, 11; *noumena* in, 228; noumenal world in, 223–37; ontological arguments in, 243–44; personality in, 219–20; present in, as concept, 226; principle of the highest good, 220, 232–33; Principles of Pure Practical Reason, 213; rational objects in, 11; religion in, 236; the self in, 212; skepticism in, 220, 229

Critique of Pure Reason (Kant), 8, 10–11, 15, 51, 119–20, 126, 174, 180–209, 272n107; analytical knowledge in, 184; concepts of understanding in, 191–92; cosmological arguments in, 203; empirical deduction in, 190; empirical knowledge in, 184; metaphysics in, 180; moral practice, 184–85; natural objects in, 11; ontological arguments in, 203; principle of pure reason in, 182; rational objects in, 11; reason as practice in, 200; religion in, 133; speculative reason in, critique of, 183; synthetic judgments, 184–85; teleological arguments in, 203; Transcendental Aesthetic, 179, 184, 185–86, 189; Transcendental Analytic, 179, 185; Transcendental Dialectic, 127, 179, 185–86, 192–205, 228–29, 238; unity of consciousness in, 190–91

Critique of the Power of Judgment (Kant), 257n4

Cynics, 235

Dante Alighieri, 74, 76
deductive reason, 12; empirical, 190
Defense of Poetry, A (Shelley), 12, 18–19, 29, 68–80, 263n51; ancient Greece and, modern poetry influenced by, 69; as first philosophical poem, 69; imagination in, 70, 75; morality in, 71; original forms of opinion and action in, 73; pleasure in, 75–76; posthumous publication of, 69–70; *The Prelude* and, 69; reason in, 70; Self in, 77; utility in, 75–76

Descartes, Rene, 6, 68, 209, 211, 266n63; modern philosophy influenced by, 119–20; on reason, 119; separation of mind, 120
desire: in *Critique of Practical Reason,* 213; imagination and, 129; Spinoza on, 67
dialectical illusion, 230–31, 240
dignity, in *The Prelude,* 106–7
Ding an sich (human spirit), 7
Discourse on Method (Descartes), 119
divine love, 108
doctrine of the soul, 197
dogmatic absolutism, 208–9
dogmatism, 154, 165, 177; in *Critique of Practical Reason,* 229; metaphysics and, 241–42
dualism. *See* Neoplatonic dualism
duty, 218–19
Dynamic Philosophy, 53

Ecce Homo (Nietzsche), 264n59
Either/Or (Kierkegaard), 52
Eliot, T. S., 5
empirical deductive reason, 190
empirical knowledge, in *Critique of Pure Reason*, 184
empiricists, critique of, 222
English poetry, Romantic period of, 8
Enlightenment, definition of, difficulty in, 8
Enquiry Concerning Human Understanding, An (Kant), 207
enthusiasm, 183; moral, 224; religious, 224
Epicureans, 234–35
equality, principle of, 74
"Essay, Supplementary to the Preface" *(Lyrical Ballads)* (Wordsworth), 37
eternity, as *saecula saeculorum*, 3
"ethical science," 72
Ethics (Spinoza), 66–67, 175, 204, 211, 262n46
ethics, good compared to, 122
eudaimonism, 220
evil: in *Critique of Practical Reason*, 215; from freedom, 164; God as responsible for, 4; in *Groundwork of the Metaphysics of Morals*, 164–65; in moral law, 145; origins of, 144, 164–65, 170; in The Prelude, relationship with good, 97; in *Religion within the Bounds of Mere Reason*, 142–44
Excursion, The (Wordsworth), 26, 35–36
existence, as concept, 238–39; for God, 255; thought and, relationship between, 254

Fairie Queene (Spenser), 260n30
faith: moral, in Hebrew Bible, 153; scriptural, 152–53. *See also* religion

fancy: Coleridge on, 57; in *The Prelude*, 101
fatalism, 183
Fear and Trembling (Kierkegaard), 7, 261n36, 269n81
felix culpa paradox, 40
Fichte, Johann Gottlieb, 8, 51
fiction: scope of, 5; tragic, 76
finite objects, 242
Four Ages of Poetry, The (Peacock), 79
France, Reign of Terror in, 14
free will. *See* will
freedom, 271n103; causality as, 225; in *Critique of Practical Reason*, 69, 213, 225, 228–29; human, 200; for Kant, 54; mind as agent of, 126; natural, 200; rational liberty, 264n53; in Transcendental Dialectic, 201–2; as transcendental idea, 201–2; unconditional, 178; unconditional world of, 176
French Revolution, 14, 99–100

Galileo, Galilei, 181–82, 241
Gamester, The (Moore), 260n24
general logic, 12–13, 231–32; foundations of, 189. *See also* Greek logic
Genesis (Old Testament): 1:2, 268n76; 1:26-27, 3; 2-6, 128; 2:23, 128
German idealism, 50
German philosophy, 8
German poetry, Romantic period of, 8
Germany. *See* Königsberg
Gibbon, Edward, 76
Gill, Stephen, 258n11, 258n13
God: Aristotelian idea of, 81, 97, 123; changeability of, 113; in *Critique of Practical Reason*, 69, 228, 233–34, 238; evil and, responsibility of, 4; existence of, 255;

good and, responsibility
for, 4; as highest good,
157; of history, 3; Kant
on, ontological arguments
for, 127, 209; Kierkegaard
on, 124; metaphysics and,
208; morality and, 242;
ontological argument for,
175
good, the: in *Critique of Practical
Reason*, 215, 231; ethics
compared to, 122; God as,
157; God as responsible for,
4; Kant on, 122; in moral
law, 145; origins of, 122;
Plato on, 122–23; in *The
Prelude*, relationship with
evil, 97; principle of highest
good, 220, 232–33; in
*Religion within the Bounds of
Mere Reason*, 142–43
Greek logic, of contradiction, 13
*Groundwork of the Metaphysics of
Morals* (Kant), 118, 122–24,
156–67, 174, 243, 250–51;
evil in, origins of, 164–65;
free will in, 157, 166; God
as highest good in, 157;
miracles in, 158–59; moral
law in, 157, 159–61; moral
truth in, 159; social contract
in, 159–60, 162; state of
peace in, 160

happiness, highest good and, 232
Hebrew Bible. *See* Old Testament
Hebrew Scriptures, 125–26
Hegel, Georg Wilhelm Friedrich, 82,
221; on absolute knowledge
of Spirit, 165; on metaphor,
4; on "philosophic mind,"
24–25; on universal human
being, 61
Heidegger, Martin, 13
Herder, Johann Gottfried, 221
heteronomy. *See* moral heteronomy
hierophant, poet as, 81

highest good, principle of: in
Critique of Practical Reason,
220, 232–33; happiness and,
232; virtue and, 232
historical religion, 140–41, 147
historical self, 86–87
history: God of, 3; temporal nature
of, 3. *See also* eternity
Hobbes, Thomas, 121, 267n69
holiness, as concept, 213–14
Holy Scripture (Scripture): divine
language of, 44; metaphor
in, 2, 117, 122; spirit of,
151–55
Homer, 3, 71–73
Horace, 95
human beings: as divine, 124; as
sensately-psychic, 1–2
human freedom, 200
human pathos, 39
human spirit. *See Ding an sich*
Hume, David, 76, 184, 207, 231
Hutchenson, Mary, 88

Ideal of Pure Reason, 179; in
Transcendental Dialectic,
197, 202–5
idealism, 183; German, 50
idolatry: Kant on, 137; metaphor
and, 45; in Old Testament,
critique of, 47; paganism as
distinct from, 157; religion
and, 45; speech and, 248
illusion: dialectical, 230–31, 240;
"logic of illusion," 196; in
Transcendental Dialectic,
196–99
imagination, 257n4; in *Biographia
Literaria*, 36; Coleridge on,
57, 64–65, 262n39; in *A
Defense of Poetry*, 70, 75;
desire created by, 129; Kant
on, 57; as mental action,
70; in *The Prelude*, 31, 111;
primary, 57; secondary, 57;
Wordsworth on, 37
"imagination of the whole," 85
imaginative self, 86–87

immorality, of poetry, 72
immortality: in *Critique of Practical Reason*, 69; metaphysics of, 22; Platonic conception of, 24
incarnational language, of metaphor, 44–45
"indefinite objects," in religion, 43–44
independence themes, in *The Prelude*, 110
individuality, in *The Prelude*, 110
inductive reason, 12
infinite objects, 242
inner intuition, 186–87
inspiration, theological language of, 10
intellectual love, 109
intuition, 186–88; inner, 186–87; outer, 186–87, 198

Jerome (Saint), 3
Jerusalem Delivered (Tasso), 79
Jesus Christ, Plato and, conflation between, 12
John (Old Testament), 3:5, 268n76
1 John, 156–57; 4:18, 156; 16, 156
Jowett, Benjamin, 136
Judaism: as cult, 155–56. *See also* anti-Judaism; Hebrew Scriptures; Old Testament

Kant, Immanuel, 4; on Adam and Eve, 124; anti-Judaism of, 12, 126, 155–56, 269n80; Coleridge on, 11, 53; *The Conflict of the Faculties*, 14, 118, 133–40, 268n74; "The Conflict of the Philosophy Faculty with the Theology Faculty," 133–34; "Conjectural Beginning of Human History," 118, 124, 126, 128–33, 143, 223; critical philosophy and, 50; critique of empiricists, 222; critique of metaphor for, 41; *Critique of the Power of Judgment*, 257n4; on dogmatism, 154, 165, 177; *An Enquiry Concerning Human Understanding*, 207; on exposition of space and time, 187–88; freedom for, 54; general logic, 12–13; on the good, origins of, 122; *Groundwork of the Metaphysics of Morals*, 118, 122–24, 156–67; on idolatry, 137; on imagination, 57; kingdom of ends, 10; metaphor of critique for, 41; on morality, development of, 137; on natural world of sensibility and understanding, 2; on nature, 54, 129–30; on paganism, 137; "Perpetual Peace," 118, 159, 162–64, 168, 181; "The Philosophical Doctrine of Religion," 140–41; pre-critical work of, 56; on private law, 160–61; *Prolegomena of a Future Metaphysics*, 174, 178, 180; on proof of God, 127; on public law, 160–61; on reality of space, 186; on religion, 128–72; *Religion within the Bounds of Mere Reason*, 14, 118, 123, 140–56, 163; as sage of Königsberg, 51; on skepticism, 154, 165, 177; on sociability, 128; on Stoics, 168–69; on transcendental, as mental concept, 112; transcendental realm and, 11; on unconditional conjecture, 165; on understanding, 2, 191, 267n72; "What is Enlightenment," 118, 172. *See also Critique of Practical Reason*; *Critique of Pure Reason*

Kierkegaard, Sören, 4; on Christianity, pagan foundations of, 68; *Either/Or*, 52; *Fear and Trembling*, 7, 261n36, 269n81; on God, 124; *logos*, 118; "Love Builds Up," 1; on nature, 117; on practice of metaphor, 1–3; on sensate-psychic acting beings, 1, 3; on spirit, 6, 117; on spiritual language, 5; on spiritual persons, 1–2; on transferred language, 2; on truth, 15, 87; *Works of Love*, 1, 6
kingdom of ends, 10
"Know Thyself" (Coleridge), 68–69
knowledge: analytical, 184; empirical, 184; mathematics, 181, 270n94; natural sciences, 181–82; of nature, paradoxes of, 175–77; objective, 176; physics, 181; as pleasure, 33; practical, 204; scientific, 177; theoretical, 204. *See also* being and knowledge
Königsberg, Germany, Kant and, 51

language: of Holy Scripture, 44; incarnational, of metaphor, 44–45; in *Lyrical Ballads*, 30; metaphorical, in *The Prelude*, 87; metrical, in poetry, 35; of Milton, 59; in philosophy, 59–60; in poetry, 35; poets' use of, 34; "real language," 30, 60; religious, 2, 113–14. *See also* metaphor; *specific types of language*
Latin Vulgate, The Bible and, 3
laudanum, 264n54
law: antimony and, 199; concepts of, 170; covenantal, 171–73; in *Critique of Practical Reason*, 213; unconditional practical, 213; universal, 213. *See also* moral law
learned religion, 140–41
Leaves of Grass (Whitman), 9
Lectures on the Philosophy of Religion (Hegel), 82
Lessing, Gotthold Ephraim, 11, 51, 262n44
Liebniz, Gottfried Wilhelm, 163, 208
Locke, John, 76
logic: Greek, 13; for Kant, 12–13. *See also specific topics*
"logic of illusion," 196
logos, 118, 133
logosophia: for Coleridge, 53–56; Theses in, 55–56
love: divine, 108; intellectual, 109; paradoxes of, 109–10; in *The Prelude*, 107–9; universal worth and, 177
"Love Builds Up" (Kierkegaard), 1, 9
love of wisdom. *See philosophia*
Lyrical Ballads (Wordsworth and Coleridge), 8, 27–31, 86, 91, 248, 259n16, 259n20; anonymous publication of, 49; "Essay, Supplementary to the Preface," 37; literary legacy of, 27; prefatory materials in, 30–31; published versions of, 27; "real language of men" in, 30

making. *See poesis*
Marx, Karl, 221
materialism, 183
Matthew (New Testament), 6:24, 42
meditative pathos, 39
memory: in "Immortality Ode," 23–24; in *The Prelude*, 104
metaphor, practice of: in ancient Greece, 3–4; in The Bible, 2; critique of, 41, 47, 246–55; Hegel on, 4; in Holy Scripture, 2, 117, 122; idolatry and, 45;

metaphor, practice of (*continued*)
as incarnational, 44–45;
Kierkegaard on, 1–3; in *The Prelude*, 116; reason and, 116; spirit in, speech about, 2; transferred language in, 2
metaphor of critique, 41, 47
metaphorical language, in *The Prelude*, 87
metaphysics: in ancient Greece, 13; Aristotle and, origins of, 189; cosmology in, 195; in *Critique of Practical Reason*, 210–12, 237; in *Critique of Pure Reason*, 180; dogmatism and, 241–42; foundations of, 250; God and, 208; of immortality, 22; in "Immortality Ode," 22; of mind, 121; of modern poetry, 13–14; nature in, 208; origins of, 14; of philosophy, 13–14; Plato and, origins of, 189; possibility of, 253–54; as practice, 121; psychology in, 195; skeptics and, 241–42; soul as part of, 195, 208; theology in, 195
metrical language, in poetry, 35
Michelangelo, 76
Milton, John, 4, 36, 71, 76; language of, 59; *Paradise Lost*, 45, 56, 78, 87, 97, 258n10, 265n60, 267n69–70
mind: as agent of freedom, 126; body and, distinction between, 131–32; metaphysics of, 121; separation of, 120; as will, 120
miracles, 158–59
modernity, as secular, 2–3
Moore, Edward, 260n24
moral autonomy, 214
moral enthusiasm, 224
moral heteronomy, 214

moral law, 252–53; Christendom and, 123; conflict as result of, 224; in *The Conflict of the Faculties*, 136; in *Critique of Practical Reason*, 212, 215–19, 222–25, 229, 235–37, 239–40; evil and, 145; good in, 145; in *Groundwork of the Metaphysics of Morals*, 157, 159–61; natural, 170; ontological argument for, 254; origins of, 222–23; paradox of, 215–16; principle of, 121, 123–24; in *Religion within the Bounds of Mere Reason*, 153–54; truth and, 172
moral necessity, 170, 225, 234
moral truth, 159
morality: Aristotle on, 235; in *Critique of Practical Reason*, 82, 213, 221, 229, 235; in *Critique of Pure Reason*, 184–85; as foundation of religion, 154–55; God from, 242; Kant on, development of, 137; origins of, 235; Plato on, origins of, 235; reason and, 10; of Stoics, 234
mortality, in "Immortality Ode," 24

natural freedom, 200
natural law, 170; in *Critique of Practical Reason*, 240–41
natural necessity, 170, 225–27
natural objects, in Kant works, 11
natural religion, 150
natural world of sensibility and understanding, 2
naturalist philosophy, 150
nature: conditional world of, 176; in "Immortality Ode," 25; Kant on, 54, 129–30; Kierkegaard on, 117; in metaphysics, 208; paradox of knowledge of, 175–77; in *The Prelude*, 32, 85, 88, 90–91, 111–12; Prophets

of Nature, 111; scientific knowledge of, 177; in social contract, 122. *See also* natural world of sensibility and understanding
necessity. *See* moral necessity; natural necessity
Neoplatonic dualism, 73
New Science (Vico), 263n51
New Testament: as poetic, 6. *See also* specific books
Newton, Isaac, 182, 241
Nietzsche, Friedrich, 264n59
nihilism. *See* skeptical nihilism
noumena, 194–95, 207; in *Critique of Practical Reason*, 228
noumenal world, in *Critique of Practical Reason*, 223–37

objective knowledge, 176
objects. *See* finite objects; "indefinite objects"; infinite objects; natural objects; rational objects
"Ode: Intimations of Immortality from Recollects of Early Childhood" ("Immortality Ode") (Wordsworth), 17–25, 64; adulthood in, 23; childhood in, 23; high arguments in, 25; human love of nature, 25; *Literaria Biographia* and, 18; memory in, 23–24; metaphysics of immortality in, 22; mortality themes in, 24; natural piety in, 28; origins of, 20–21; paradoxes in, 21, 23; parental relationships in, 21; "philosophic mind," 23–25; temporal elements of, 22–23; thematic center of, 28
"Ode to Duty" (Wordsworth), 265n61
Old Testament (Hebrew Bible): critique of idolatry in, 47; moral faith in, 153; parallelism in, 34; as poetic, 6. *See also* specific books
ontological arguments: in *Critique of Practical Reason*, 243; in *Critique of Pure Reason*, 203; for God, 127, 175, 209; by Kant, 127, 209; for moral law, 254; for philosophy, origins of, 13–14
ontological motifs, in *The Prelude*, 86
oracular ignorance, 53
original sin: in "Conjectural Beginning of Human History," 130–32, 143. *See also* Adam and Eve
outer intuition, 186–87, 198

paganism: Christianity and, 68, 131; idolatry as distinct from, 157; Kant on, 137
Paradise Lost (Milton), 45, 56, 78, 258n10, 265n60, 267n69–70; *The Prelude* and, 87, 97
paradoxes: in "Immortality Ode," 21, 23; of knowledge of nature, 175–77; of love, 109–10; of moral law, 215–16; in *The Prelude*, 85; of revelation, 148
parallelism, 34
paralogisms, 197
Pascal, Blaise, 132
Peacock, Thomas Love, 79, 262n49
Pensées (Pascal), 132
"Perpetual Peace" (Kant), 118, 159, 162–64, 168, 181
personality, 219–20
Petrarch, 75
phenomena, 194
philosophers, poets as, 70
philosophia (love of wisdom), 4
"philosophic mind," in "Immortality Ode," 23–25
"Philosophical Doctrine of Religion, The" (Kant), 140–41
philosophical language: as poetic, 2; of reason and truth, 10

philosophy: in *Biographia Literaria*, 50; Christianity and, incompatibility with, 65–66; critical, 50; definition of, 5; Descartes as major influence on, 119–20; Dynamic, 53; historical origins of, 13–14; language of, 59–60; metaphoric critique of, 246–55; metaphysics of, 13–14; modern, 6; naturalist, 150; ontological origins of, 13–14; rationalist, 150; religion and, 80; theology and, 126; truth of poetry in, 19. *See also* German philosophy

plagiarism, 51

Plato, 3, 131, 258n13; Coleridge influenced by, 63; on the good, 122–23; on immortality, 24; Jesus Christ and, conflation between, 12; metaphysics and, 189; on moral concepts, origins of, 235; Neoplatonic dualism, 73; principle of equality and, application of, 74; Shelley on, 71–72, 74

pleasure: in *A Defense of Poetry*, 75–76; definition of, 76; knowledge as, 33; rationality and, 30; of self-realization, 41; from tragic fiction, 76; types of, 75–76

Pliny, 167–68

poesis (making), 4

poetic diction, 34

poetic language: as philosophical, 2; religious, 2

poetical faculty, 77–79

poetics: The Bible, 6; definition of, 5; Wordsworth on, 40, 57–59

Poetics (Aristotle), 60, 63

poetry: abuses of, 43–44; aim and purpose of, 59; Aristotle on, 60; in *Biographia Literaria*, critique of, 20, 28–29; Coleridge on, 58–59; creation of, 28; cultivation of, 77; definition of, 5, 69–70; as divine, 77–78; divine origins of, 44; as homage, 33; human pathos and, 39; as image of man, 33; immorality of, 72; language structure in, 35; meditative pathos and, 39; metaphoric critique of, 246–55; origins of civilization and, 70; poetic diction, 34; proofs of, 58; prose and, relationship between, 32, 35, 62, 260n24; religion and, 42–44, 70–71, 80; truth of philosophy in, 19; Wordsworth on, popular poetry as distinct from his work, 32. *See also* English poetry; German poetry

poetry of creation, 28

poets: audience for, 34; common language for, 34; as hierophant, 81; moral views of, lack of, 81; as philosophers, 70; in *The Prelude*, 33–34; self-reflection for, 88

polis (political rule), 120–21, 263n51

political rule. *See polis*

possibility: of metaphysics, 253–54; in Transcendental Dialectic, 193–94

practical knowledge, 204

practical reason, critique of, 173, 178–79

practical understanding, 149

practice of metaphor. *See* metaphor

Prelude, The (Wordsworth), 8–10, 16, 68, 244, 246, 249, 251–52; Adam and Eve in, 97, 114; anonymity of cities in, 93; autobiographical elements of, 26, 89, 92; Book 1, 25, 87–91; Book 7, 91–93; Book 8, 93–95, 98–99; Book 9, 99; Book 10, 99–100, 102; Book 11, 102–3; Book

12, 99, 104–5, 107; Book 13, 9, 83–85, 99, 107–11; childhood experiences in, 89; Coleridge in, 91; creation in, 107; dual themes in, 88; false education in, 264n56; fancy in, 101; as foundational poetic work, 20; French Revolution in, 99–100; good and evil in, relationship between, 97; historical motifs in, 86; historical self in, 86–87; *Home in Grasmere*, 25–26; human dignity in, 106–7; imagination in, 31, 111; "imagination of the whole" in, 85; imaginative self in, 86–87; independence as theme in, 110; individuality as theme in, 110; inspiration for, 83–84; London in, 96–97; love in, 107–9; metaphor in, 116; metaphorical language in, 87; methodological approach to, 85–86; narrative tales in, 87; nature in, 32, 85, 88, 90–91, 111–12; ontological motifs in, 86; *Paradise Lost* references in, 87, 97; paradoxes in, 85; poet in, 33–34; poetic mind in, 112; Preface of 1815, 45–46; "principal object" in, 31; pure reason in, critique of, 114–15, 173; *The Recluse* and, 25–26; religious language in, 113–14; remembering in, 104; self-reflection for poets, 88; shepherd's life in, 93–95; "spots of time" in, 103–4; structure of, 19, 86
present, as concept, 226
primary imagination, 57
"principal object," in *The Prelude*, 31

principle of being and knowledge. *See* being and knowledge
principle of equality. *See* equality
principle of moral law. *See* moral law
principle of self-consciousness. *See* self-consciousness
principles of criticism. *See* criticism
Principles of Pure Practical Reason, 213
private law, 160–61
Prolegomena of a Future Metaphysics (Kant), 174, 178, 180
"Prophets of Nature," 9, 111
prose, poetry and, relationship between, 32, 35, 62, 260n24
Provençal Troubadours, 75
Psalms (Old Testament), 8:4–5, 3
psychology, 195
public law, 160–61
pure reason, critique of, 114–15, 173, 178; in *Critique of Pure Reason*, 182; Ideal of Pure Reason, 179, 197, 202–5. *See also Critique of Pure Reason*
Pythagoras, 53

Raphael, 76
rational liberty, 264n53
rational objects: in *Critique of Practical Reason*, 11; in *Critique of Pure Reason*, 11
rationalist philosophy, 150
rationality, pleasure and, 30
readers of superior judgment, 29–30
"real language," Wordsworth on, 60
realism, transcendental, 197
reason: causality of, 201–2; in *The Conflict of the Faculties*, 135, 137; deductive, 12; in *A Defense of Poetry*, 70; Descartes on, 119; elements of, 249; Ideal of Pure Reason, 179, 197, 202–5; inductive, 12; as mental action, 70; metaphor as domain of, 116; morality and, 10; philosophical language of, 10;

reason: causality of (*continued*)
practical, critique of, 173, 178–79; as practice, 54, 200; pure, in *The Prelude*, critique of, 114–15, 173, 178–79; religion and, 125–26, 138, 269n88; "religion of reason," 126; revelation of, 148; speculative, 183
Recluse, The (Wordsworth), 25–27; Book II, 26; Book III, 26; structure of, 27
Reign of Terror, 14
religion: allegory in, 71; in *The Conflict of the Faculties*, 133–40; in *Critique of Practical Reason*, 236; in *Critique of Pure Reason*, 133; historical, 140–41, 147; idolatry and, 45; "indefinite objects" in, 43–44; Kant on, 128–72; learned, 140–41; moral foundations of, 154–55; natural, 150; philosophy and, 80; poetry and, 42–44, 70–71, 80; reason and, 125–26, 138, 269n88. *See also* anti-Judaism; Christianity/Christendom
"religion of reason": in The Bible, 126; in *Religion within the Bounds of Mere Reason*, 141, 154
Religion within the Bounds of Mere Reason (Kant), 14, 118, 123, 140–56, 163; Adam and Eve in, 146; Christianity in, 146, 153; "Concerning the Battle of Good Against the Evil Principle for Dominion over the Human Being," 168; evil in, 142–44; the good in, 142–43; historical religion in, 140–41, 147; learned religion in, 140–41; moral law in, 153–54; natural religion in, 150; naturalist philosophy, 150; "The Philosophical Doctrine of Religion," 140–41; practical understanding in, 149; rationalist philosophy, 150; religion of reason in, 141, 154; revelation in, 147–48; scriptural faith in, 152–53; structure of, 140–41; theoretical understanding in, 149
religious enthusiasm, 224
religious language: as philosophical, 2; as poetic, 2; in *The Prelude*, 113–14
Republic (Plato), 74
revelation: creation and, 171; paradox of, 148; of reason, 148; in *Religion within the Bounds of Mere Reason*, 147–48
Reynolds, Joshua, 30
Richardson, Samuel, 260n24
"Rime of the Ancient Mariner, The" (Coleridge), 262n39
Romantic period, 8
Romanticism, definition of, difficulty in, 8
Rousseau, Jean-Jacques, 68–69, 76, 121, 267n69; on fall of Man, 40–41; social contract and, 41

saecula saeculorum (ages of ages), 3, 82, 171, 227, 245
Schelling, Friedrich Wilhelm Joseph, 8, 11, 51
scriptural faith, 152–53
Scripture. *See* Holy Scripture
secondary imagination, 57
secular, as modern, 2–3
the Self: consciousness of, 192; in *Critique of Practical Reason*, 212; in *A Defense of Poetry*, 77; historical, 86–87; imaginative, 86–87; in *The Prelude*, 86–87
self-alienation, 69
self-consciousness, principle of, 56

self-knowledge, Coleridge on, 52–53
self-realization, pleasure of, 41
self-reflection, for poets, 88
Seneca, 265n61
sensate-psychical beings, 1–3
sensibility: Kant on, 2; natural world of, 2
separation of mind, 120
Shakespeare, William, 4, 28, 36, 61, 71
Shelley, Percy Bysshe: *A Defense of Poetry*, 12, 18–19, 29, 68–80, 263n51; on Jesus Christ, conflation with Plato, 12; on Plato, 71–72, 74; on poetical faculty, 77–79; on poetry as divine, 77–78
skeptical nihilism, 208–9
skepticism, 154, 165, 177, 183; in *Critique of Practical Reason*, 220, 229; metaphysics and, 241–42
sociability, of man, 128
social contract: in *Groundwork of the Metaphysics of Morals*, 159–60, 162; nature in, 122; Rousseau and, 41
Social Contract, The (Rousseau), 41
Socrates, 3, 74, 231; oracular ignorance, 53; on "philosophic mind," 24–25
Socratic tradition, 53
"Song of Myself" (Whitman), 9
soul: doctrine of the soul, 197; in metaphysics, 195, 208
Southey, Robert, 258n10
speculative reason, 183
Spenser, Edmund, 36, 260n30
Spinoza, Baruch, 6–7, 211; on desire, 67; *Ding an sich* (human spirit), 7; *Ethics*, 66–67, 175, 204, 211, 262n46; *Theologico-Political Treatise*, 4, 6, 66–67, 121, 126, 263n51, 267n69
spirit: of Holy Scripture, 151–55; Kierkegaard on, 6, 117
spiritual language, Kierkegaard on, 5

spiritual persons, sensate-psychical beings and, 1–2
"spots of time", in *The Prelude*, 103–4
Stevens, Wallace, 4–5
Stoics, 168–69, 234–35, 265n61; doctrine for, 67; moral concepts of, 234
supersensible human being, 138–39
superstition, 183
Synesius, 56
synthetic judgments, 184–85
synthetic reason. *See* inductive reason

Tantalus, 260n27, 265n60
Tasso, Torquato, 79
taste, Wordsworth on, 37–38
teleological arguments, 203
temporality, time and: in "Immortality Ode," 22–23; present as concept, 226
theodicy, 162–64, 166–68; The Bible as, 166; creation and, 170–71
Theodicy (Liebniz), 163
theological language, of inspiration, 10
Theologico-Political Treatise (Spinoza), 4, 6, 66–67, 121, 126, 263n51, 267n69
theology, 185; in metaphysics, 195; philosophy and, 126; theodicy and, 162–64
theoretical knowledge, 204
theoretical understanding, 149
thought, existence and, relationship between, 254
time. *See* temporality
timocracy, 266n64
"To William Wordsworth" (Coleridge), 18–19, 26–27, 47–52, 102, 112; prayers in, 49
tragic fiction, 76
Transcendental Aesthetic, 179, 184, 185–86, 189
Transcendental Analytic, 179, 185

Transcendental Dialectic, in *Critique of Pure Reason*, 127, 179, 185–86, 192–205, 228–29, 238; "The Antimony of Pure Reason," 199–204; boundary concepts in, 195; freedom in, 201–2; Ideal of Pure Reason in, 197, 202–5; illusion in, 196–99; as "logic of illusion," 196; *noumena* in, 194–95, 207; outer intuition in, 198; *phenomena* in, 194; possibility in, 193–94
transcendental realism, 197
transcendental realm, Kant and, 11
Treatise on Human Nature, A (Hume), 207
truth: Kierkegaard on, 15, 87; moral, 159; moral law and, 172; philosophical language of, 10; subjectivity of, 15, 87

unbelief, 183
unconditional freedom, 178
unconditional practical law, 213
understanding: Kant on, 2, 191, 267n72; natural world of, 2; practical, 149; theoretical, 149
unity of consciousness, 190–91
universal law, 213
utility, in *A Defense of Poetry*, 75–76

Vallon, Annette, 88
Vico, Giambattista, 4, 263n51
Virgil, 95
virtue, highest good and, 232

Voltaire, 76, 163

"What is Enlightenment" (Kant), 118, 172
Whitman, Walt, 4, 8–9
will, 271n103; in *Groundwork of the Metaphysics of Morals*, 157, 166; mind as, 120
Wolff, Christian, 208
Wordsworth, William, 4–5, 258n10; on Adam and Eve, 40; Coleridge on, 47–69; defects of poetic works, 65–66; "Essay, Supplementary to the Preface," 37; *The Excursion*, 26; on imagination, 37; "Immortality Ode," 17–25; metaphor as domain of reason for, 116; "Ode to Duty," 265n61; on pleasure of self-realization, 41; poetic theory of, 65; on poetics, 40, 57–59; on poetry and prose, relationship between, 35; on popular poetry, his works as distinct from, 32; as "Prophet of Nature," 9, 111; on readers of superior judgment, 29–30; on "real language," 60; *The Recluse*, 25–26; on religion's relationship with poetry, 42–44; on taste, 37–38; timeline of life, 88–89. See also *Lyrical Ballads*; *The Prelude*
Works of Love (Kierkegaard), 1, 6

www.ingramcontent.com/pod-product-compliance
Lightning Source LLC
Chambersburg PA
CBHW061431300426
44114CB00014B/1638